【Contents:】

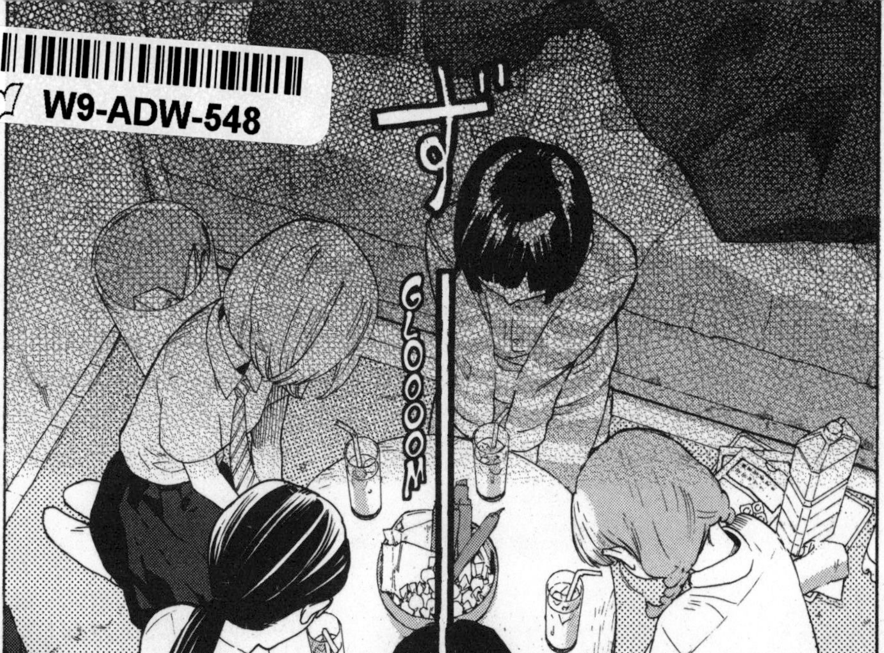
す
GLOOOOOM

Meeting 5

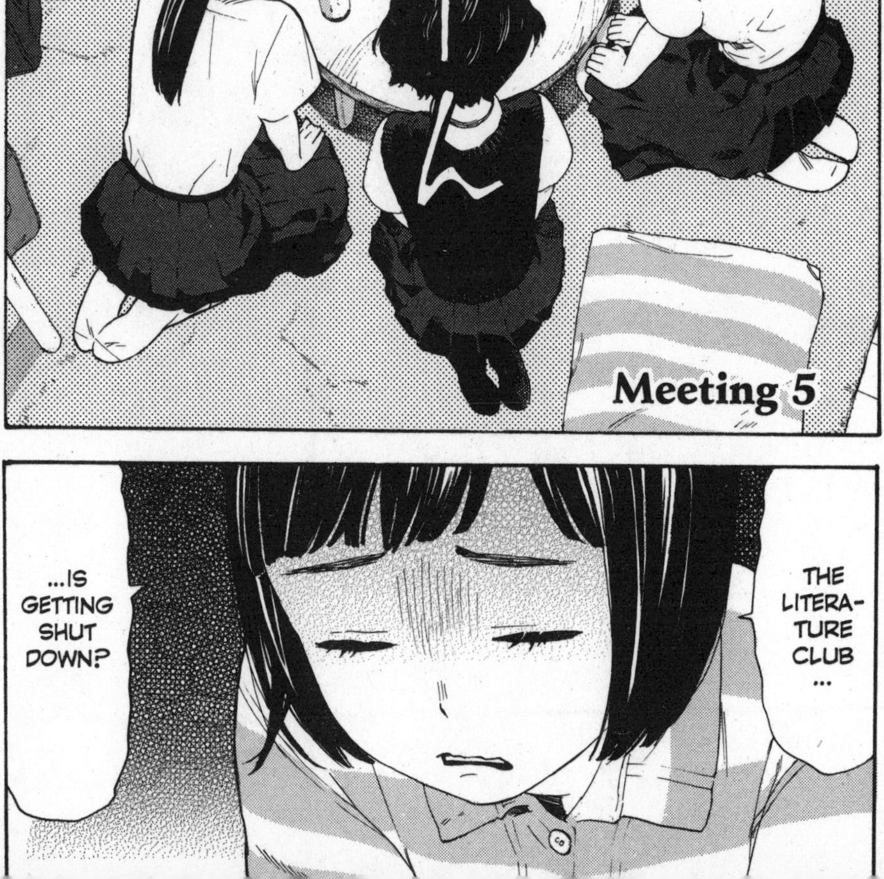
THE LITERA-TURE CLUB...
...IS GETTING SHUT DOWN?

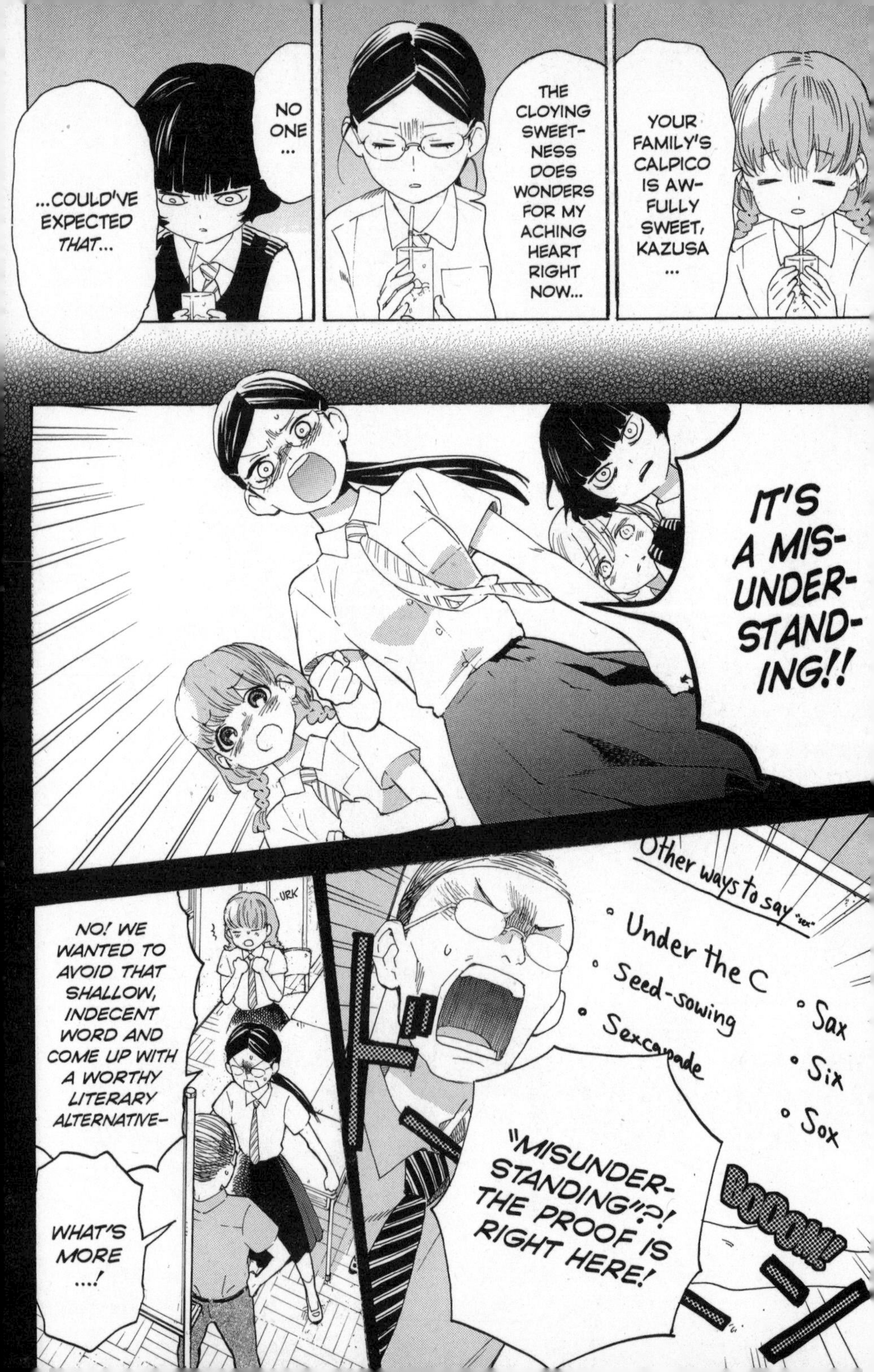
YOUR FAMILY'S CALPICO IS AW-FULLY SWEET, KAZUSA ...
THE CLOYING SWEET-NESS DOES WONDERS FOR MY ACHING HEART RIGHT NOW...
NO ONE ...
...COULD'VE EXPECTED THAT...
IT'S A MIS-UNDER-STANDING!!
Other ways to say "sex"
• Under the C
• Seed-sowing
• Sexcapade
• Sax
• Six
• Sox
"MISUNDER-STANDING"?! THE PROOF IS RIGHT HERE!
...URK
NO! WE WANTED TO AVOID THAT SHALLOW, INDECENT WORD AND COME UP WITH A WORTHY LITERARY ALTERNATIVE-
WHAT'S MORE ...!

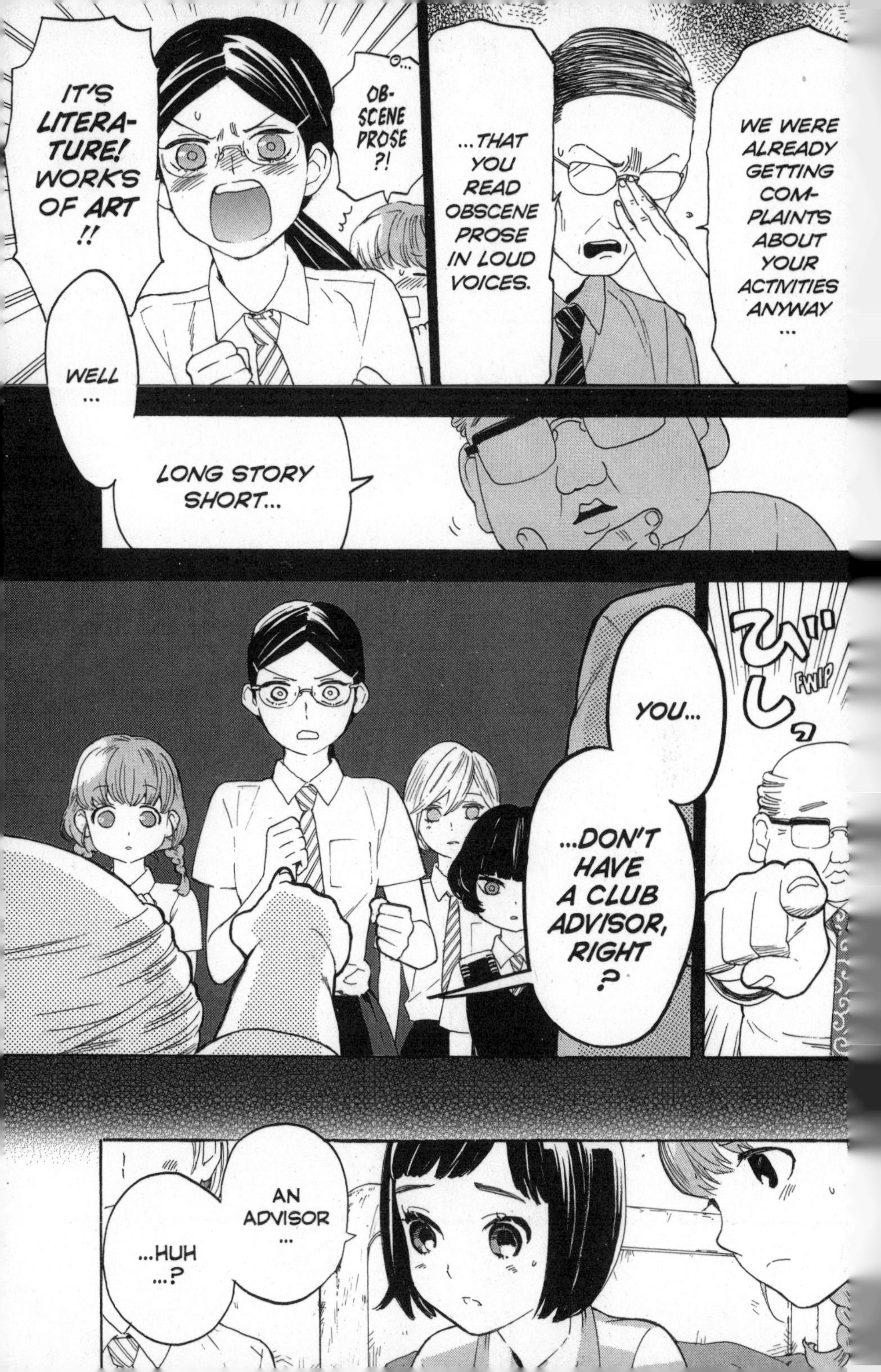
WE WERE ALREADY GETTING COM-PLAINTS ABOUT YOUR ACTIVITIES ANYWAY...
...THAT YOU READ OBSCENE PROSE IN LOUD VOICES.
O...
OB-SCENE PROSE?!
IT'S LITERA-TURE! WORKS OF ART!!
WELL...
LONG STORY SHORT...
FWIP
YOU...
...DON'T HAVE A CLUB ADVISOR, RIGHT?
AN ADVISOR...
...HUH...?

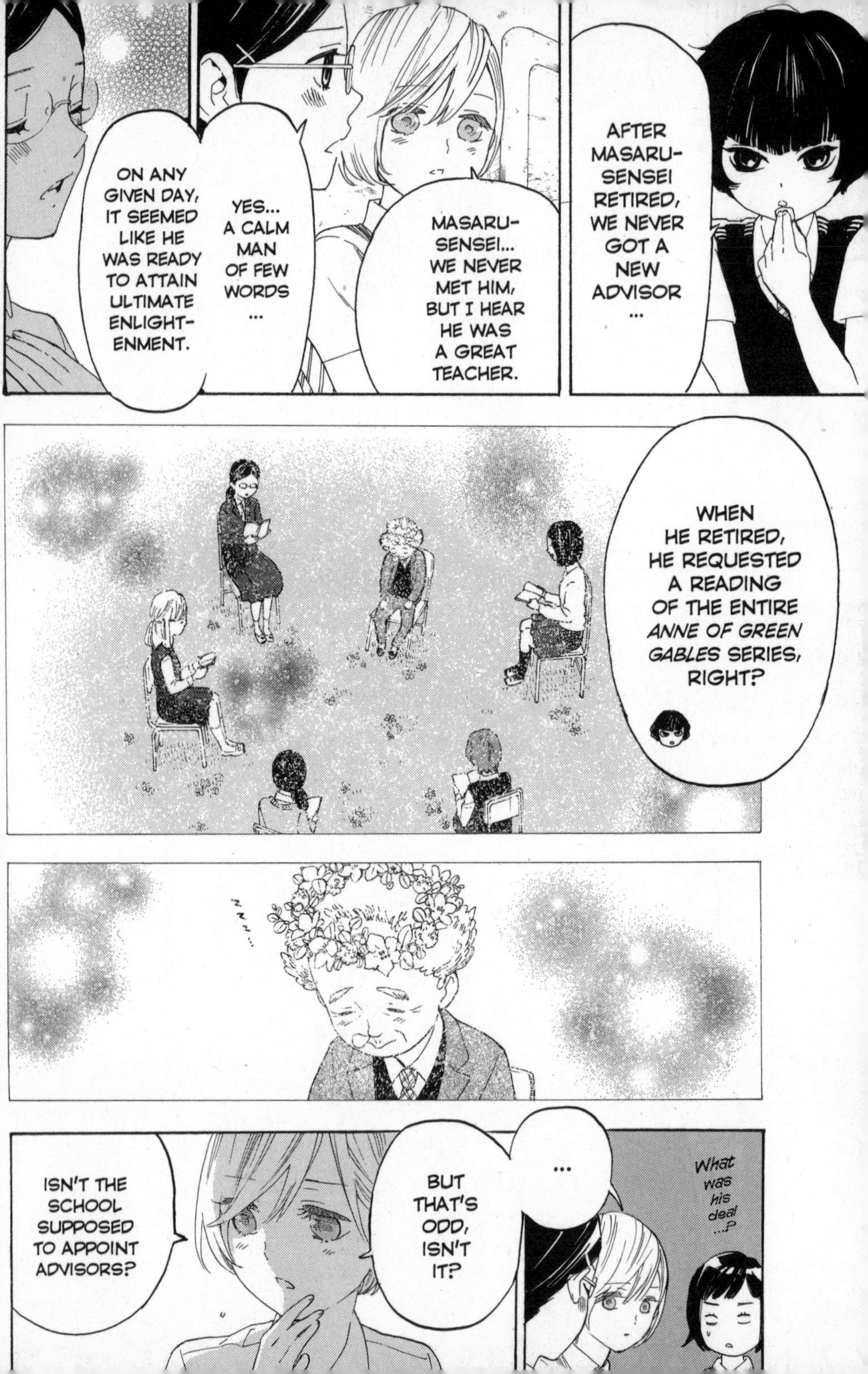
AFTER MASARU-SENSEI RETIRED, WE NEVER GOT A NEW ADVISOR ...
MASARU-SENSEI... WE NEVER MET HIM, BUT I HEAR HE WAS A GREAT TEACHER.
YES... A CALM MAN OF FEW WORDS ...
ON ANY GIVEN DAY, IT SEEMED LIKE HE WAS READY TO ATTAIN ULTIMATE ENLIGHT-ENMENT.
WHEN HE RETIRED, HE REQUESTED A READING OF THE ENTIRE *ANNE OF GREEN GABLES* SERIES, RIGHT?
NNH...
What was his deal ...?
...
BUT THAT'S ODD, ISN'T IT?
ISN'T THE SCHOOL SUPPOSED TO APPOINT ADVISORS?

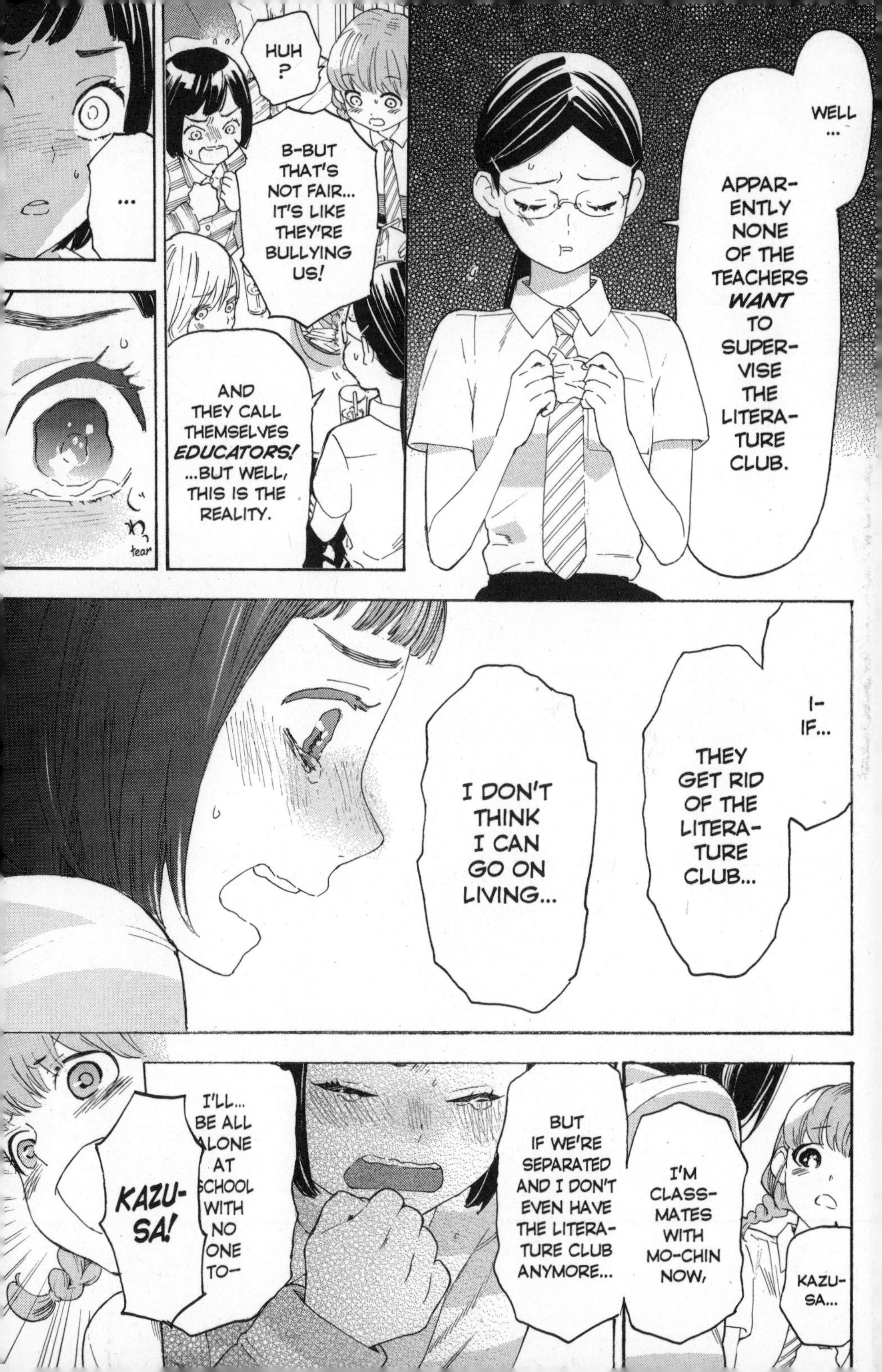
WELL...
APPARENTLY NONE OF THE TEACHERS *WANT* TO SUPERVISE THE LITERATURE CLUB.
HUH?
B-BUT THAT'S NOT FAIR... IT'S LIKE THEY'RE BULLYING US!
AND THEY CALL THEMSELVES *EDUCATORS!* ...BUT WELL, THIS IS THE REALITY.
...
tear
I- IF...
THEY GET RID OF THE LITERATURE CLUB...
I DON'T THINK I CAN GO ON LIVING...
KAZUSA...
I'M CLASSMATES WITH MO-CHIN NOW,
BUT IF WE'RE SEPARATED AND I DON'T EVEN HAVE THE LITERATURE CLUB ANYMORE...
I'LL... BE ALL ALONE AT SCHOOL WITH NO ONE TO-
KAZUSA!

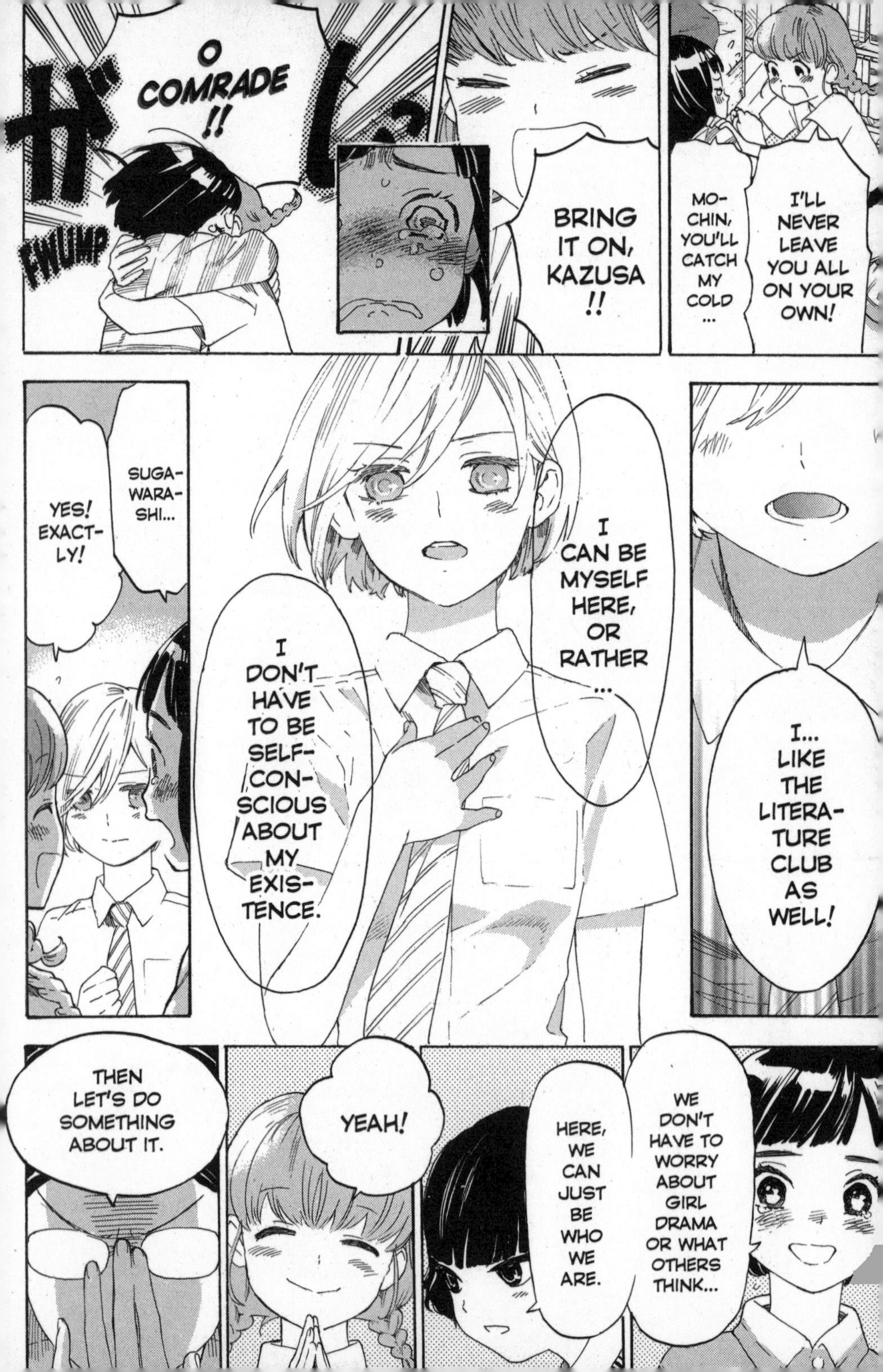
I'LL NEVER LEAVE YOU ALL ON YOUR OWN!
MO-CHIN, YOU'LL CATCH MY COLD ...
BRING IT ON, KAZUSA !!
O COMRADE !!
FWUMP
I... LIKE THE LITERATURE CLUB AS WELL!
I CAN BE MYSELF HERE, OR RATHER ...
I DON'T HAVE TO BE SELF-CONSCIOUS ABOUT MY EXISTENCE.
SUGAWARA-SHI...
YES! EXACTLY!
WE DON'T HAVE TO WORRY ABOUT GIRL DRAMA OR WHAT OTHERS THINK...
HERE, WE CAN JUST BE WHO WE ARE.
YEAH!
THEN LET'S DO SOMETHING ABOUT IT.

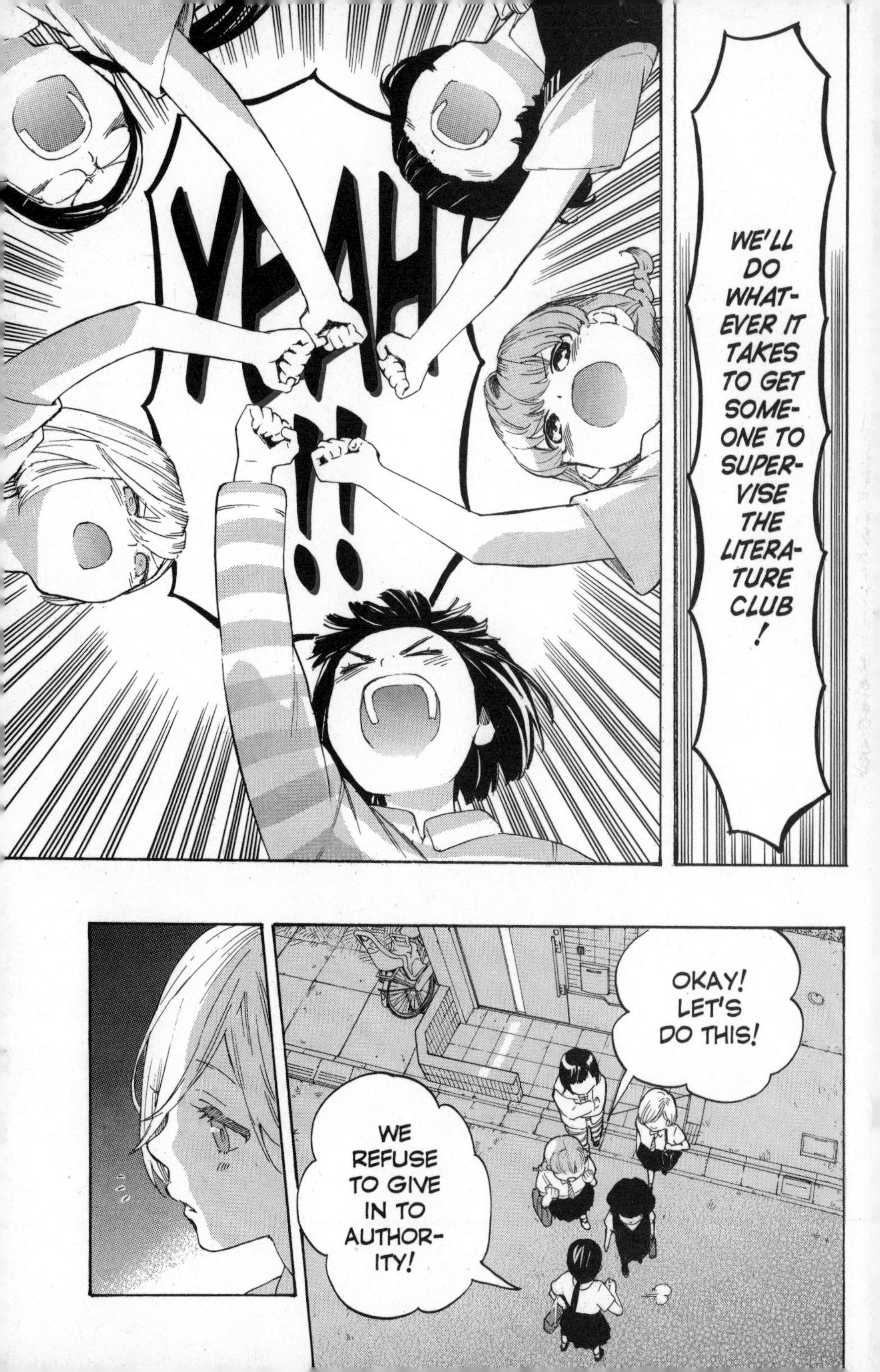
WE'LL DO WHATEVER IT TAKES TO GET SOMEONE TO SUPERVISE THE LITERATURE CLUB!
YEAH!!!
OKAY! LET'S DO THIS!
WE REFUSE TO GIVE IN TO AUTHORITY!

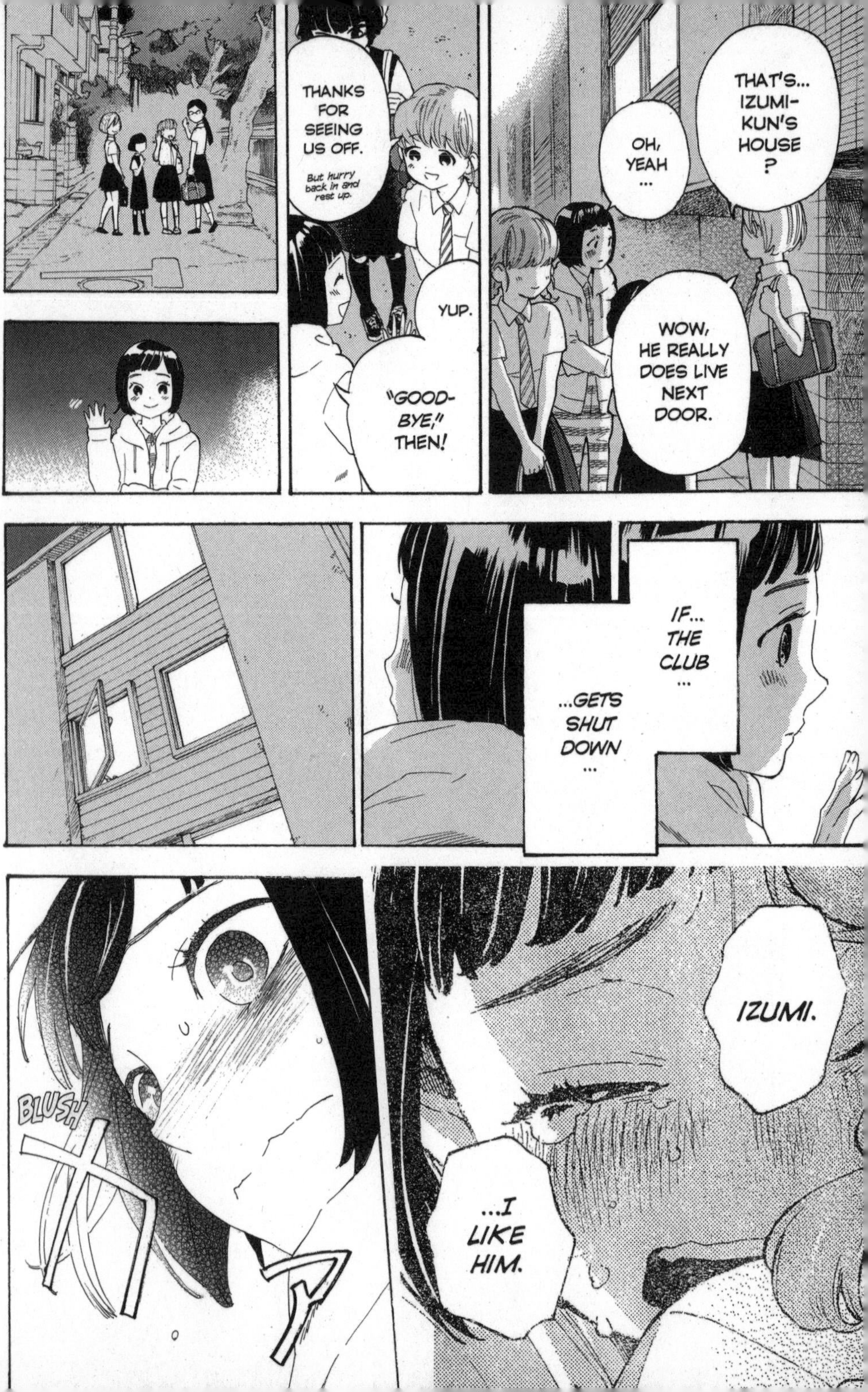
THAT'S... IZUMI-KUN'S HOUSE?
OH, YEAH...
WOW, HE REALLY DOES LIVE NEXT DOOR.
THANKS FOR SEEING US OFF.
But hurry back in and rest up.
YUP.
"GOOD-BYE," THEN!
IF... THE CLUB...
...GETS SHUT DOWN...
IZUMI.
...I LIKE HIM.
BLUSH

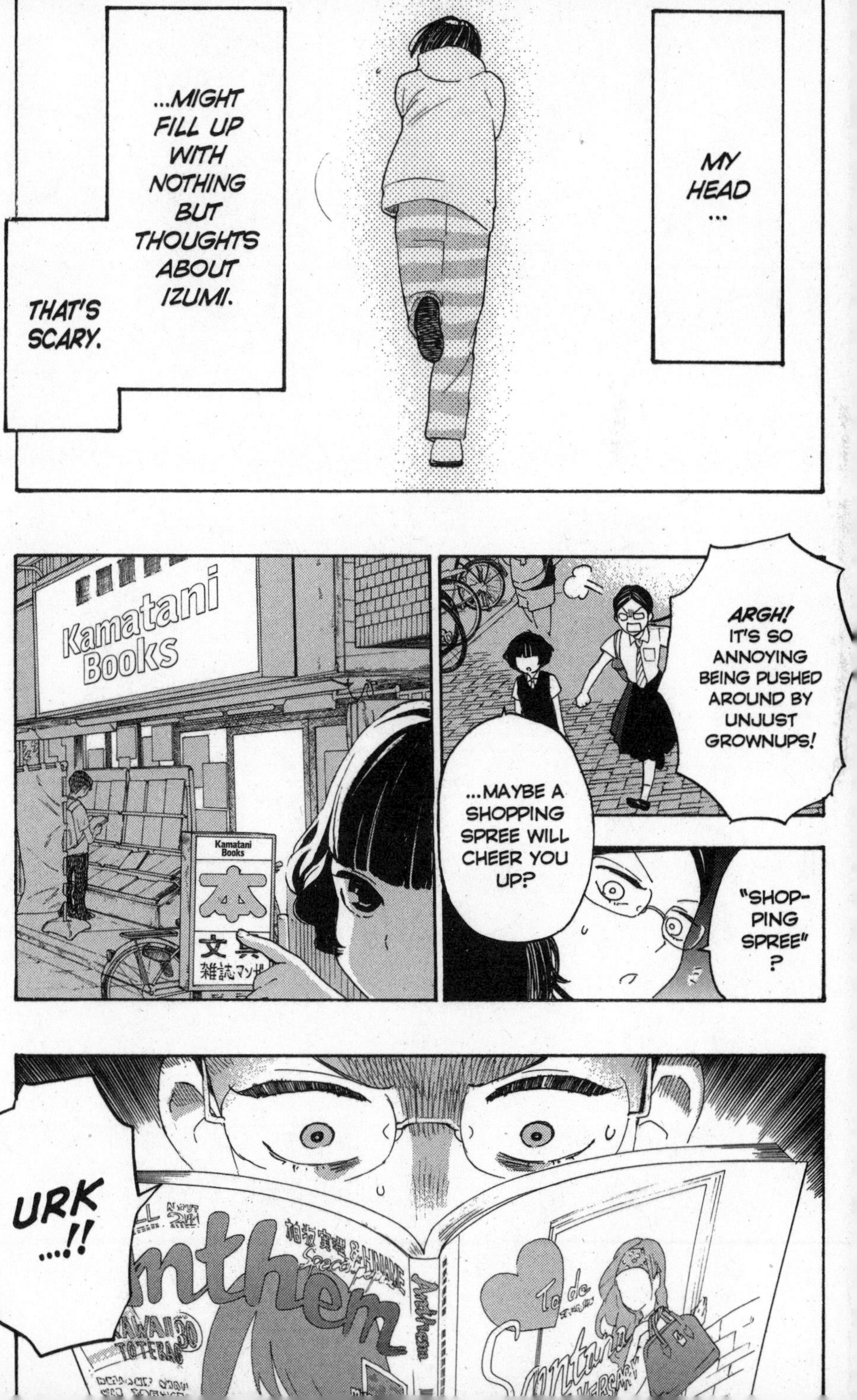
MY HEAD ...
...MIGHT FILL UP WITH NOTHING BUT THOUGHTS ABOUT IZUMI.
THAT'S SCARY.
ARGH! IT'S SO ANNOYING BEING PUSHED AROUND BY UNJUST GROWNUPS!
...MAYBE A SHOPPING SPREE WILL CHEER YOU UP?
"SHOP-PING SPREE" ?
Kamatani Books
Kamatani Books
本
URK ...!!

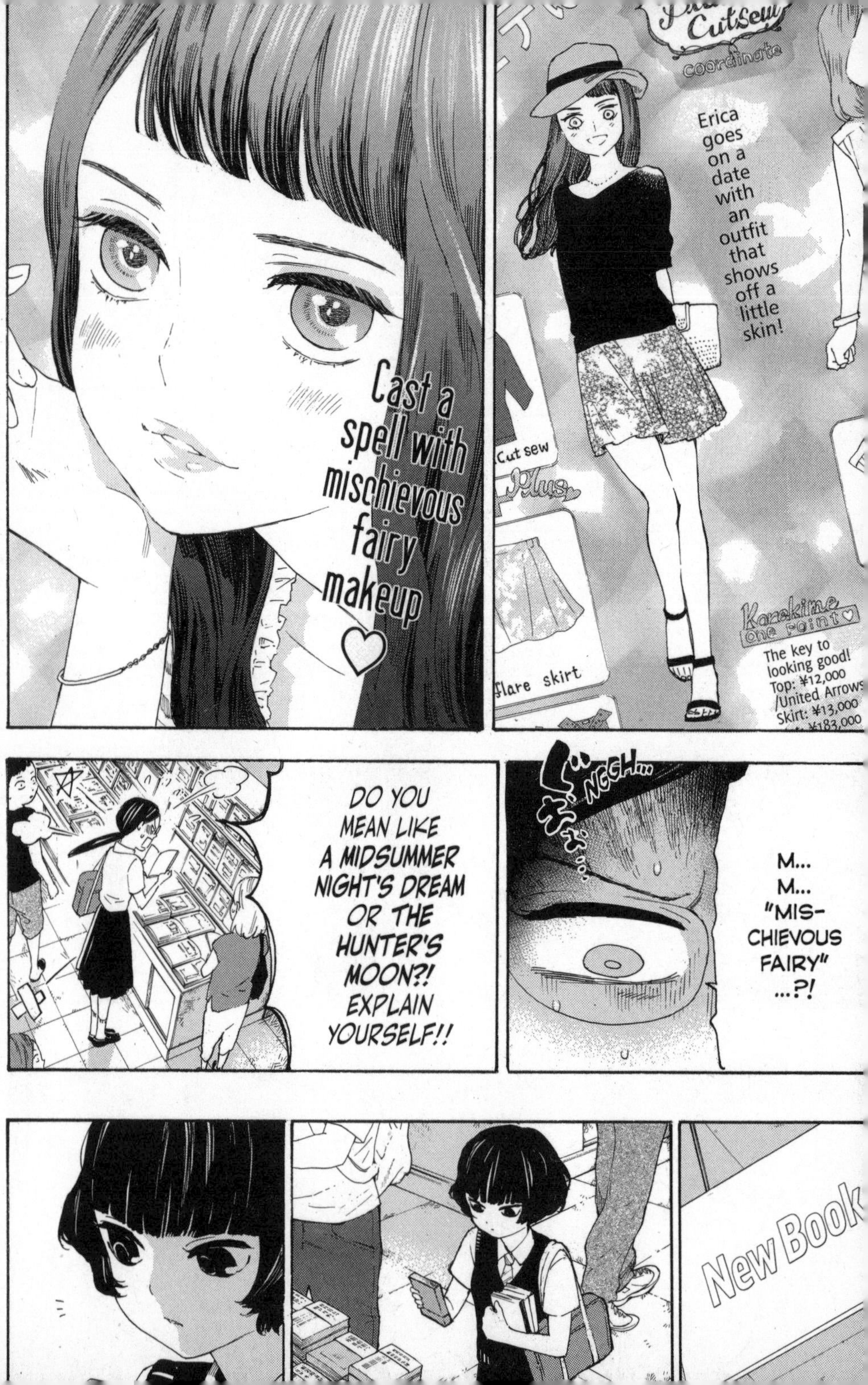
Cutsew
coordinate
Erica goes on a date with an outfit that shows off a little skin!
Cut sew
flare skirt
Korekime
one point
The key to looking good!
Top: ¥12,000
/United Arrows
Skirt: ¥13,000
Cast a spell with mischievous fairy makeup ♡
NGGH...
M... M... "MIS-CHIEVOUS FAIRY" ...?!
DO YOU MEAN LIKE A MIDSUMMER NIGHT'S DREAM OR THE HUNTER'S MOON?! EXPLAIN YOURSELF!!
New Book

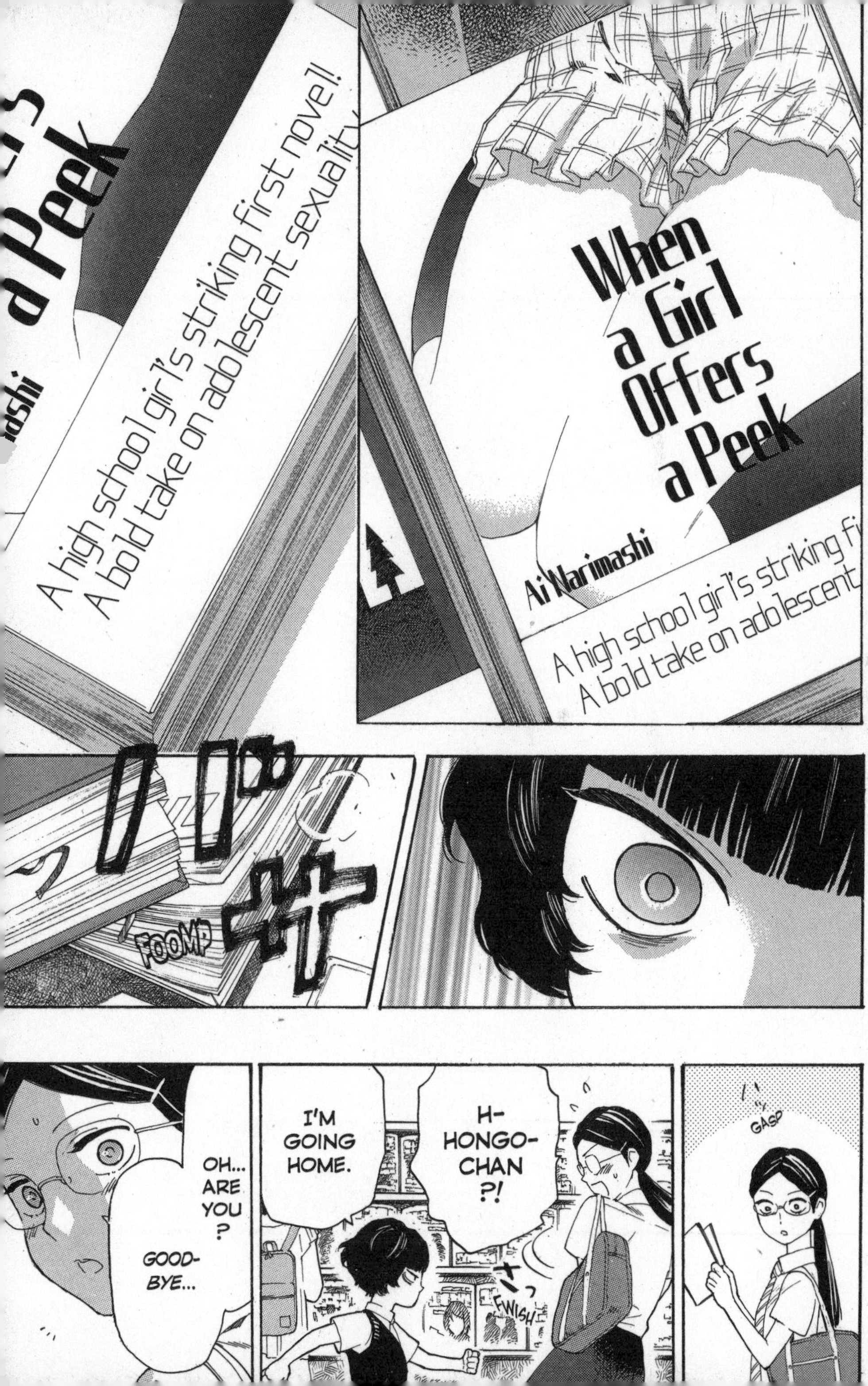
When a Girl Offers a Peek
Ai Warimashi
A high school girl's striking fi
A bold take on adolescent
a Peek
A high school girl's striking first novel!
A bold take on adolescent sexuality
FOOMP
GASP
H-HONGO-CHAN?!
I'M GOING HOME.
FWISH
OH... ARE YOU?
GOOD-BYE...

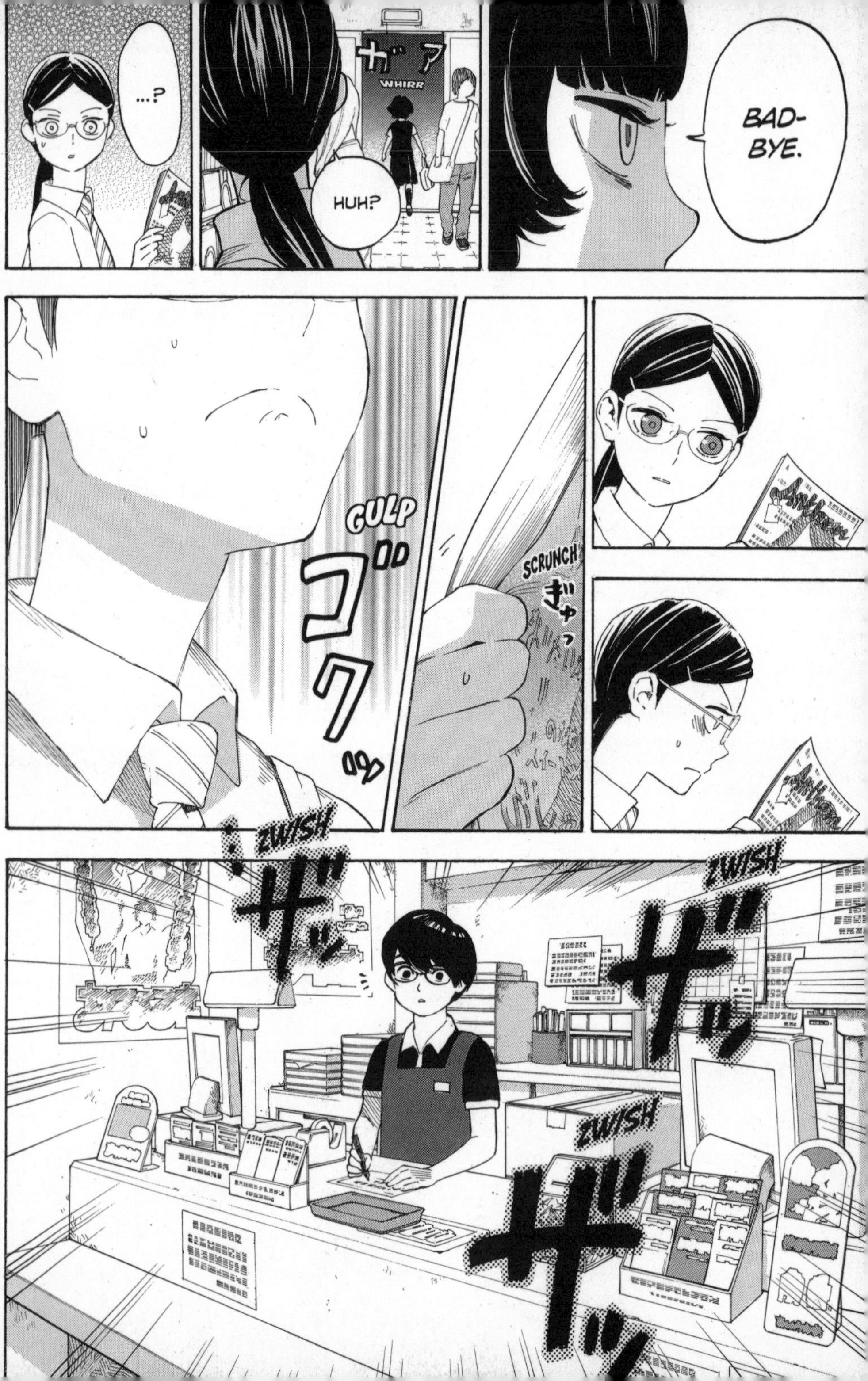
BAD-BYE.
ガァ
WHIRR
HUH?
...?
SCRUNCH
ぎゅっ
GULP
ゴクッ
ZWISH
ザッ
ZWISH
ザッ
ZWISH
ザッ

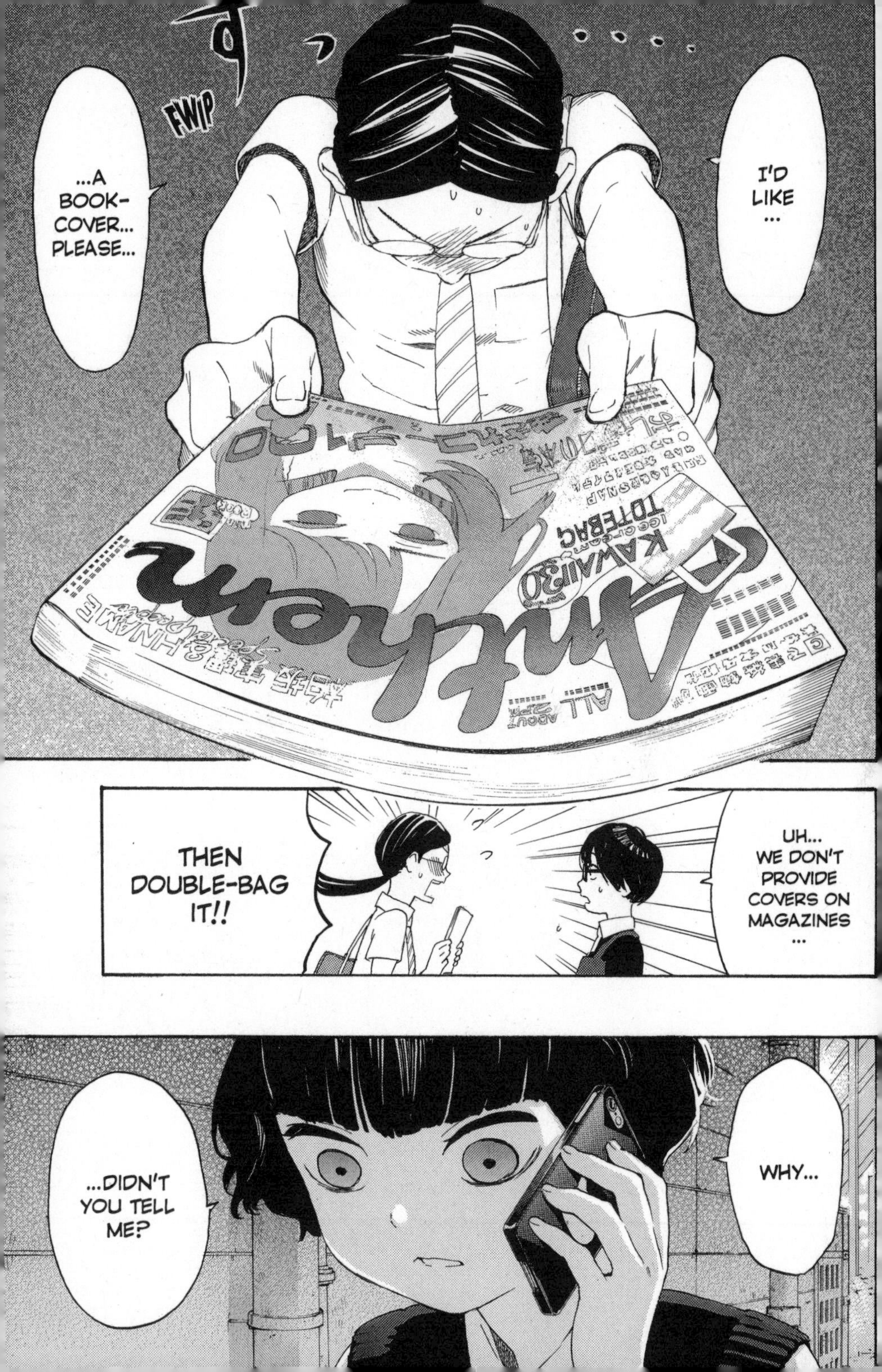
I'D LIKE ...
FWIP
...A BOOK-COVER... PLEASE...
UH... WE DON'T PROVIDE COVERS ON MAGAZINES ...
THEN DOUBLE-BAG IT!!
WHY...
...DIDN'T YOU TELL ME?

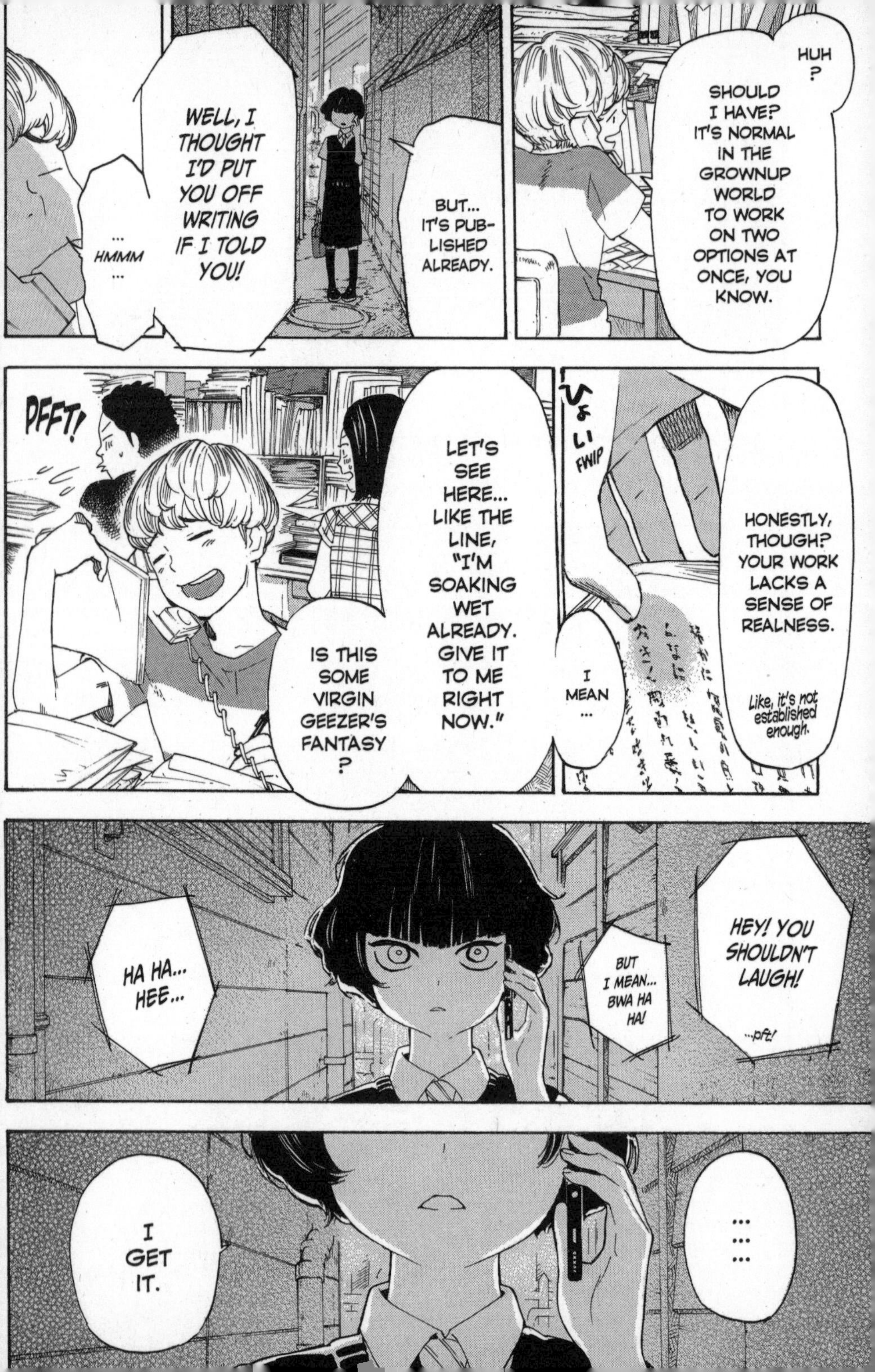
HUH?
SHOULD I HAVE? IT'S NORMAL IN THE GROWNUP WORLD TO WORK ON TWO OPTIONS AT ONCE, YOU KNOW.
BUT... IT'S PUB-LISHED ALREADY.
WELL, I THOUGHT I'D PUT YOU OFF WRITING IF I TOLD YOU!
... HMMM ...
HONESTLY, THOUGH? YOUR WORK LACKS A SENSE OF REALNESS.
Like, it's not established enough.
ひょい
FWIP
I MEAN ...
LET'S SEE HERE... LIKE THE LINE, "I'M SOAKING WET ALREADY. GIVE IT TO ME RIGHT NOW."
IS THIS SOME VIRGIN GEEZER'S FANTASY?
PFFT!
HEY! YOU SHOULDN'T LAUGH!
...pft!
BUT I MEAN... BWA HA HA!
HA HA... HEE...
... ...
I GET IT.

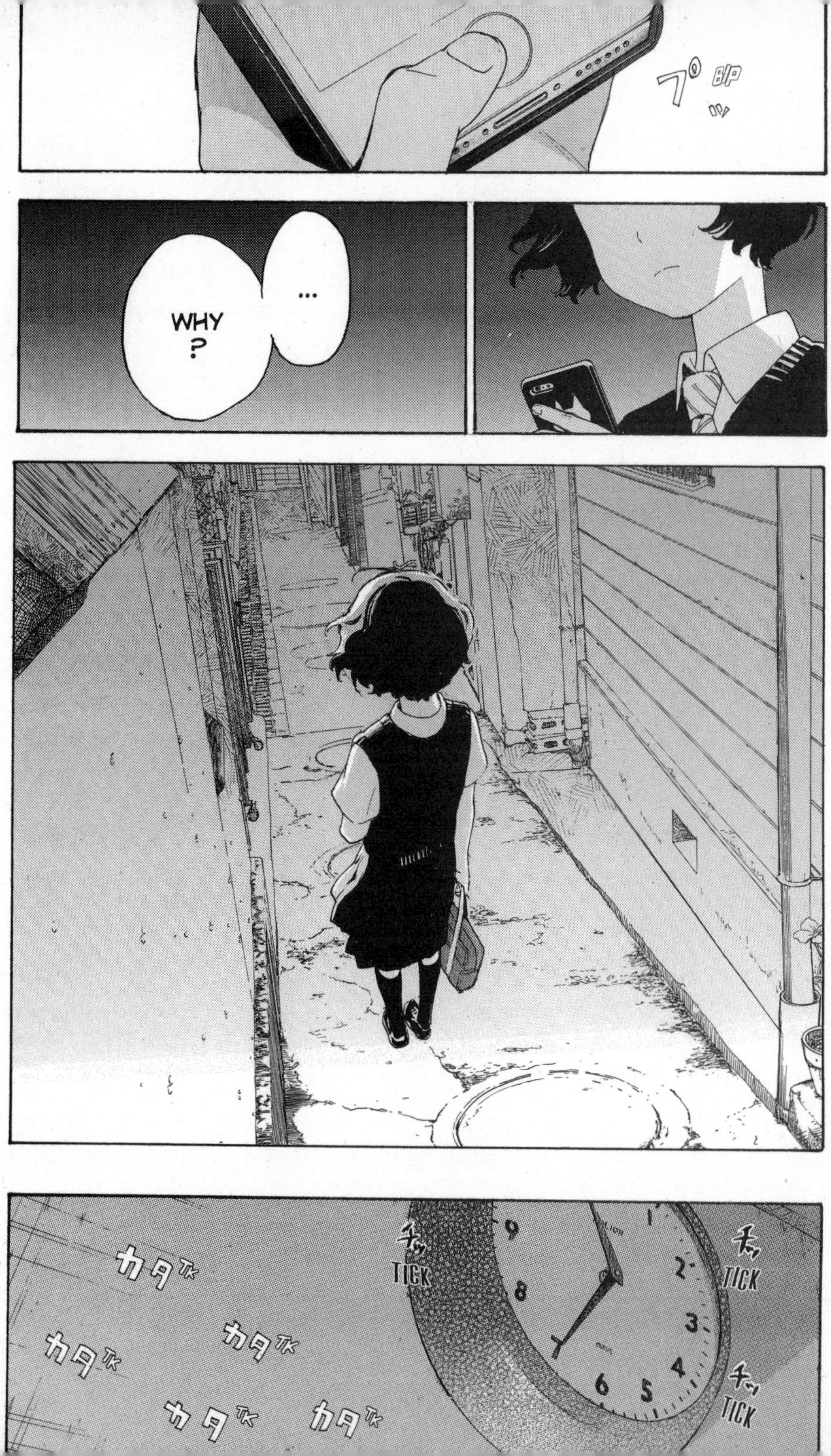

プ BIP
...
WHY ?
チッ TICK
チッ TICK
カタ TK
チッ TICK
カタ TK
カタ TK
カタ TK
カタ TK

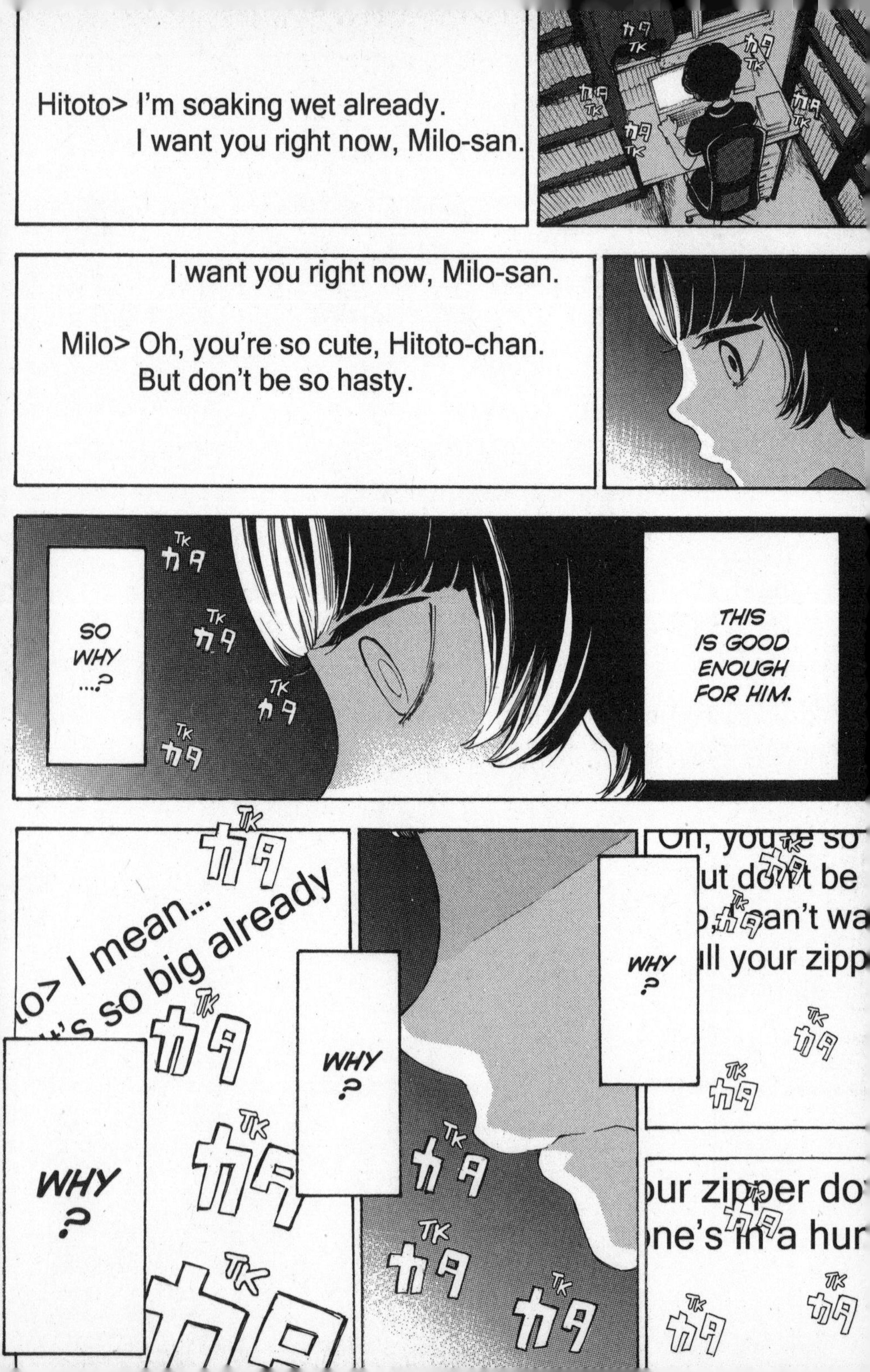
TK カタ
Hitoto> I'm soaking wet already.
I want you right now, Milo-san.
I want you right now, Milo-san.
Milo> Oh, you're so cute, Hitoto-chan.
But don't be so hasty.
THIS IS GOOD ENOUGH FOR HIM.
TK カタ
SO WHY ...?
Oh, you're so
ut don't be
o, can't wa
ull your zipp
WHY ?
our zipper do
ne's in a hur
TK カタ
WHY ?
TK カタ
o> I mean...
t's so big already
WHY ?
TK カタ

WHY?

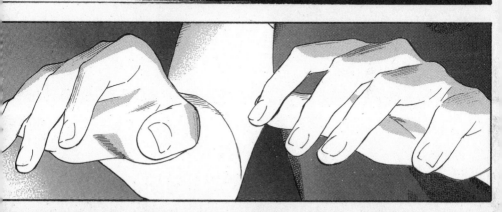

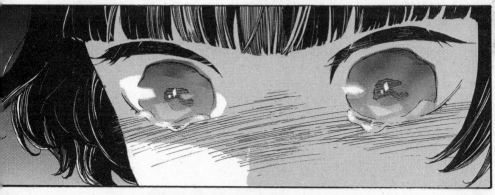

Milo> Hitoto-chan, are you not really in the mood today?

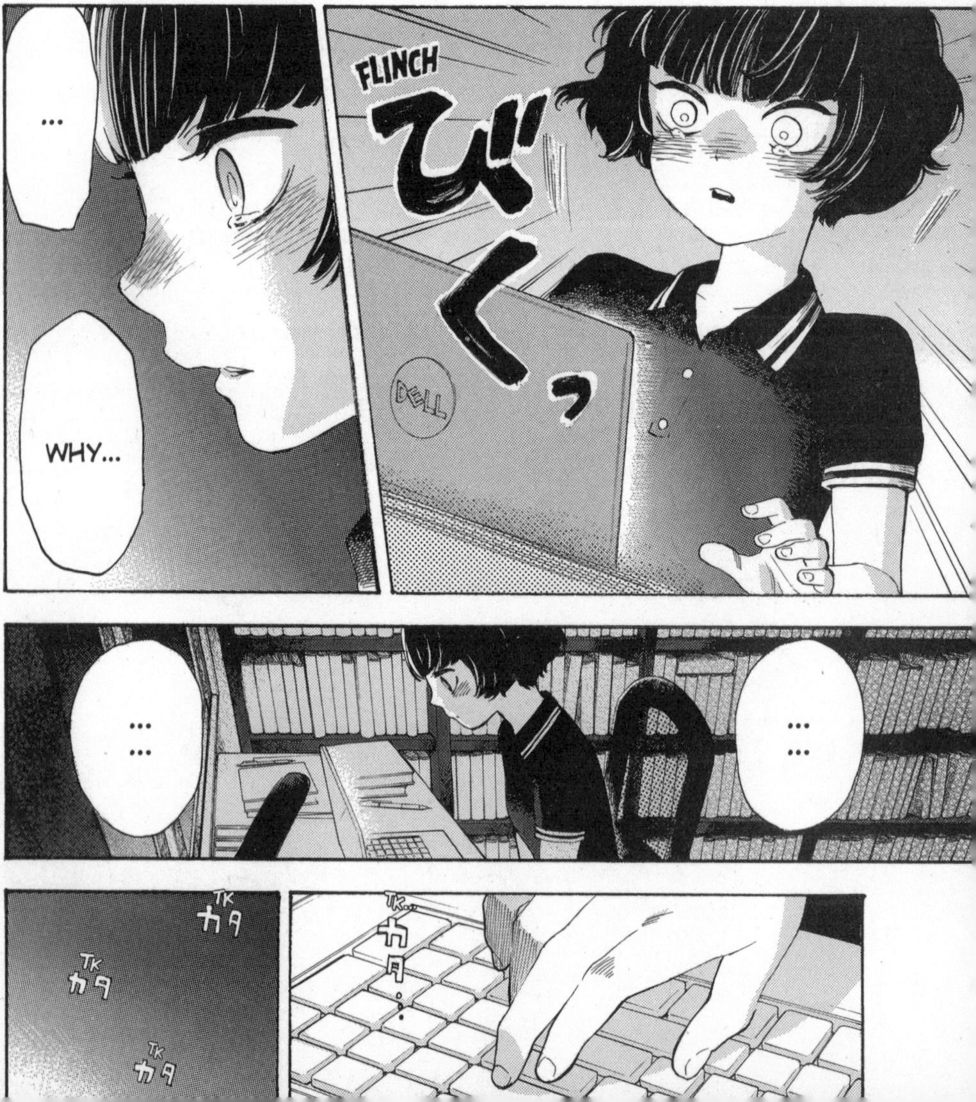
FLINCH
びくっ
...
WHY...
... ...
... ...
TK...
カタ...
TK
カタ
TK
カタ
TK
カタ

Hitoto> I don't know.

TK カタ
TK カタ
TK カタ
TK カタ
TK カタ

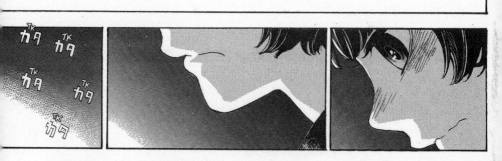

Hitoto> Chatting isn't enough.

I want to really do it with you, Milo-san

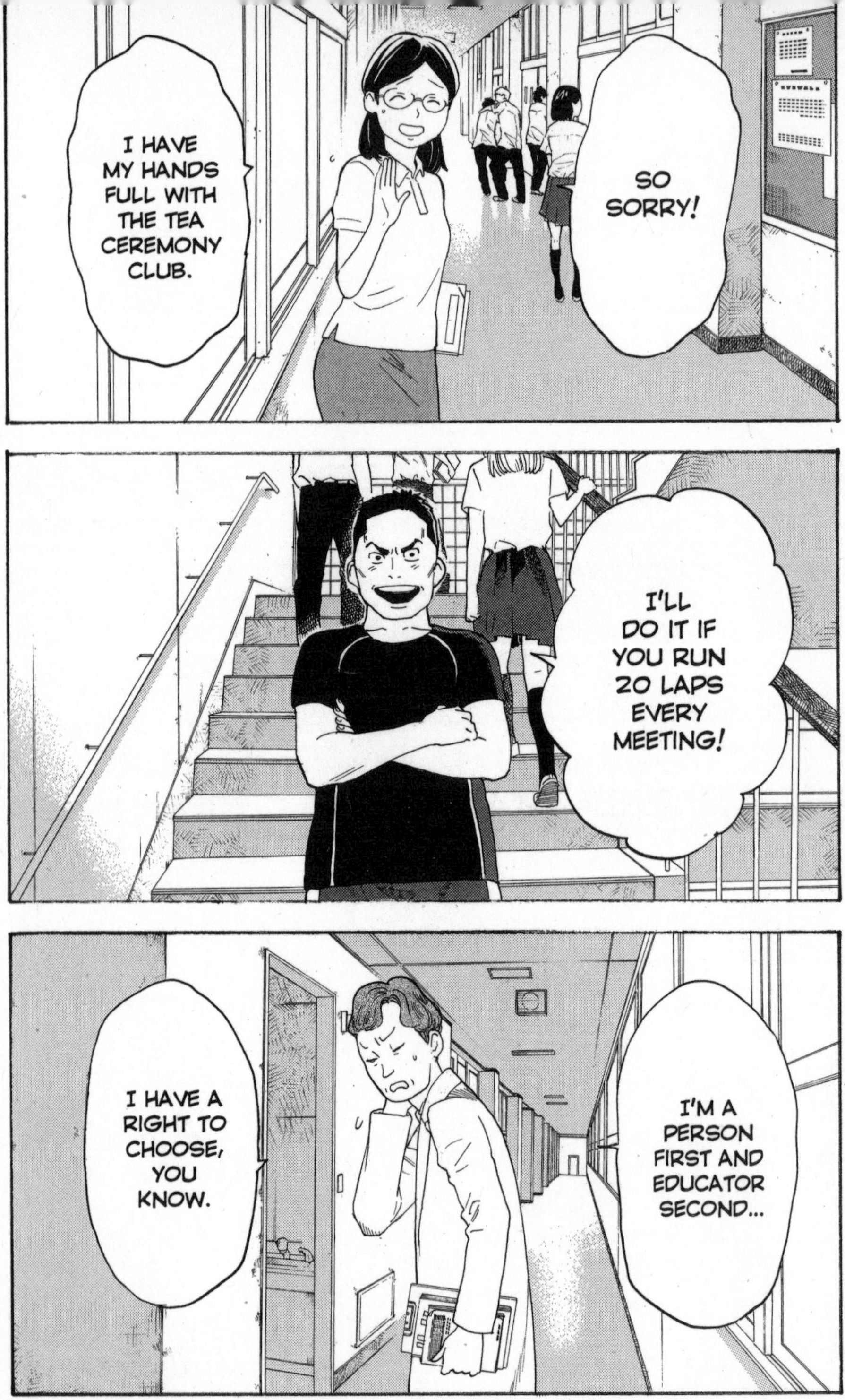
SO SORRY!
I HAVE MY HANDS FULL WITH THE TEA CEREMONY CLUB.
I'LL DO IT IF YOU RUN 20 LAPS EVERY MEETING!
I'M A PERSON FIRST AND EDUCATOR SECOND...
I HAVE A RIGHT TO CHOOSE, YOU KNOW.

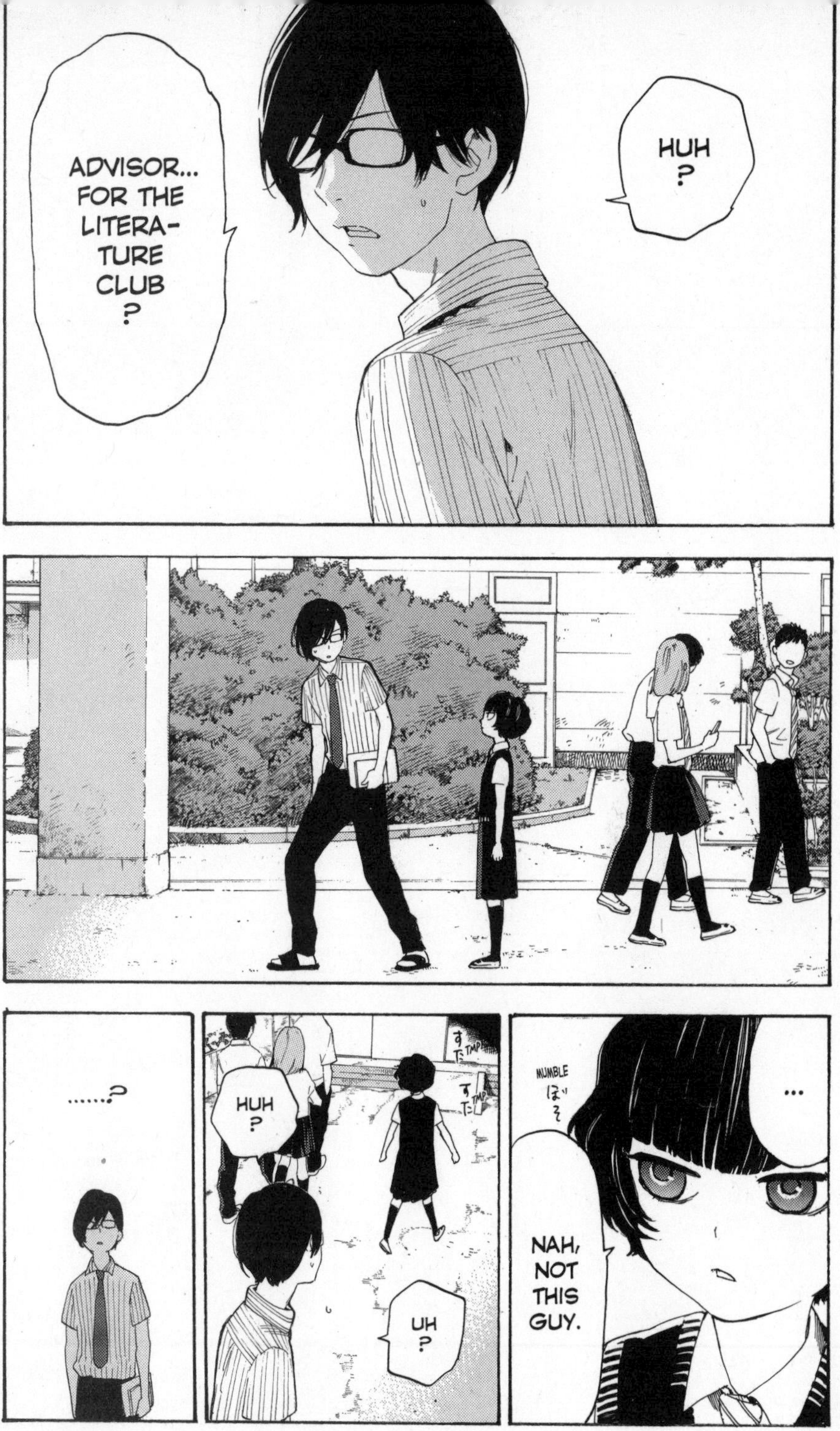
HUH?
ADVISOR... FOR THE LITERA-TURE CLUB?
...
MUMBLE
NAH, NOT THIS GUY.
TMP
TMP
HUH?
UH?
......?

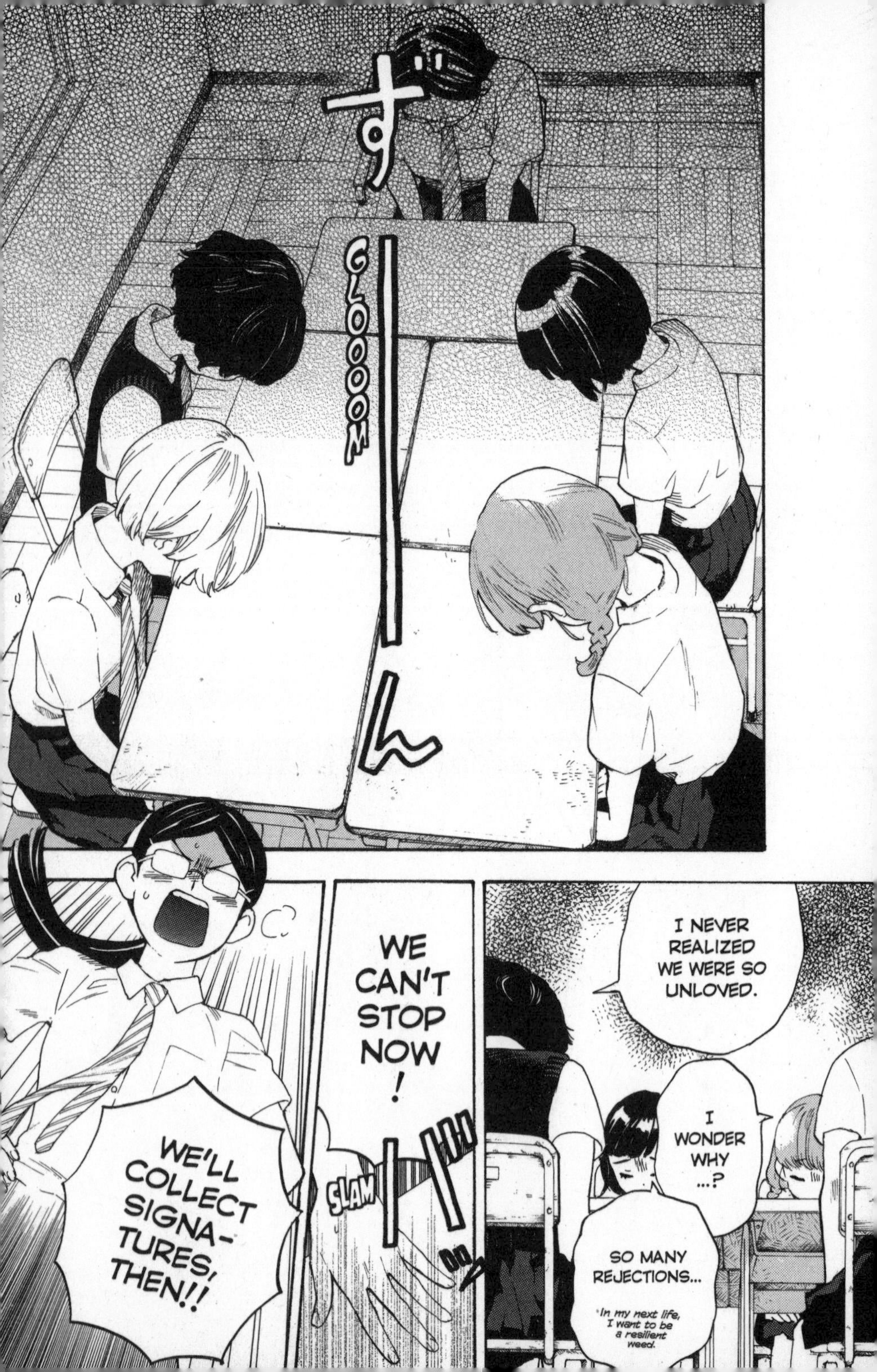
すーーん
GLOOOOOM
I NEVER REALIZED WE WERE SO UNLOVED.
I WONDER WHY ...?
SO MANY REJECTIONS...
In my next life, I want to be a resilient weed.
WE CAN'T STOP NOW!
SLAM
WE'LL COLLECT SIGNATURES, THEN!!

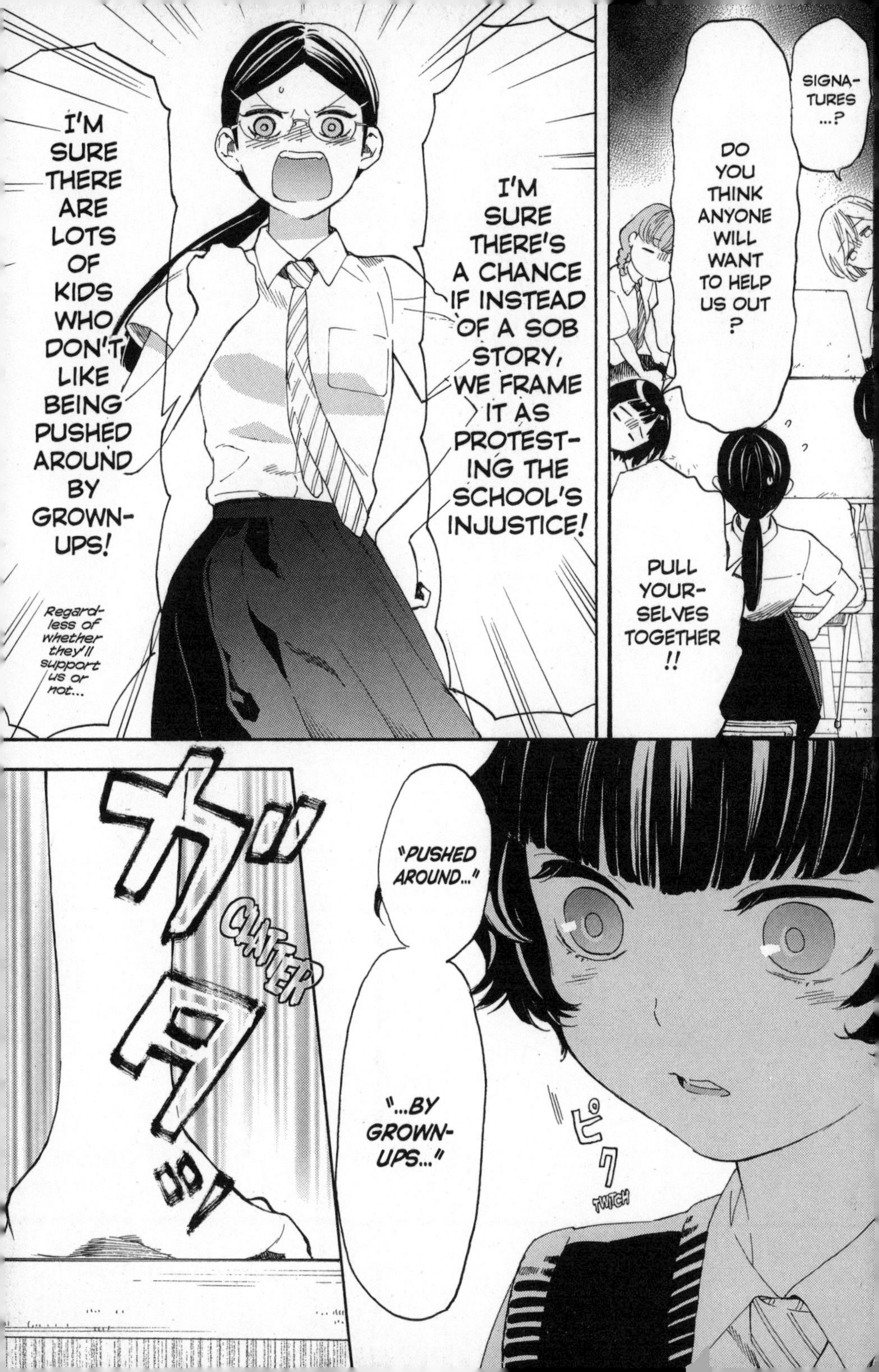
SIGNA-TURES ...?
DO YOU THINK ANYONE WILL WANT TO HELP US OUT ?
PULL YOUR-SELVES TOGETHER !!
I'M SURE THERE'S A CHANCE IF INSTEAD OF A SOB STORY, WE FRAME IT AS PROTEST-ING THE SCHOOL'S INJUSTICE!
I'M SURE THERE ARE LOTS OF KIDS WHO DON'T LIKE BEING PUSHED AROUND BY GROWN-UPS!
Regard-less of whether they'll support us or not...
"PUSHED AROUND..."
"...BY GROWN-UPS..."
ピク
TWITCH
ガタッ
CLATTER

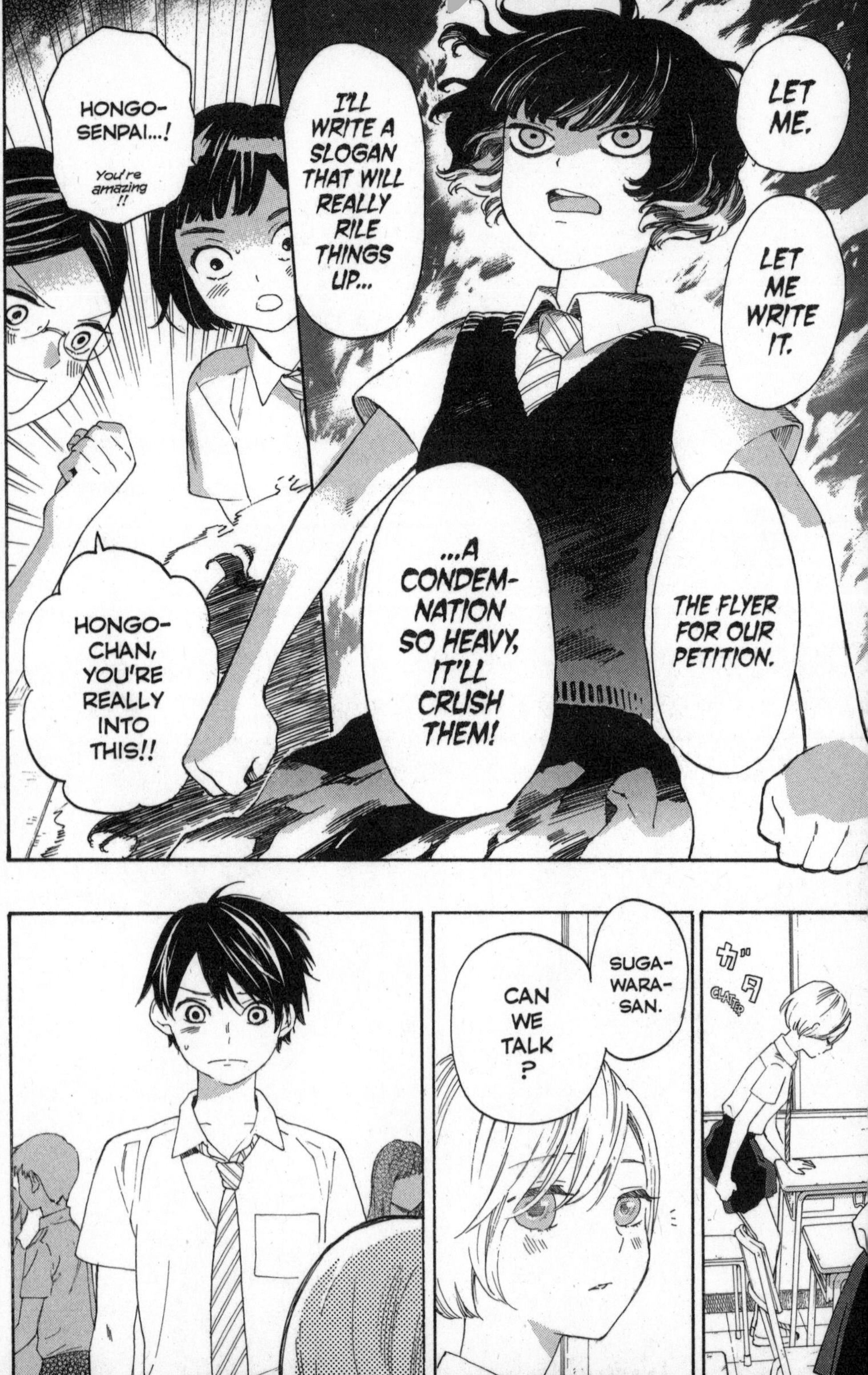
LET ME.
LET ME WRITE IT.
THE FLYER FOR OUR PETITION.
...A CONDEMNATION SO HEAVY, IT'LL CRUSH THEM!
I'LL WRITE A SLOGAN THAT WILL REALLY RILE THINGS UP...
HONGO-SENPAI...!
You're amazing!!
HONGO-CHAN, YOU'RE REALLY INTO THIS!!
カタ
CLATTER
SUGAWARA-SAN.
CAN WE TALK?

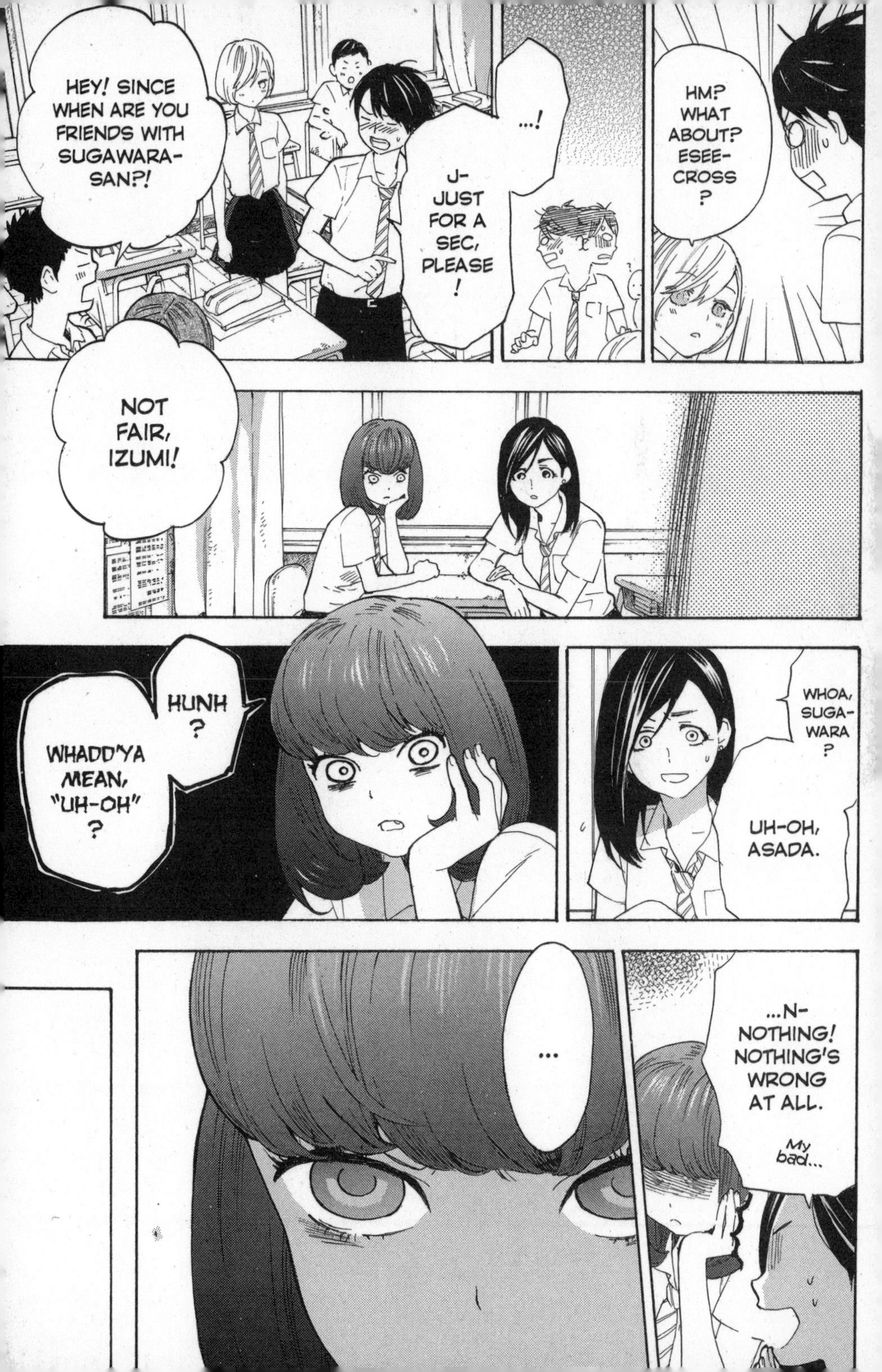
HM? WHAT ABOUT? ESEE-CROSS?
...!
J-JUST FOR A SEC, PLEASE!
HEY! SINCE WHEN ARE YOU FRIENDS WITH SUGAWARA-SAN?!
NOT FAIR, IZUMI!
WHOA, SUGAWARA?
UH-OH, ASADA.
HUNH?
WHADD'YA MEAN, "UH-OH"?
...N-NOTHING! NOTHING'S WRONG AT ALL.
My bad...
...

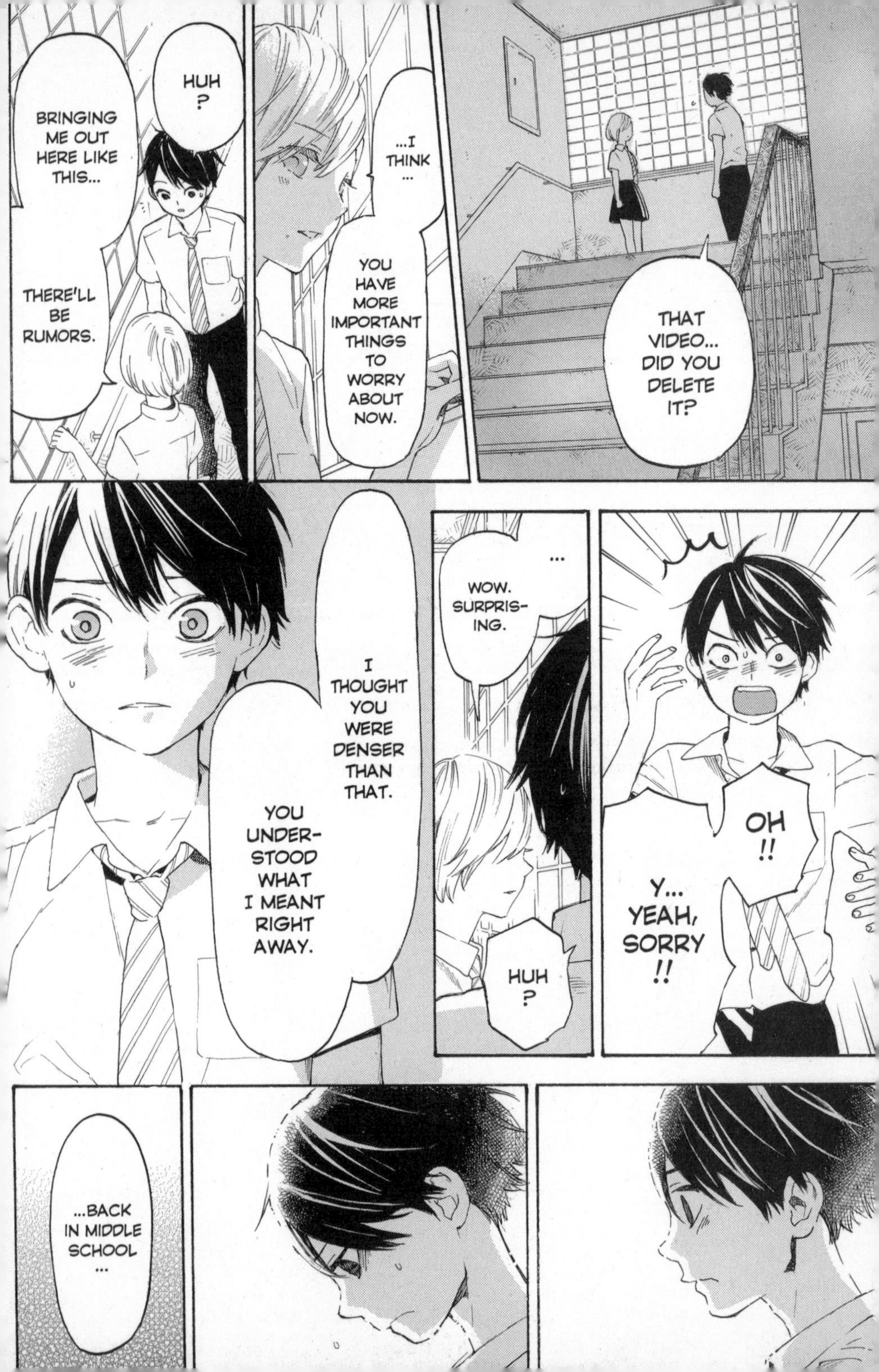
THAT VIDEO... DID YOU DELETE IT?
...I THINK ...
YOU HAVE MORE IMPORTANT THINGS TO WORRY ABOUT NOW.
HUH ?
BRINGING ME OUT HERE LIKE THIS...
THERE'LL BE RUMORS.
OH !!
Y... YEAH, SORRY !!
...
WOW. SURPRIS-ING.
HUH ?
I THOUGHT YOU WERE DENSER THAN THAT.
YOU UNDER-STOOD WHAT I MEANT RIGHT AWAY.
...BACK IN MIDDLE SCHOOL ...

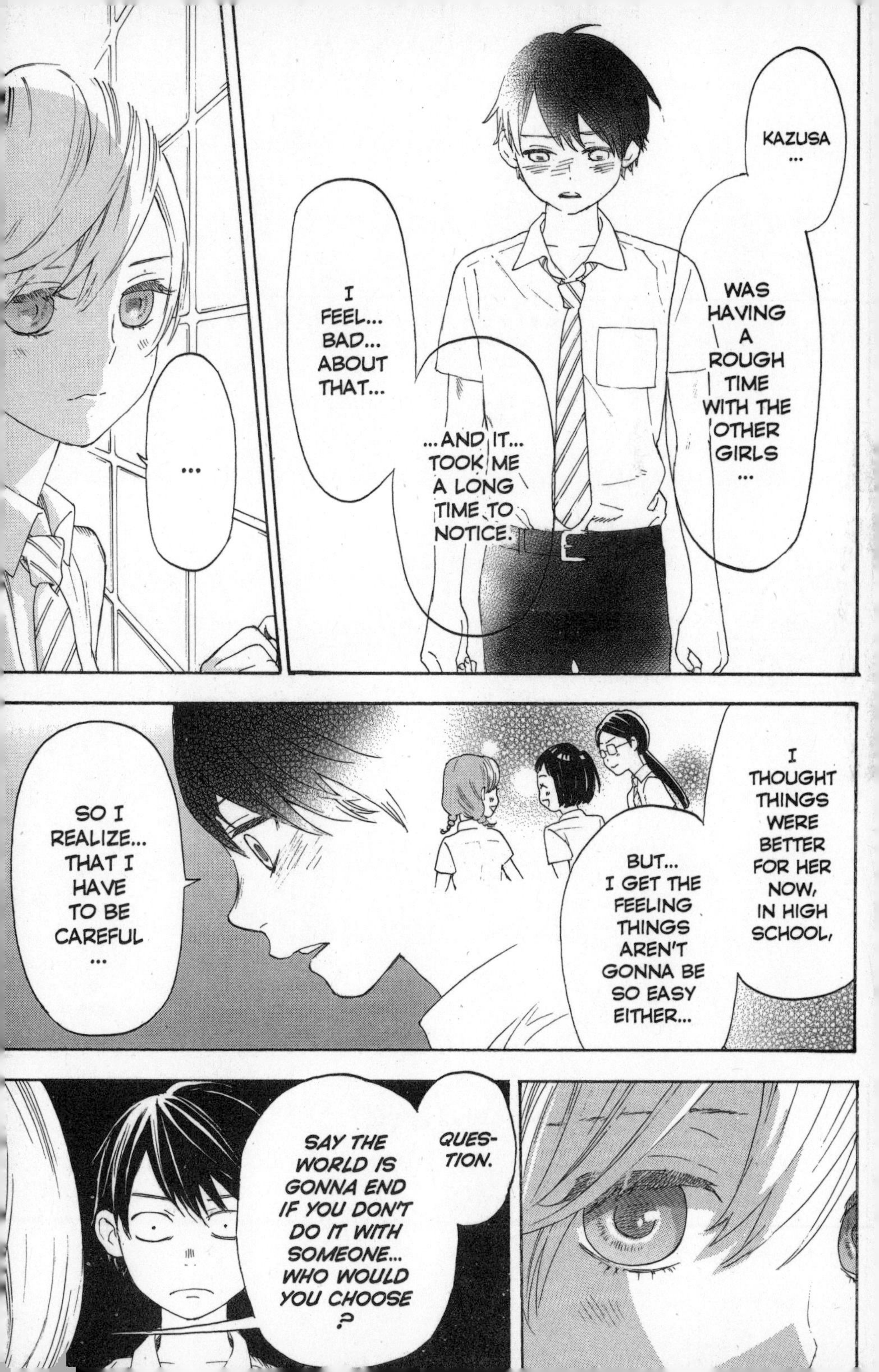
KAZUSA ...
WAS HAVING A ROUGH TIME WITH THE OTHER GIRLS ...
...AND IT... TOOK ME A LONG TIME TO NOTICE.
I FEEL... BAD... ABOUT THAT...
...
I THOUGHT THINGS WERE BETTER FOR HER NOW, IN HIGH SCHOOL,
BUT... I GET THE FEELING THINGS AREN'T GONNA BE SO EASY EITHER...
SO I REALIZE... THAT I HAVE TO BE CAREFUL ...
QUES-TION.
SAY THE WORLD IS GONNA END IF YOU DON'T DO IT WITH SOMEONE... WHO WOULD YOU CHOOSE ?

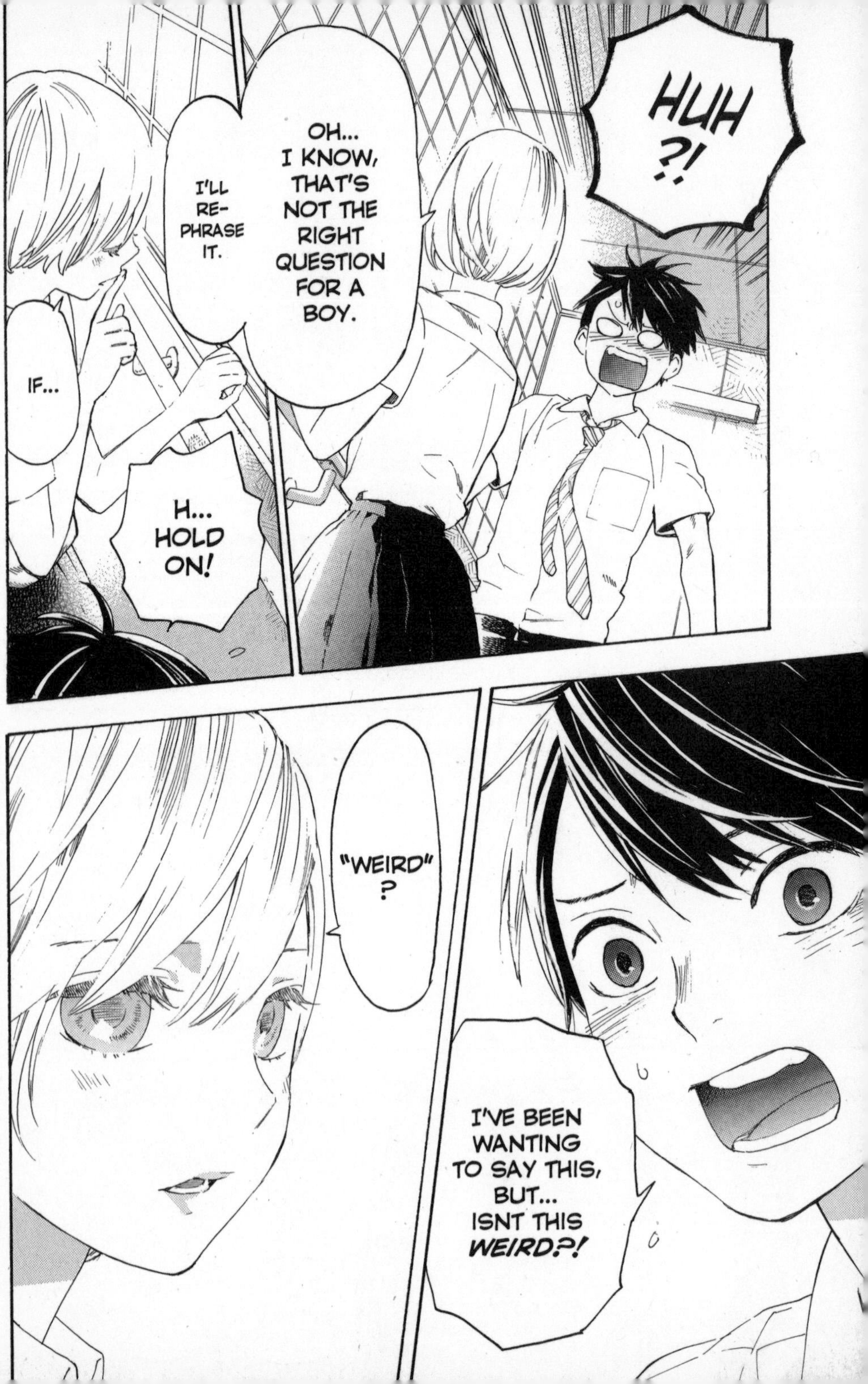
HUH?!
OH... I KNOW, THAT'S NOT THE RIGHT QUESTION FOR A BOY.
I'LL RE-PHRASE IT.
IF...
H... HOLD ON!
I'VE BEEN WANTING TO SAY THIS, BUT... ISNT THIS *WEIRD?!*
"WEIRD"?

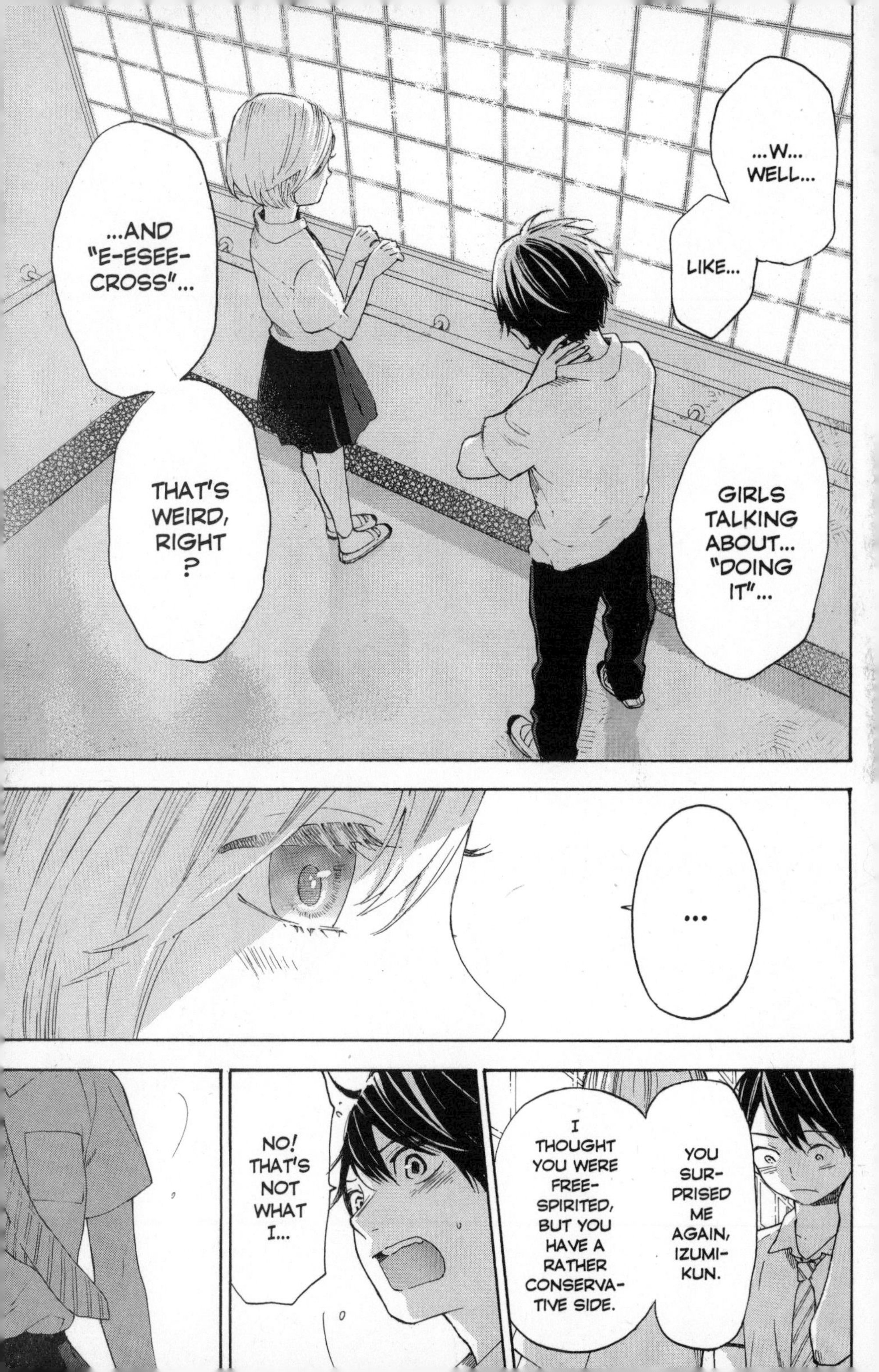
...W... WELL...
LIKE...
GIRLS TALKING ABOUT... "DOING IT"...
...AND "E-ESEE-CROSS"...
THAT'S WEIRD, RIGHT?
...
YOU SUR-PRISED ME AGAIN, IZUMI-KUN.
I THOUGHT YOU WERE FREE-SPIRITED, BUT YOU HAVE A RATHER CONSERVA-TIVE SIDE.
NO! THAT'S NOT WHAT I...

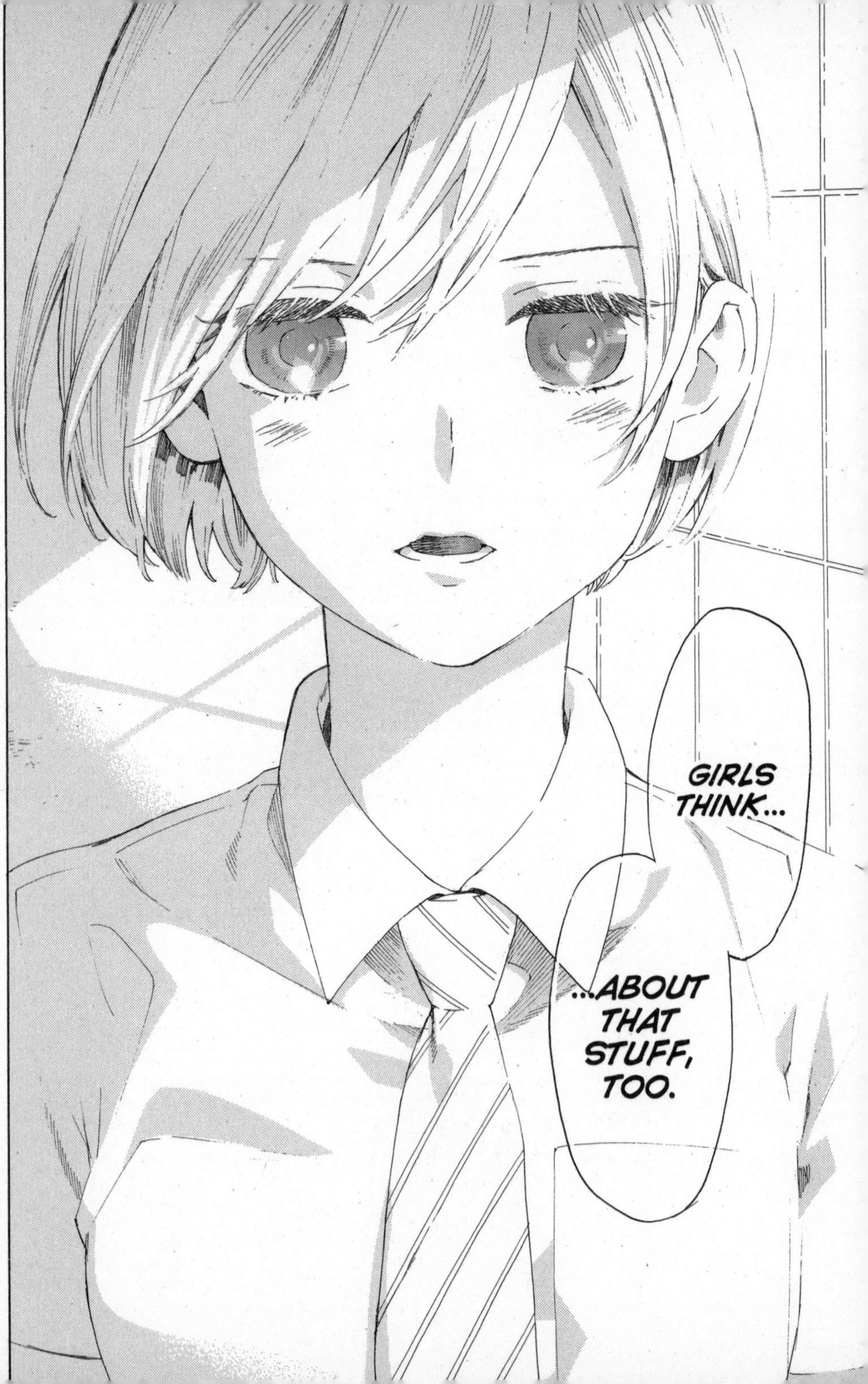
GIRLS THINK...
...ABOUT THAT STUFF, TOO.

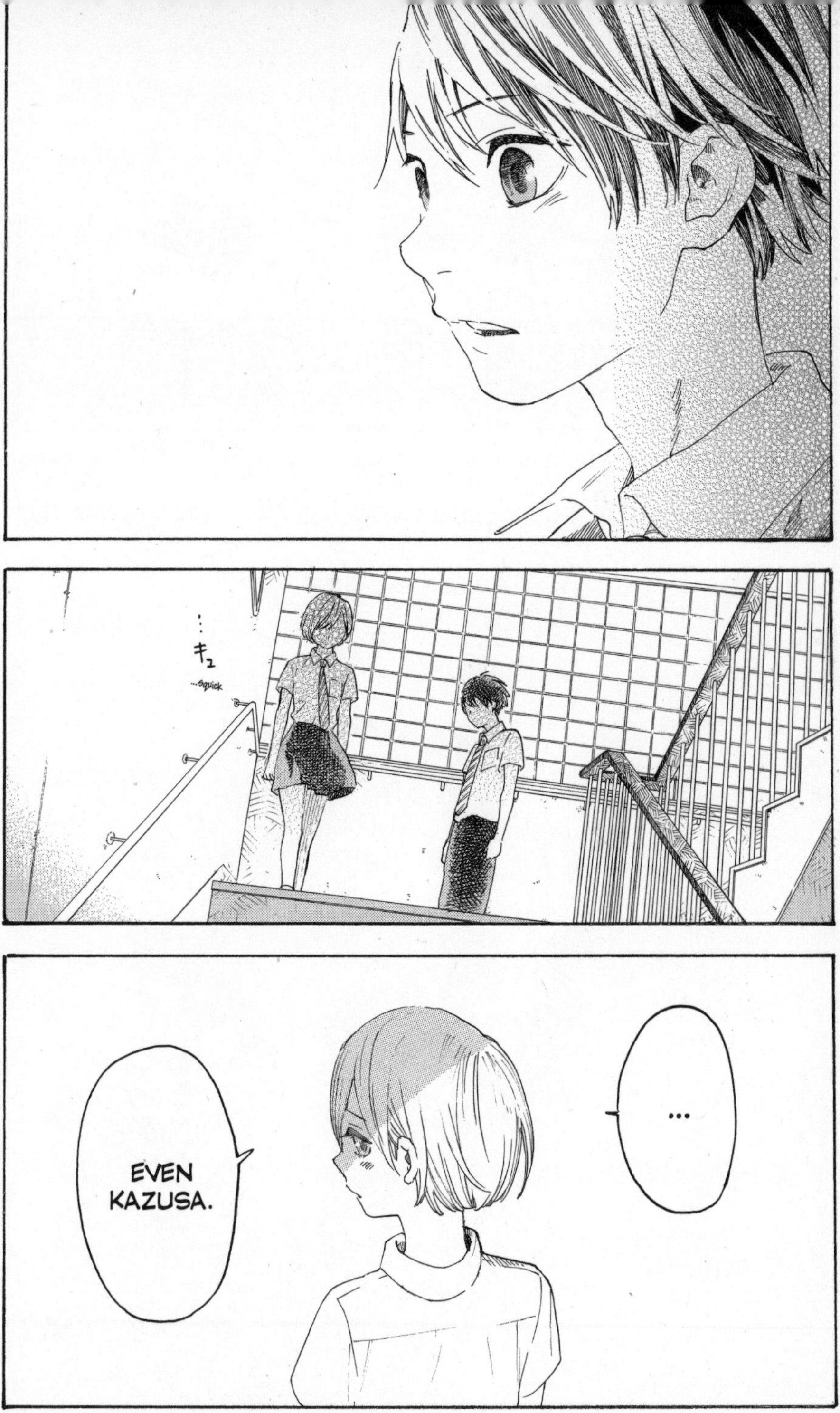
…キュ
...squick
...
EVEN KAZUSA.

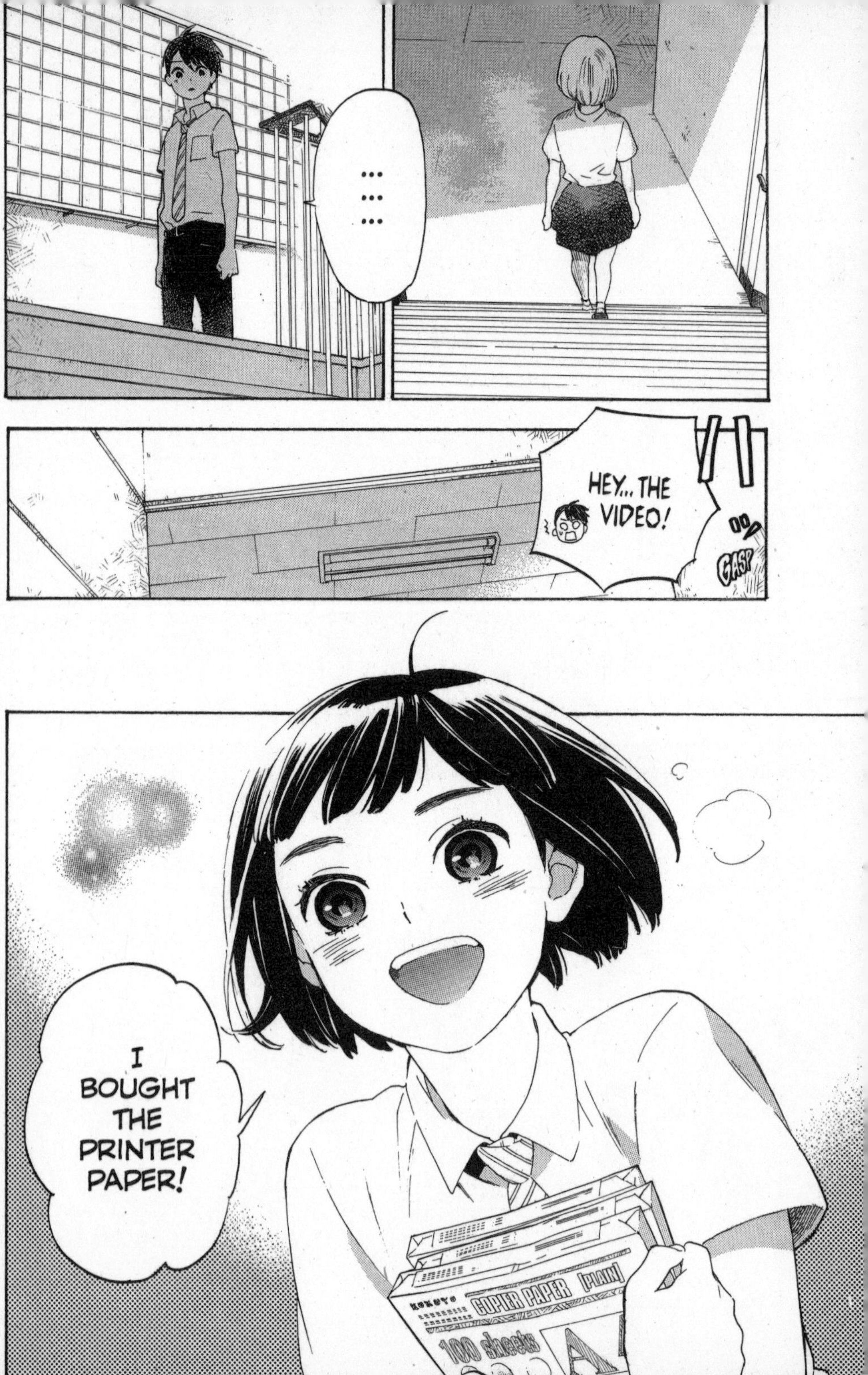
... ...
HEY... THE VIDEO!
GASP
I BOUGHT THE PRINTER PAPER!
COPIER PAPER [PLAIN]
100 sheets

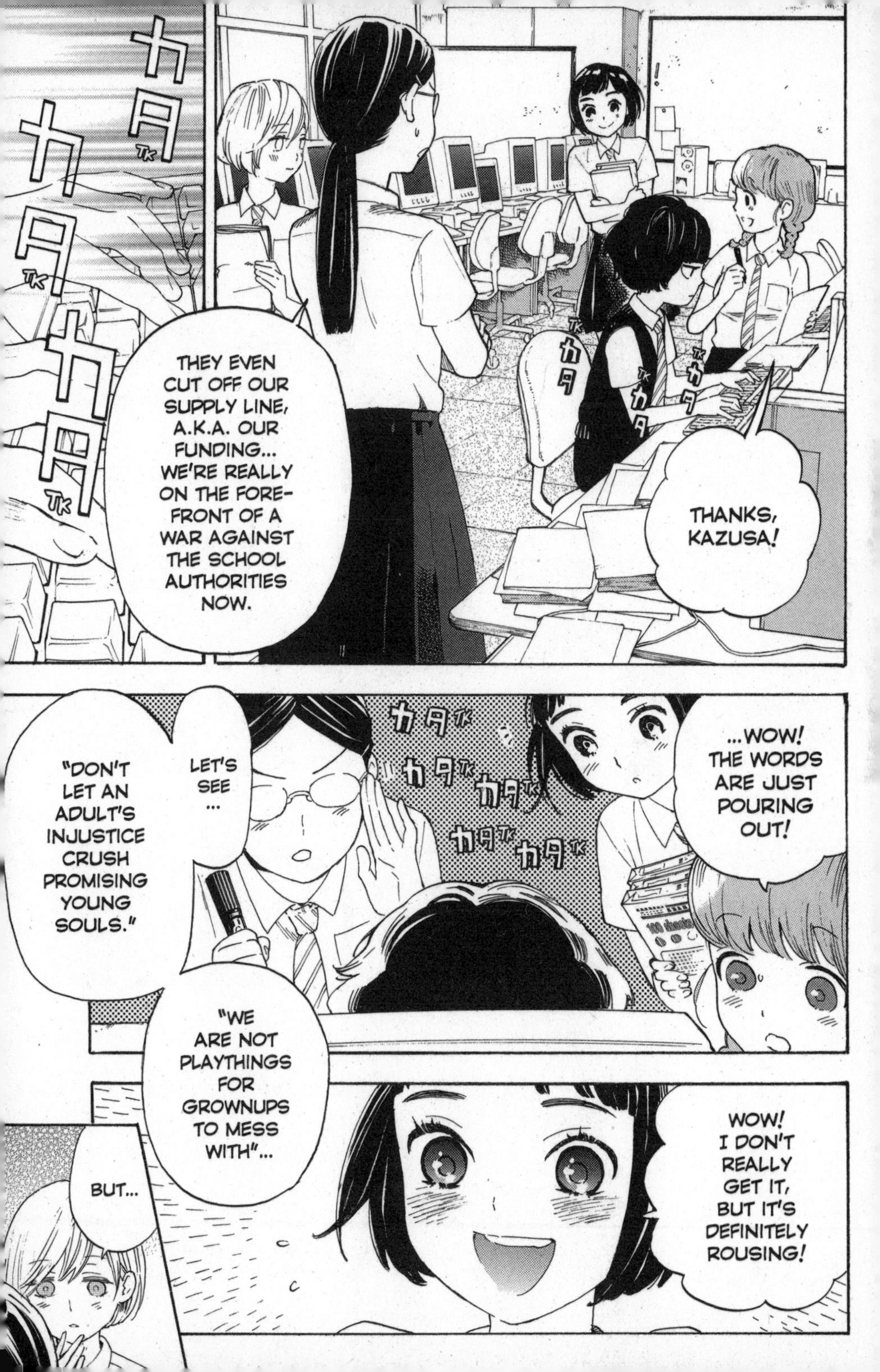
カタ TK
カタ TK
カタ TK
カタ TK
THANKS, KAZUSA!
THEY EVEN CUT OFF OUR SUPPLY LINE, A.K.A. OUR FUNDING... WE'RE REALLY ON THE FORE-FRONT OF A WAR AGAINST THE SCHOOL AUTHORITIES NOW.
...WOW! THE WORDS ARE JUST POURING OUT!
カタ TK
LET'S SEE ...
"DON'T LET AN ADULT'S INJUSTICE CRUSH PROMISING YOUNG SOULS."
"WE ARE NOT PLAYTHINGS FOR GROWNUPS TO MESS WITH"...
WOW! I DON'T REALLY GET IT, BUT IT'S DEFINITELY ROUSING!
BUT...

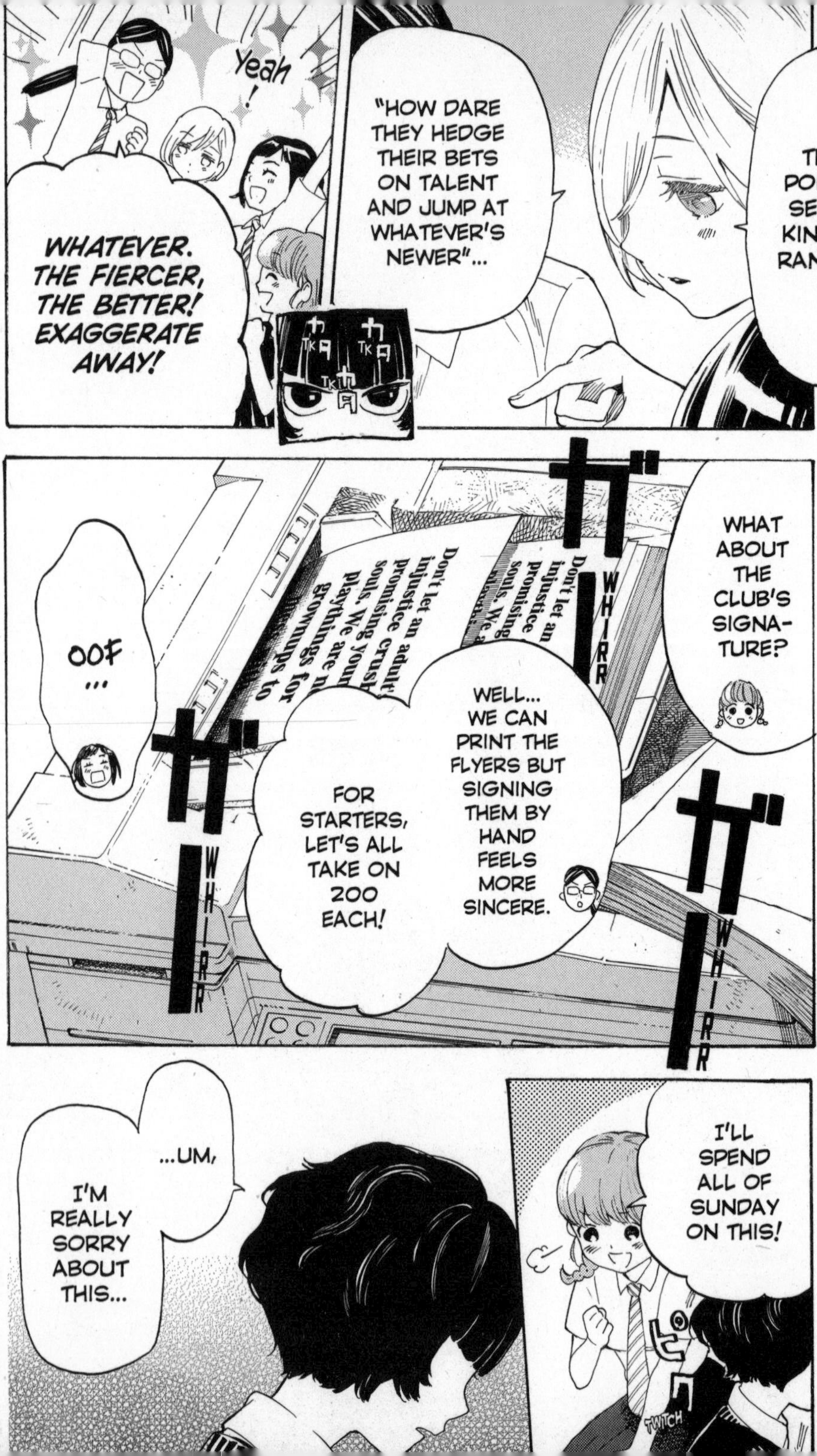
THIS POINT... SEEMS KIND OF RANDOM?
"HOW DARE THEY HEDGE THEIR BETS ON TALENT AND JUMP AT WHATEVER'S NEWER"...
Yeah!
WHATEVER. THE FIERCER, THE BETTER! EXAGGERATE AWAY!
TK TK TK
WHAT ABOUT THE CLUB'S SIGNATURE?
WHIRR
WELL... WE CAN PRINT THE FLYERS BUT SIGNING THEM BY HAND FEELS MORE SINCERE.
WHIRR
FOR STARTERS, LET'S ALL TAKE ON 200 EACH!
WHIRR
OOF...
I'LL SPEND ALL OF SUNDAY ON THIS!
TWITCH
...UM,
I'M REALLY SORRY ABOUT THIS...

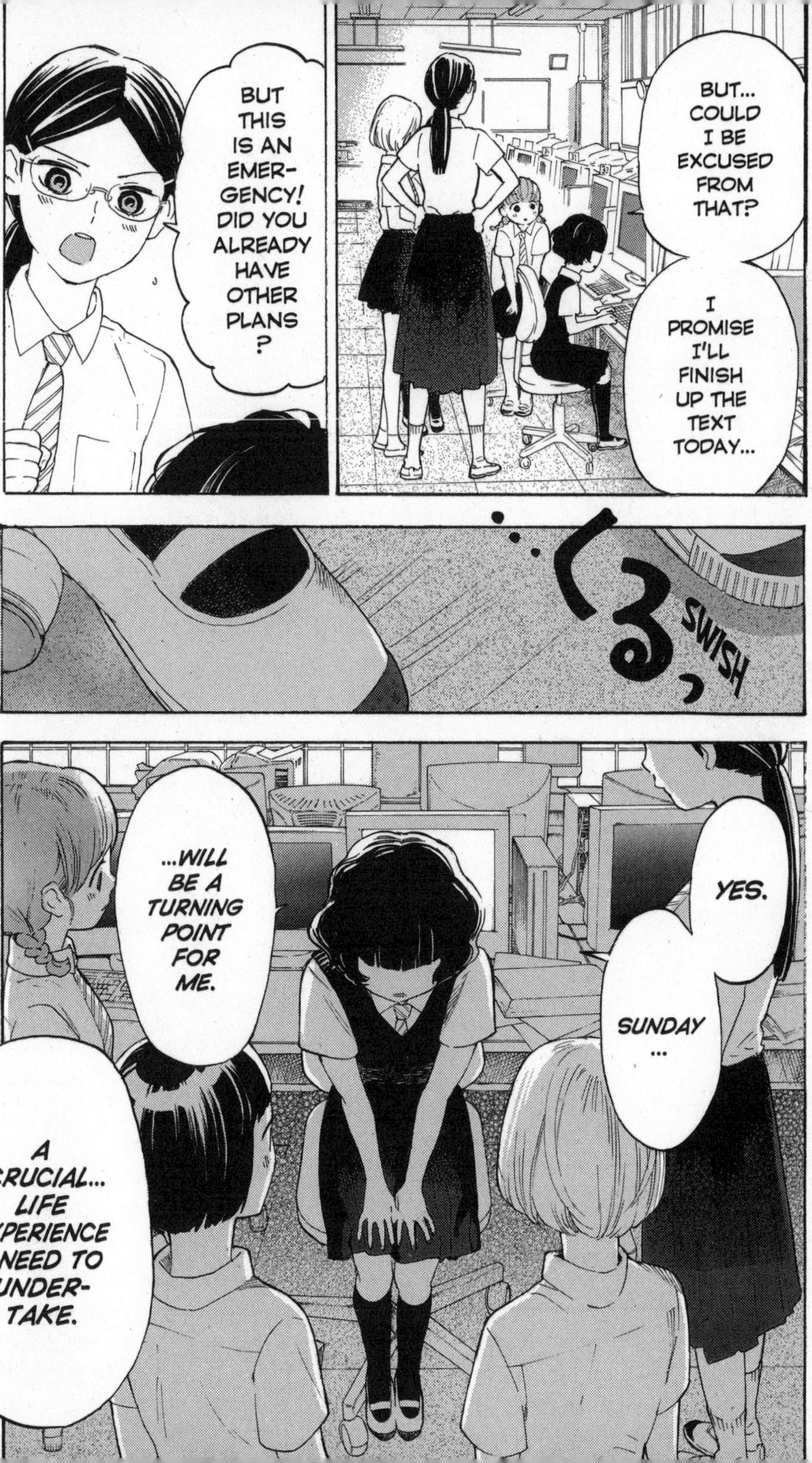
BUT... COULD I BE EXCUSED FROM THAT?
I PROMISE I'LL FINISH UP THE TEXT TODAY...
BUT THIS IS AN EMERGENCY! DID YOU ALREADY HAVE OTHER PLANS ?
くる
SWISH
YES.
SUNDAY ...
...WILL BE A TURNING POINT FOR ME.
A CRUCIAL... LIFE EXPERIENCE I NEED TO UNDERTAKE.

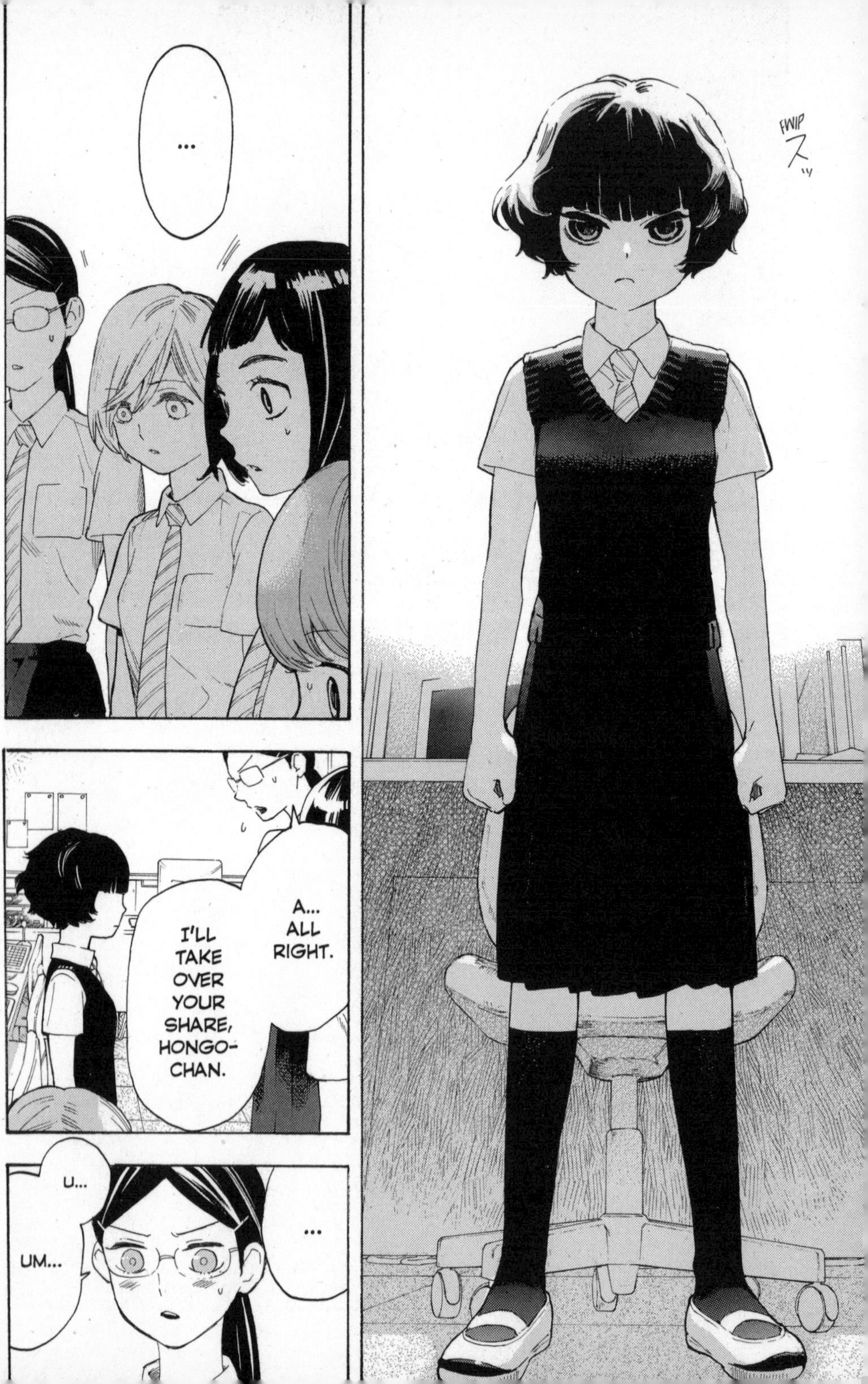
FWIP
スッ
...
A... ALL RIGHT.
I'LL TAKE OVER YOUR SHARE, HONGO-CHAN.
U...
UM...
...

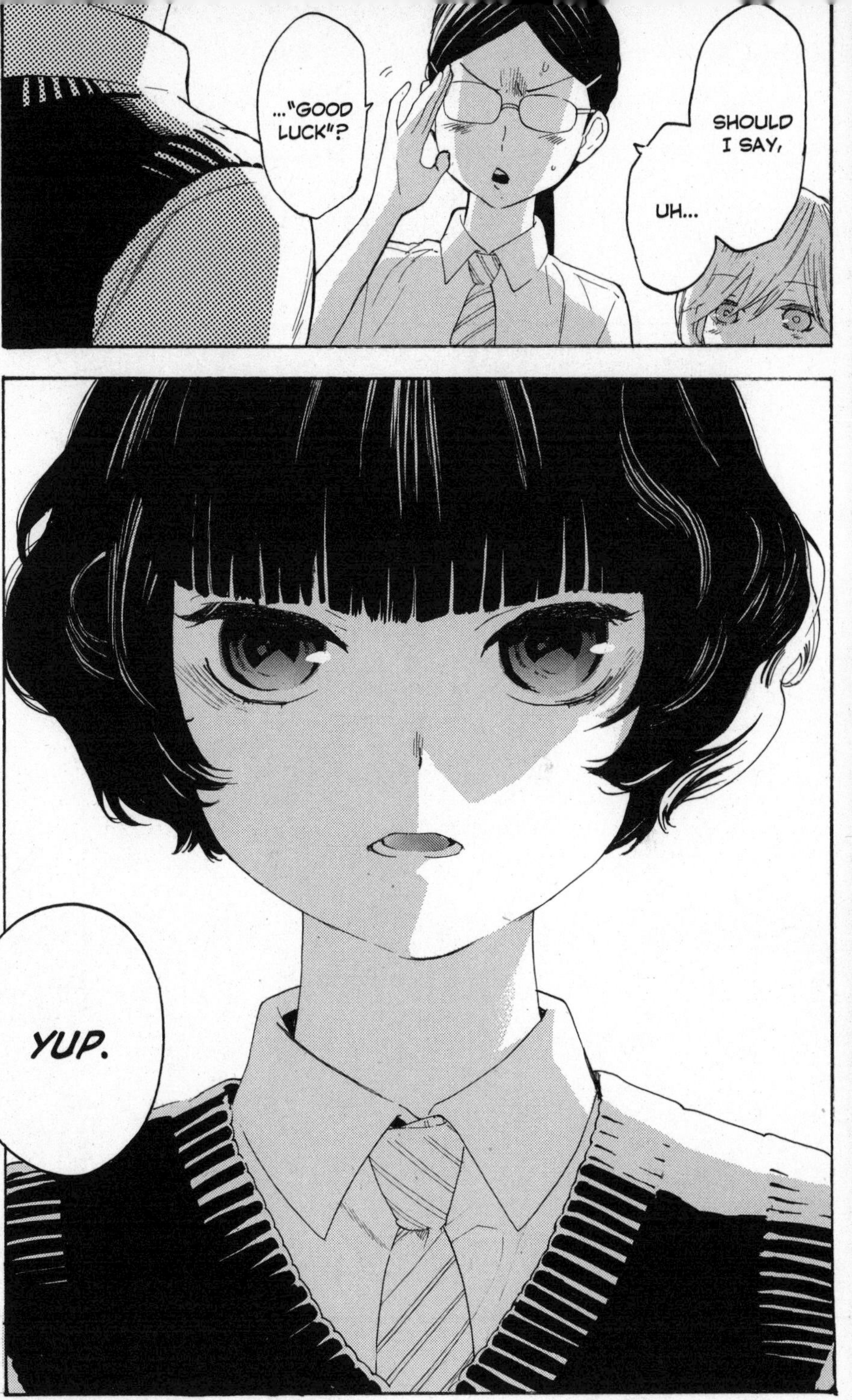
SHOULD I SAY, UH...
..."GOOD LUCK"?
YUP.

Meeting 6

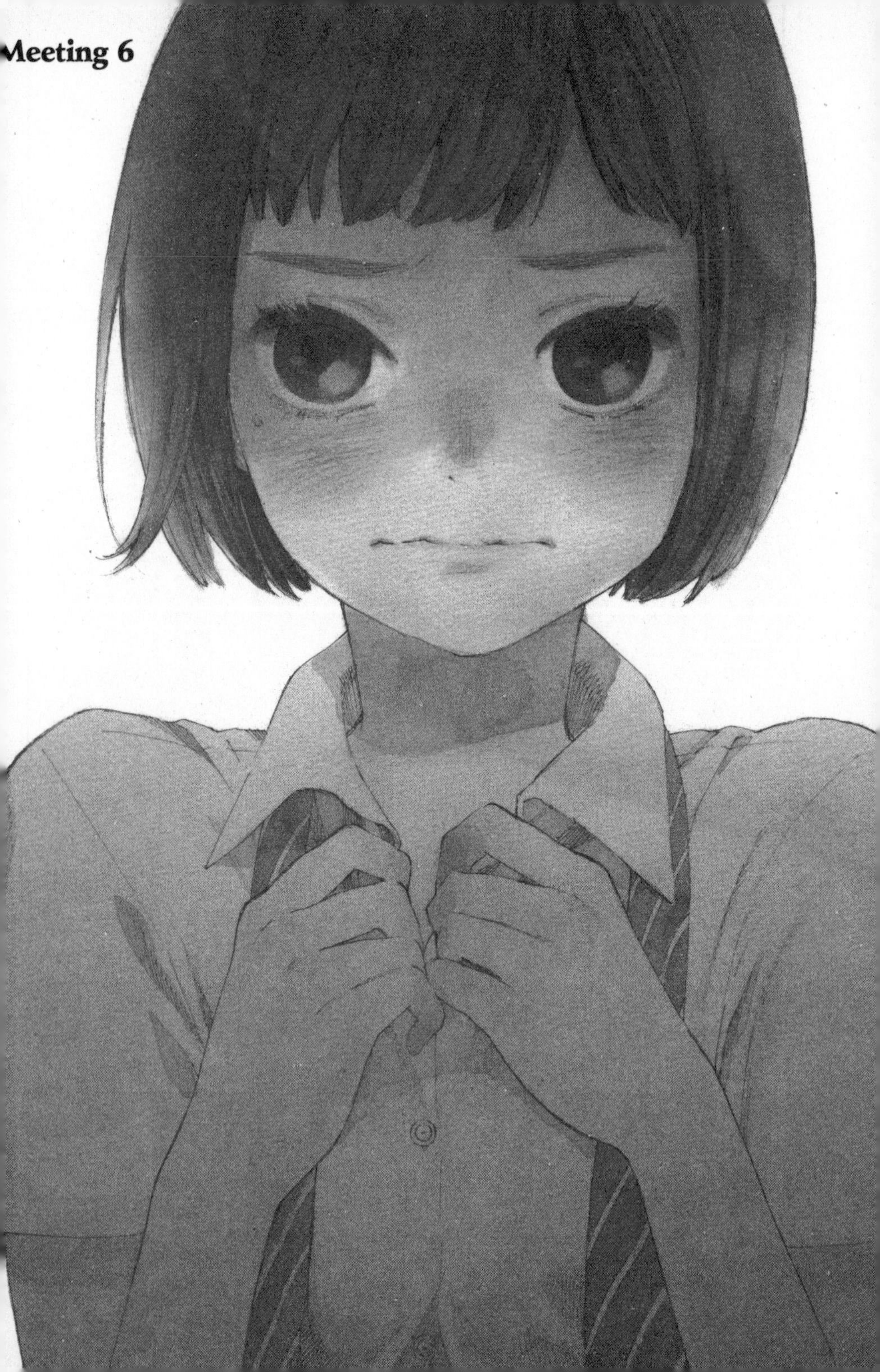

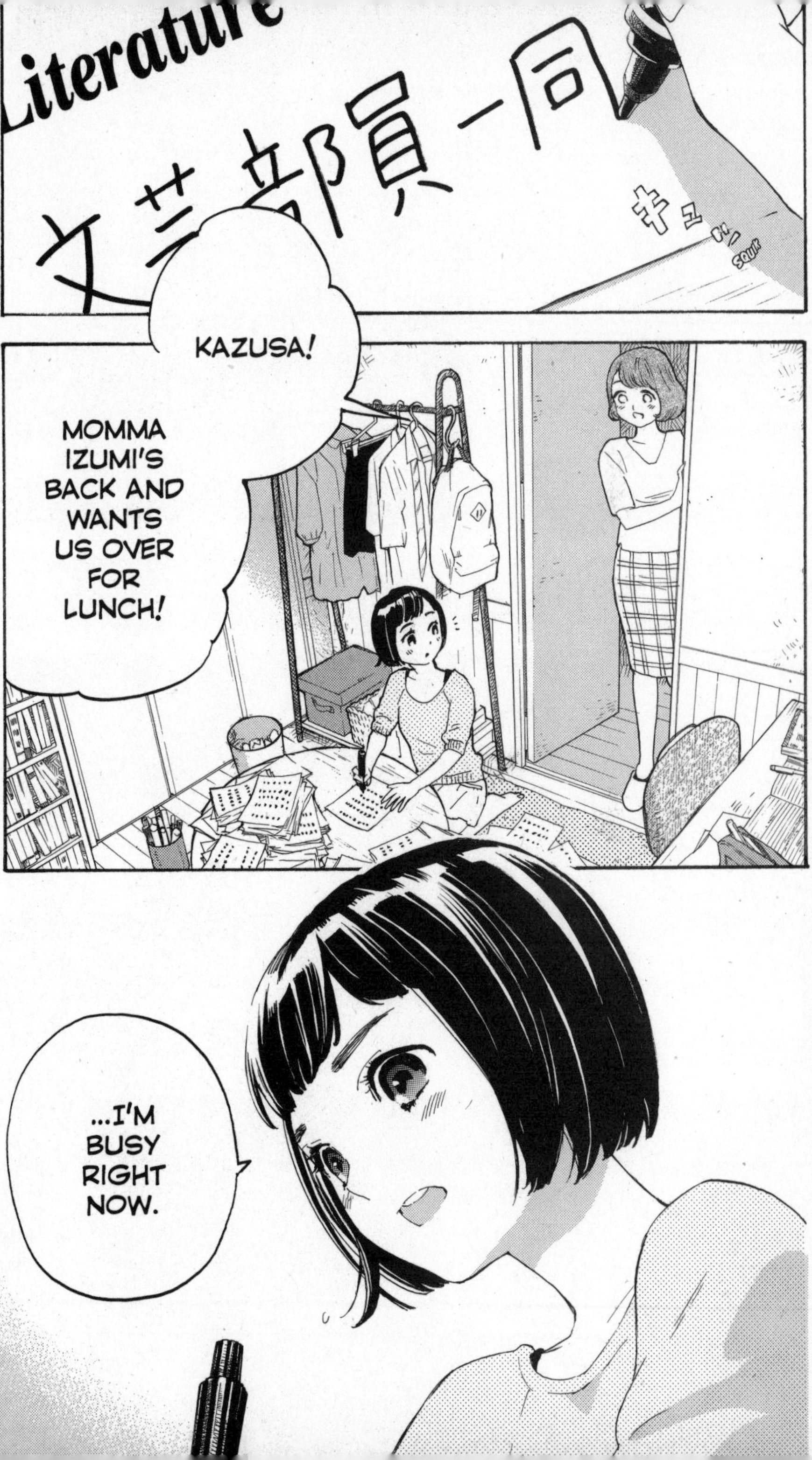
Literature
文芸部員一同
キュッ
SQUIK
KAZUSA!
MOMMA IZUMI'S BACK AND WANTS US OVER FOR LUNCH!
...I'M BUSY RIGHT NOW.

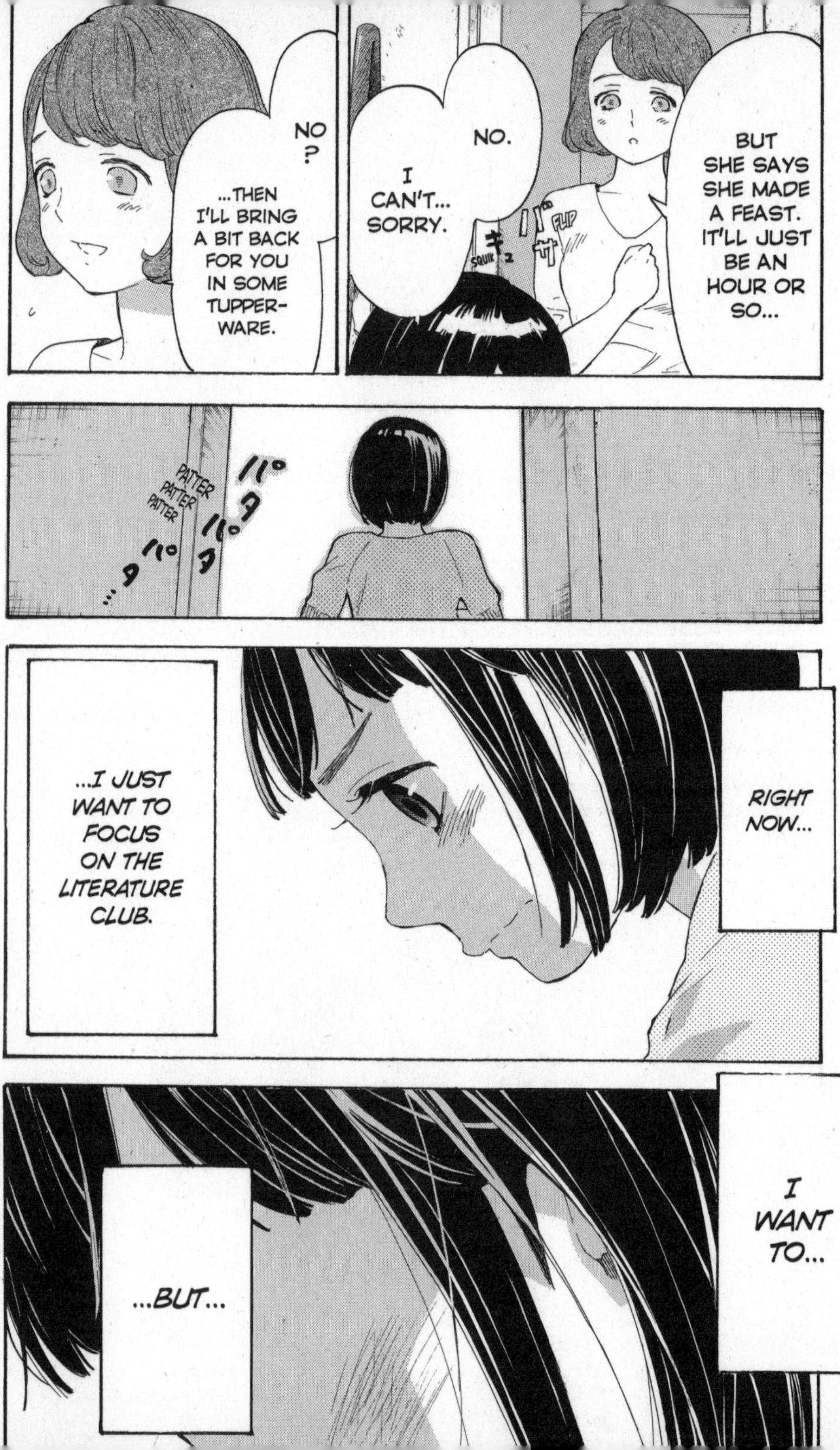
BUT SHE SAYS SHE MADE A FEAST. IT'LL JUST BE AN HOUR OR SO...
FLIP
NO.
I CAN'T... SORRY.
SQUIK
NO?
...THEN I'LL BRING A BIT BACK FOR YOU IN SOME TUPPER-WARE.
PATTER PATTER PATTER
RIGHT NOW...
...I JUST WANT TO FOCUS ON THE LITERATURE CLUB.
I WANT TO...
...BUT...

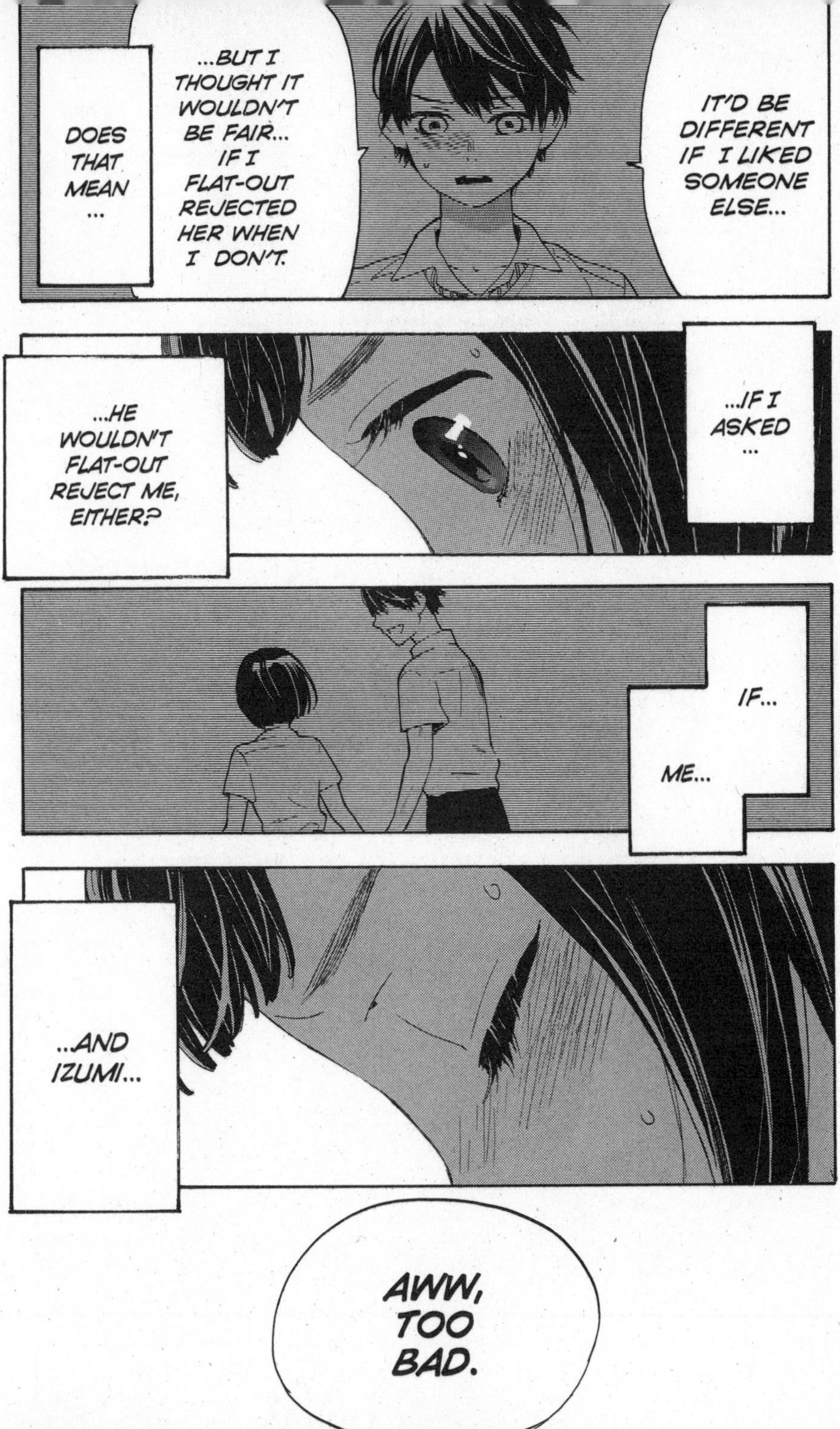
IT'D BE DIFFERENT IF I LIKED SOMEONE ELSE...
...BUT I THOUGHT IT WOULDN'T BE FAIR... IF I FLAT-OUT REJECTED HER WHEN I DON'T.
DOES THAT MEAN ...
...IF I ASKED ...
...HE WOULDN'T FLAT-OUT REJECT ME, EITHER?
IF...
ME...
...AND IZUMI...
AWW, TOO BAD.

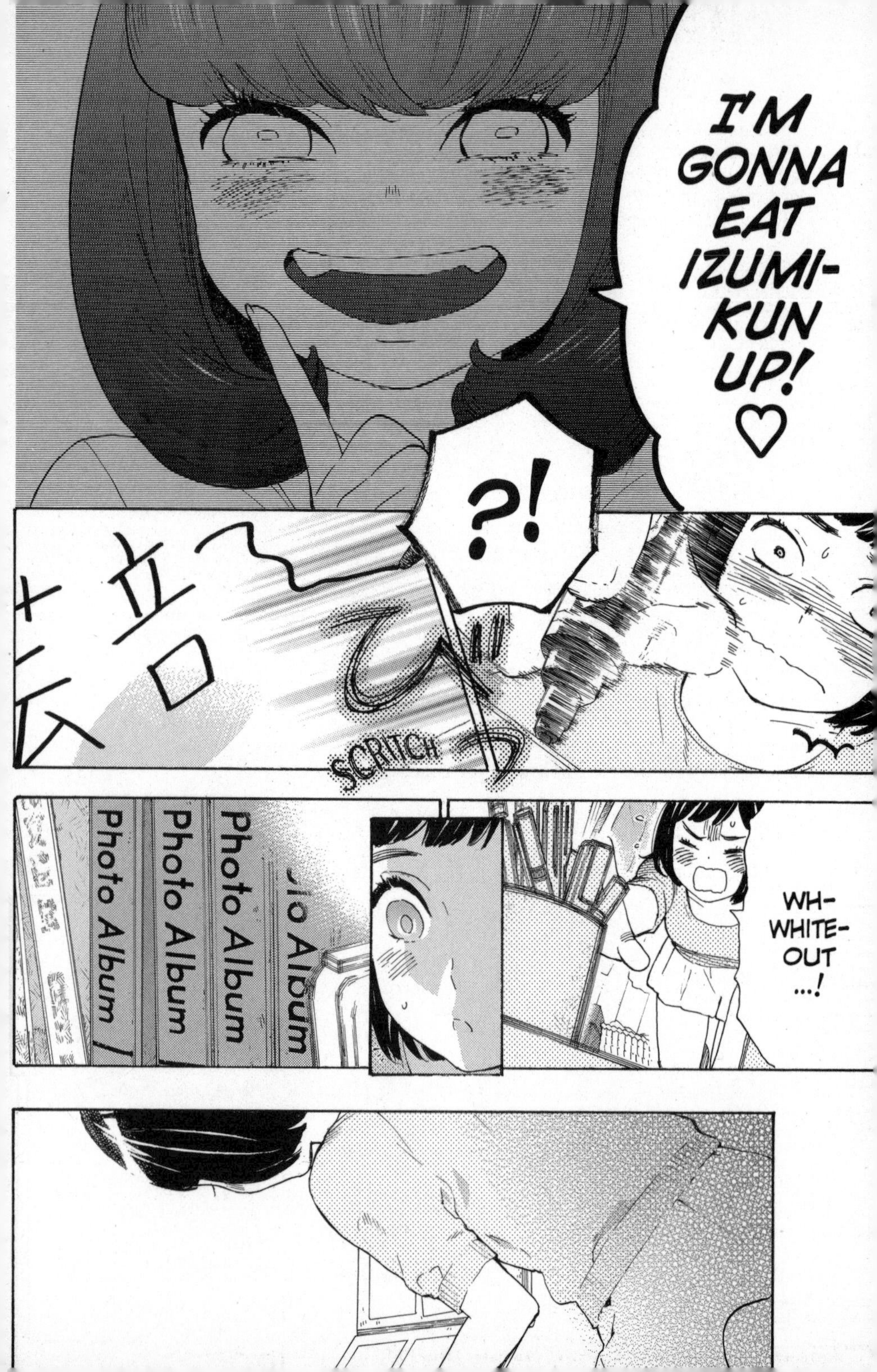
I'M GONNA EAT IZUMI-KUN UP! ♡
?!
SCRITCH
WH- WHITE-OUT ...!
Photo Album
Photo Album
Photo Album

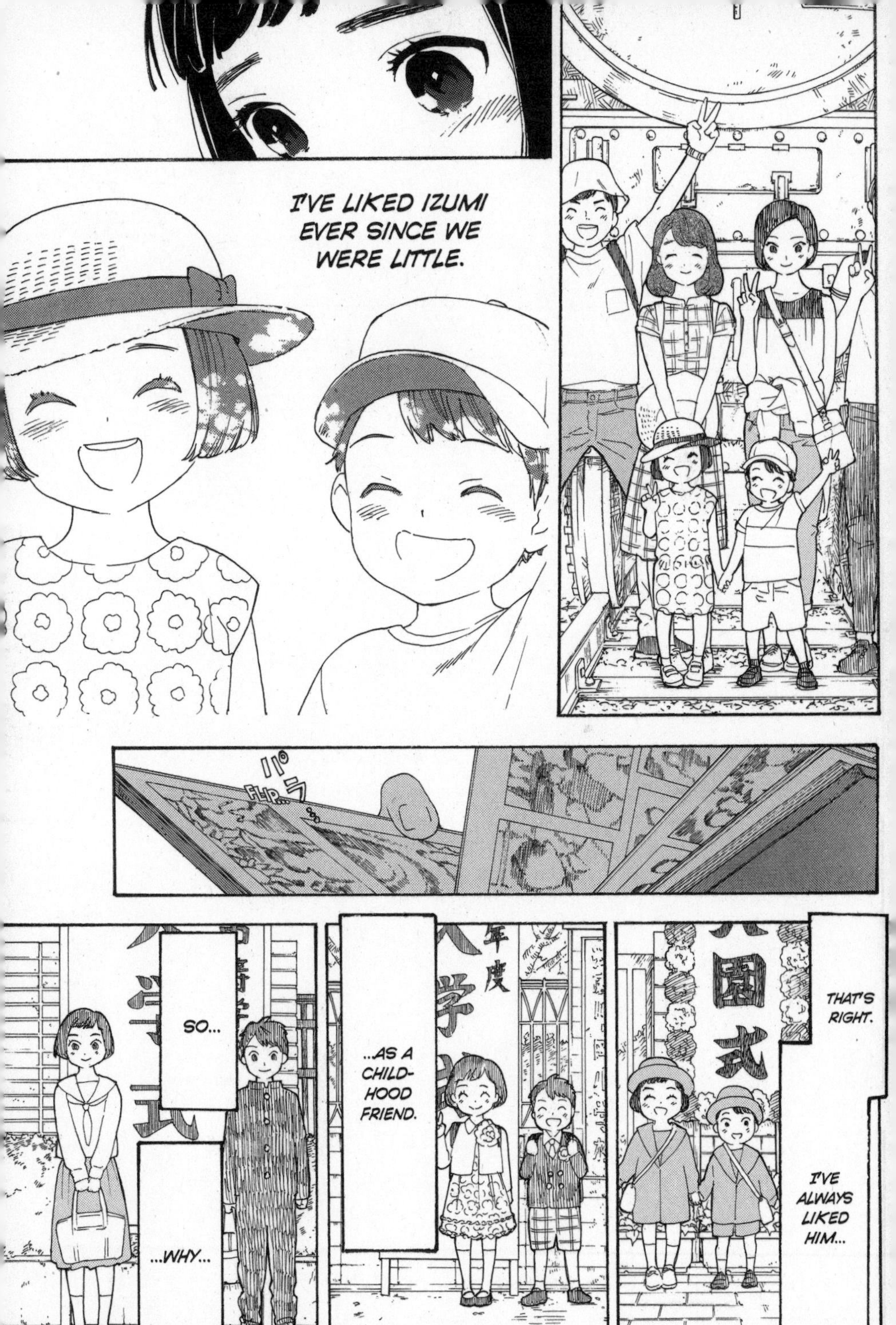
I'VE LIKED IZUMI EVER SINCE WE WERE LITTLE.
パラ
FLIP...
THAT'S RIGHT.
I'VE ALWAYS LIKED HIM...
...AS A CHILD-HOOD FRIEND.
SO...
...WHY...

SIGNS (R to L): Entrance ceremony for Preschool, Elementary, Junior High.

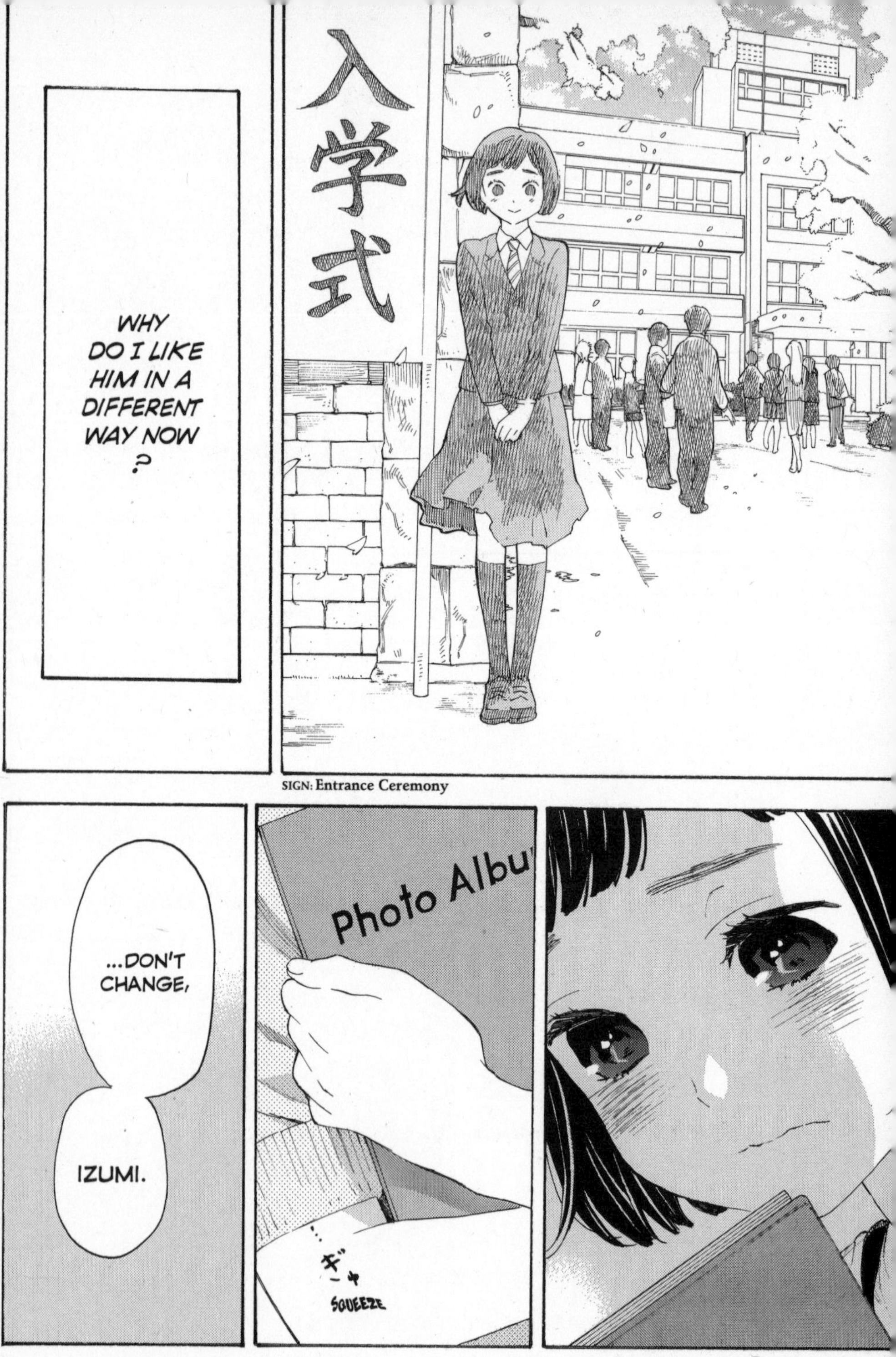
入学式
WHY DO I LIKE HIM IN A DIFFERENT WAY NOW?
SIGN: Entrance Ceremony
Photo Albu
ギュ
SQUEEZE
...DON'T CHANGE,
IZUMI.

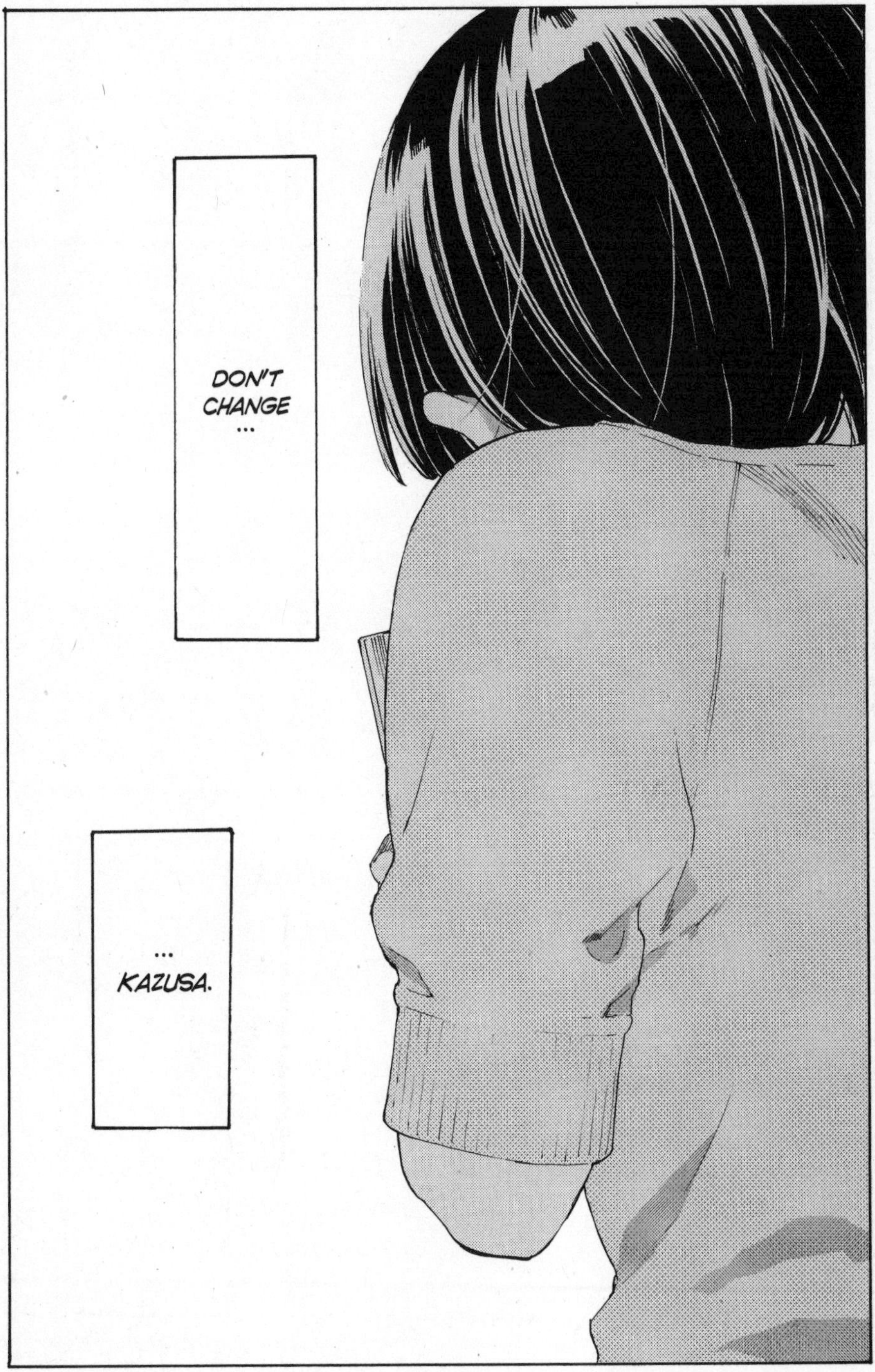
DON'T CHANGE ...
... KAZUSA.

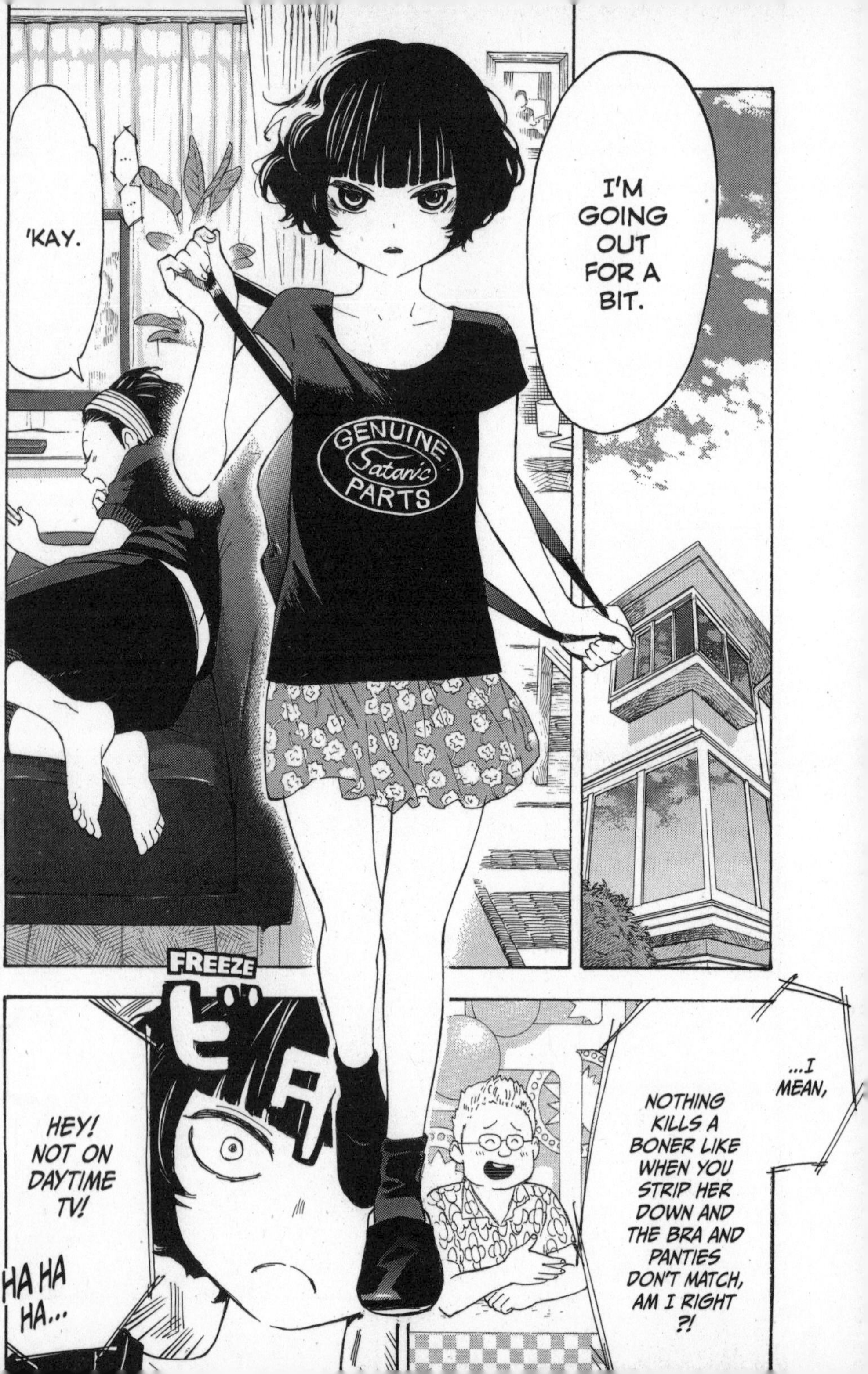
I'M GOING OUT FOR A BIT.
GENUINE Satanic PARTS
'KAY.
...I MEAN,
NOTHING KILLS A BONER LIKE WHEN YOU STRIP HER DOWN AND THE BRA AND PANTIES DON'T MATCH, AM I RIGHT ?!
FREEZE
ピタ
HEY! NOT ON DAYTIME TV!
HA HA HA...

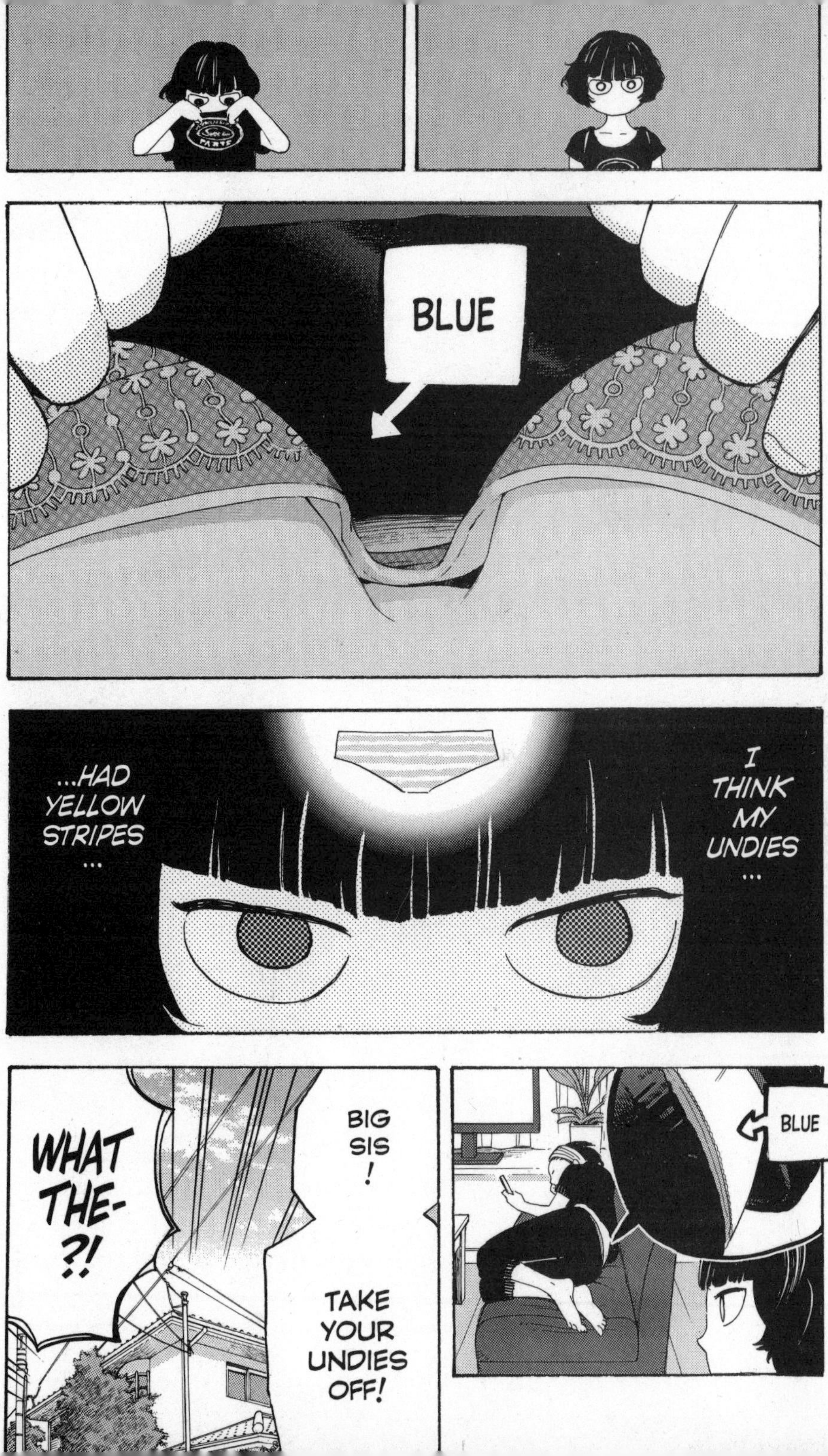
BLUE
I THINK MY UNDIES...
...HAD YELLOW STRIPES...
BLUE
BIG SIS! TAKE YOUR UNDIES OFF!
WHAT THE-?!

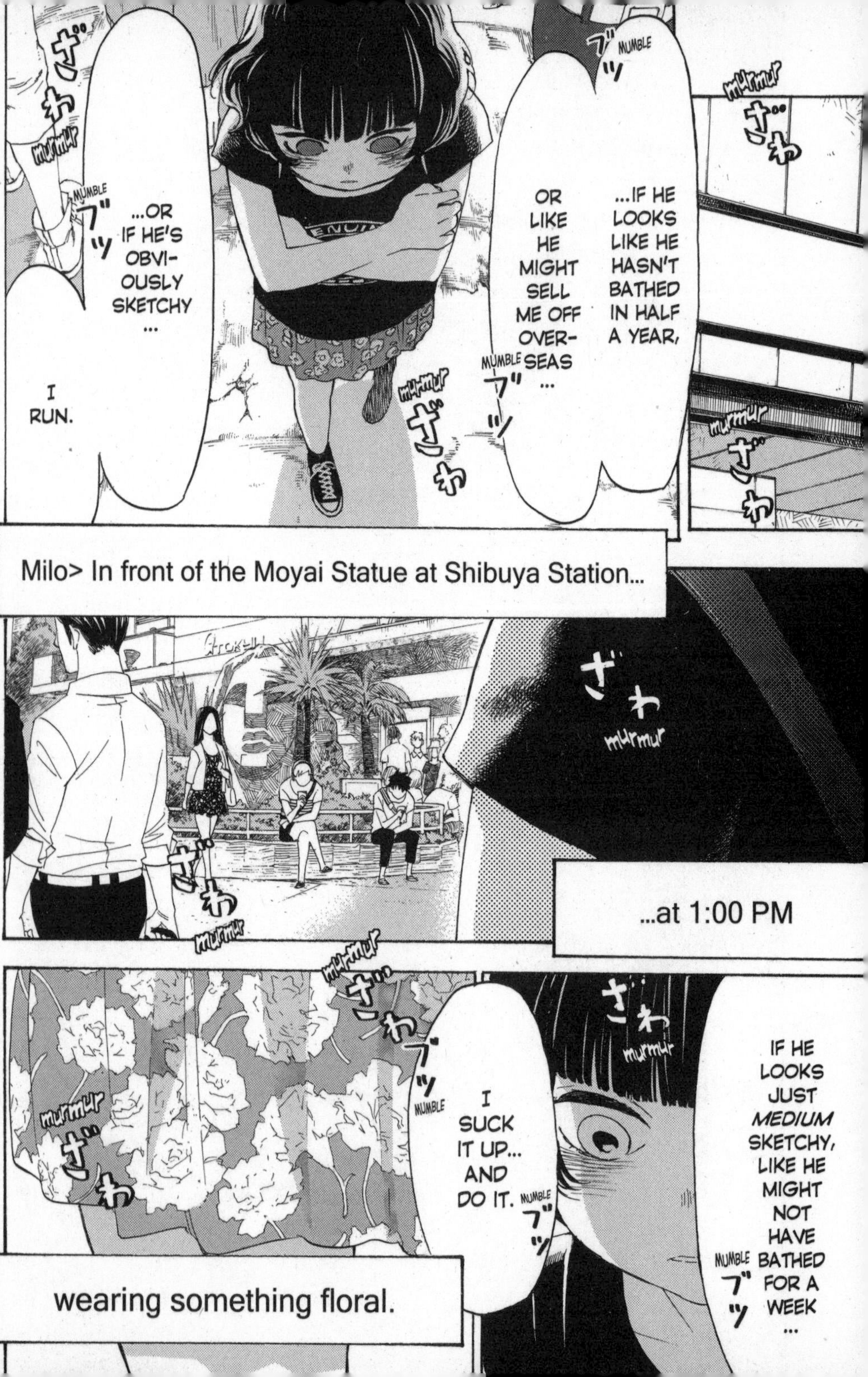
murmur
...IF HE LOOKS LIKE HE HASN'T BATHED IN HALF A YEAR,
OR LIKE HE MIGHT SELL ME OFF OVER-SEAS ...
...OR IF HE'S OBVI-OUSLY SKETCHY ...
I RUN.
Milo> In front of the Moyai Statue at Shibuya Station...
...at 1:00 PM
IF HE LOOKS JUST *MEDIUM* SKETCHY, LIKE HE MIGHT NOT HAVE BATHED FOR A WEEK ...
I SUCK IT UP... AND DO IT.
wearing something floral.

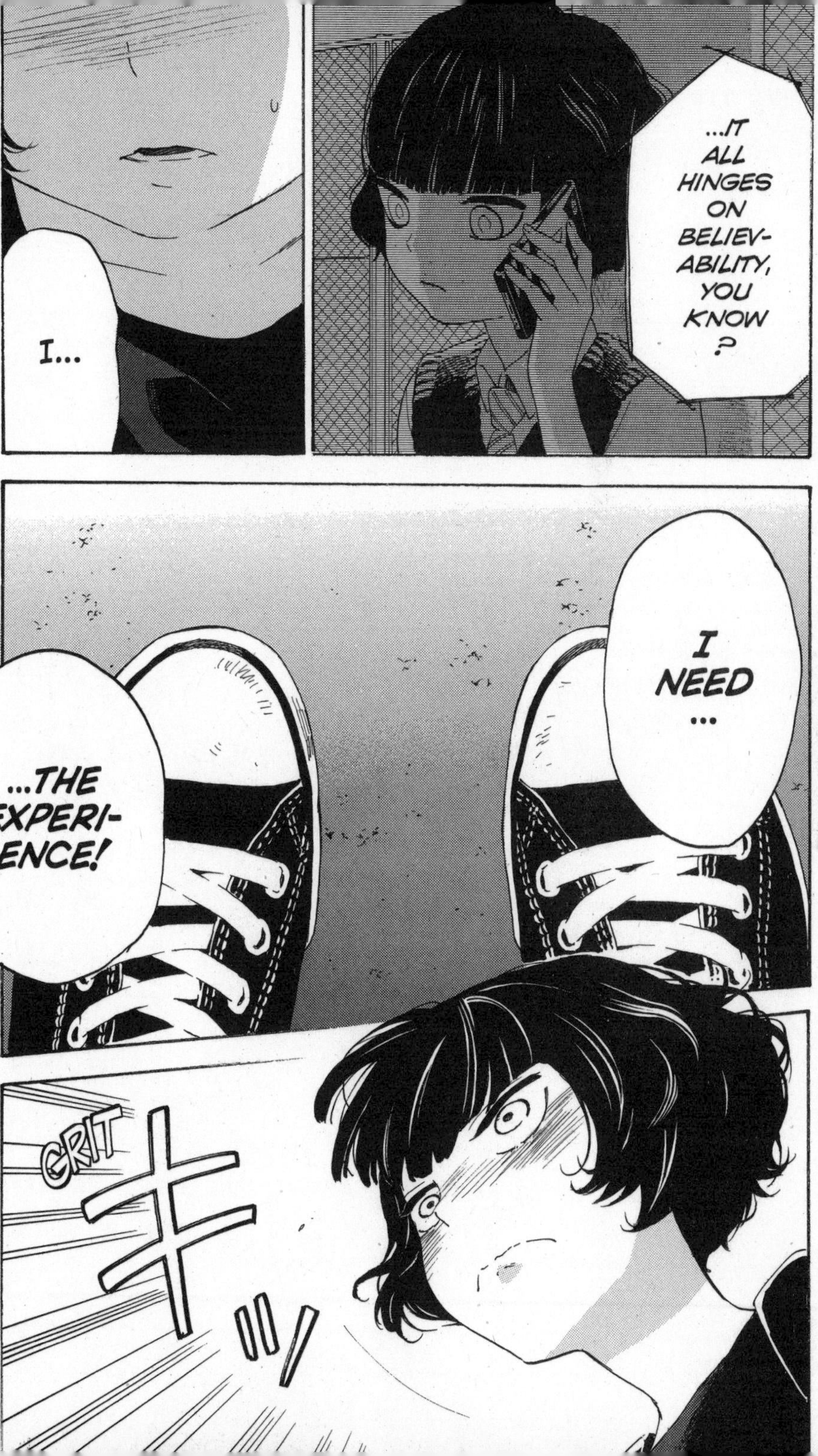
...IT ALL HINGES ON BELIEV-ABILITY, YOU KNOW?
I...
I NEED...
...THE EXPERI-ENCE!
CRIT

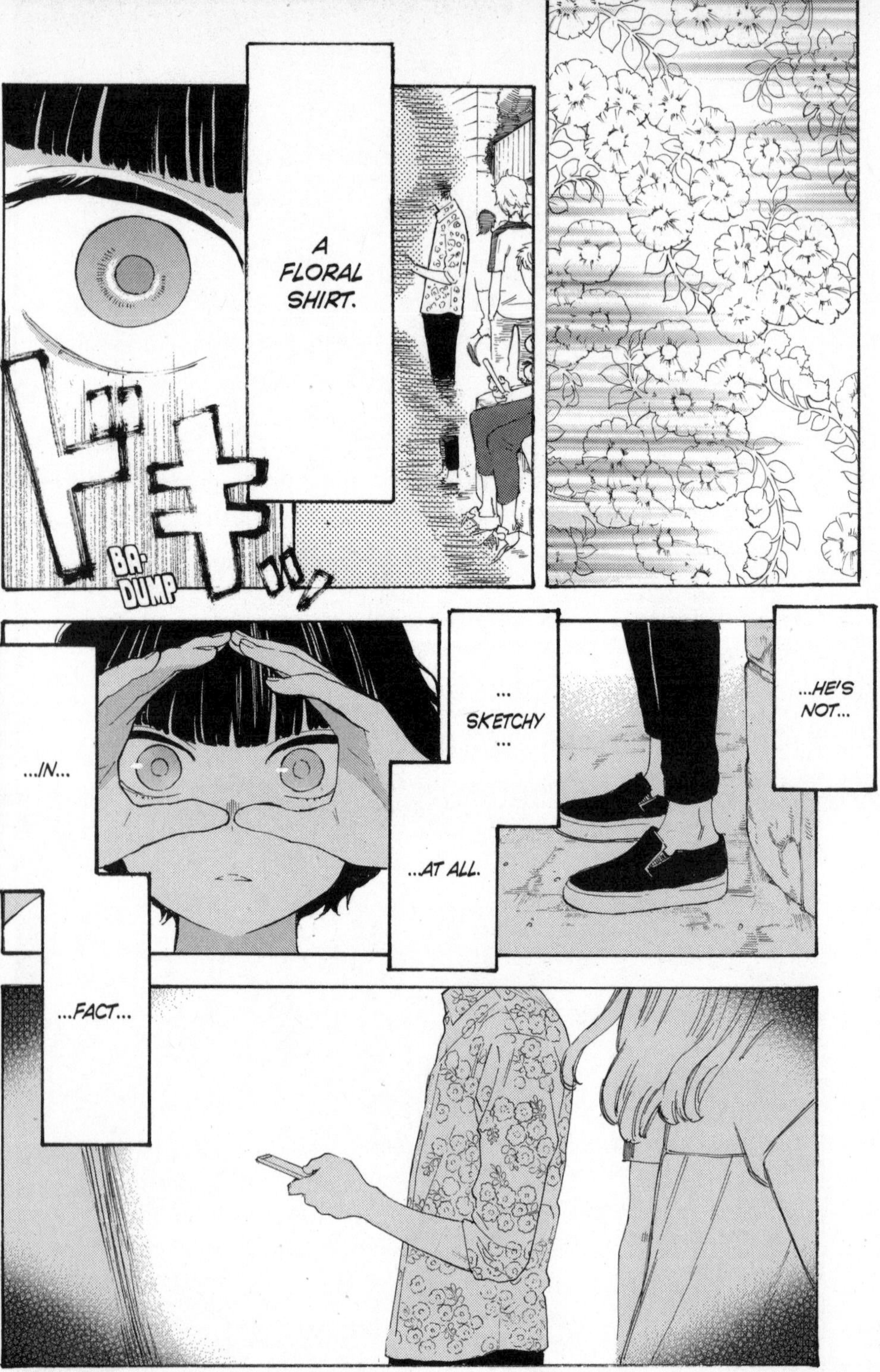
A FLORAL SHIRT.
ドキッ
BA-DUMP
...HE'S NOT...
... SKETCHY ...
...AT ALL.
...IN...
...FACT...

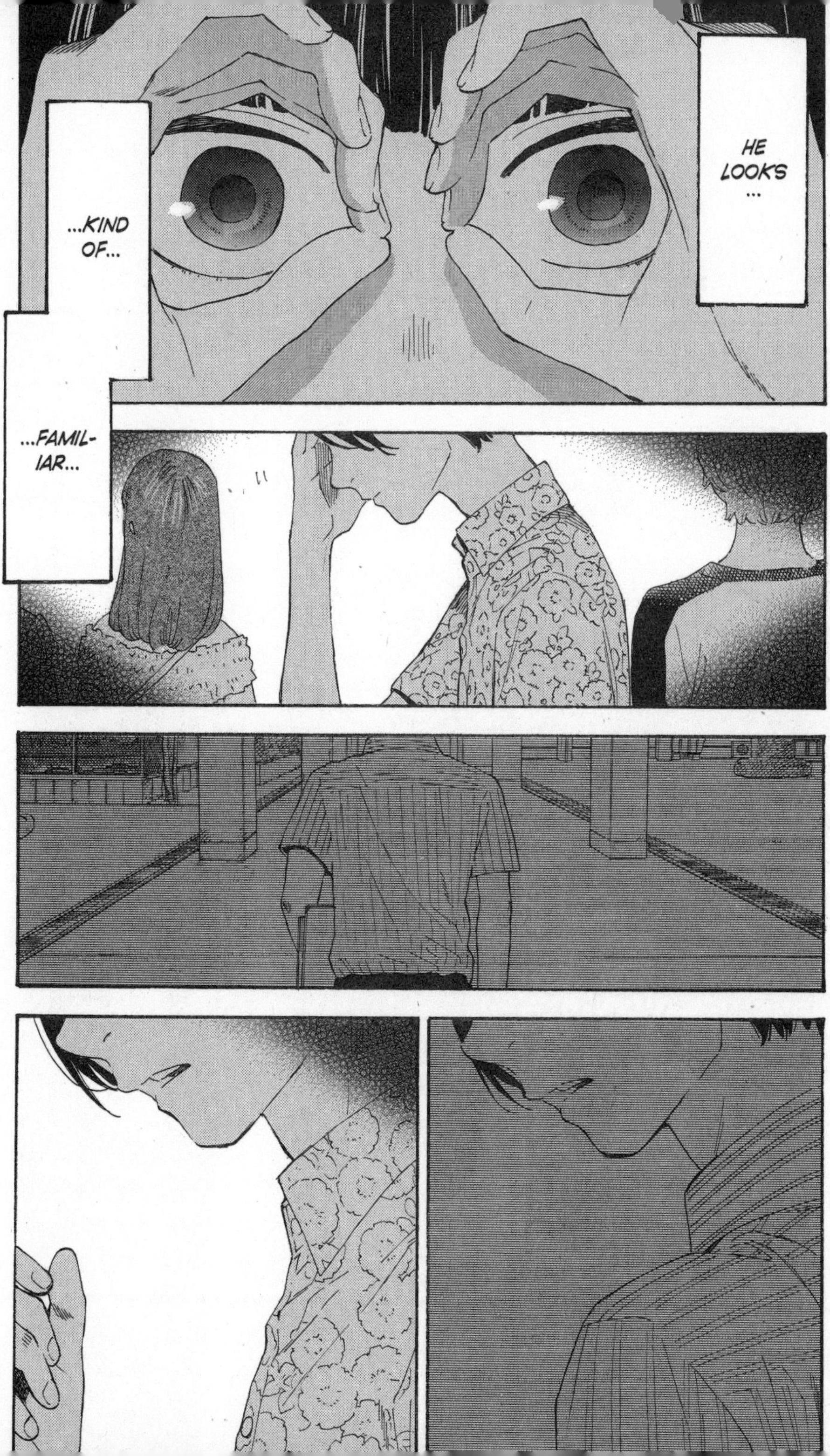
HE LOOKS ...
...KIND OF...
...FAMIL-IAR...

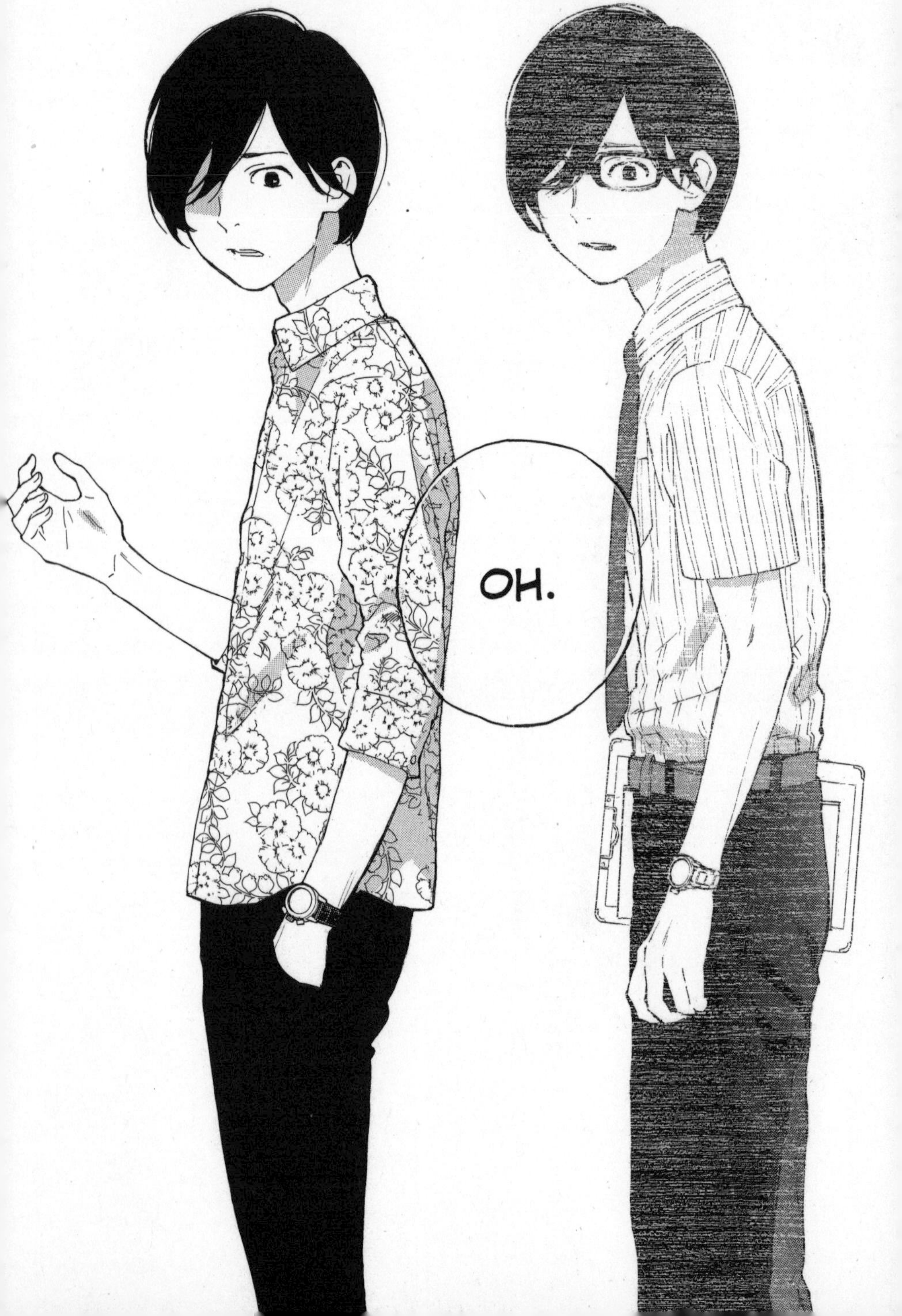
OH.

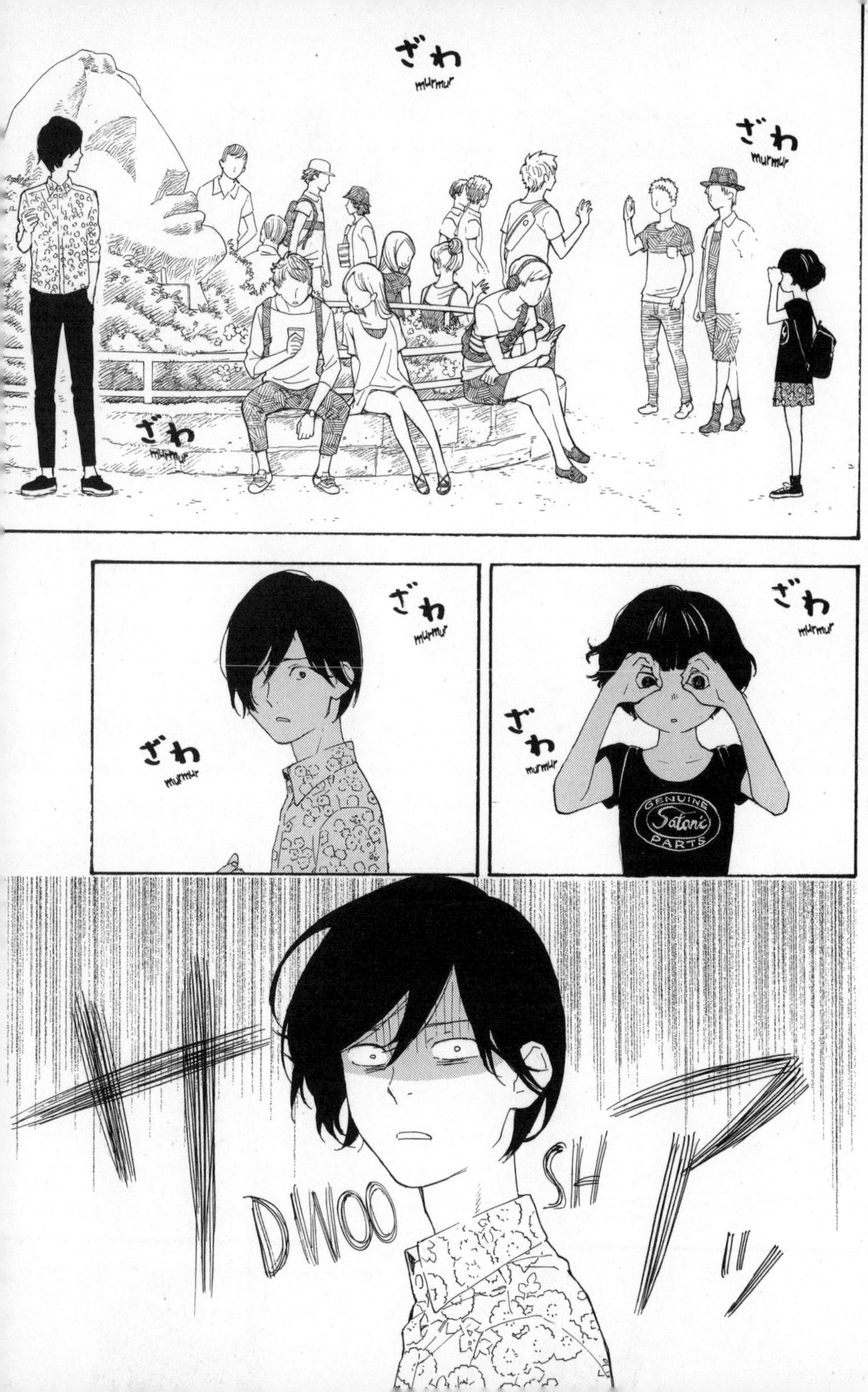
ざわ
murmur
ざわ
murmur
ざわ
murmur
ざわ
murmur
ざわ
murmur
GENUINE Satanic PARTS
ざわ
murmur
ざわ
murmur
DWOOSH

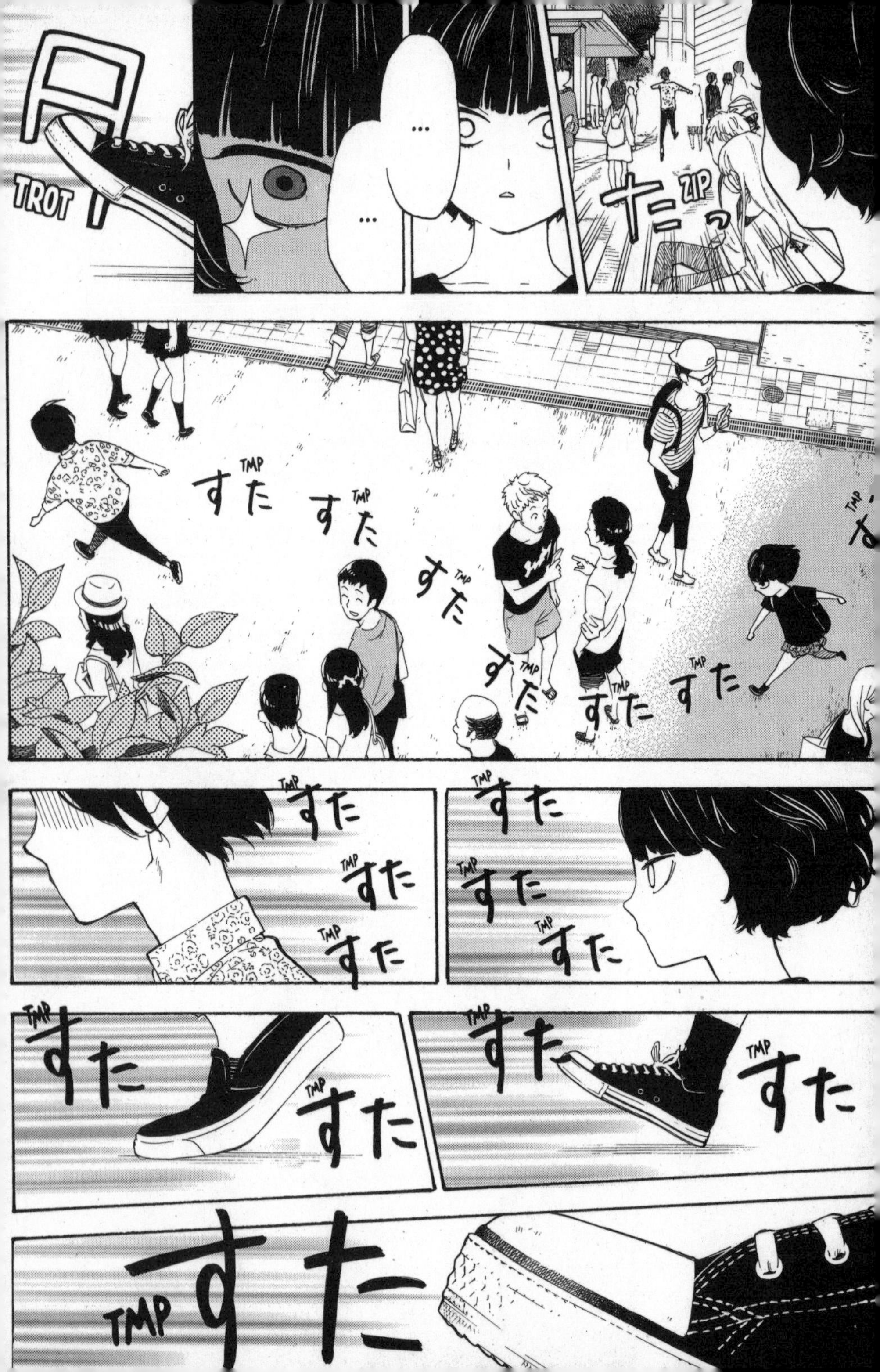

たっ
ZIP
...
...
TROT
TMP
すた
TMP
すた
TMP
すた
TMP
すた
TMP
すた
TMP
すた
TMP
すた
TMP
すた
TMP
すた
TMP
すた
TMP
すた
TMP
すた
TMP
すた
TMP
すた
TMP
すた
TMP
すた
TMP
すた
TMP
すた
TMP
すた

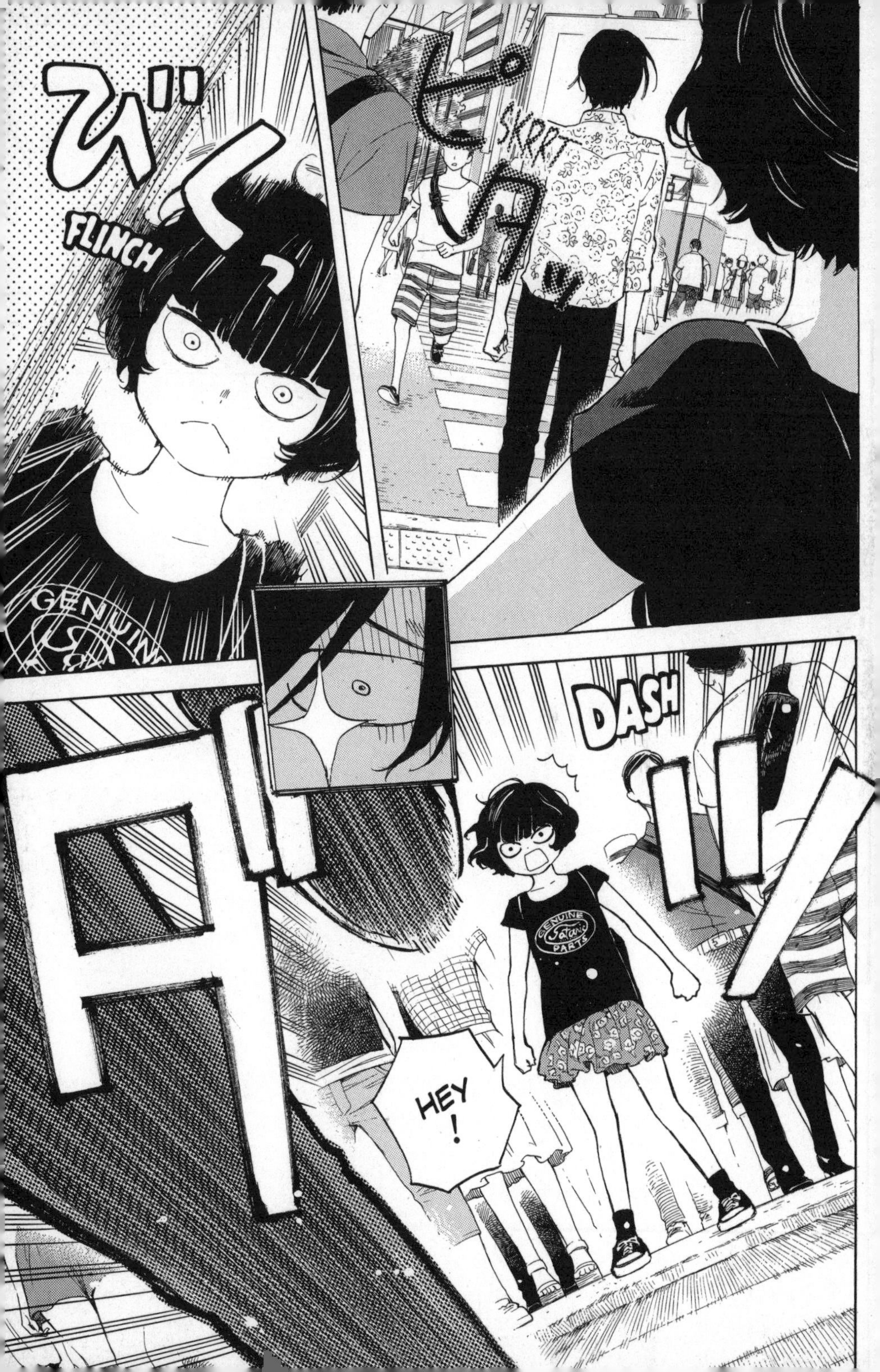
ピタッ
SKRRT
びくっ
FLINCH
ダッ
DASH
HEY!

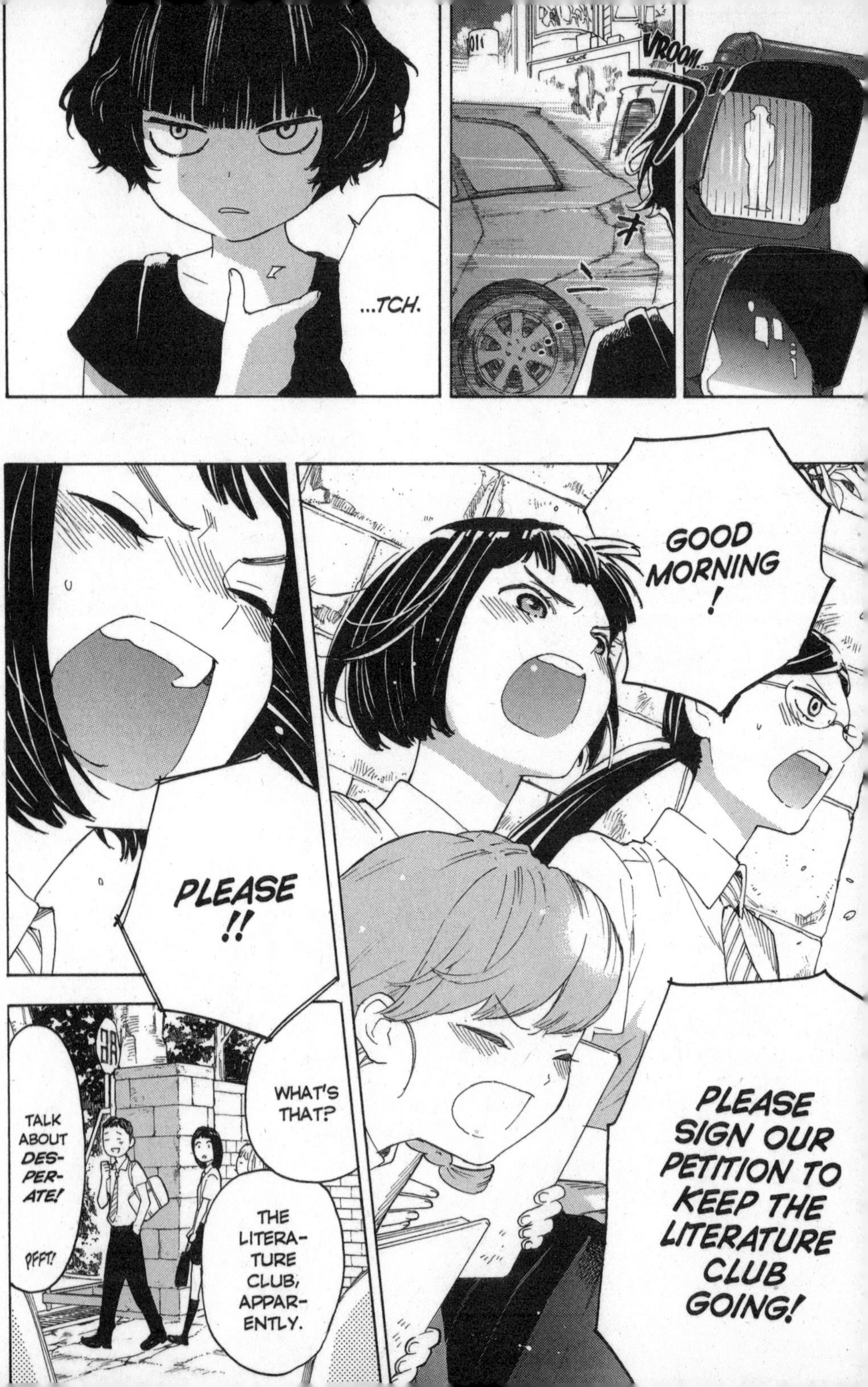
VROOM...
...TCH.
GOOD MORNING!
PLEASE SIGN OUR PETITION TO KEEP THE LITERATURE CLUB GOING!
PLEASE!!
WHAT'S THAT?
THE LITERATURE CLUB, APPARENTLY.
TALK ABOUT DESPERATE!
PFFT!

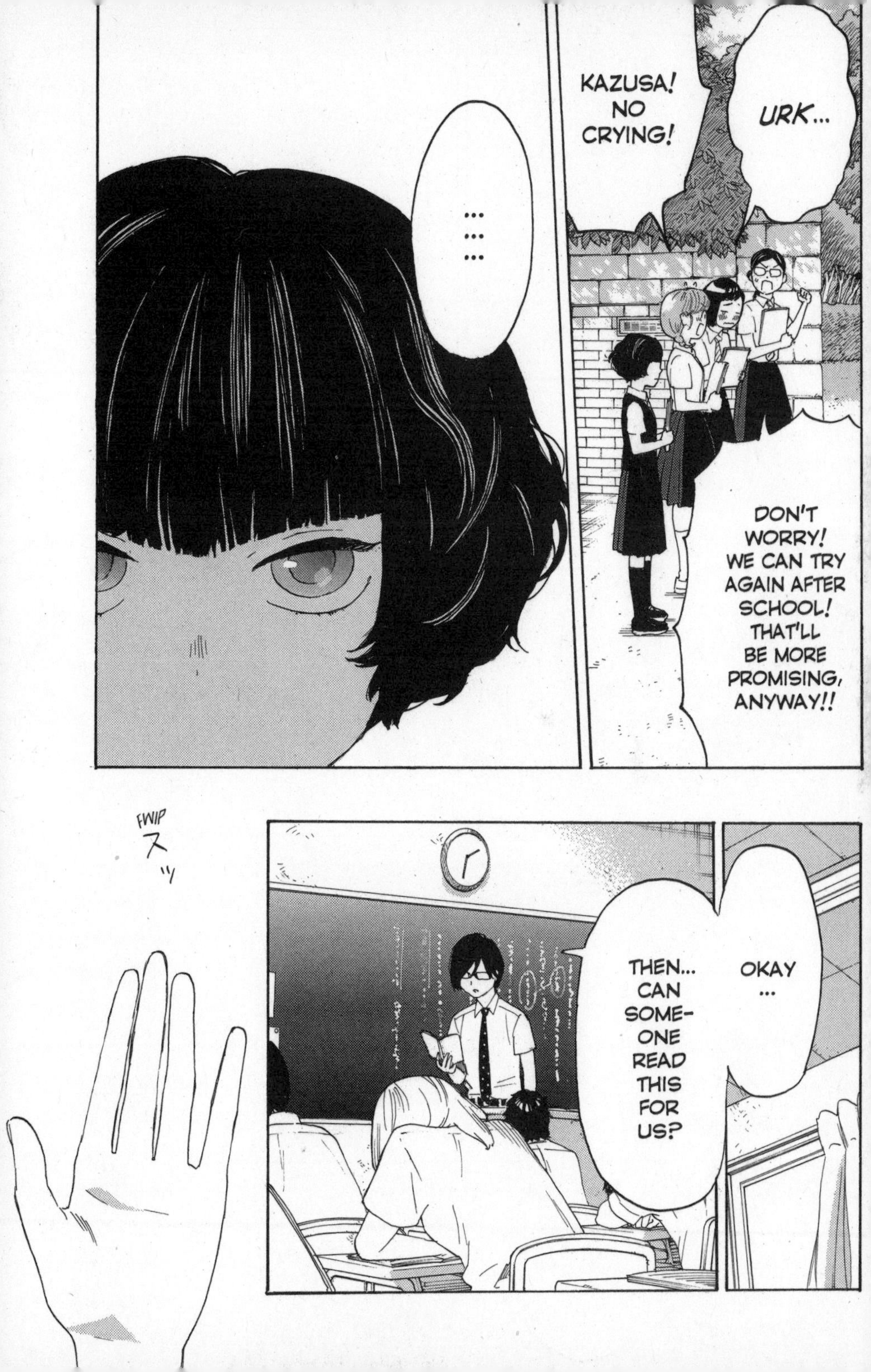
URK...
KAZUSA! NO CRYING!
DON'T WORRY! WE CAN TRY AGAIN AFTER SCHOOL! THAT'LL BE MORE PROMISING, ANYWAY!!
......
OKAY...
THEN... CAN SOME-ONE READ THIS FOR US?
FWIP
スッ

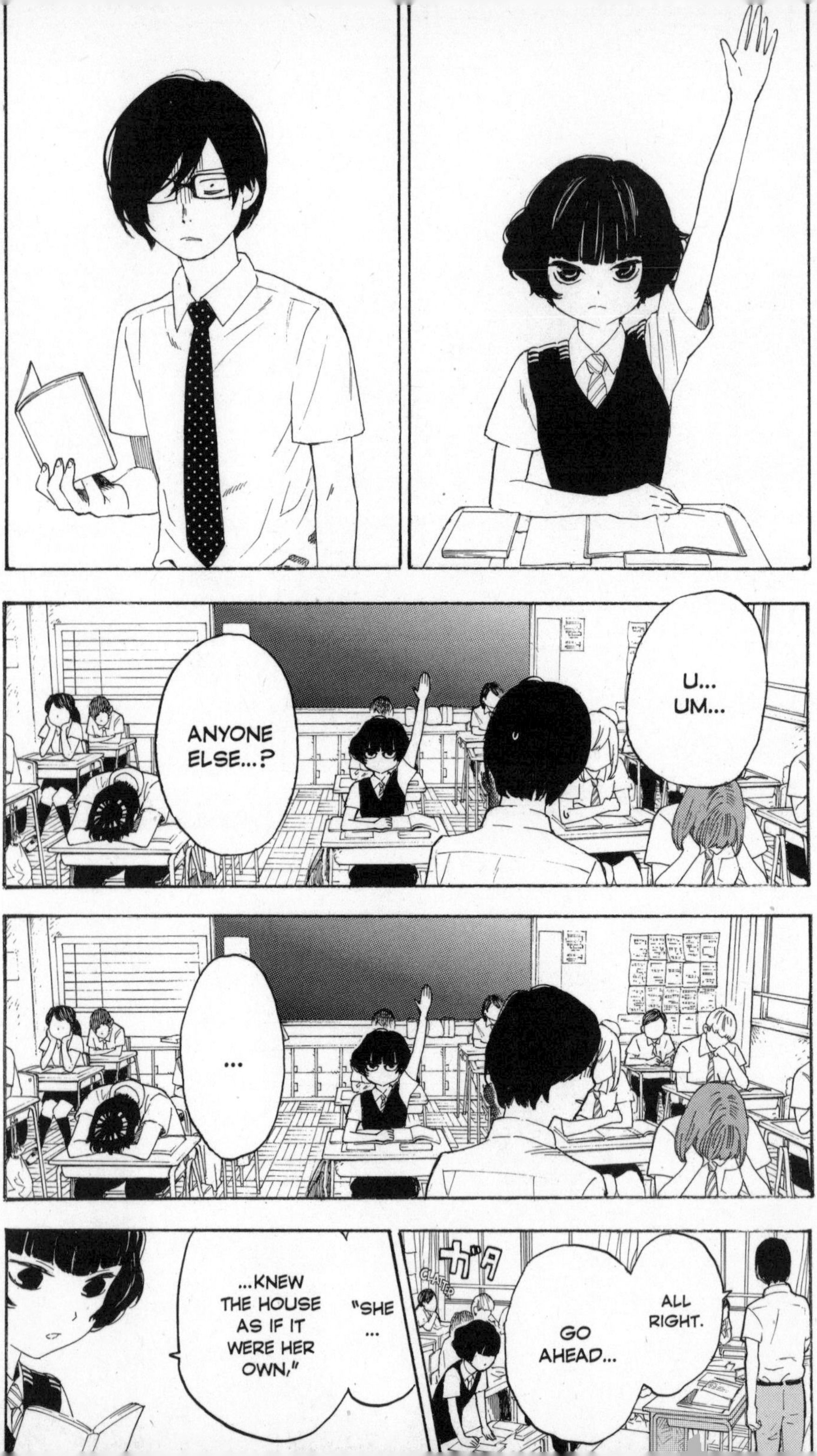
U... UM...
ANYONE ELSE...?
...
ALL RIGHT.
GO AHEAD...
ガタ
CLATTER
"SHE ...
...KNEW THE HOUSE AS IF IT WERE HER OWN,"

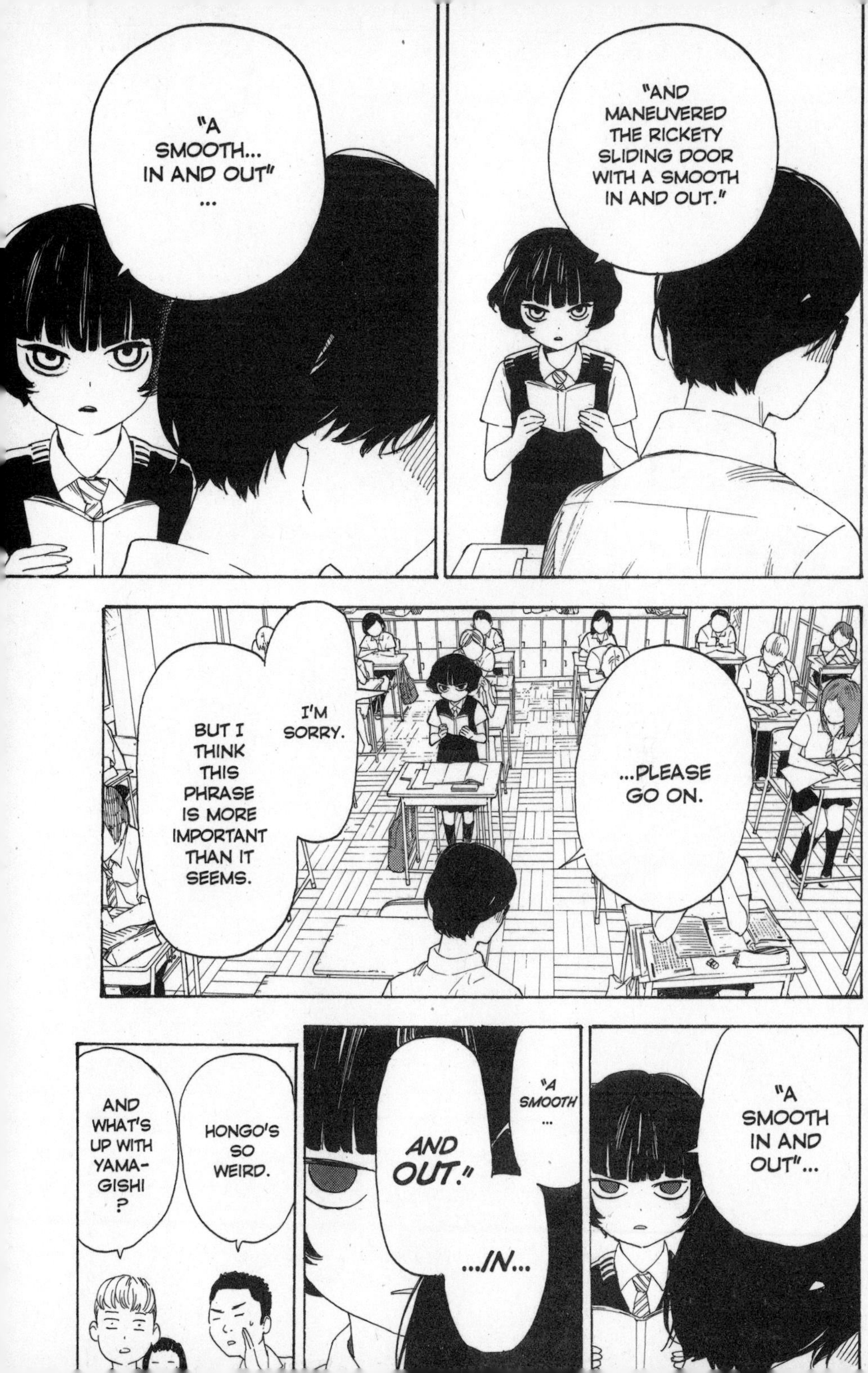
"AND MANEUVERED THE RICKETY SLIDING DOOR WITH A SMOOTH IN AND OUT."
"A SMOOTH... IN AND OUT" ...
I'M SORRY.
BUT I THINK THIS PHRASE IS MORE IMPORTANT THAN IT SEEMS.
...PLEASE GO ON.
"A SMOOTH IN AND OUT"...
"A SMOOTH ...
...IN...
AND OUT."
HONGO'S SO WEIRD.
AND WHAT'S UP WITH YAMAGISHI?

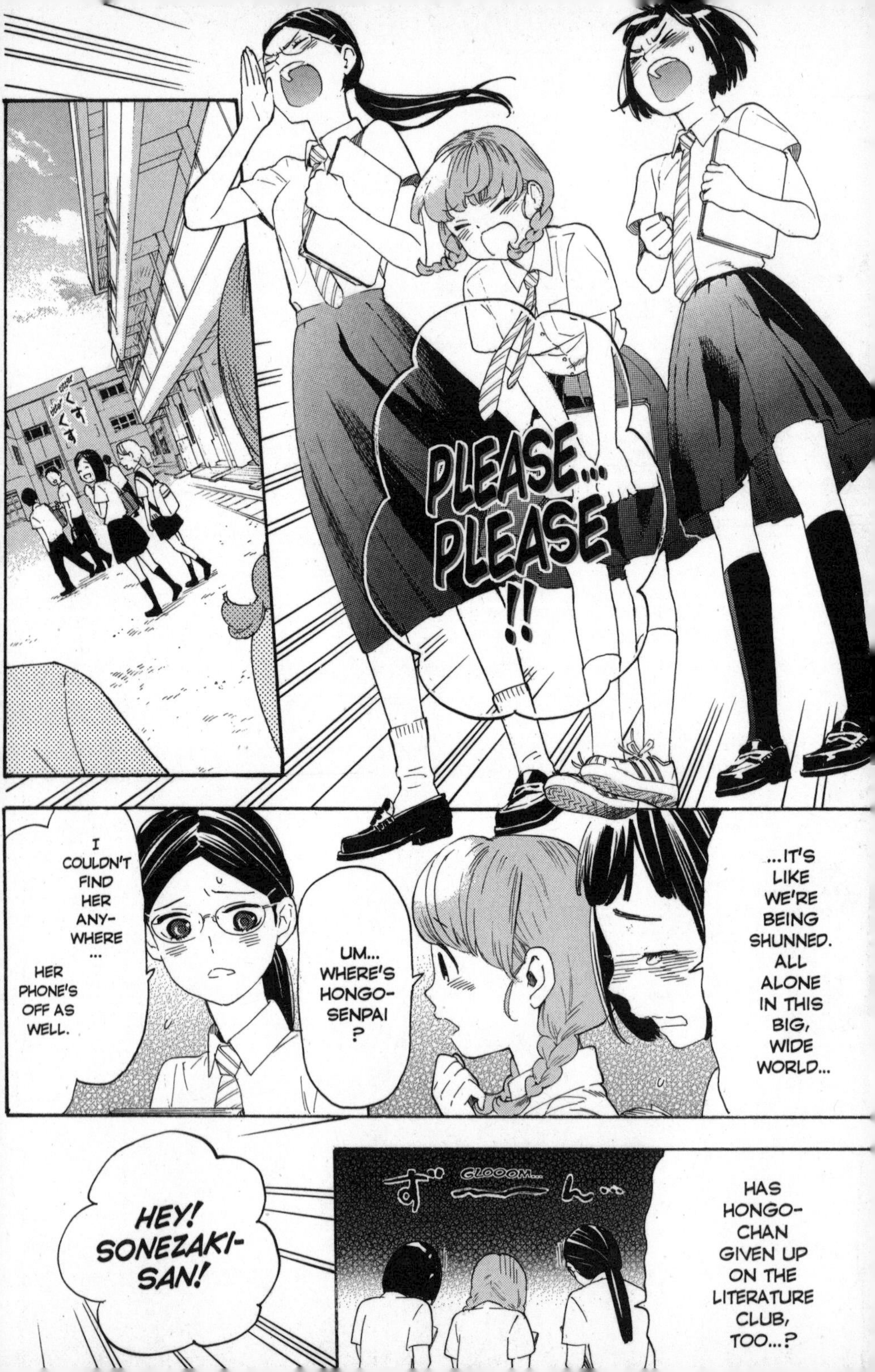
PLEASE... PLEASE!!
くすくす titter titter
...IT'S LIKE WE'RE BEING SHUNNED. ALL ALONE IN THIS BIG, WIDE WORLD...
UM... WHERE'S HONGO-SENPAI?
I COULDN'T FIND HER ANYWHERE...
HER PHONE'S OFF AS WELL.
HAS HONGO-CHAN GIVEN UP ON THE LITERATURE CLUB, TOO...?
ずーーん GLOOOM...
HEY! SONEZAKI-SAN!

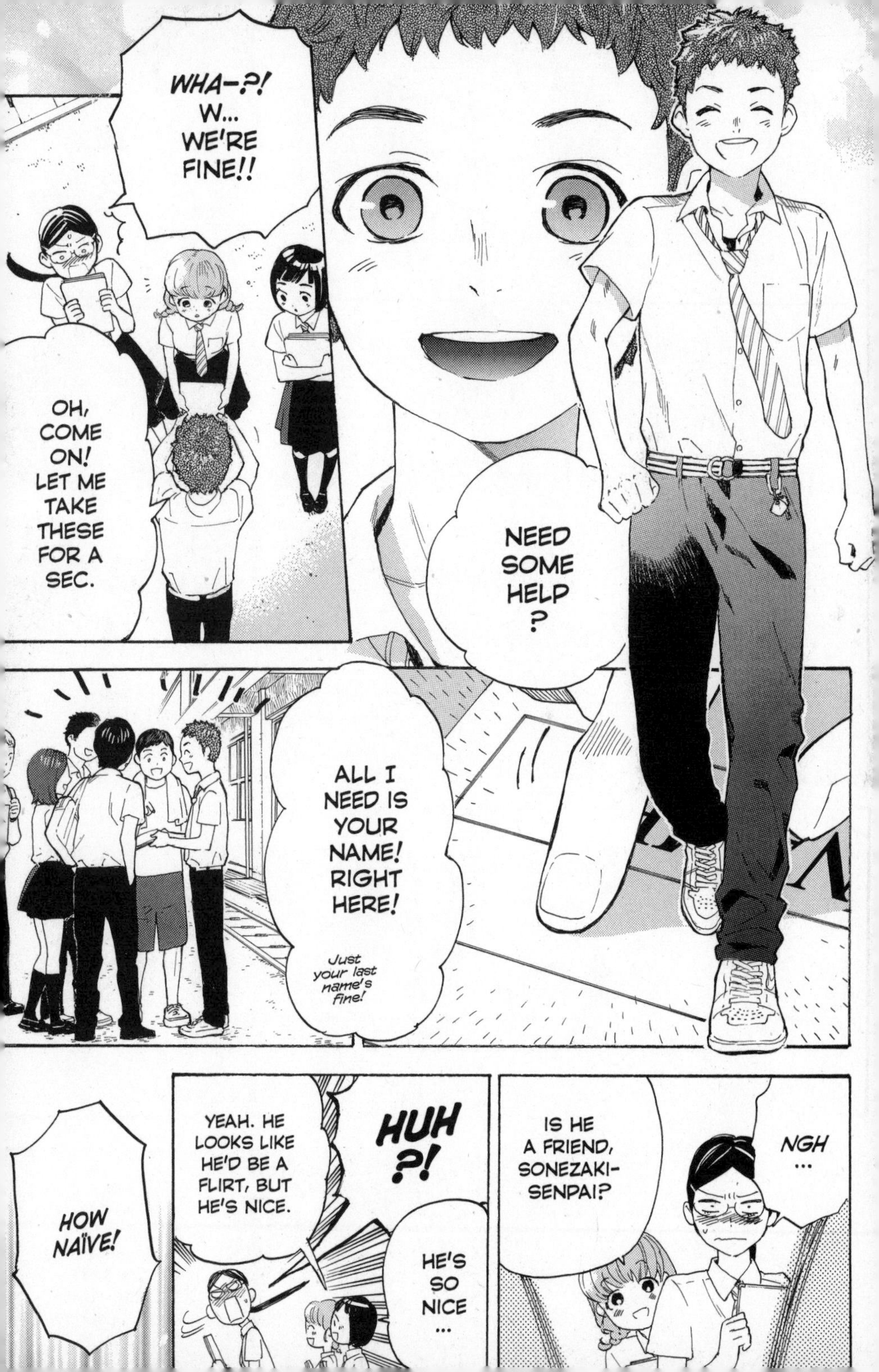
NEED SOME HELP?
WHA-?! W... WE'RE FINE!!
OH, COME ON! LET ME TAKE THESE FOR A SEC.
ALL I NEED IS YOUR NAME! RIGHT HERE!
Just your last name's fine!
NGH ...
IS HE A FRIEND, SONEZAKI-SENPAI?
HUH ?!
YEAH. HE LOOKS LIKE HE'D BE A FLIRT, BUT HE'S NICE.
HE'S SO NICE ...
HOW NAÏVE!

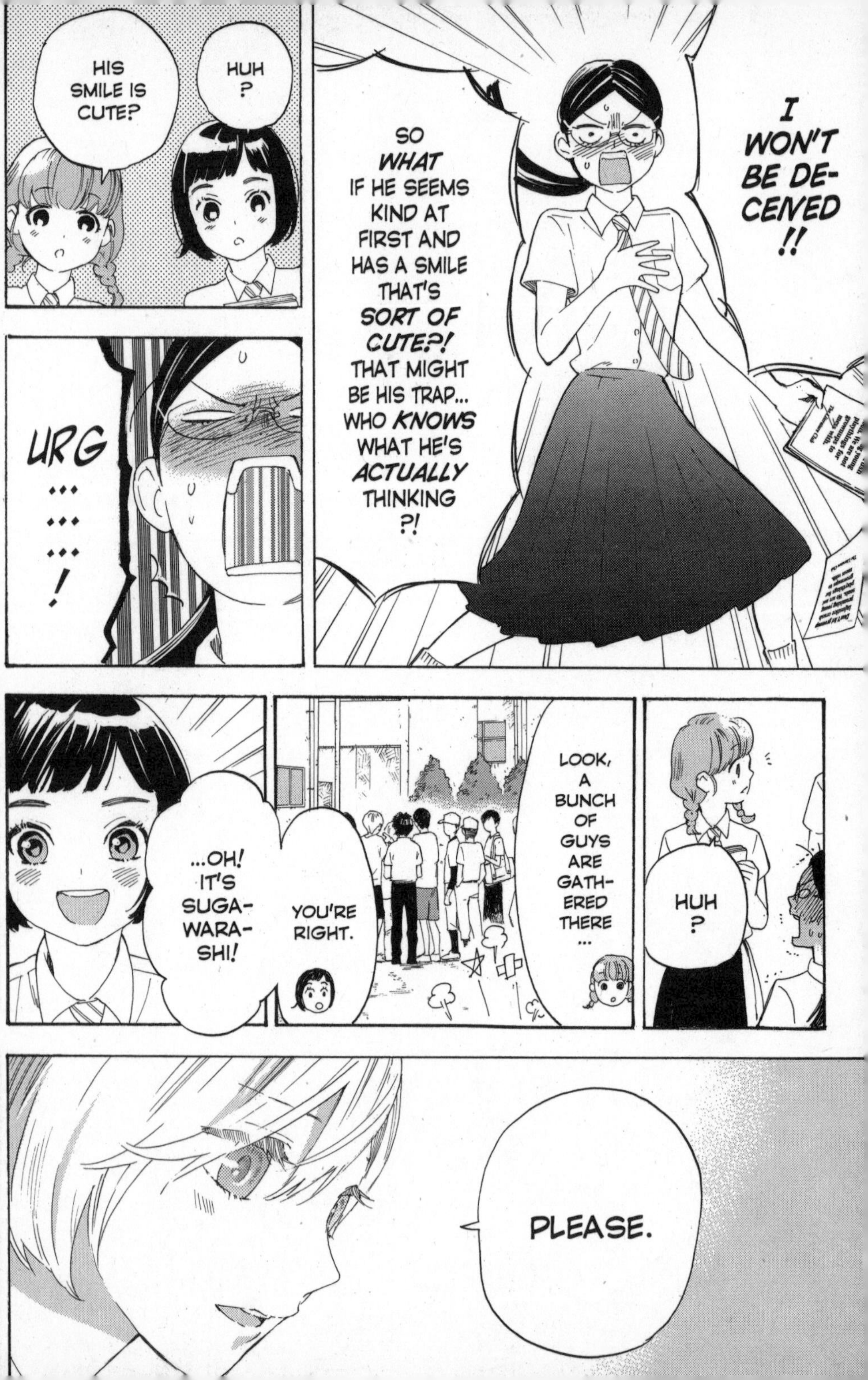
I WON'T BE DE-CEIVED!!
SO WHAT IF HE SEEMS KIND AT FIRST AND HAS A SMILE THAT'S SORT OF CUTE?! THAT MIGHT BE HIS TRAP... WHO KNOWS WHAT HE'S ACTUALLY THINKING?!
HUH?
HIS SMILE IS CUTE?
URG.........!
HUH?
LOOK, A BUNCH OF GUYS ARE GATH-ERED THERE...
YOU'RE RIGHT.
...OH! IT'S SUGA-WARA-SHI!
PLEASE.

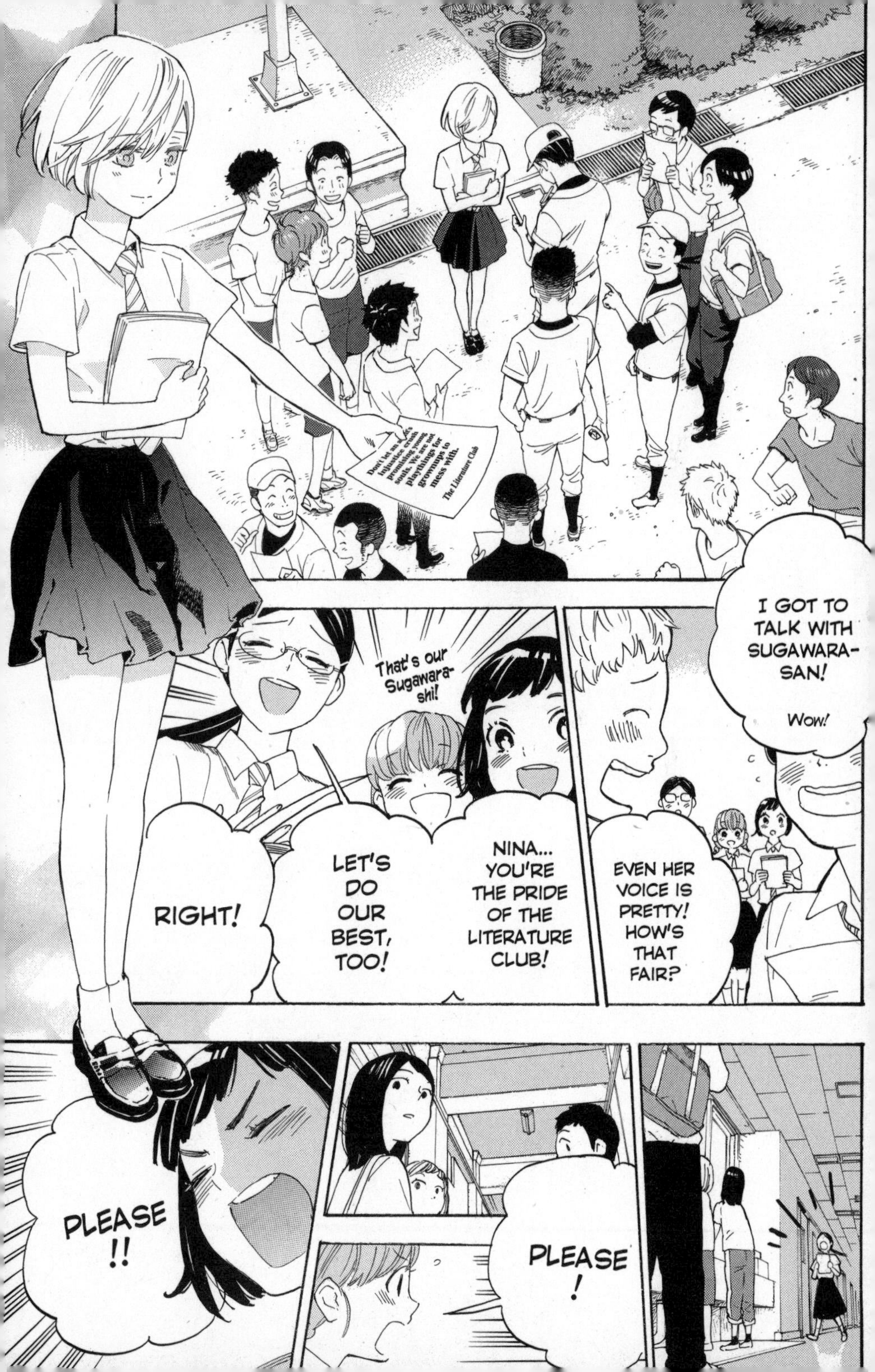
Don't let an
injustice crush promising young souls. We are not playthings for grownups to mess with.
The Literature Club
I GOT TO TALK WITH SUGAWARA-SAN!
Wow!
EVEN HER VOICE IS PRETTY! HOW'S THAT FAIR?
That's our Sugawara-shi!
NINA... YOU'RE THE PRIDE OF THE LITERATURE CLUB!
LET'S DO OUR BEST, TOO!
RIGHT!
PLEASE !
PLEASE !!

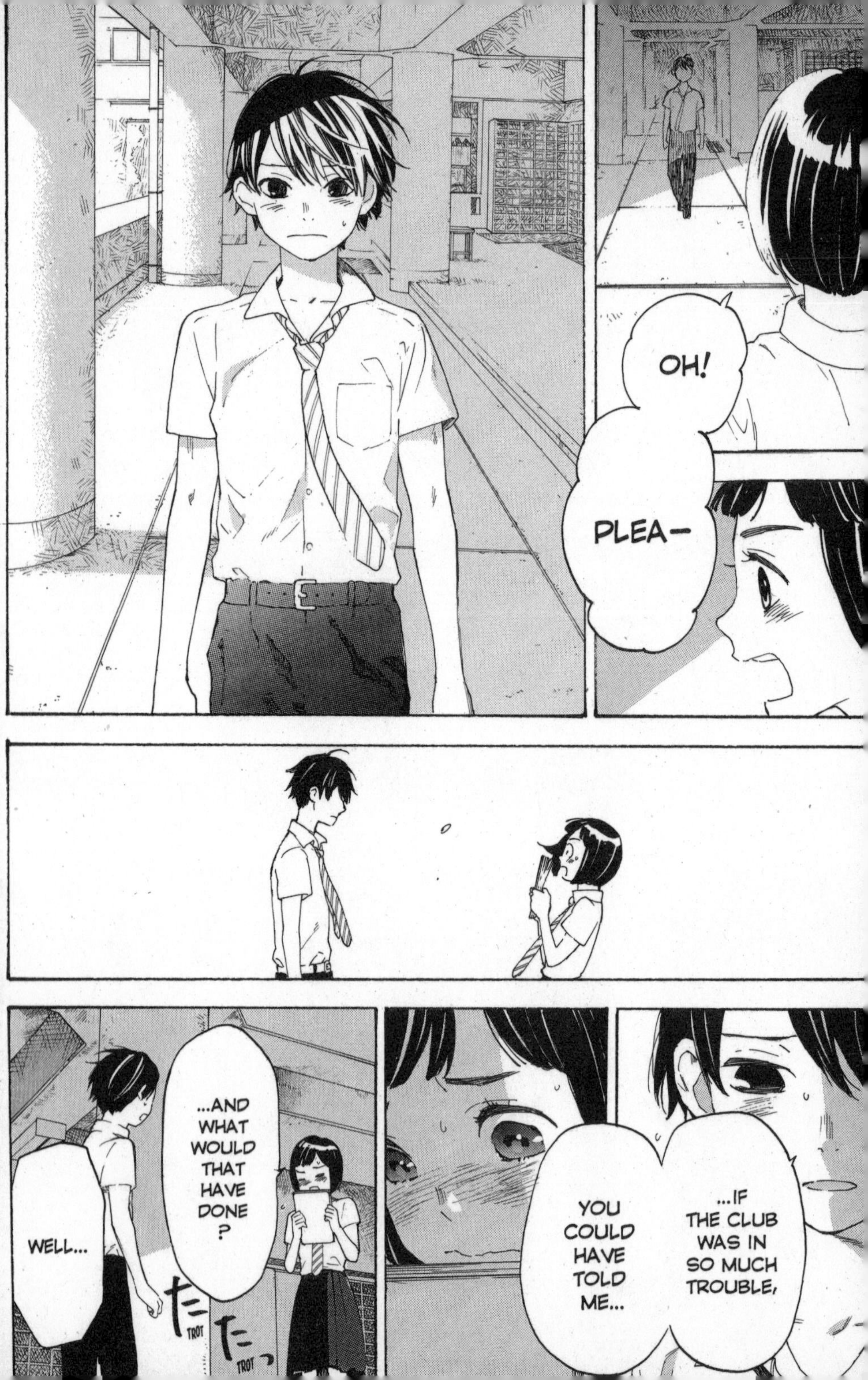
OH!
PLEA-
...IF THE CLUB WAS IN SO MUCH TROUBLE,
YOU COULD HAVE TOLD ME...
...AND WHAT WOULD THAT HAVE DONE?
WELL...
TROT
TROT

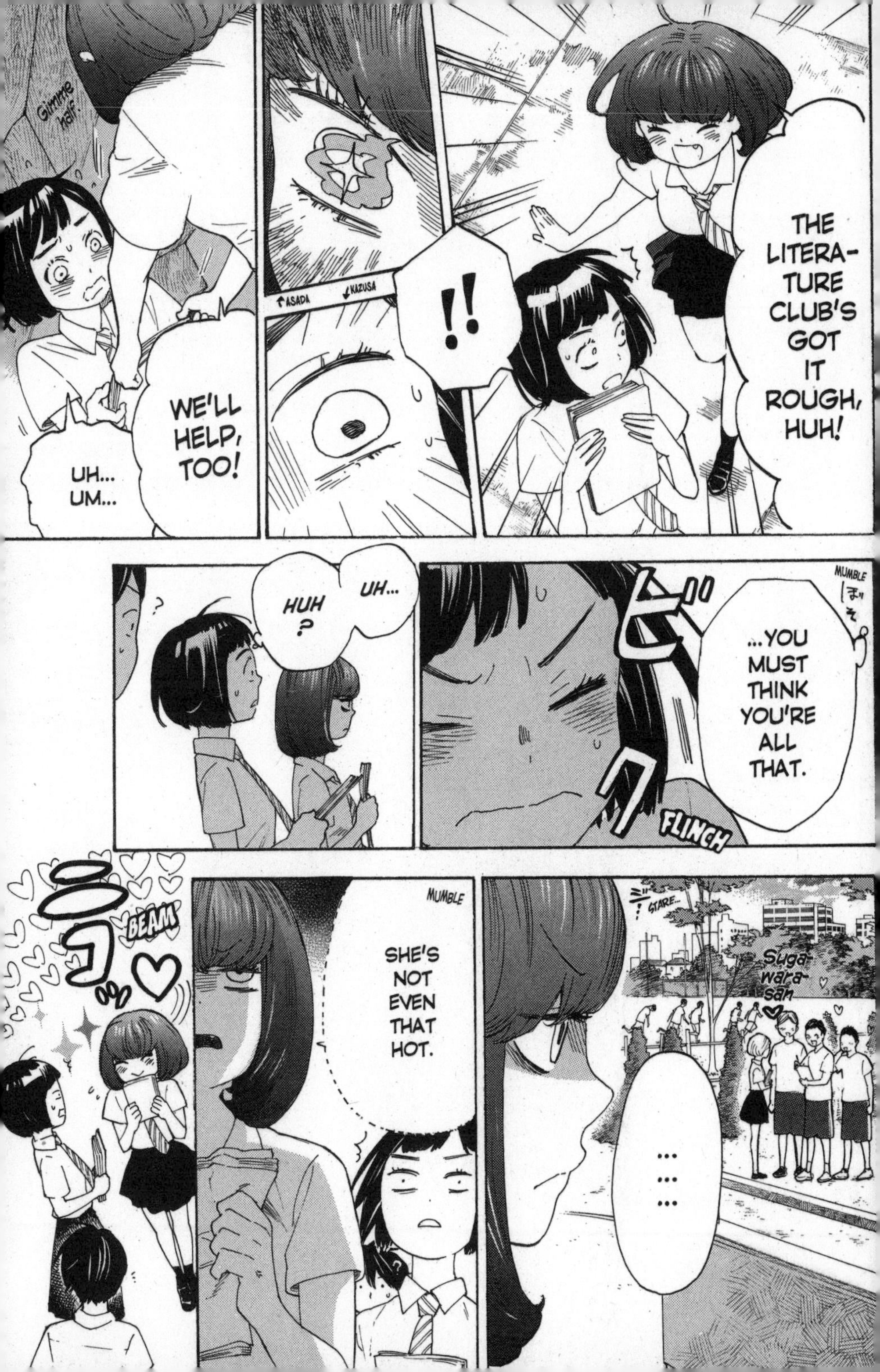

THE LITERA-TURE CLUB'S GOT IT ROUGH, HUH!
!!
↑ASADA ↓KAZUSA
Gimme half.
WE'LL HELP, TOO!
UH... UM...
MUMBLE
...YOU MUST THINK YOU'RE ALL THAT.
FLINCH
UH...
HUH?
STARE...
Suga-wara-san
... ...
MUMBLE
SHE'S NOT EVEN THAT HOT.
BEAM

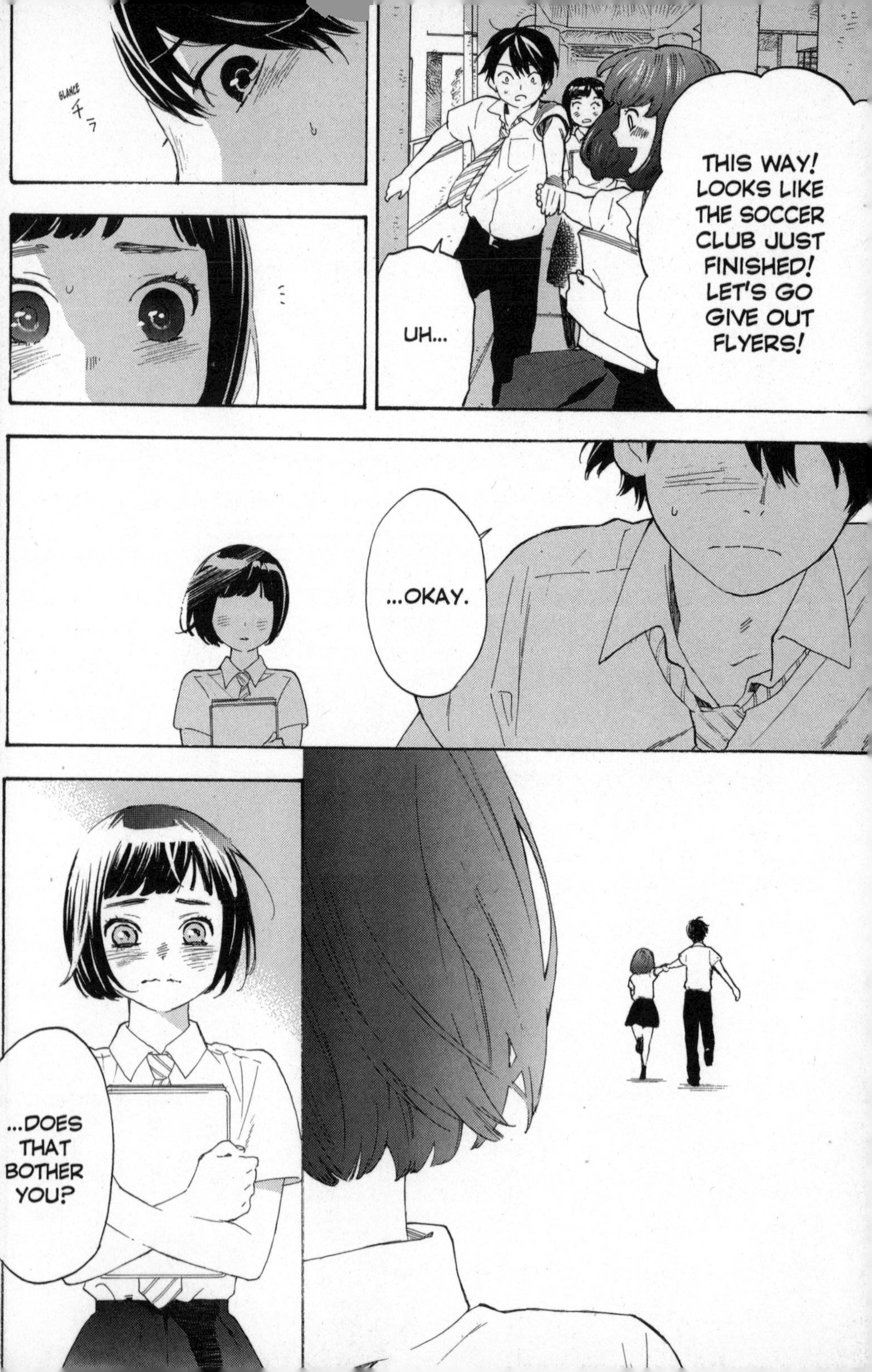
THIS WAY! LOOKS LIKE THE SOCCER CLUB JUST FINISHED! LET'S GO GIVE OUT FLYERS!
UH...
GLANCE
チラ
...OKAY.
...DOES THAT BOTHER YOU?

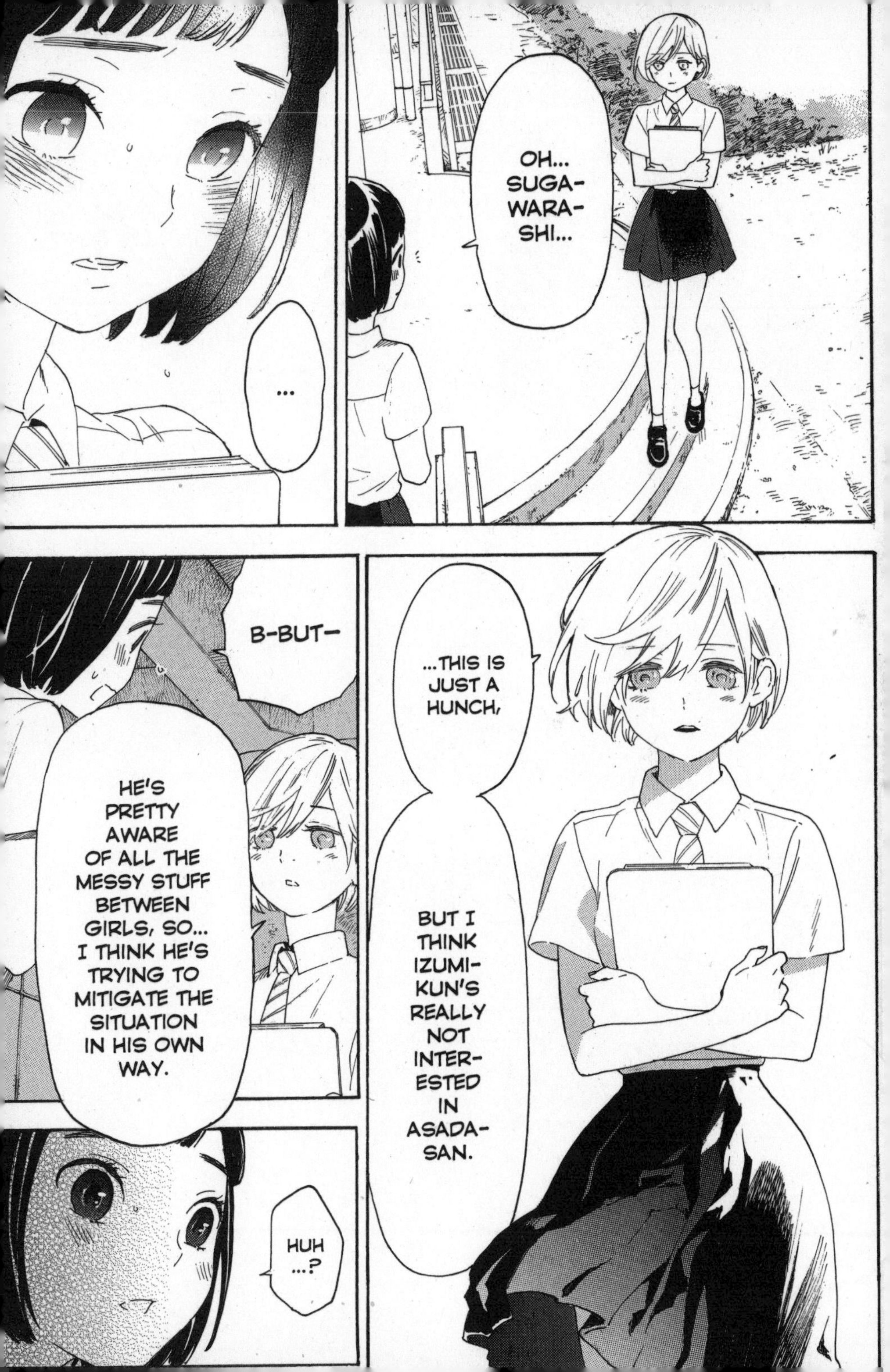
OH... SUGA-WARA-SHI...
...
...THIS IS JUST A HUNCH,
BUT I THINK IZUMI-KUN'S REALLY NOT INTER-ESTED IN ASADA-SAN.
B-BUT—
HE'S PRETTY AWARE OF ALL THE MESSY STUFF BETWEEN GIRLS, SO... I THINK HE'S TRYING TO MITIGATE THE SITUATION IN HIS OWN WAY.
HUH ...?

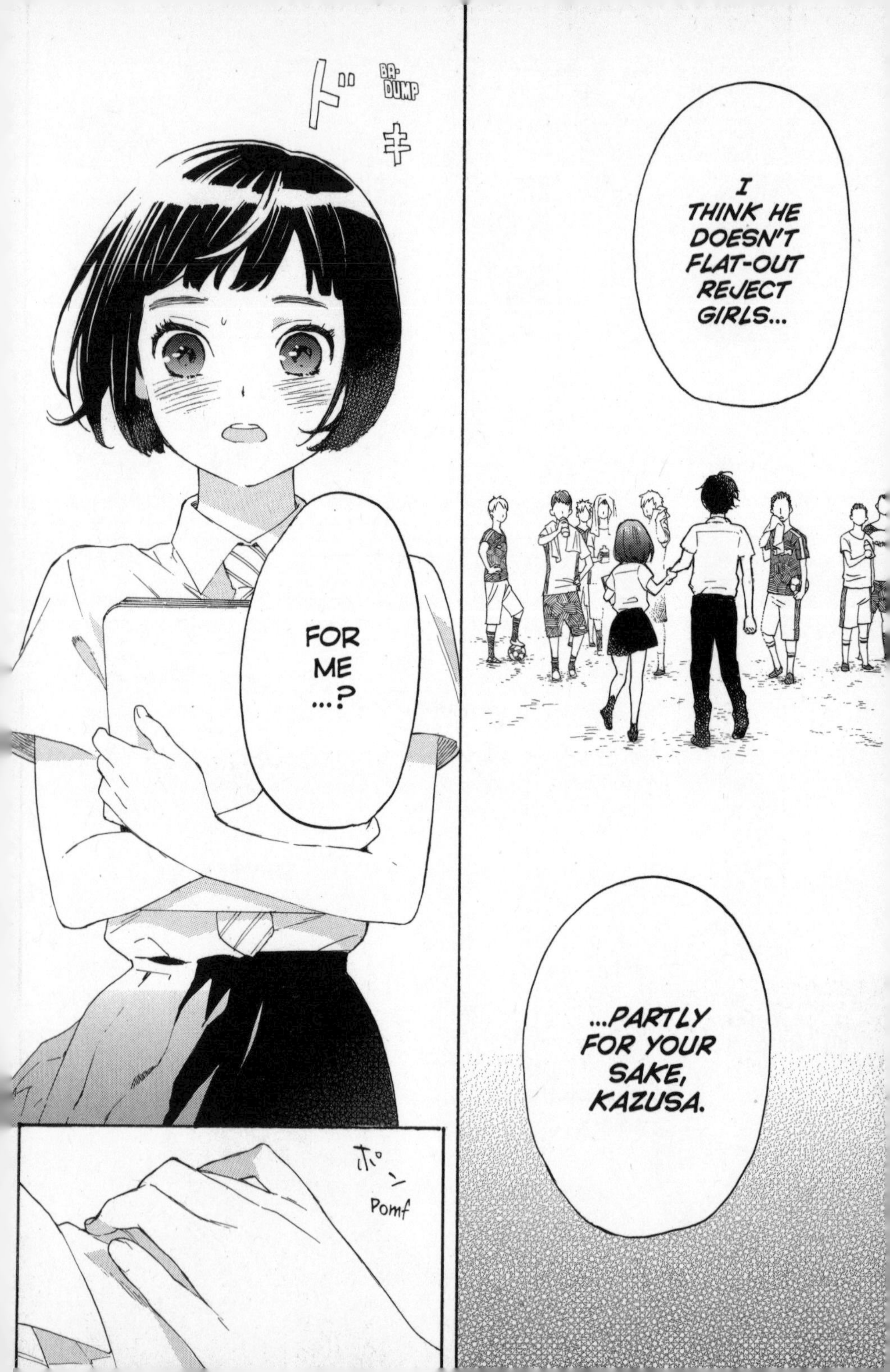
I THINK HE DOESN'T FLAT-OUT REJECT GIRLS...
...PARTLY FOR YOUR SAKE, KAZUSA.
ドキ
BA-DUMP
FOR ME ...?
ポン
Pomf

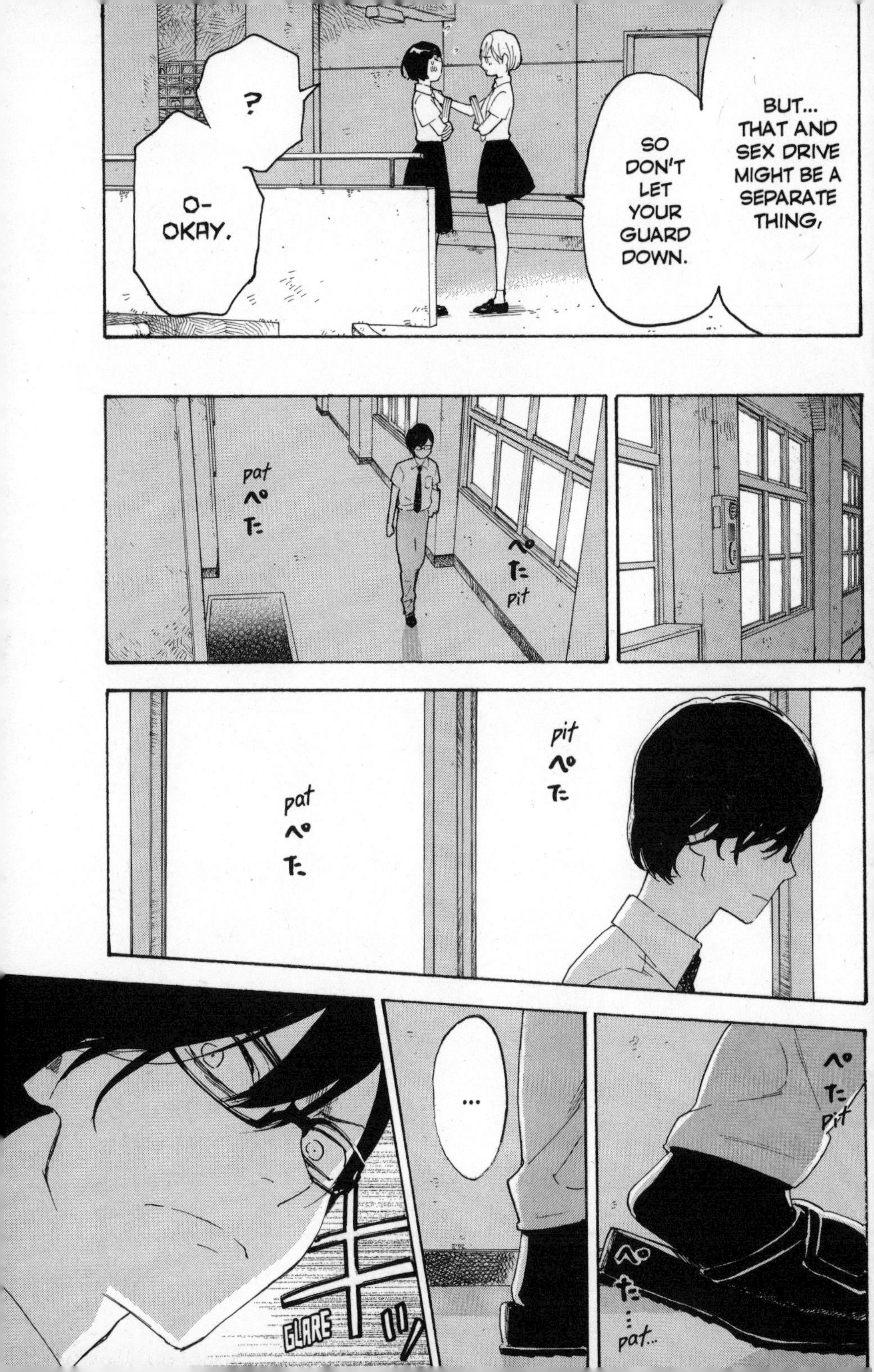
BUT... THAT AND SEX DRIVE MIGHT BE A SEPARATE THING,
SO DON'T LET YOUR GUARD DOWN.
?
O- OKAY.
pat ぺた
ぺた pit
pit ぺた
pat ぺた
ぺた pit
ぺた... pat...
...
GLARE

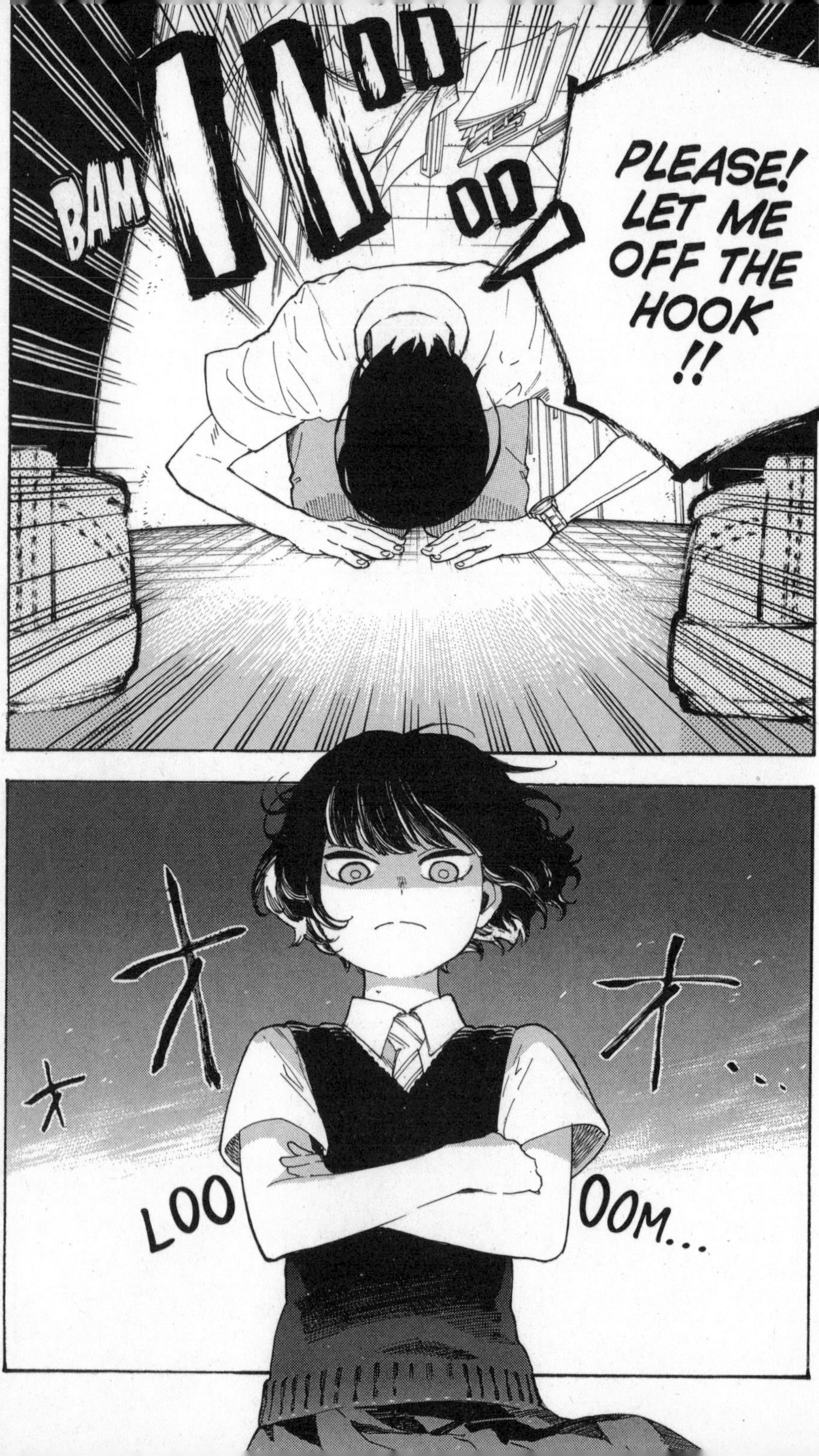
PLEASE! LET ME OFF THE HOOK !!
BAM
LOO OOM...

ON ONE CONDITION.

...FINE.

HUH ...?!

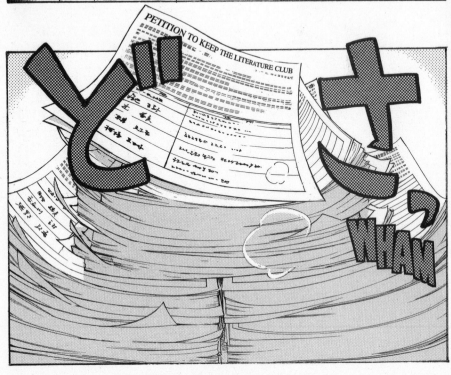

PETITION TO KEEP THE LITERATURE CLUB

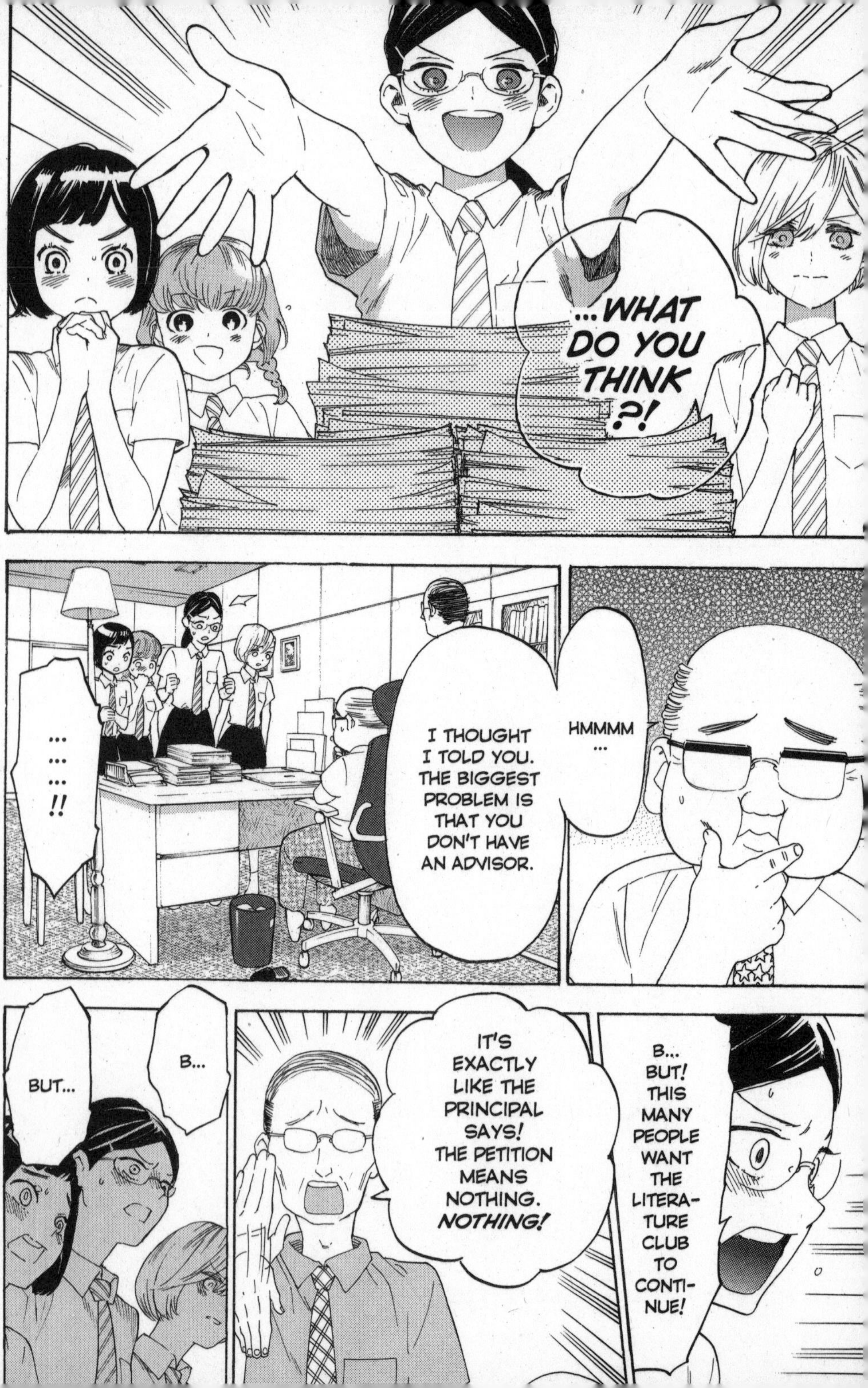
...WHAT DO YOU THINK ?!
HMMMM ...
I THOUGHT I TOLD YOU. THE BIGGEST PROBLEM IS THAT YOU DON'T HAVE AN ADVISOR.
... ... !!
B... BUT! THIS MANY PEOPLE WANT THE LITERATURE CLUB TO CONTINUE!
IT'S EXACTLY LIKE THE PRINCIPAL SAYS! THE PETITION MEANS NOTHING. *NOTHING!*
B...
BUT...

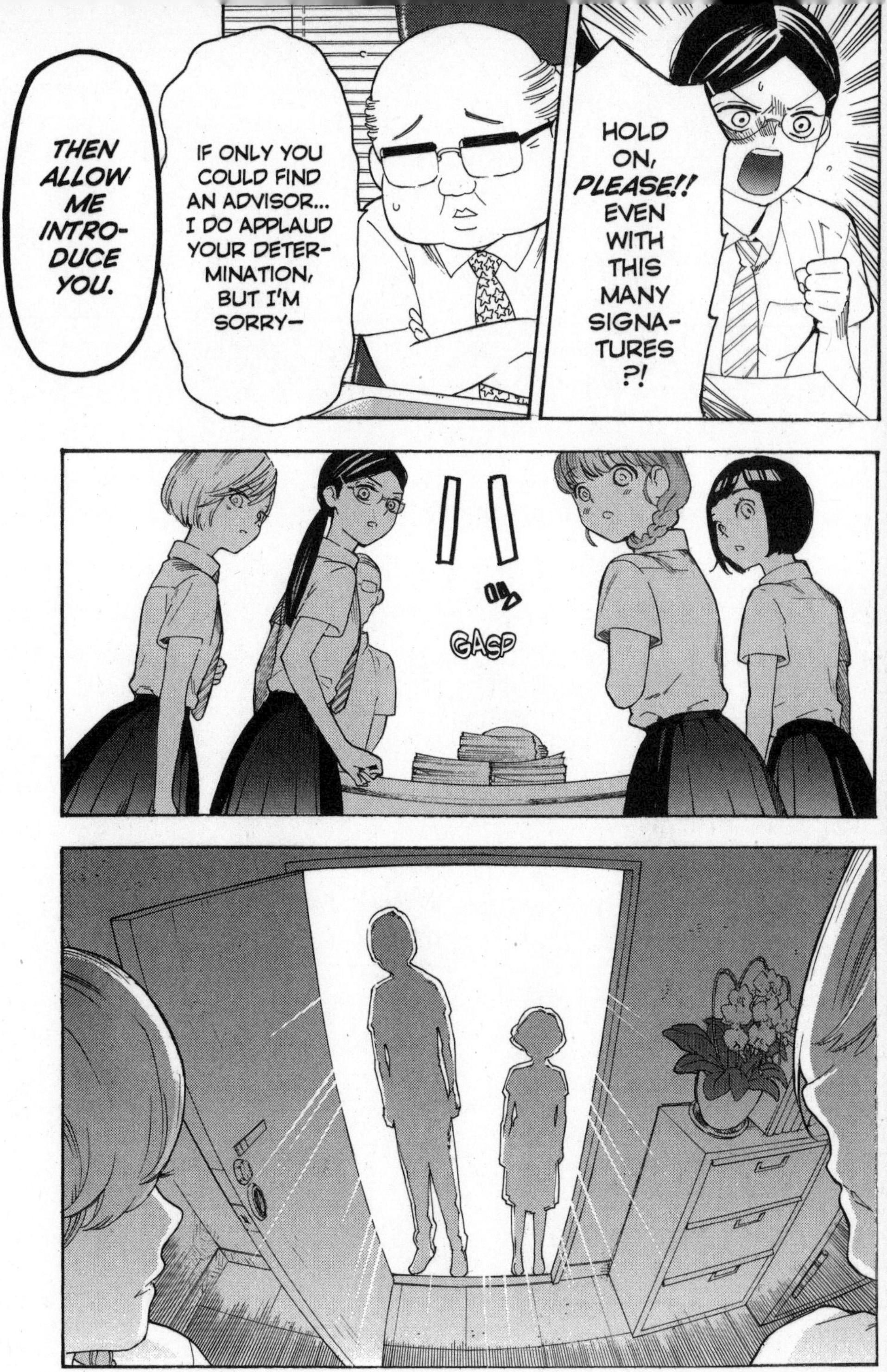
HOLD ON, PLEASE!! EVEN WITH THIS MANY SIGNATURES?!
IF ONLY YOU COULD FIND AN ADVISOR... I DO APPLAUD YOUR DETERMINATION, BUT I'M SORRY—
THEN ALLOW ME INTRODUCE YOU.
GASP

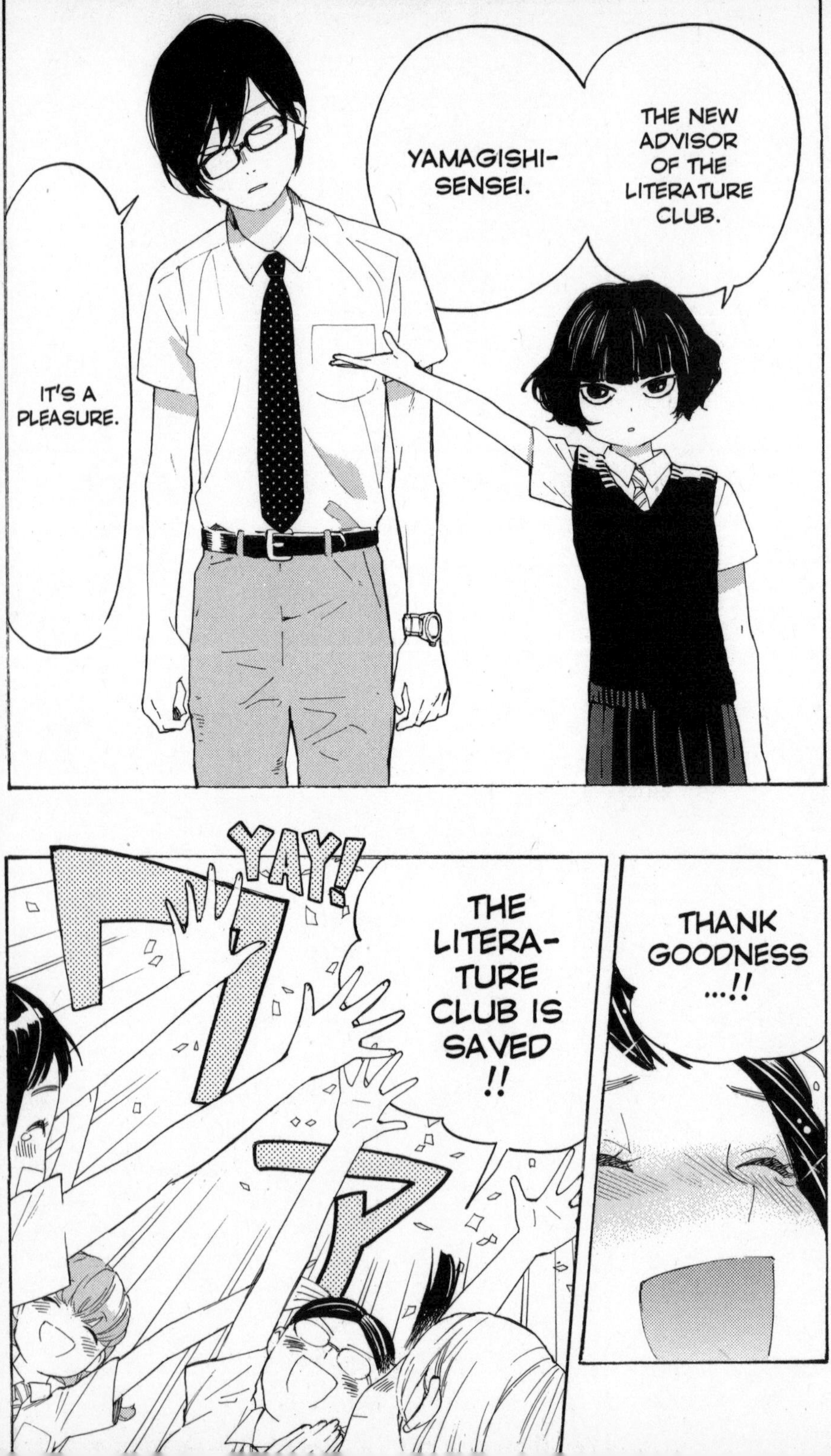
THE NEW ADVISOR OF THE LITERATURE CLUB.
YAMAGISHI-SENSEI.
IT'S A PLEASURE.
THANK GOODNESS ...!!
YAY!
THE LITERA-TURE CLUB IS SAVED !!

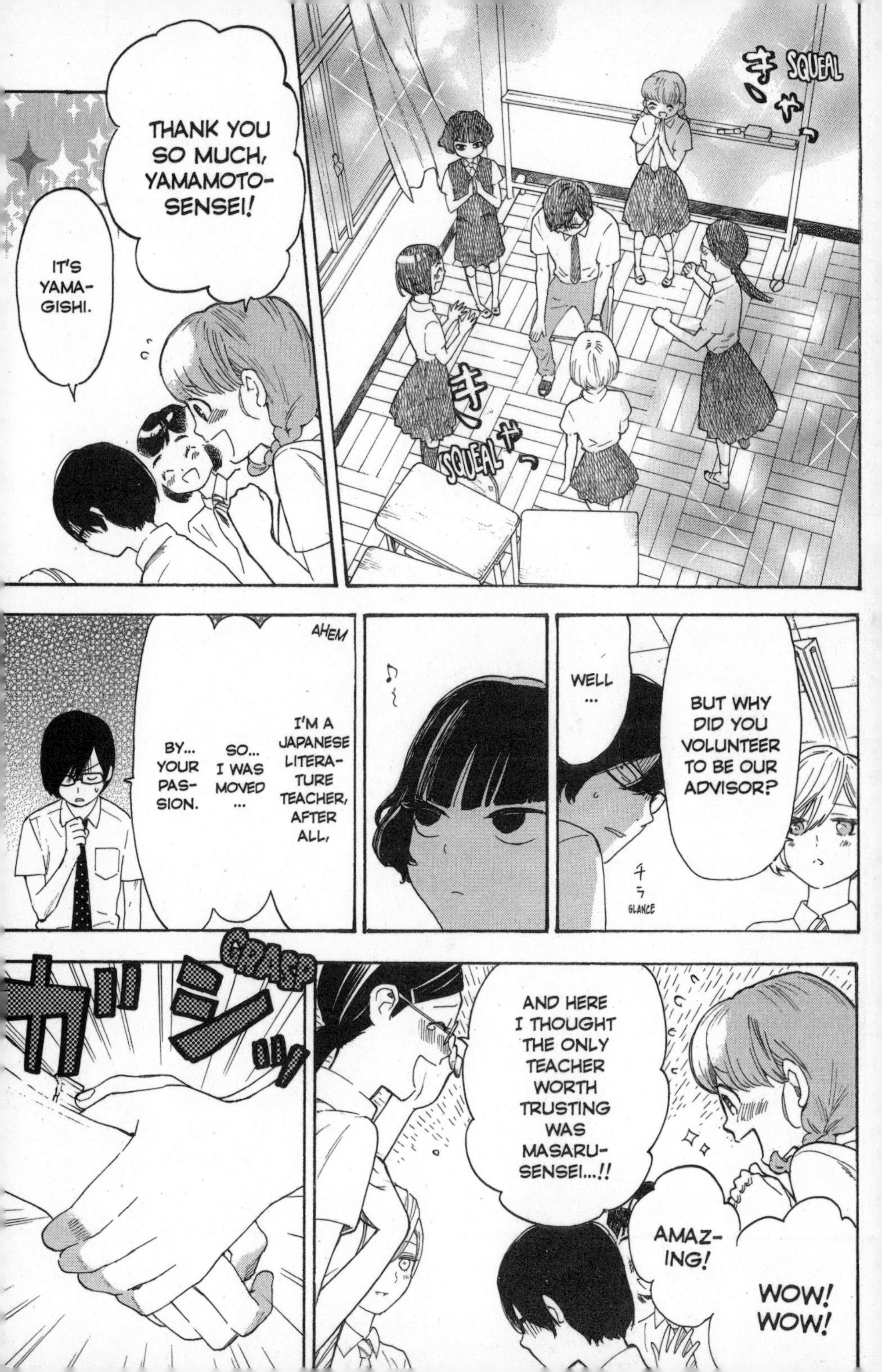
きゃ
SQUEAL
きゃー
SQUEAL
THANK YOU SO MUCH, YAMAMOTO-SENSEI!
IT'S YAMAGISHI.
BUT WHY DID YOU VOLUNTEER TO BE OUR ADVISOR?
WELL...
チラ
GLANCE
AHEM
I'M A JAPANESE LITERATURE TEACHER, AFTER ALL,
SO... I WAS MOVED...
BY... YOUR PASSION.
AND HERE I THOUGHT THE ONLY TEACHER WORTH TRUSTING WAS MASARU-SENSEI...!!
AMAZING!
WOW! WOW!
ガシッ
GRASP

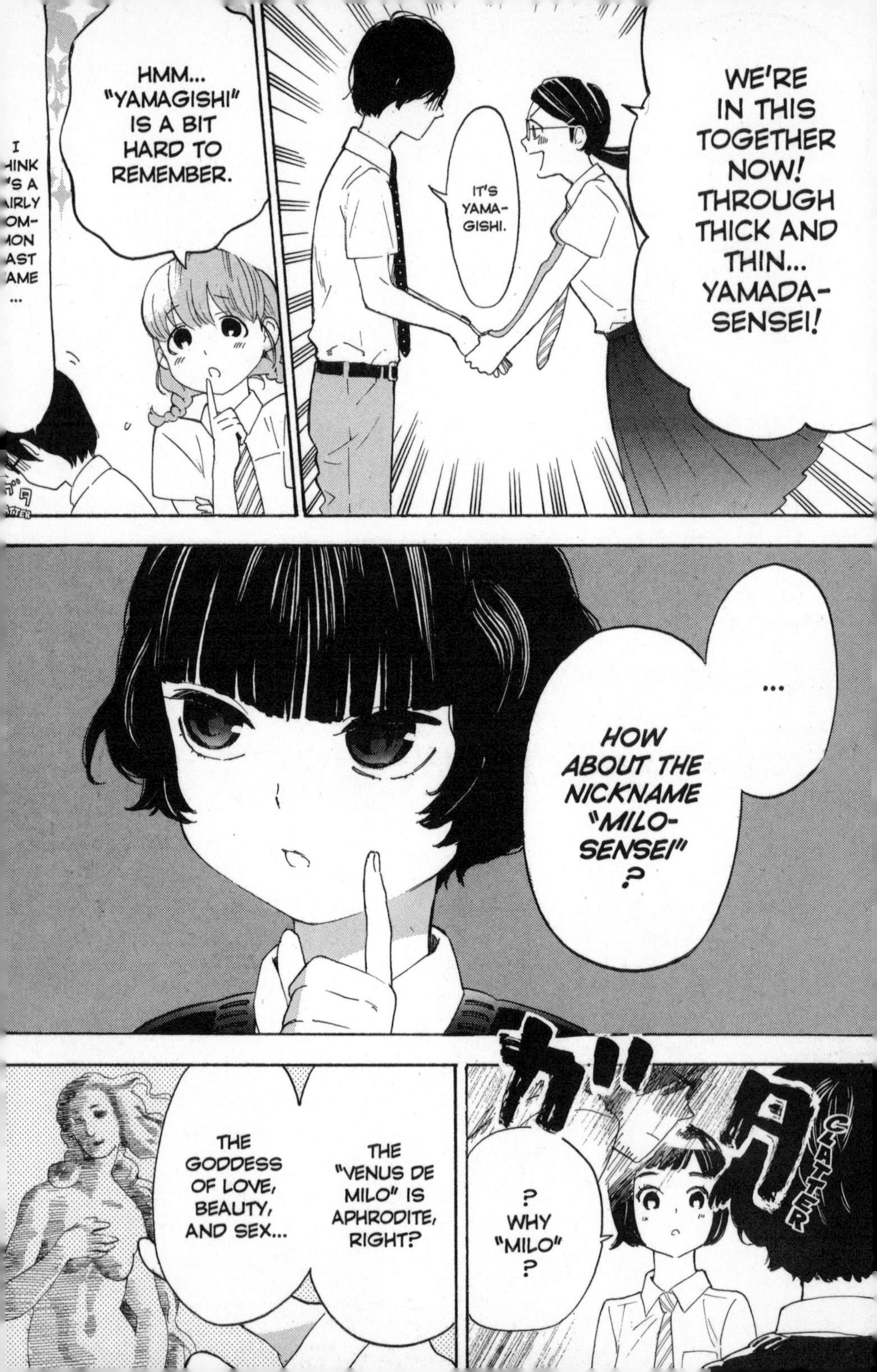
WE'RE IN THIS TOGETHER NOW! THROUGH THICK AND THIN... YAMADA-SENSEI!
IT'S YAMA-GISHI.
HMM... "YAMAGISHI" IS A BIT HARD TO REMEMBER.
...
HOW ABOUT THE NICKNAME "MILO-SENSEI"?
ガタ
GATTER
? WHY "MILO"?
THE "VENUS DE MILO" IS APHRODITE, RIGHT?
THE GODDESS OF LOVE, BEAUTY, AND SEX...

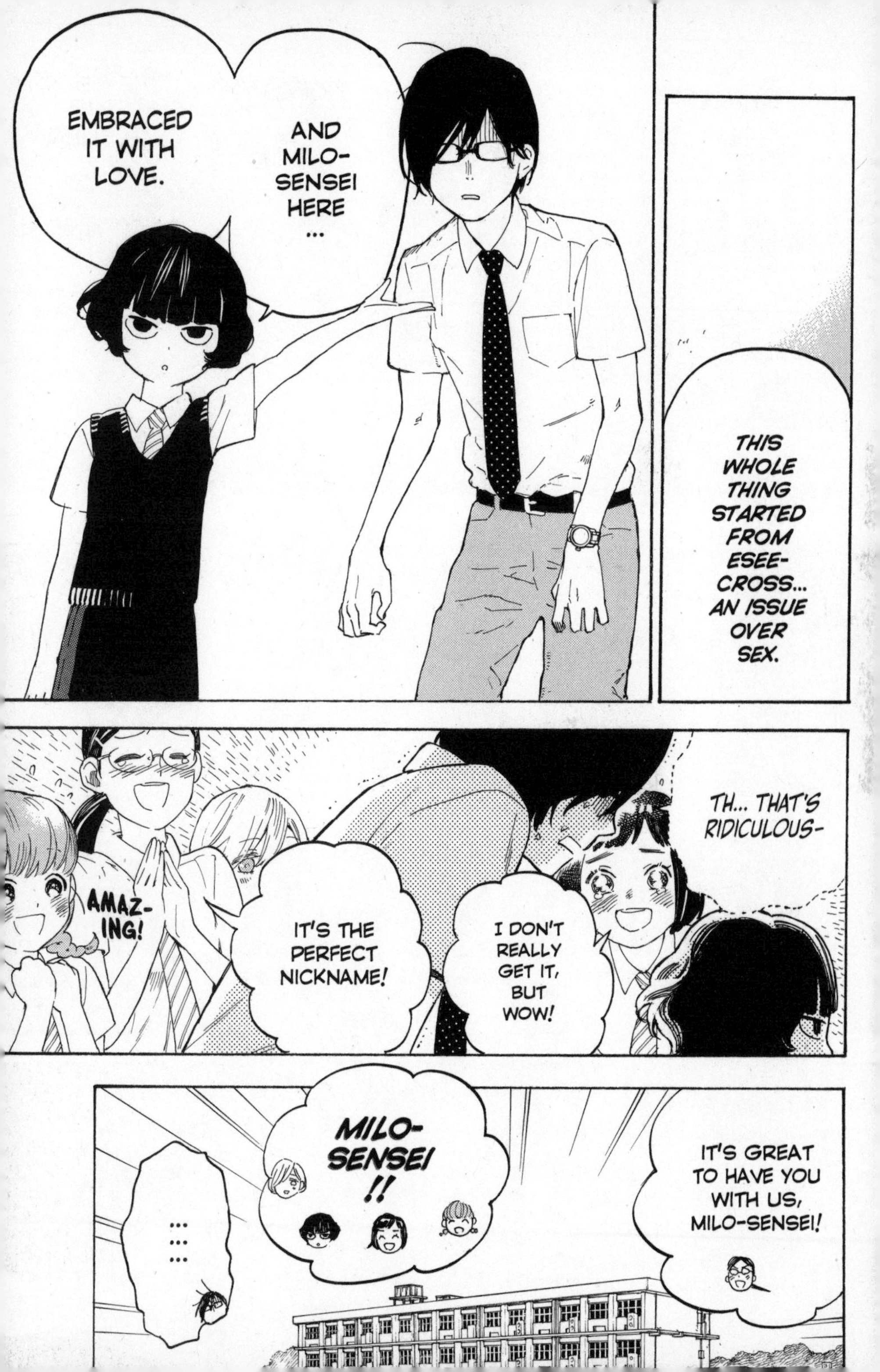
THIS WHOLE THING STARTED FROM ESEE-CROSS... AN ISSUE OVER SEX.
AND MILO-SENSEI HERE ...
EMBRACED IT WITH LOVE.
TH... THAT'S RIDICULOUS-
I DON'T REALLY GET IT, BUT WOW!
IT'S THE PERFECT NICKNAME!
AMAZ-ING!
IT'S GREAT TO HAVE YOU WITH US, MILO-SENSEI!
MILO-SENSEI!!
... ...

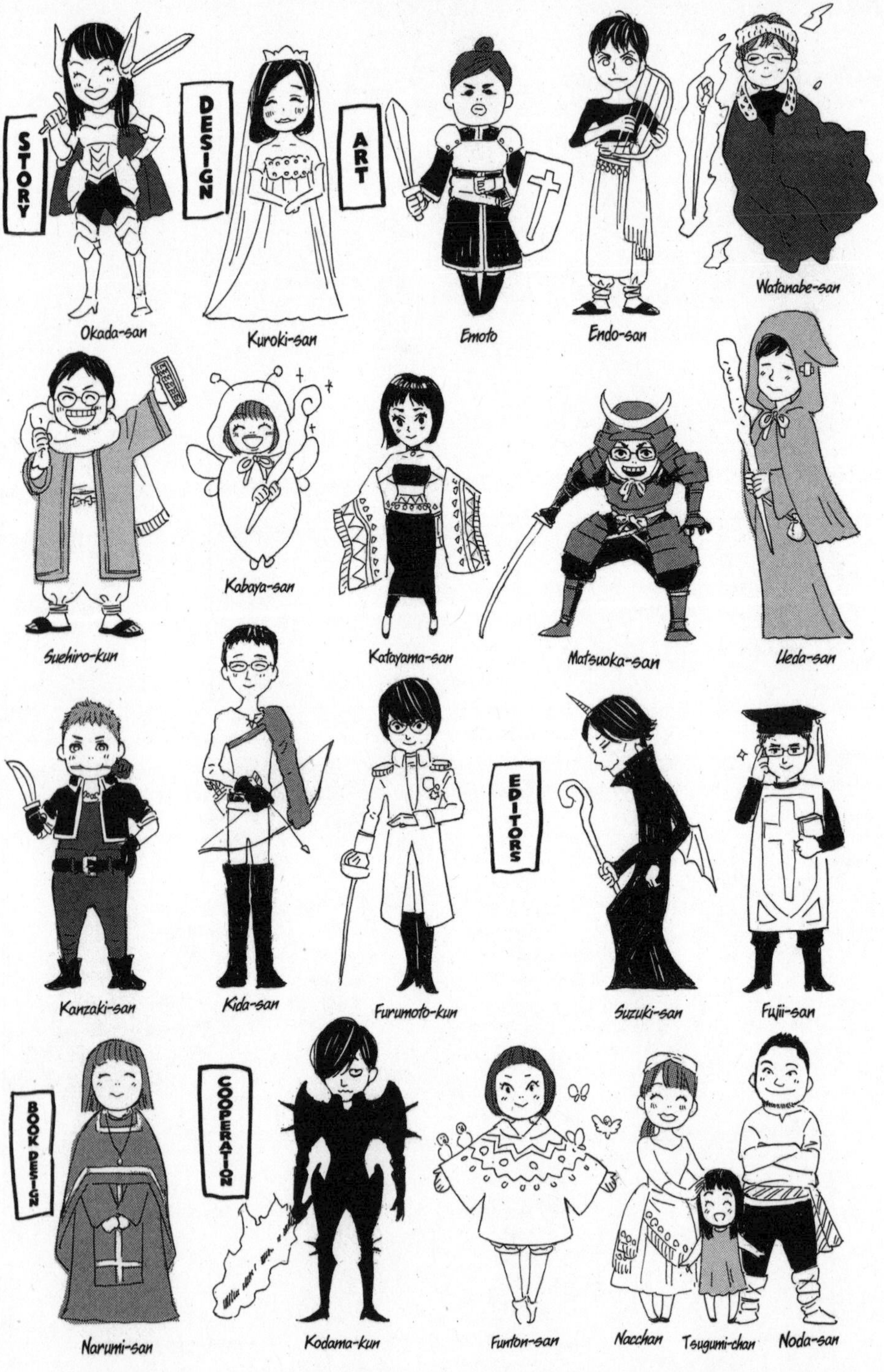
STORY
Okada-san
DESIGN
Kuroki-san
ART
Emoto
Endo-san
Watanabe-san
Suehiro-kun
Kabaya-san
Katayama-san
Matsuoka-san
Ueda-san
Kanzaki-san
Kida-san
Furumoto-kun
EDITORS
Suzuki-san
Fujii-san
BOOK DESIGN
Narumi-san
COOPERATION
Kodama-kun
Funton-san
Nacchan
Tsugumi-chan
Noda-san

Meeting 7

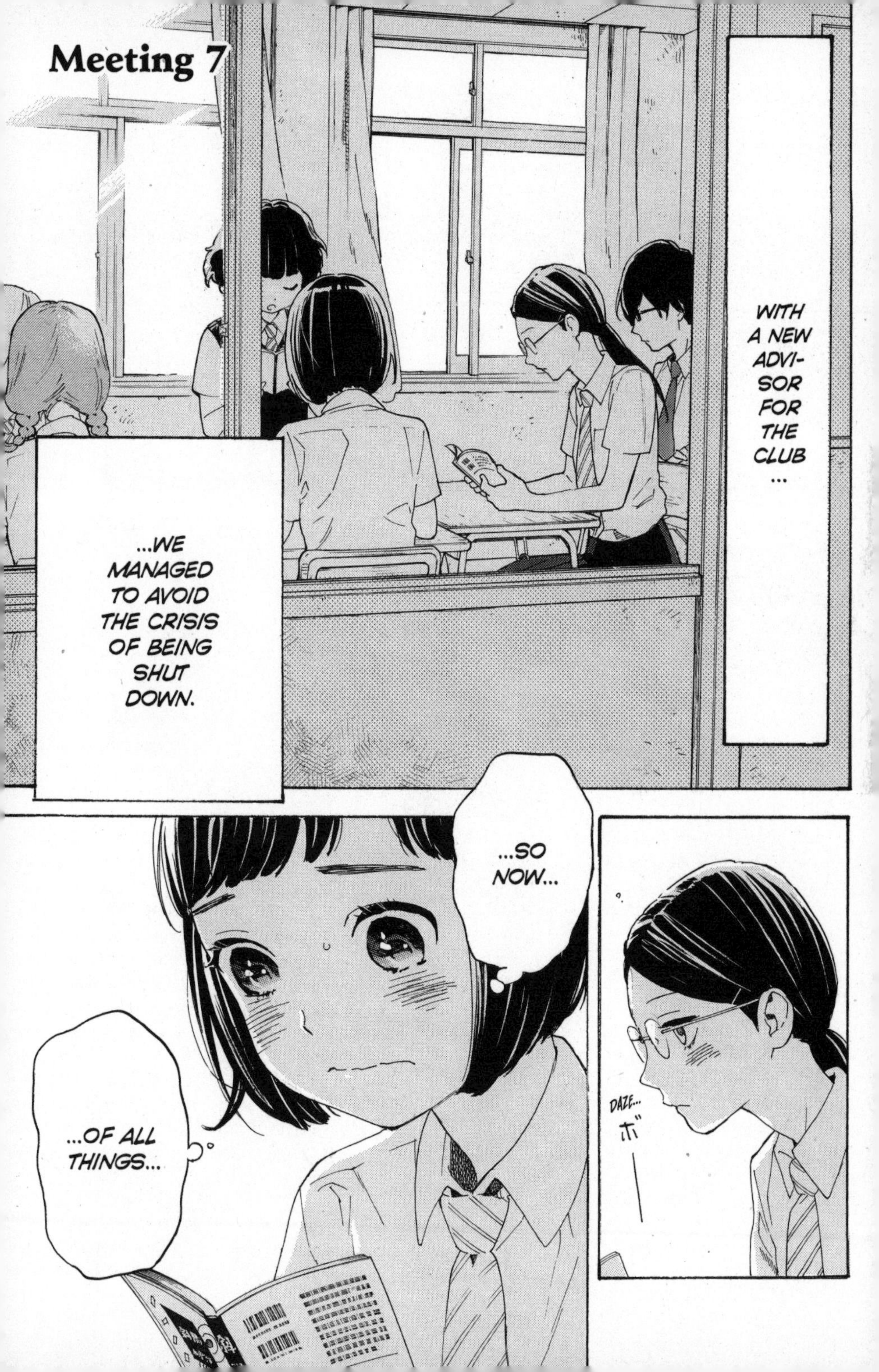
WITH A NEW ADVI-SOR FOR THE CLUB ...
...WE MANAGED TO AVOID THE CRISIS OF BEING SHUT DOWN.
DAZE... ボ
...SO NOW...
...OF ALL THINGS...

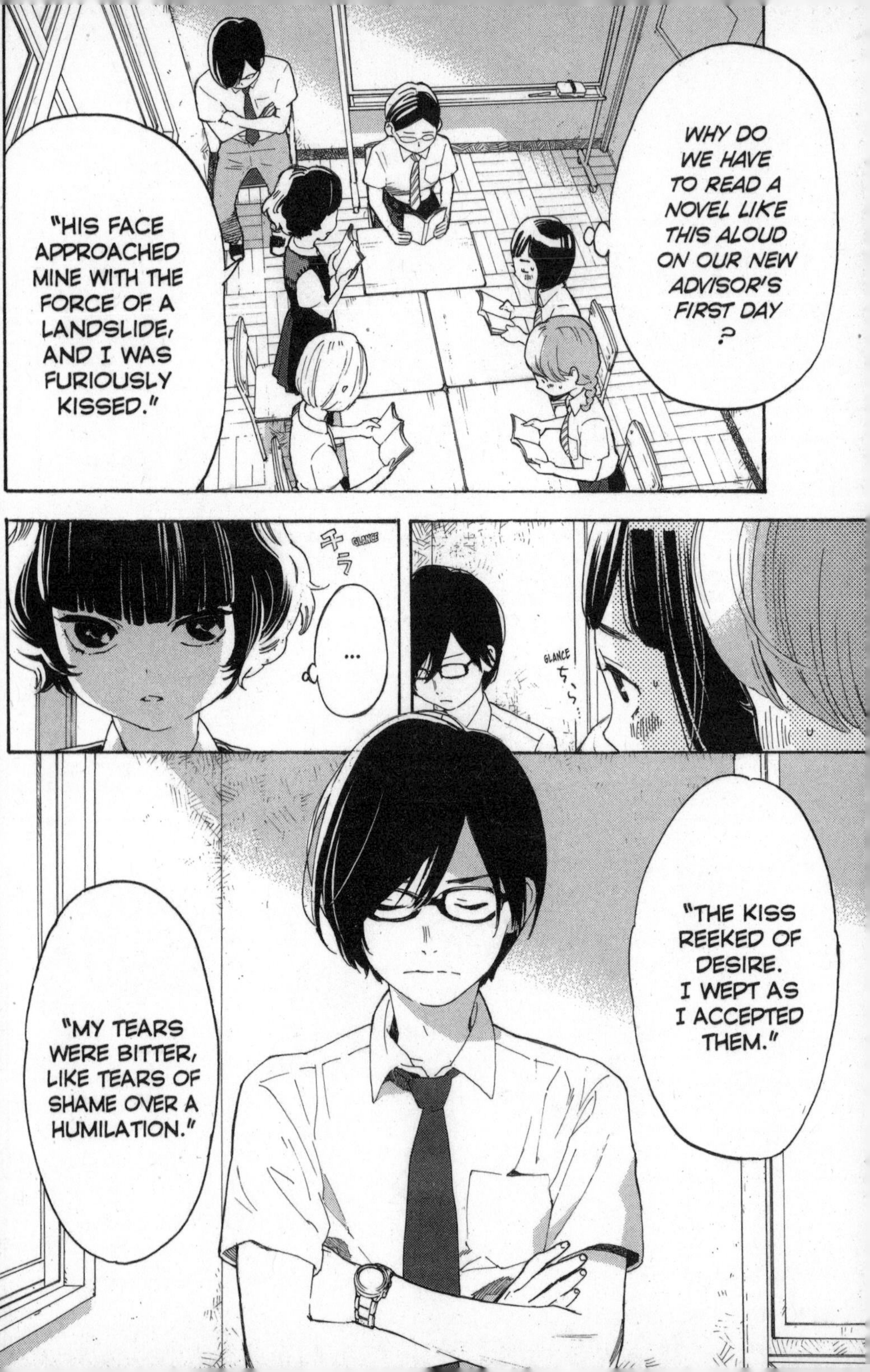
WHY DO WE HAVE TO READ A NOVEL LIKE THIS ALOUD ON OUR NEW ADVISOR'S FIRST DAY?
"HIS FACE APPROACHED MINE WITH THE FORCE OF A LANDSLIDE, AND I WAS FURIOUSLY KISSED."
GLANCE
ちら…
チラ
GLANCE
...
"THE KISS REEKED OF DESIRE. I WEPT AS I ACCEPTED THEM."
"MY TEARS WERE BITTER, LIKE TEARS OF SHAME OVER A HUMILATION."

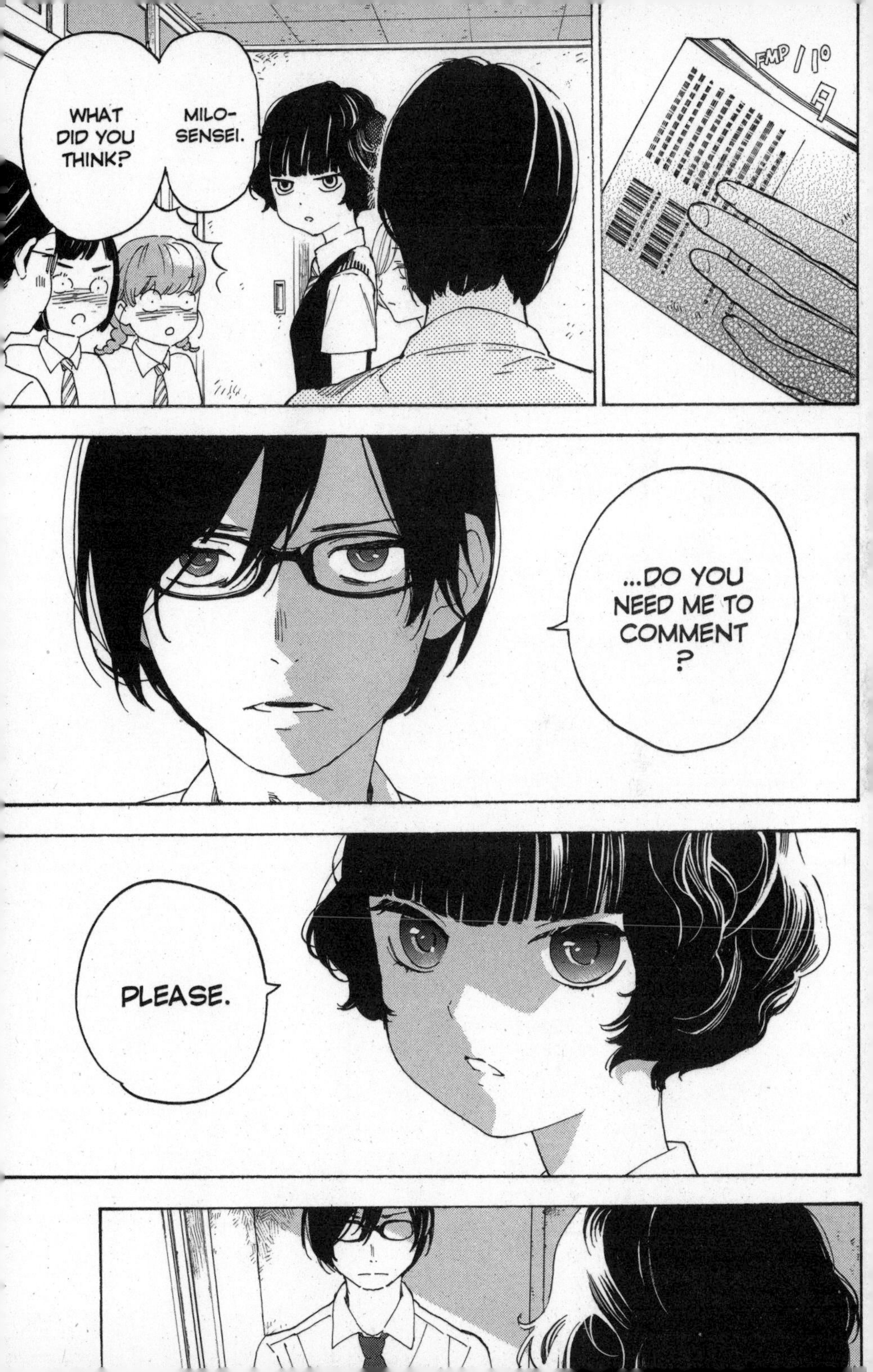
MILO-SENSEI.
WHAT DID YOU THINK?
...DO YOU NEED ME TO COMMENT?
PLEASE.

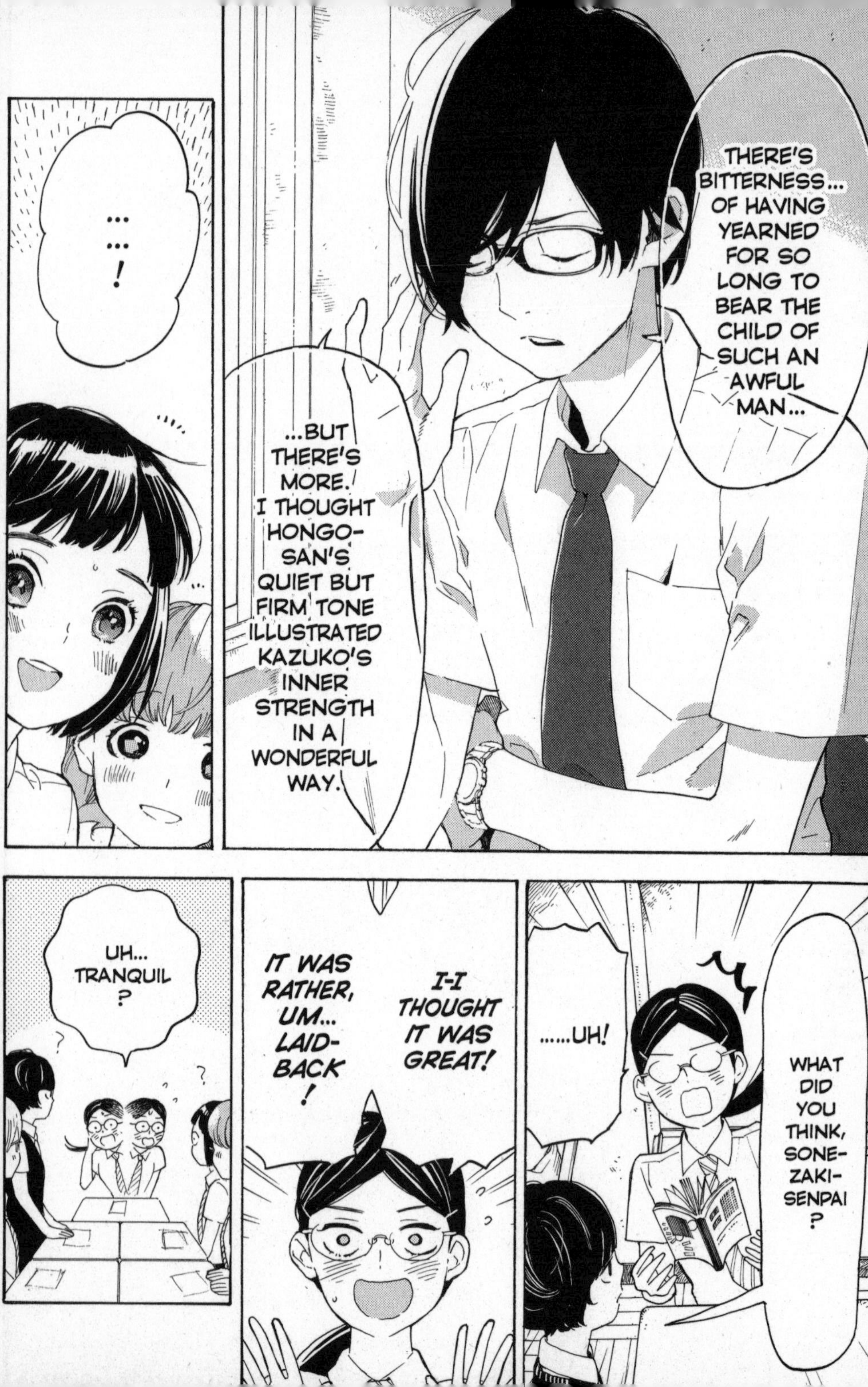
THERE'S BITTERNESS... OF HAVING YEARNED FOR SO LONG TO BEAR THE CHILD OF SUCH AN AWFUL MAN...
...BUT THERE'S MORE. I THOUGHT HONGO-SAN'S QUIET BUT FIRM TONE ILLUSTRATED KAZUKO'S INNER STRENGTH IN A WONDERFUL WAY.
......!
WHAT DID YOU THINK, SONE-ZAKI-SENPAI?
......UH!
I-I THOUGHT IT WAS GREAT!
IT WAS RATHER, UM... LAID-BACK!
UH... TRANQUIL?

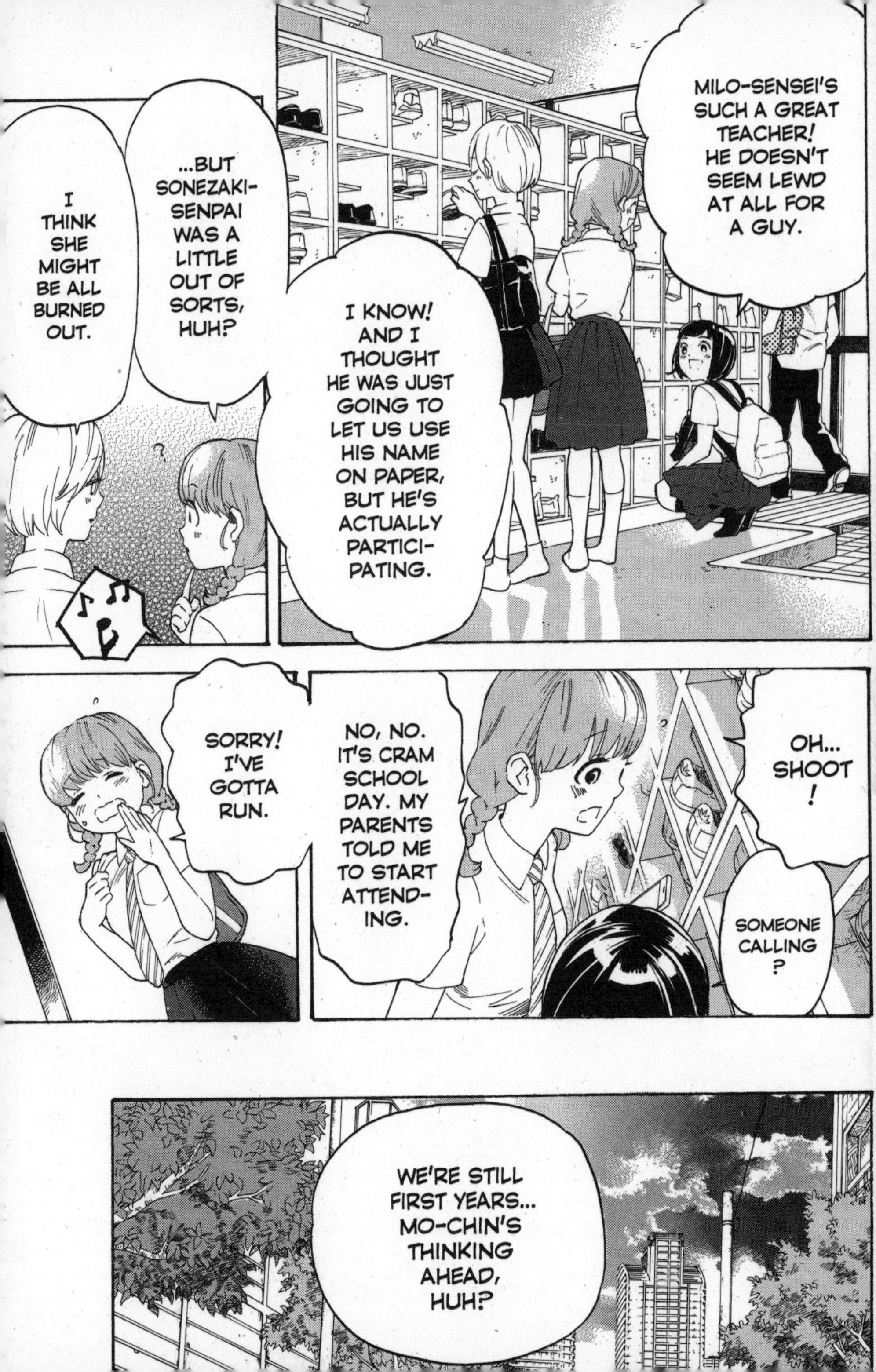
MILO-SENSEI'S SUCH A GREAT TEACHER! HE DOESN'T SEEM LEWD AT ALL FOR A GUY.
I KNOW! AND I THOUGHT HE WAS JUST GOING TO LET US USE HIS NAME ON PAPER, BUT HE'S ACTUALLY PARTICI-PATING.
...BUT SONEZAKI-SENPAI WAS A LITTLE OUT OF SORTS, HUH?
I THINK SHE MIGHT BE ALL BURNED OUT.
OH... SHOOT!
SOMEONE CALLING?
NO, NO. IT'S CRAM SCHOOL DAY. MY PARENTS TOLD ME TO START ATTEND-ING.
SORRY! I'VE GOTTA RUN.
WE'RE STILL FIRST YEARS... MO-CHIN'S THINKING AHEAD, HUH?

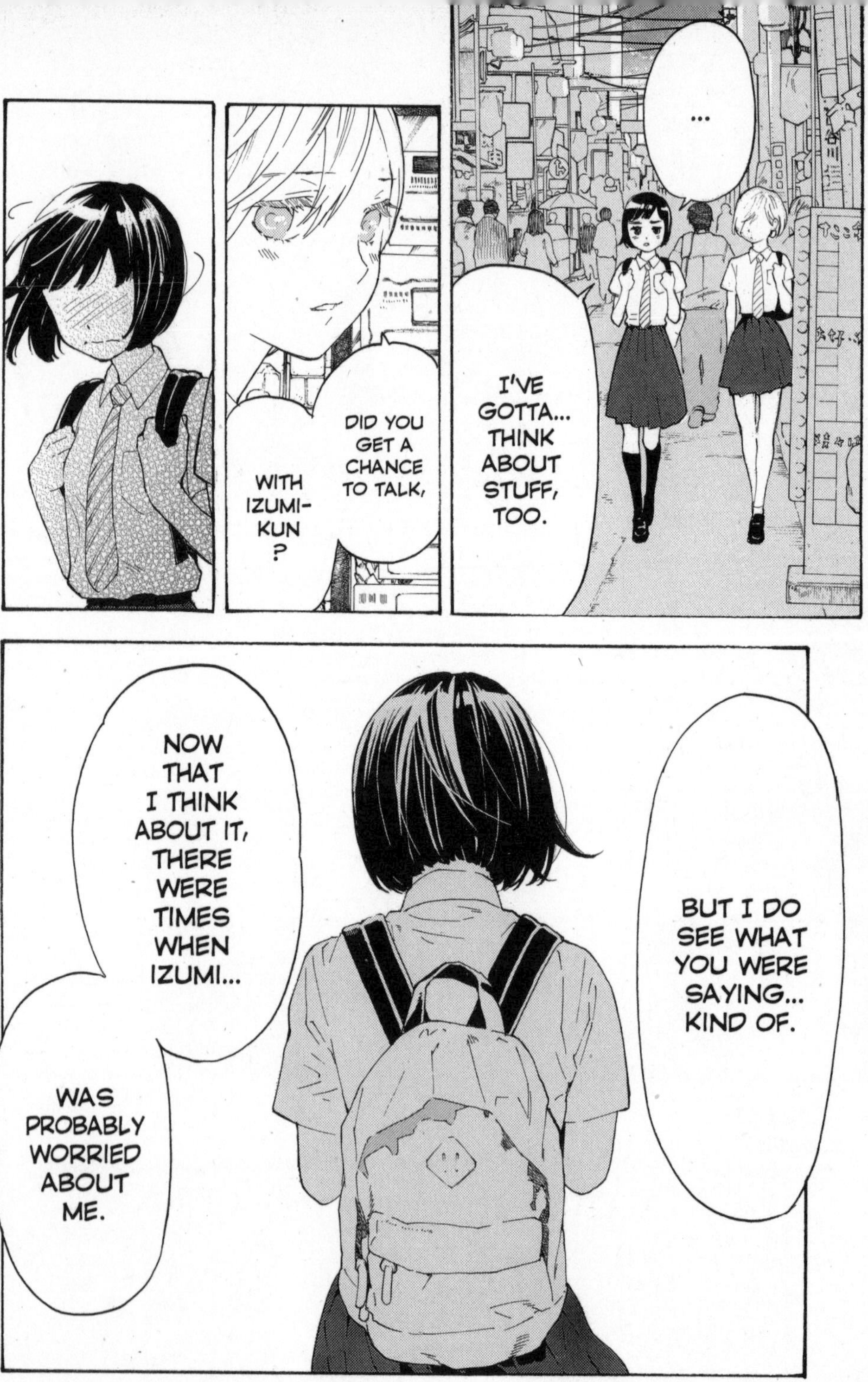
...
I'VE GOTTA... THINK ABOUT STUFF, TOO.
DID YOU GET A CHANCE TO TALK,
WITH IZUMI-KUN?
BUT I DO SEE WHAT YOU WERE SAYING... KIND OF.
NOW THAT I THINK ABOUT IT, THERE WERE TIMES WHEN IZUMI...
WAS PROBABLY WORRIED ABOUT ME.

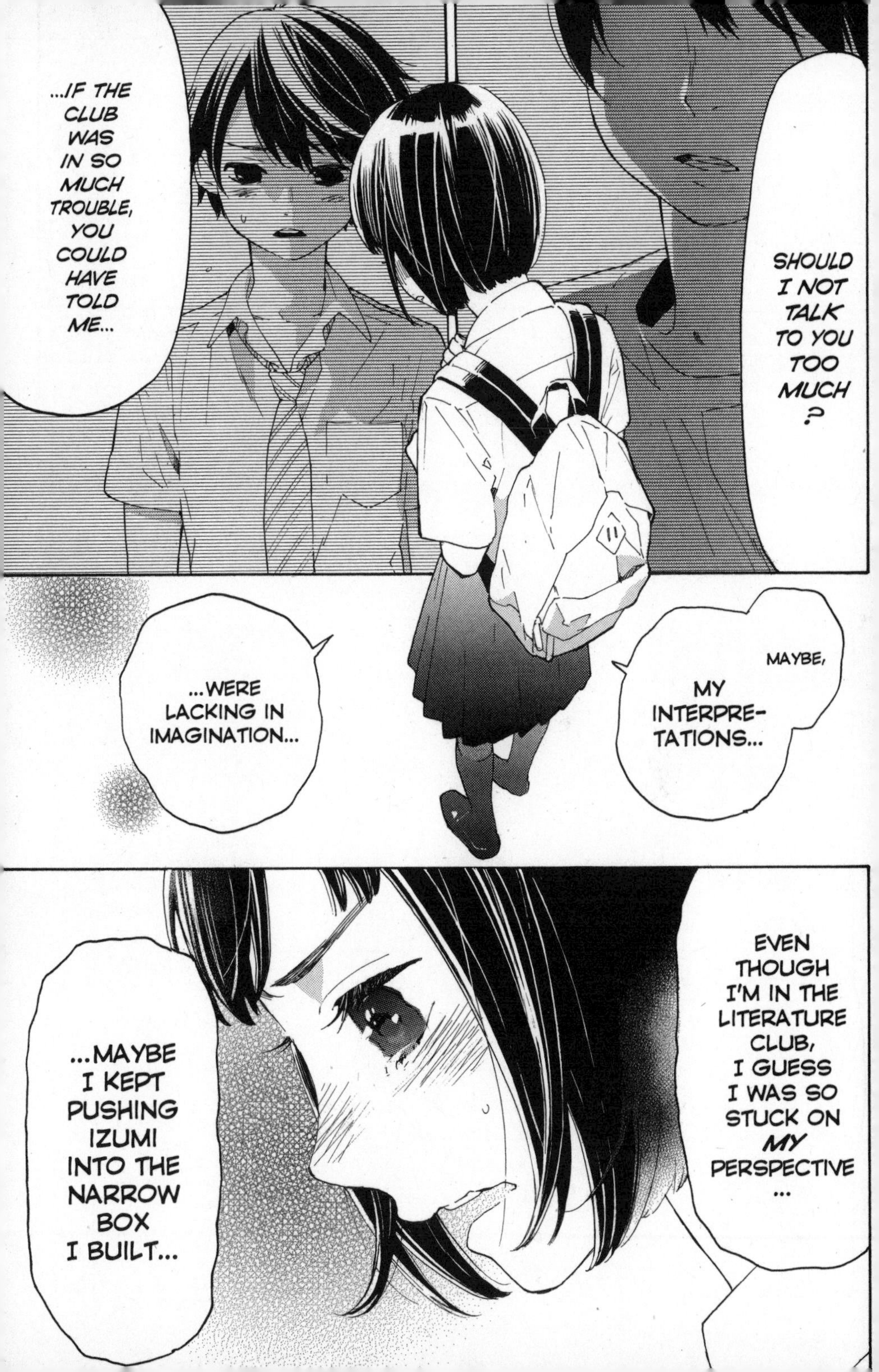
SHOULD I NOT TALK TO YOU TOO MUCH?
...IF THE CLUB WAS IN SO MUCH TROUBLE, YOU COULD HAVE TOLD ME...
MAYBE, MY INTERPRETATIONS...
...WERE LACKING IN IMAGINATION...
EVEN THOUGH I'M IN THE LITERATURE CLUB, I GUESS I WAS SO STUCK ON *MY* PERSPECTIVE...
...MAYBE I KEPT PUSHING IZUMI INTO THE NARROW BOX I BUILT...

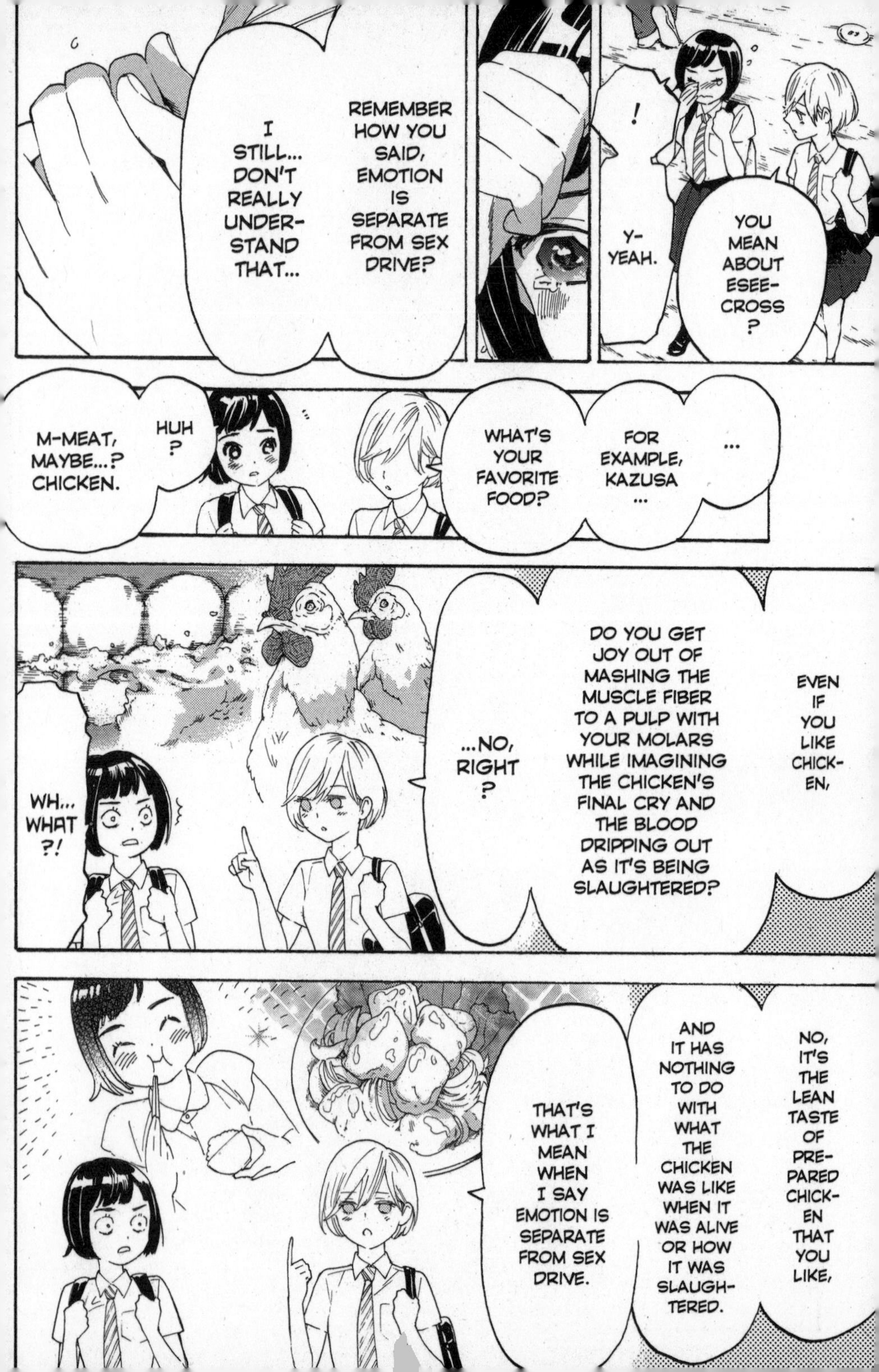
YOU MEAN ABOUT ESEE-CROSS?
Y-YEAH.
!
REMEMBER HOW YOU SAID, EMOTION IS SEPARATE FROM SEX DRIVE?
I STILL... DON'T REALLY UNDERSTAND THAT...
...
FOR EXAMPLE, KAZUSA...
WHAT'S YOUR FAVORITE FOOD?
HUH?
M-MEAT, MAYBE...? CHICKEN.
EVEN IF YOU LIKE CHICK-EN,
DO YOU GET JOY OUT OF MASHING THE MUSCLE FIBER TO A PULP WITH YOUR MOLARS WHILE IMAGINING THE CHICKEN'S FINAL CRY AND THE BLOOD DRIPPING OUT AS IT'S BEING SLAUGHTERED?
...NO, RIGHT?
WH... WHAT?!
NO, IT'S THE LEAN TASTE OF PRE-PARED CHICK-EN THAT YOU LIKE,
AND IT HAS NOTHING TO DO WITH WHAT THE CHICKEN WAS LIKE WHEN IT WAS ALIVE OR HOW IT WAS SLAUGH-TERED.
THAT'S WHAT I MEAN WHEN I SAY EMOTION IS SEPARATE FROM SEX DRIVE.

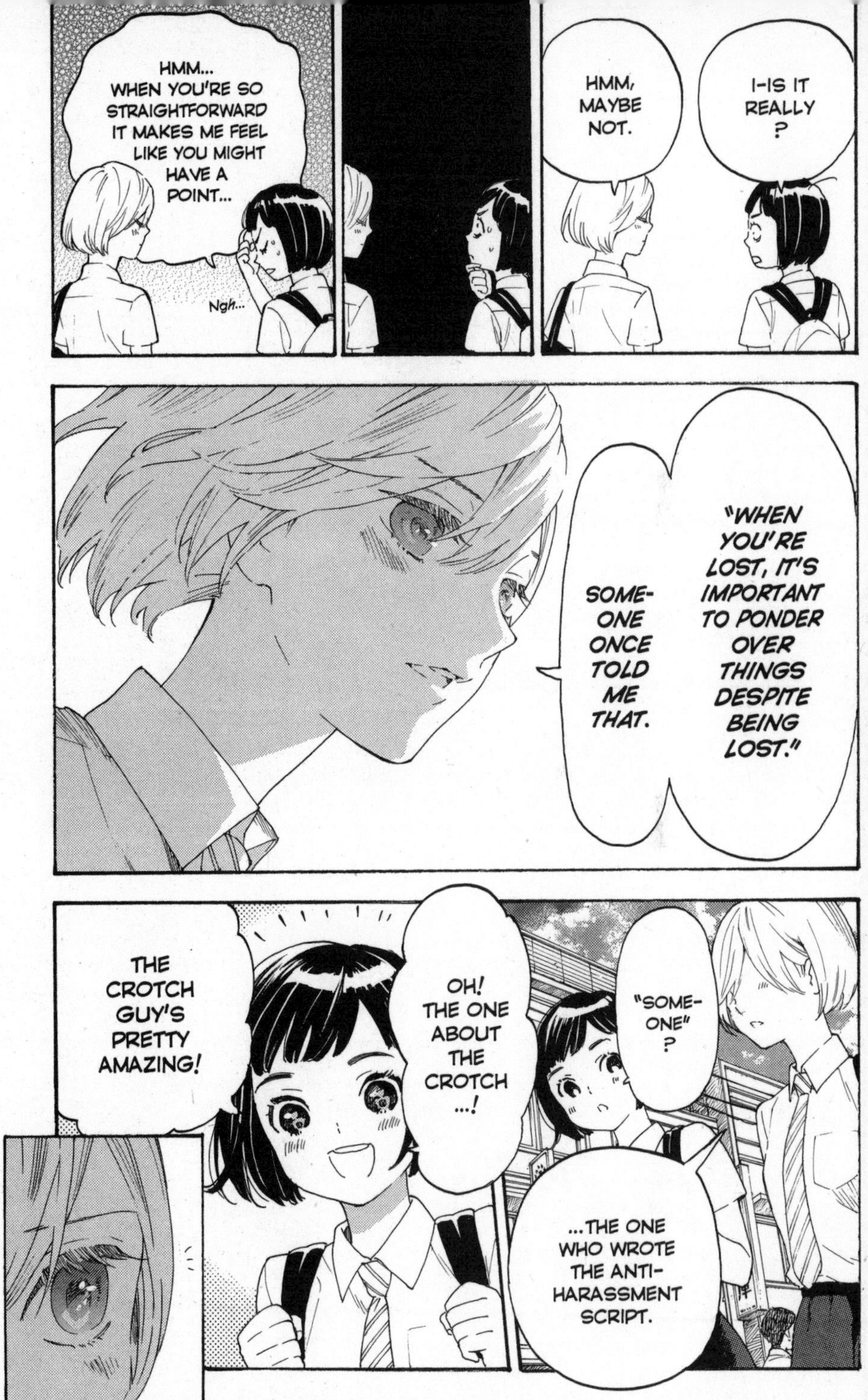
I-IS IT REALLY?
HMM, MAYBE NOT.
HMM... WHEN YOU'RE SO STRAIGHTFORWARD IT MAKES ME FEEL LIKE YOU MIGHT HAVE A POINT...
Ngh...
"WHEN YOU'RE LOST, IT'S IMPORTANT TO PONDER OVER THINGS DESPITE BEING LOST."
SOME-ONE ONCE TOLD ME THAT.
"SOME-ONE"?
...THE ONE WHO WROTE THE ANTI-HARASSMENT SCRIPT.
OH! THE ONE ABOUT THE CROTCH...!
THE CROTCH GUY'S PRETTY AMAZING!

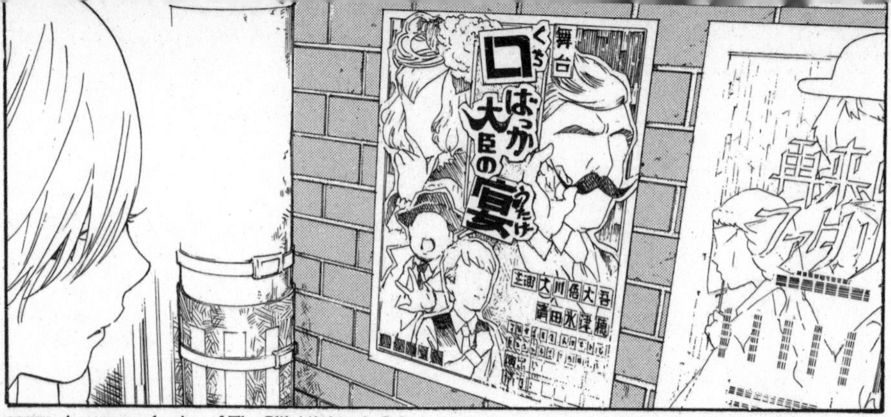
舞台
口ばっか大臣の宴
POSTER: A stage production of The Glib Minister's Gala

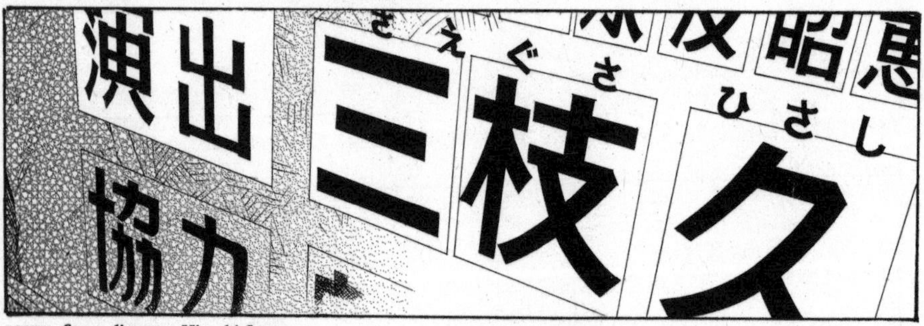
演出
三枝久
協力
POSTER: Stage director: Hisashi Saegusa

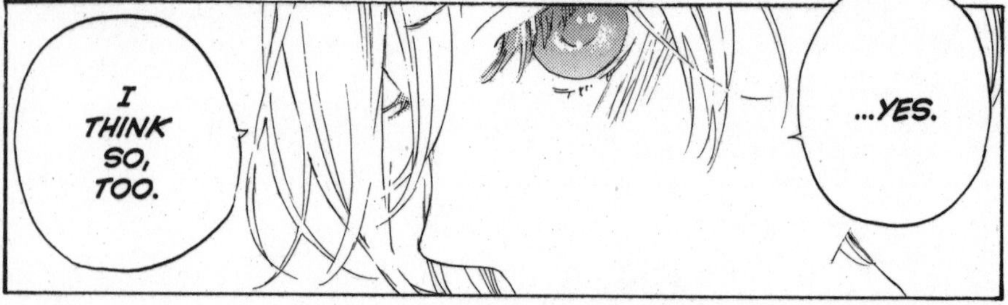
...YES.
I THINK SO, TOO.

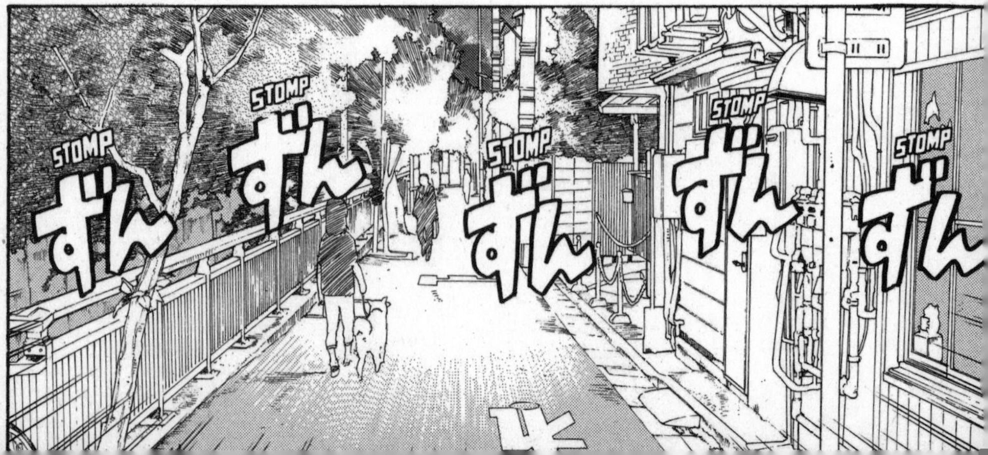
STOMP
ずん
STOMP
ずん
STOMP
ずん
STOMP
ずん
STOMP
ずん

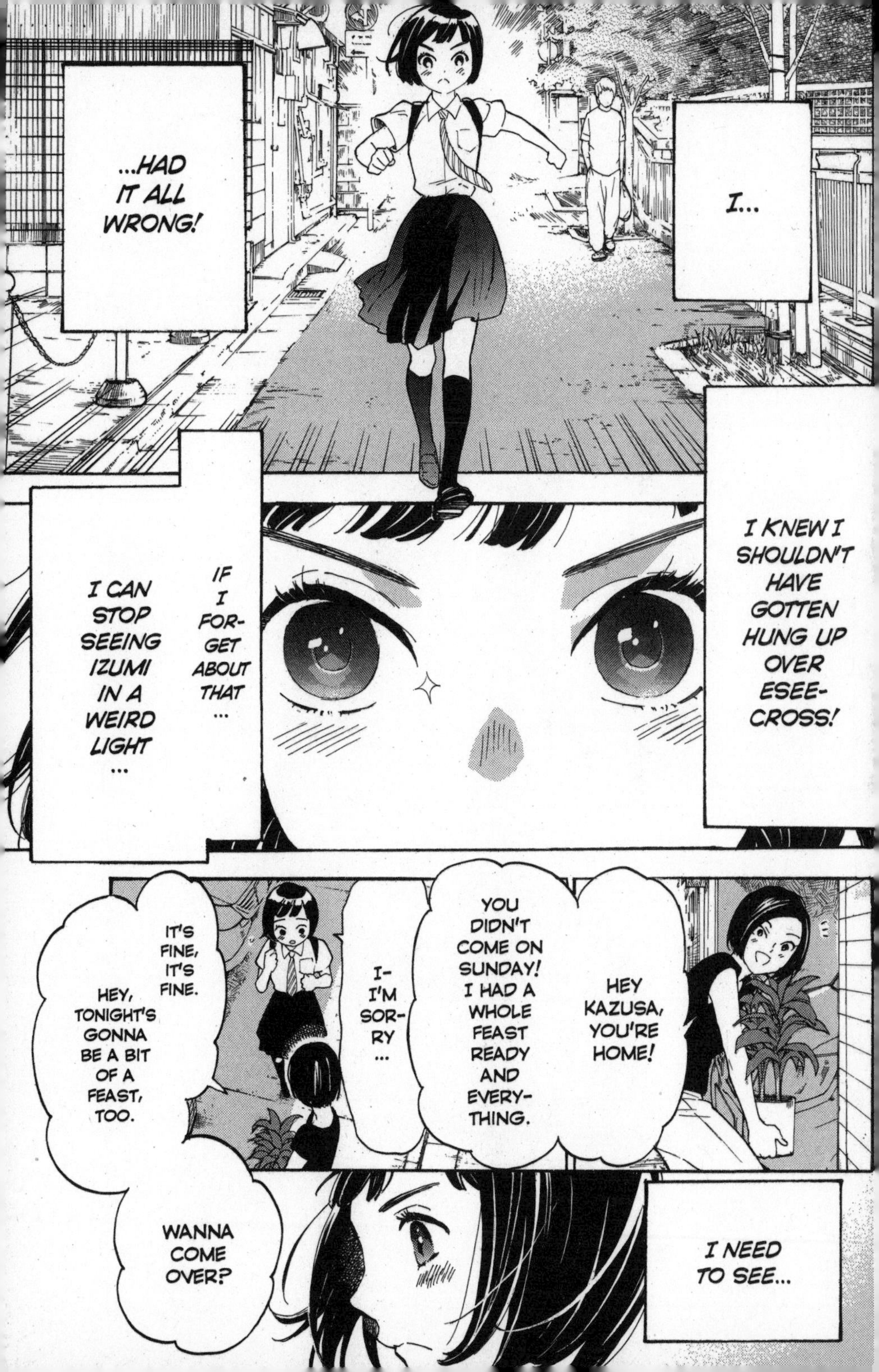
I...
...HAD IT ALL WRONG!
I KNEW I SHOULDN'T HAVE GOTTEN HUNG UP OVER ESEE-CROSS!
IF I FOR-GET ABOUT THAT...
I CAN STOP SEEING IZUMI IN A WEIRD LIGHT...
HEY KAZUSA, YOU'RE HOME!
YOU DIDN'T COME ON SUNDAY! I HAD A WHOLE FEAST READY AND EVERY-THING.
I- I'M SOR-RY...
IT'S FINE, IT'S FINE.
HEY, TONIGHT'S GONNA BE A BIT OF A FEAST, TOO.
I NEED TO SEE...
WANNA COME OVER?

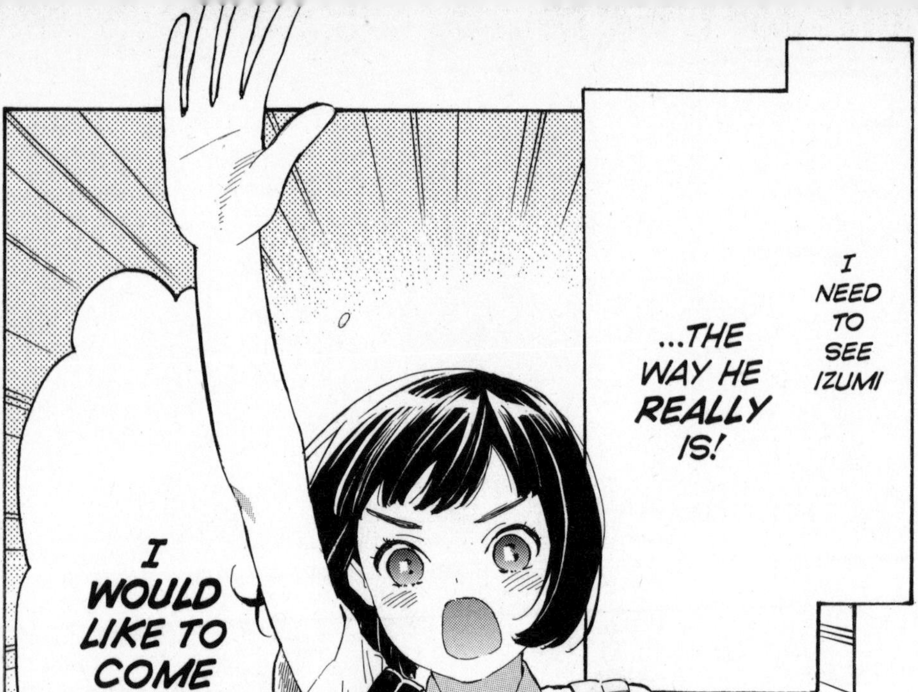
I NEED TO SEE IZUMI
...THE WAY HE REALLY IS!
I WOULD LIKE TO COME OVER!

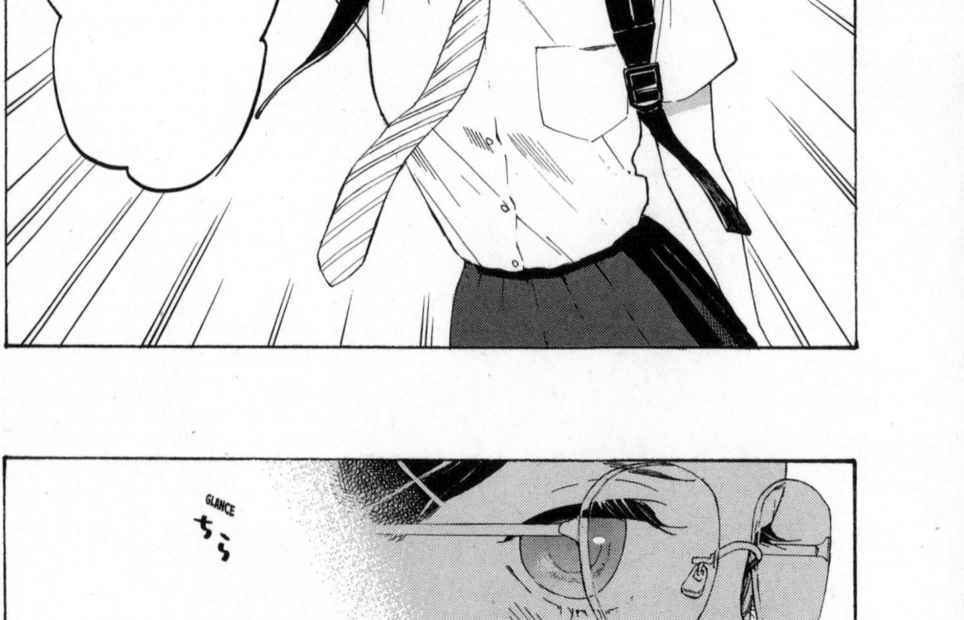
GLANCE
ちら

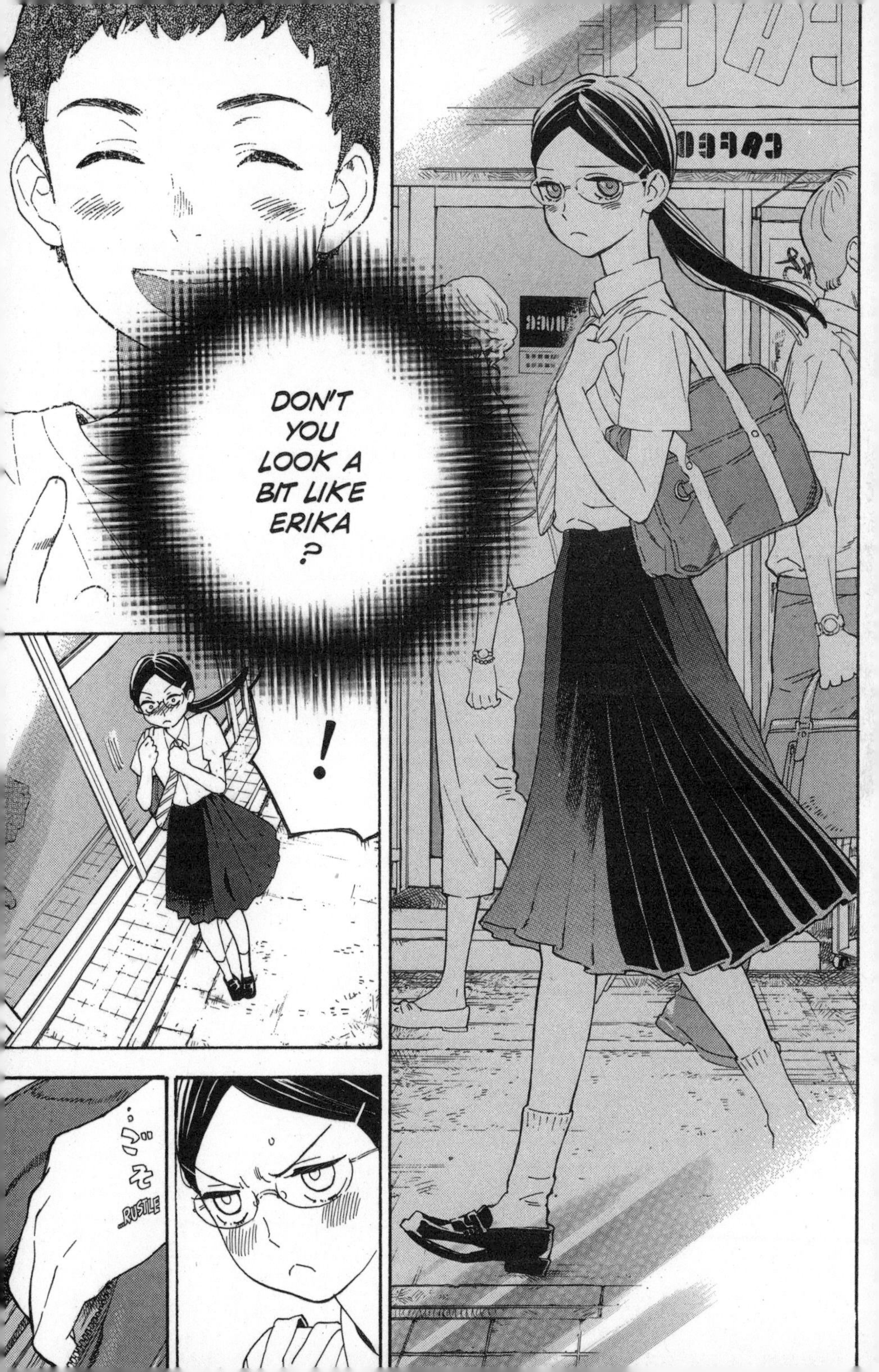
DON'T YOU LOOK A BIT LIKE ERIKA?
!
ごそ
...RUSTLE

Cast a spell with mischievous fairy makeup ♡

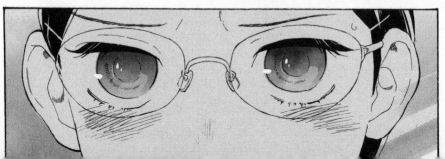

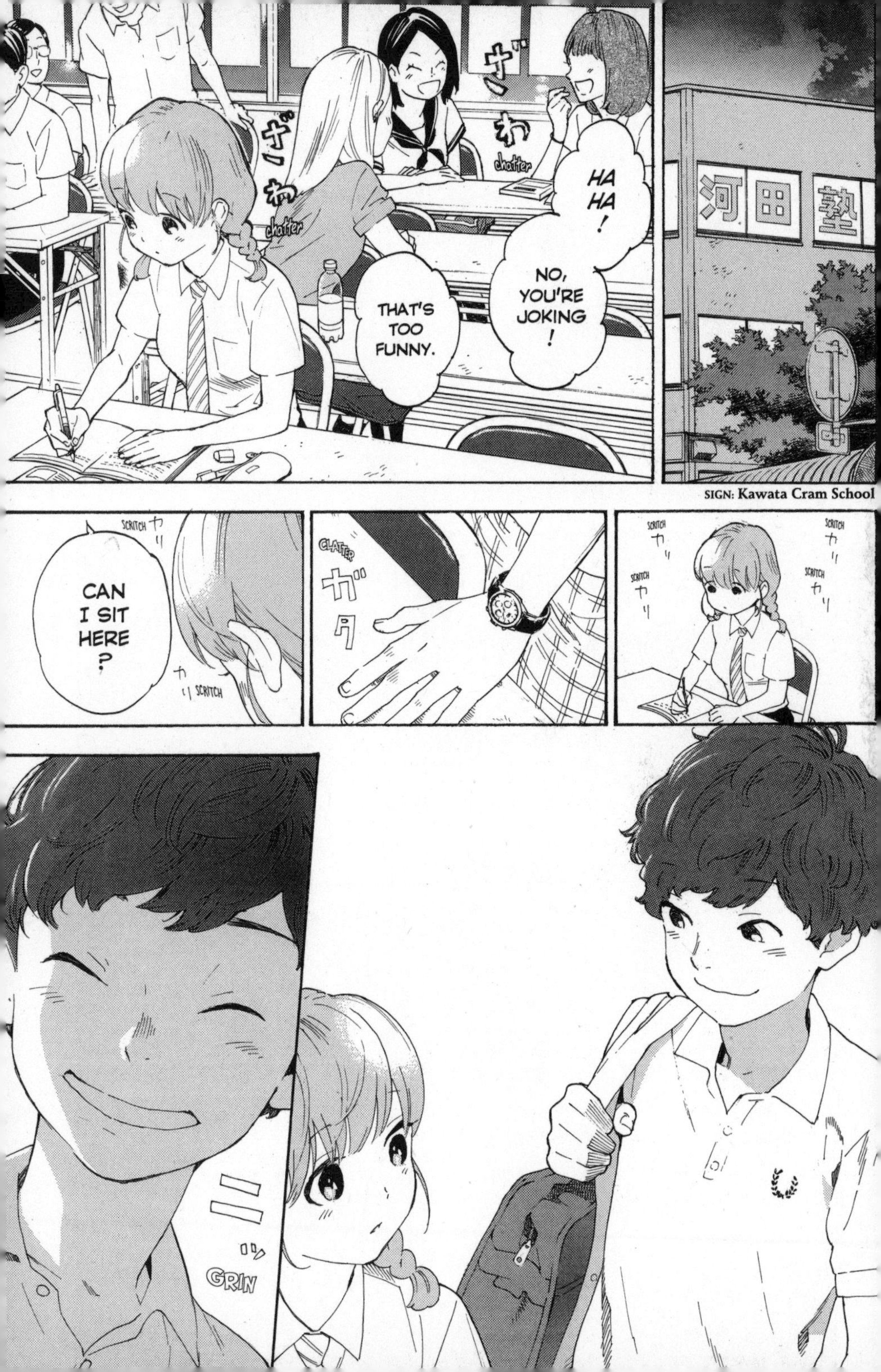
河田塾
HA HA!
ざわ chatter
NO, YOU'RE JOKING!
THAT'S TOO FUNNY.
ざわ chatter
SCRITCH カリ
SCRITCH カリ
SCRITCH カリ
SCRITCH カリ
CLATTER ガタ
SCRITCH カリ
CAN I SIT HERE?
カリ SCRITCH
ニッ GRIN

SIGN: Kawata Cram School

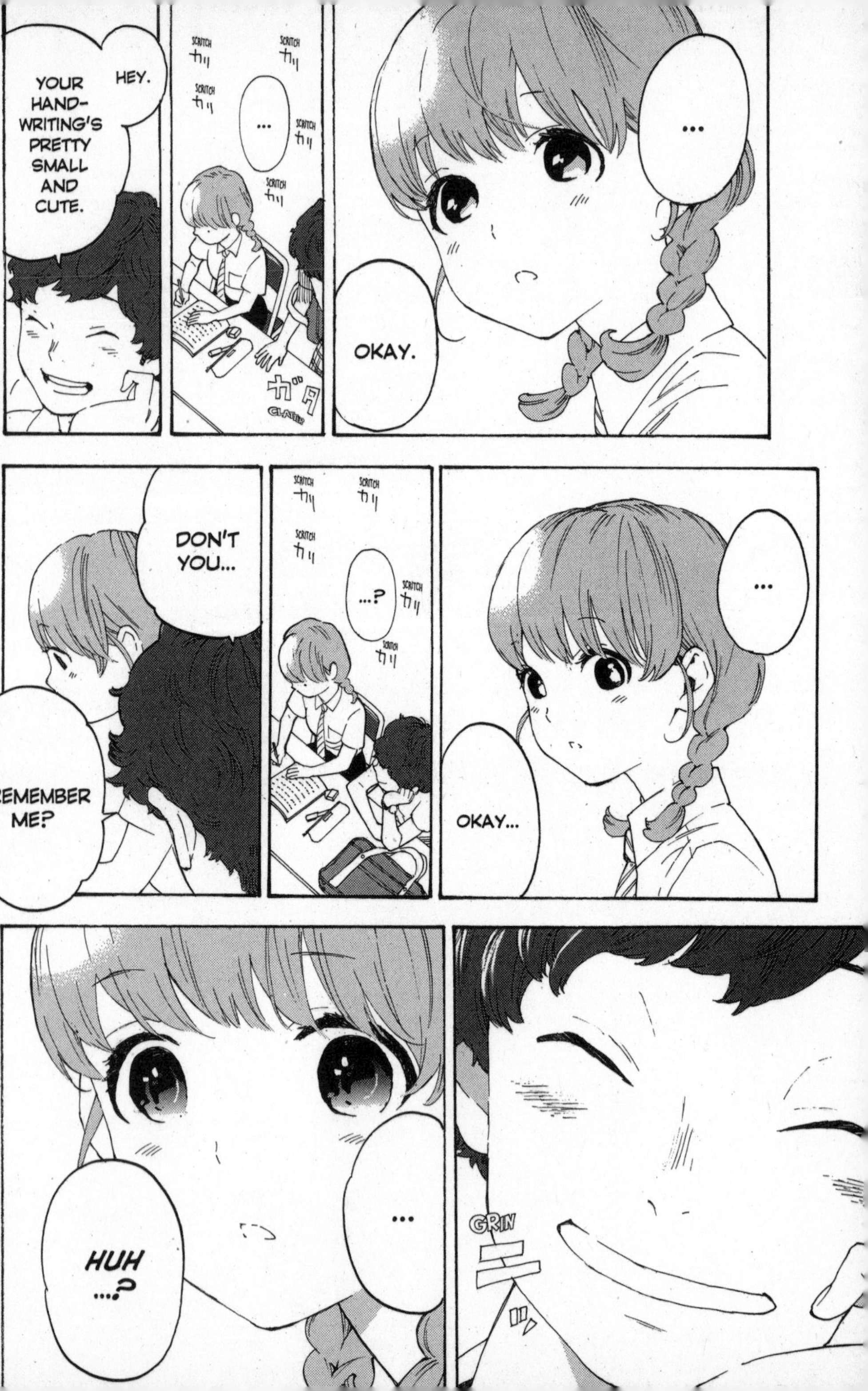
...
OKAY.
SCRITCH カリ
...
SCRITCH カリ
ガタ CLATTER
HEY.
YOUR HAND-WRITING'S PRETTY SMALL AND CUTE.
...
OKAY...
SCRITCH カリ
...?
SCRITCH カリ
DON'T YOU...
REMEMBER ME?
GRIN
...
HUH ...?

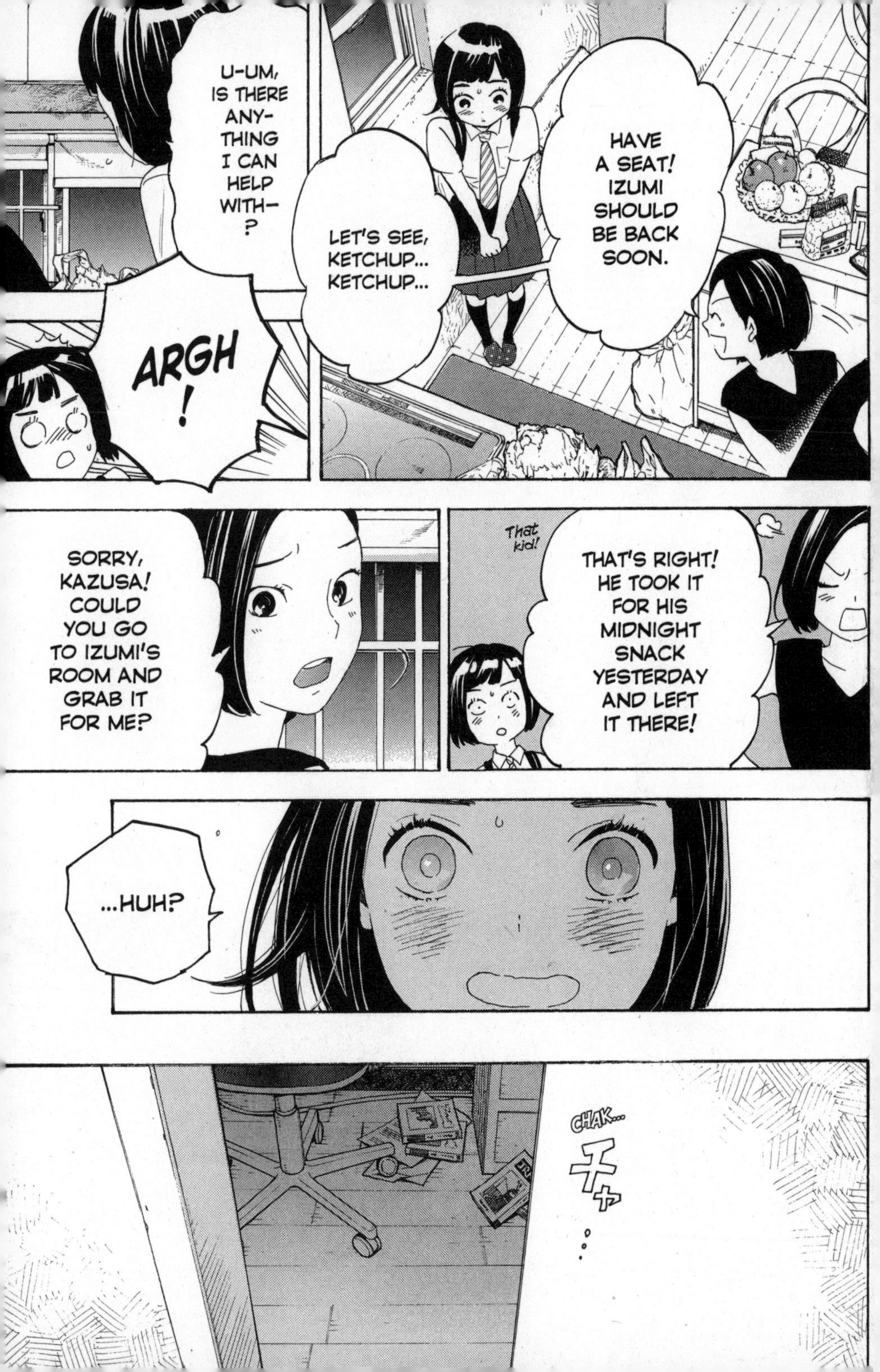
HAVE A SEAT! IZUMI SHOULD BE BACK SOON.
LET'S SEE, KETCHUP... KETCHUP...
U-UM, IS THERE ANY-THING I CAN HELP WITH—?
ARGH!
That kid!
THAT'S RIGHT! HE TOOK IT FOR HIS MIDNIGHT SNACK YESTERDAY AND LEFT IT THERE!
SORRY, KAZUSA! COULD YOU GO TO IZUMI'S ROOM AND GRAB IT FOR ME?
...HUH?
CHAK...
チャ

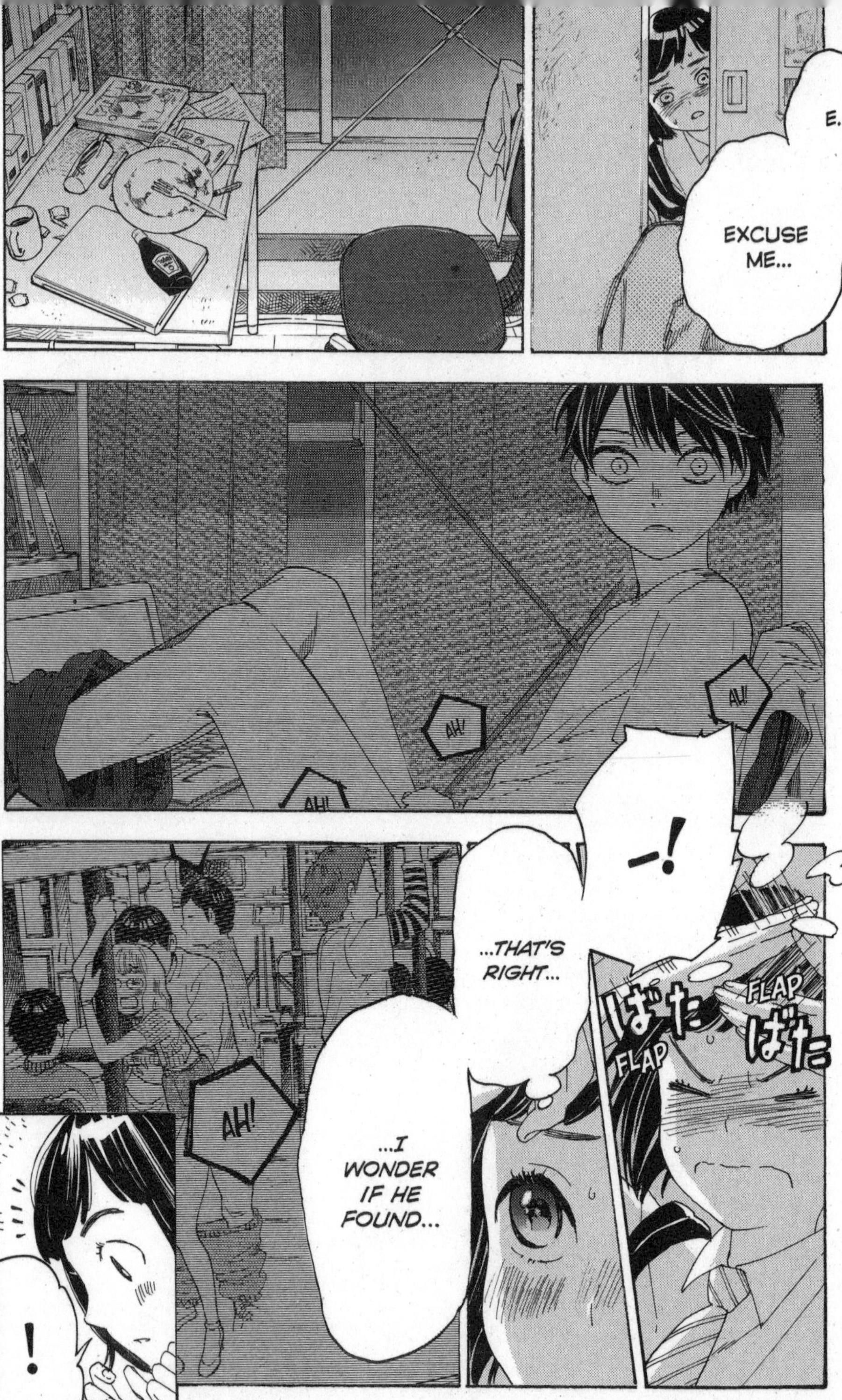
E...
EXCUSE ME...
AH!
AH!
AH!
—!
ばた
FLAP
ばた
FLAP
...THAT'S RIGHT...
...I WONDER IF HE FOUND...
AH!
!

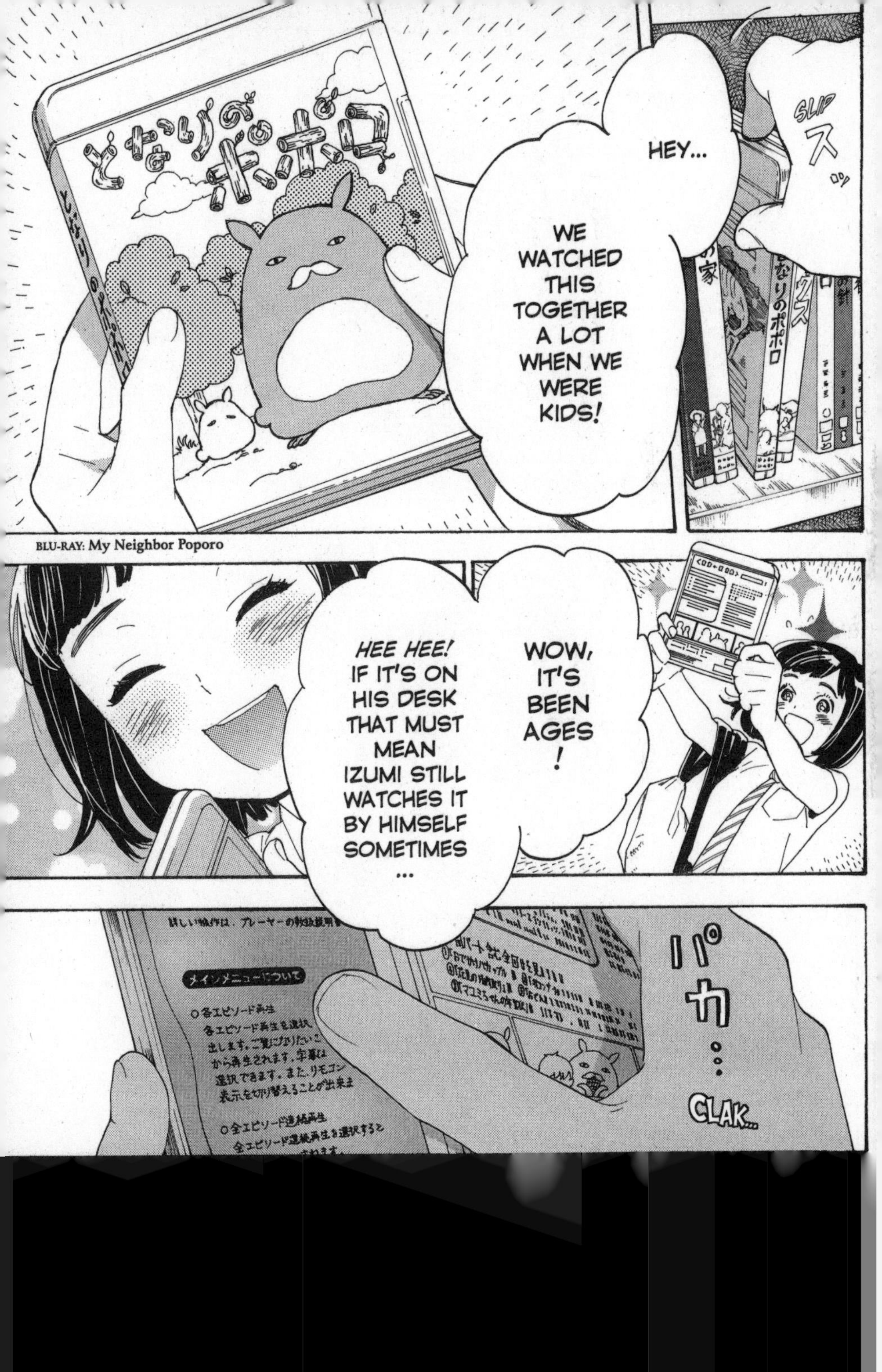
SLIP
HEY...
WE WATCHED THIS TOGETHER A LOT WHEN WE WERE KIDS!
BLU-RAY: My Neighbor Poporo
WOW, IT'S BEEN AGES!
HEE HEE! IF IT'S ON HIS DESK THAT MUST MEAN IZUMI STILL WATCHES IT BY HIMSELF SOMETIMES...
CLAK...

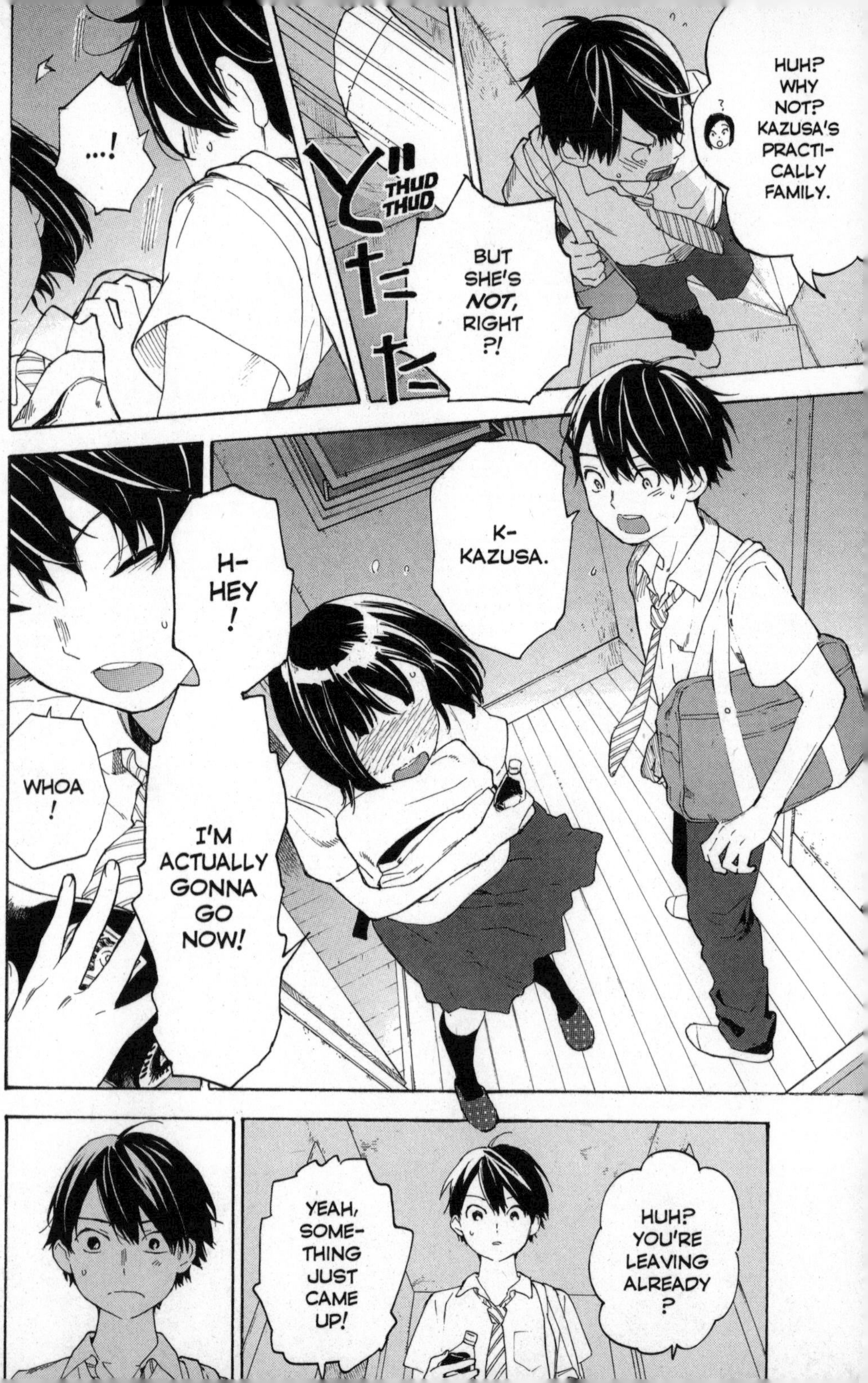
HUH? WHY NOT? KAZUSA'S PRACTI-CALLY FAMILY.
THUD THUD
BUT SHE'S NOT, RIGHT?!
...!
K-KAZUSA.
H-HEY!
I'M ACTUALLY GONNA GO NOW!
WHOA!
HUH? YOU'RE LEAVING ALREADY?
YEAH, SOME-THING JUST CAME UP!

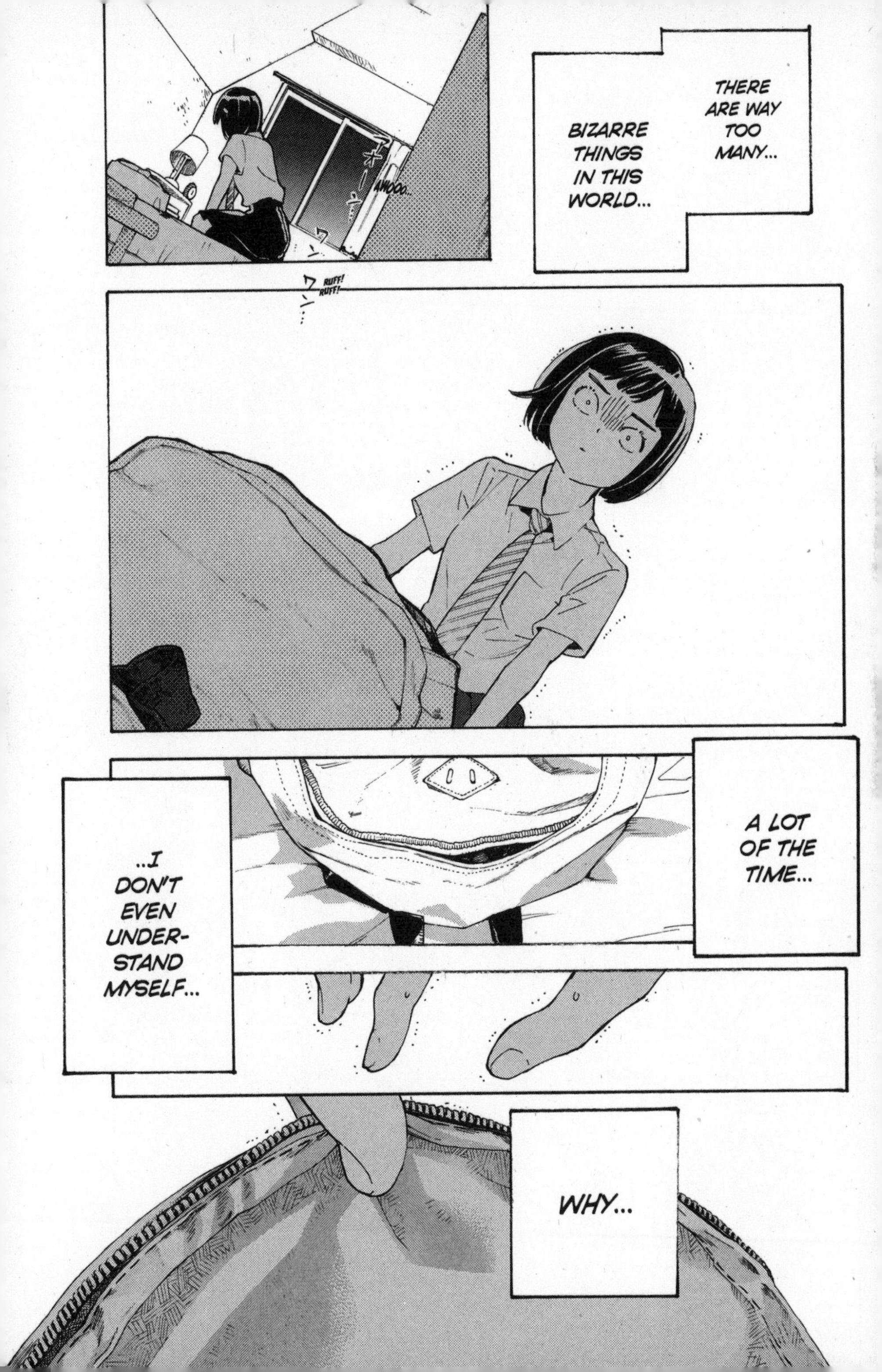
THERE ARE WAY TOO MANY...
BIZARRE THINGS IN THIS WORLD...
AWOOO...
RUFF! RUFF!
A LOT OF THE TIME...
..I DON'T EVEN UNDER-STAND MYSELF...
WHY...

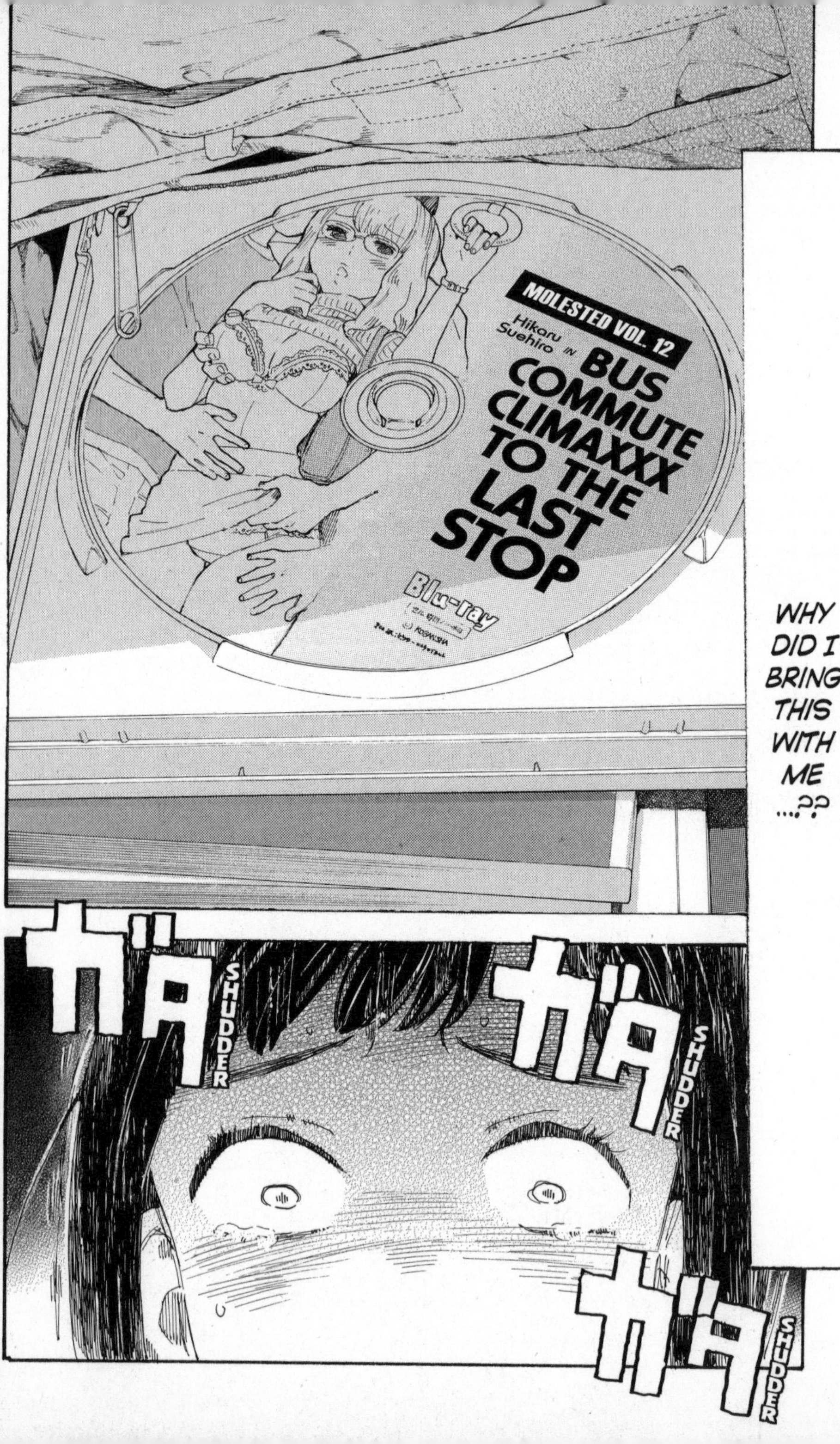
WHY DID I BRING THIS WITH ME ...??
MOLESTED VOL. 12
Hikaru Suehiro IN
BUS COMMUTE CLIMAXXX TO THE LAST STOP
Blu-ray
ガタ
SHUDDER
ガタ
SHUDDER
ガタ
SHUDDER

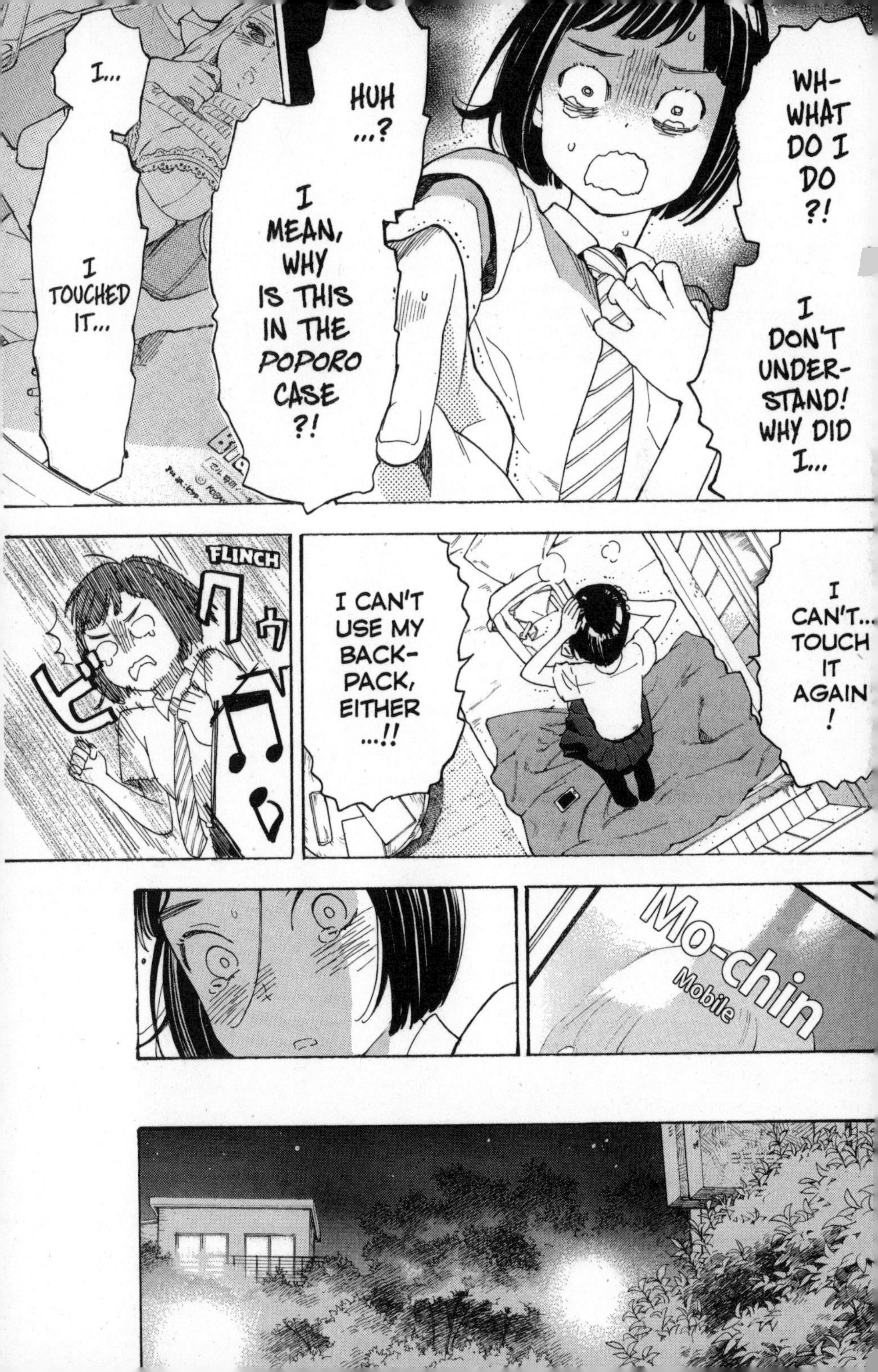
WH-WHAT DO I DO?!
I DON'T UNDERSTAND! WHY DID I...
HUH...?
I MEAN, WHY IS THIS IN THE POPORO CASE?!
I...
I TOUCHED IT...
I CAN'T... TOUCH IT AGAIN!
I CAN'T USE MY BACKPACK, EITHER...!!
FLINCH
Mo-chin
Mobile

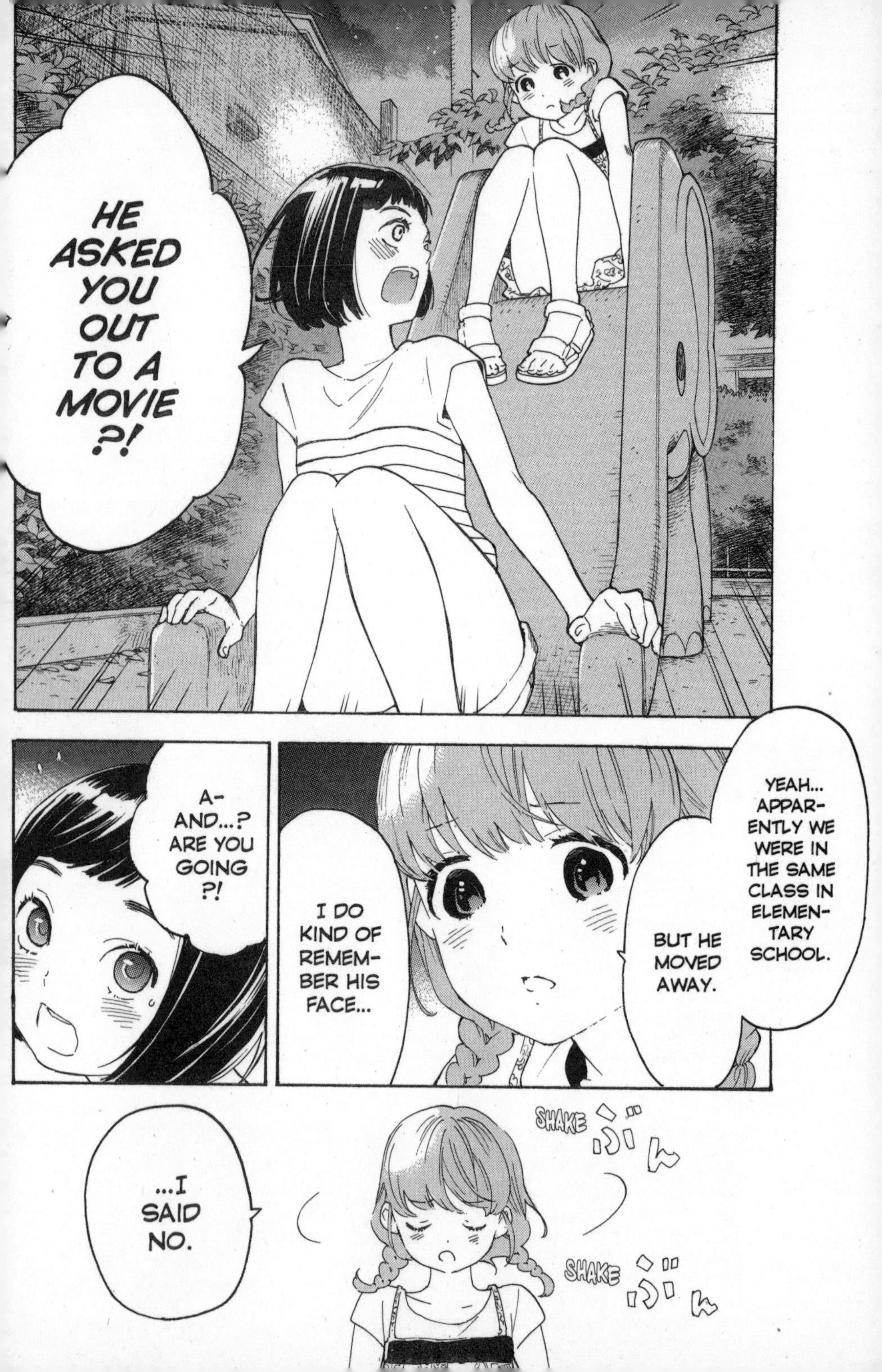
HE ASKED YOU OUT TO A MOVIE ?!
YEAH... APPARENTLY WE WERE IN THE SAME CLASS IN ELEMENTARY SCHOOL.
BUT HE MOVED AWAY.
I DO KIND OF REMEMBER HIS FACE...
A- AND...? ARE YOU GOING ?!
SHAKE
...I SAID NO.
SHAKE

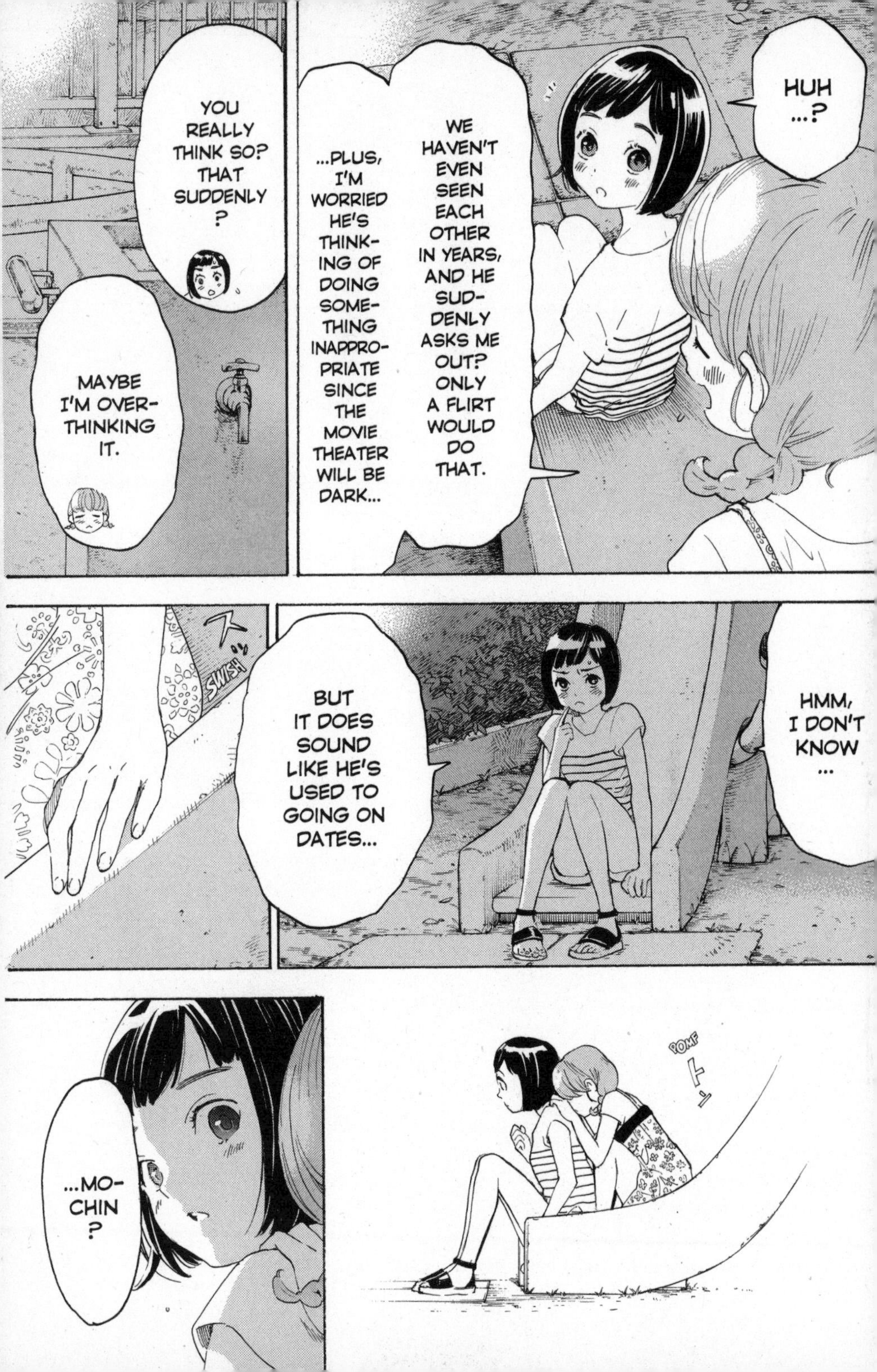
HUH ...?
WE HAVEN'T EVEN SEEN EACH OTHER IN YEARS, AND HE SUD-DENLY ASKS ME OUT? ONLY A FLIRT WOULD DO THAT.
...PLUS, I'M WORRIED HE'S THINK-ING OF DOING SOME-THING INAPPRO-PRIATE SINCE THE MOVIE THEATER WILL BE DARK...
YOU REALLY THINK SO? THAT SUDDENLY ?
MAYBE I'M OVER-THINKING IT.
HMM, I DON'T KNOW ...
BUT IT DOES SOUND LIKE HE'S USED TO GOING ON DATES...
SWISH
POMF
...MO-CHIN ?

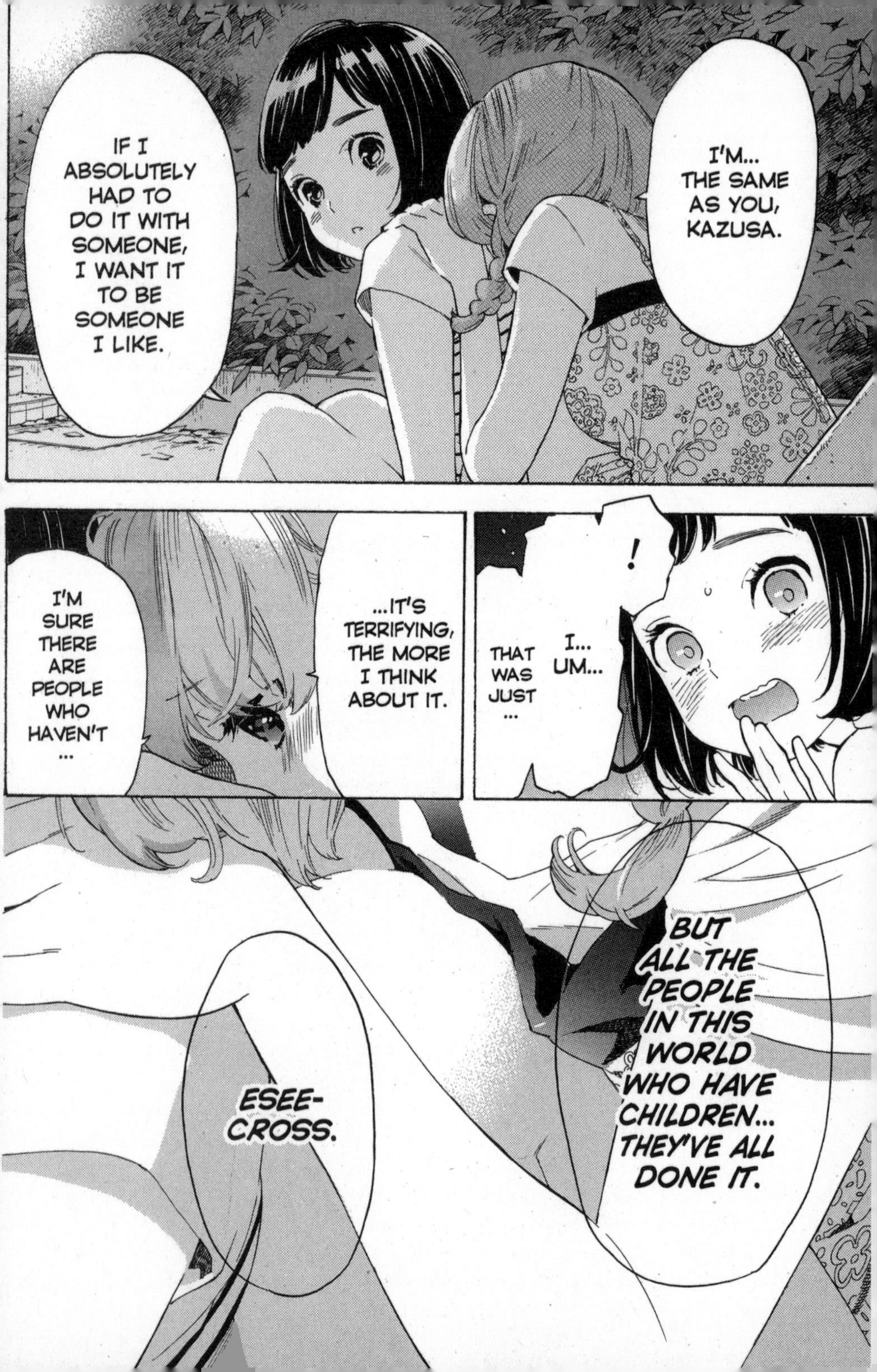
I'M... THE SAME AS YOU, KAZUSA.
IF I ABSOLUTELY HAD TO DO IT WITH SOMEONE, I WANT IT TO BE SOMEONE I LIKE.
!
I... UM...
THAT WAS JUST ...
...IT'S TERRIFYING, THE MORE I THINK ABOUT IT.
I'M SURE THERE ARE PEOPLE WHO HAVEN'T ...
BUT ALL THE PEOPLE IN THIS WORLD WHO HAVE CHILDREN... THEY'VE ALL DONE IT.
ESEE-CROSS.

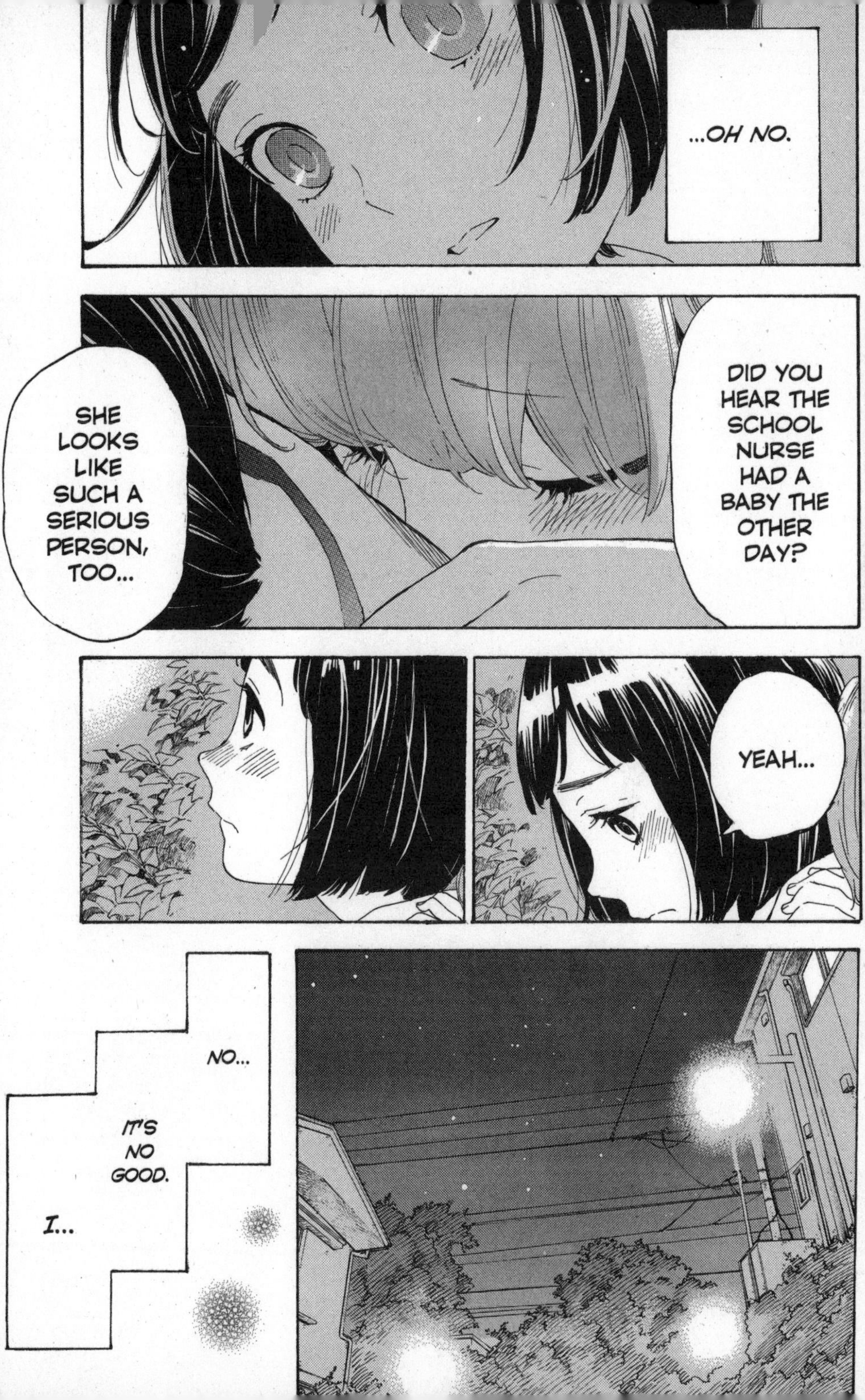
...OH NO.
DID YOU HEAR THE SCHOOL NURSE HAD A BABY THE OTHER DAY?
SHE LOOKS LIKE SUCH A SERIOUS PERSON, TOO...
YEAH...
NO...
IT'S NO GOOD.
I...

I CAN'T HELP THINKING ABOUT IT.

AFTER I TOLD MYSELF...

...I WOULDN'T THINK ABOUT ESEECROSS ANYMORE...

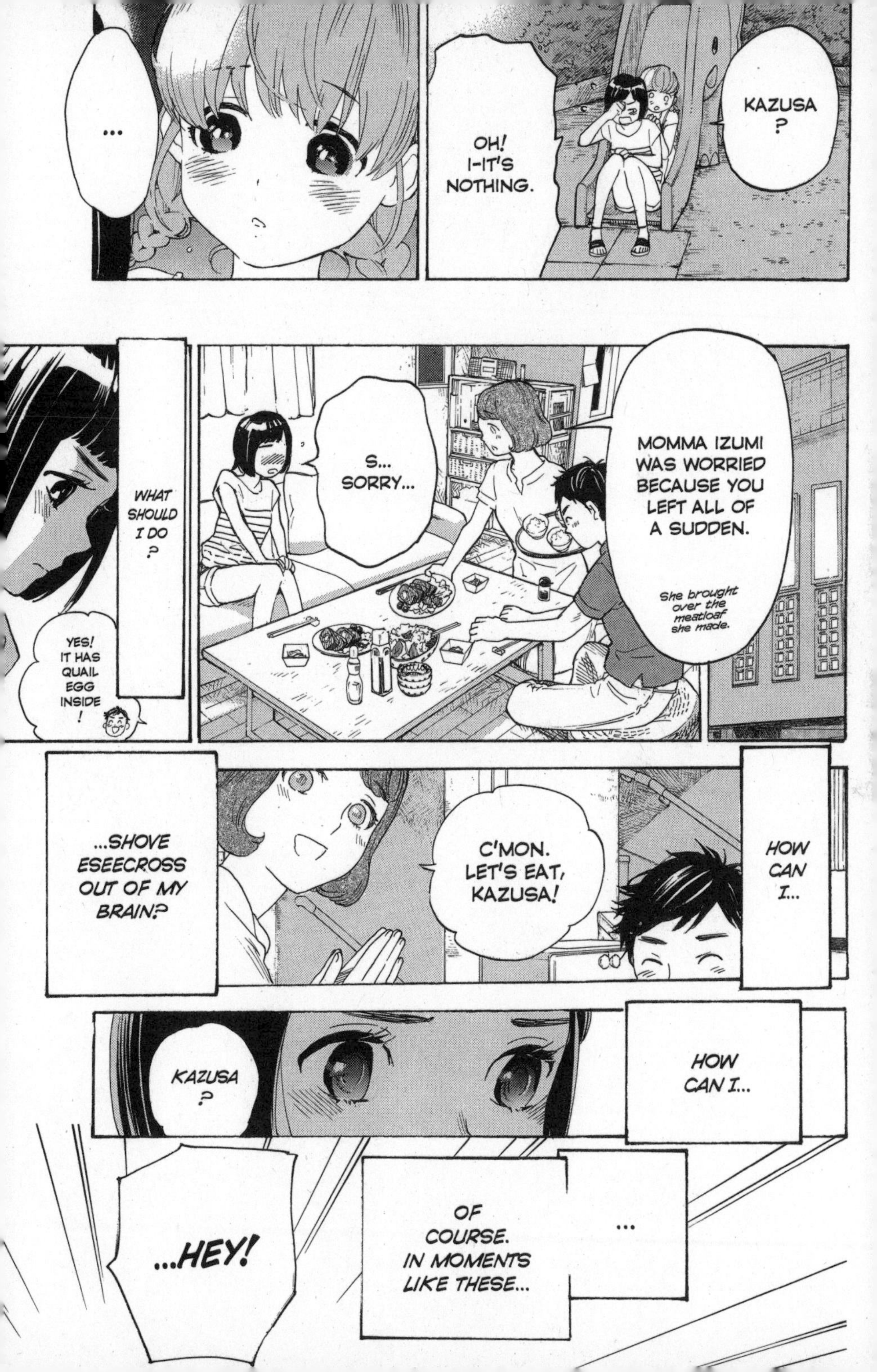
KAZUSA ?
OH! I-IT'S NOTHING.
...
MOMMA IZUMI WAS WORRIED BECAUSE YOU LEFT ALL OF A SUDDEN.
She brought over the meatloaf she made.
S... SORRY...
WHAT SHOULD I DO ?
YES! IT HAS QUAIL EGG INSIDE !
HOW CAN I...
C'MON. LET'S EAT, KAZUSA!
...SHOVE ESEECROSS OUT OF MY BRAIN?
HOW CAN I...
KAZUSA ?
...
OF COURSE. IN MOMENTS LIKE THESE...
...HEY!

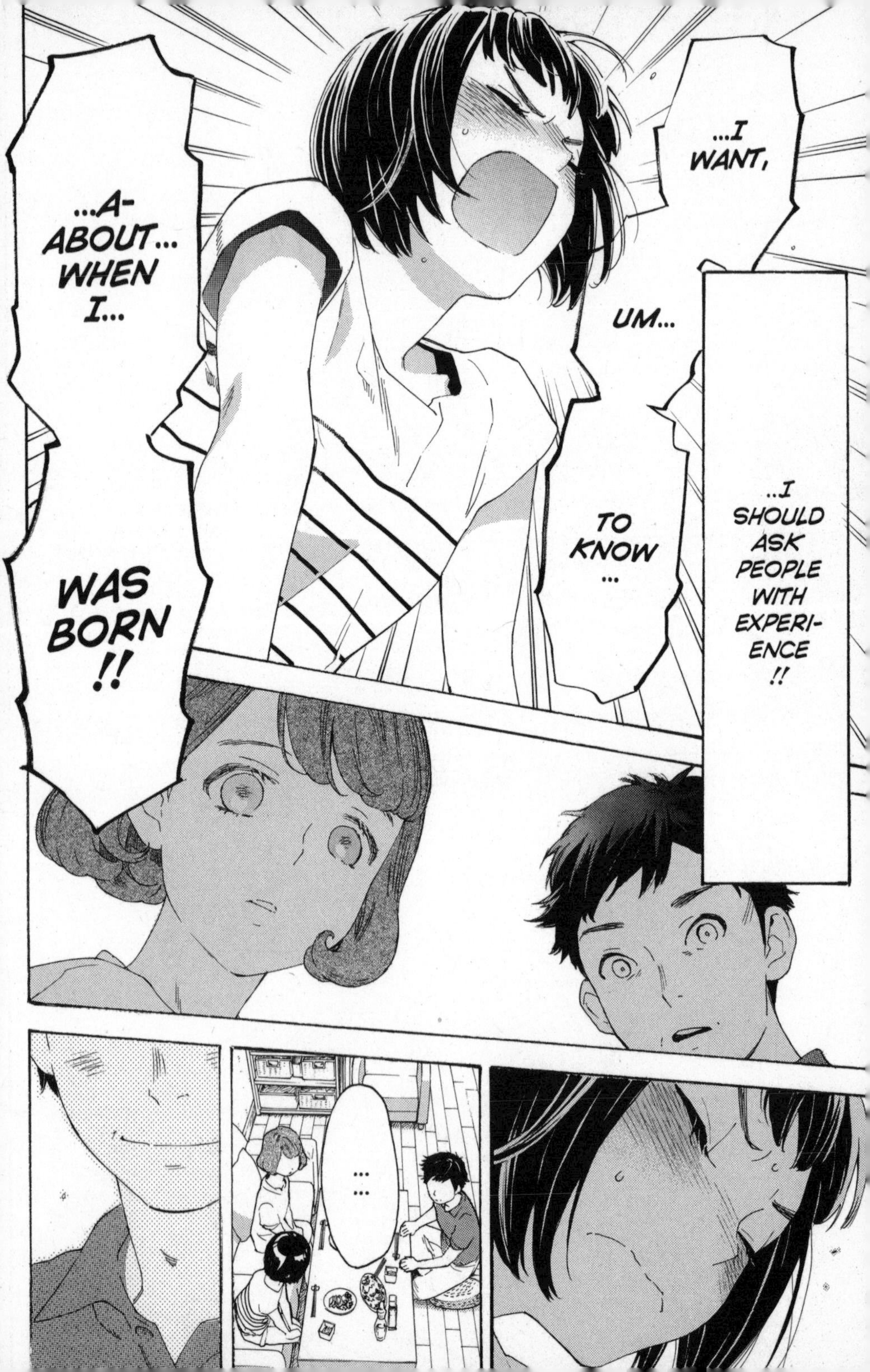
...I WANT,
UM...
TO KNOW...
...A-ABOUT... WHEN I...
WAS BORN!!
..I SHOULD ASK PEOPLE WITH EXPERI-ENCE!!
...
...

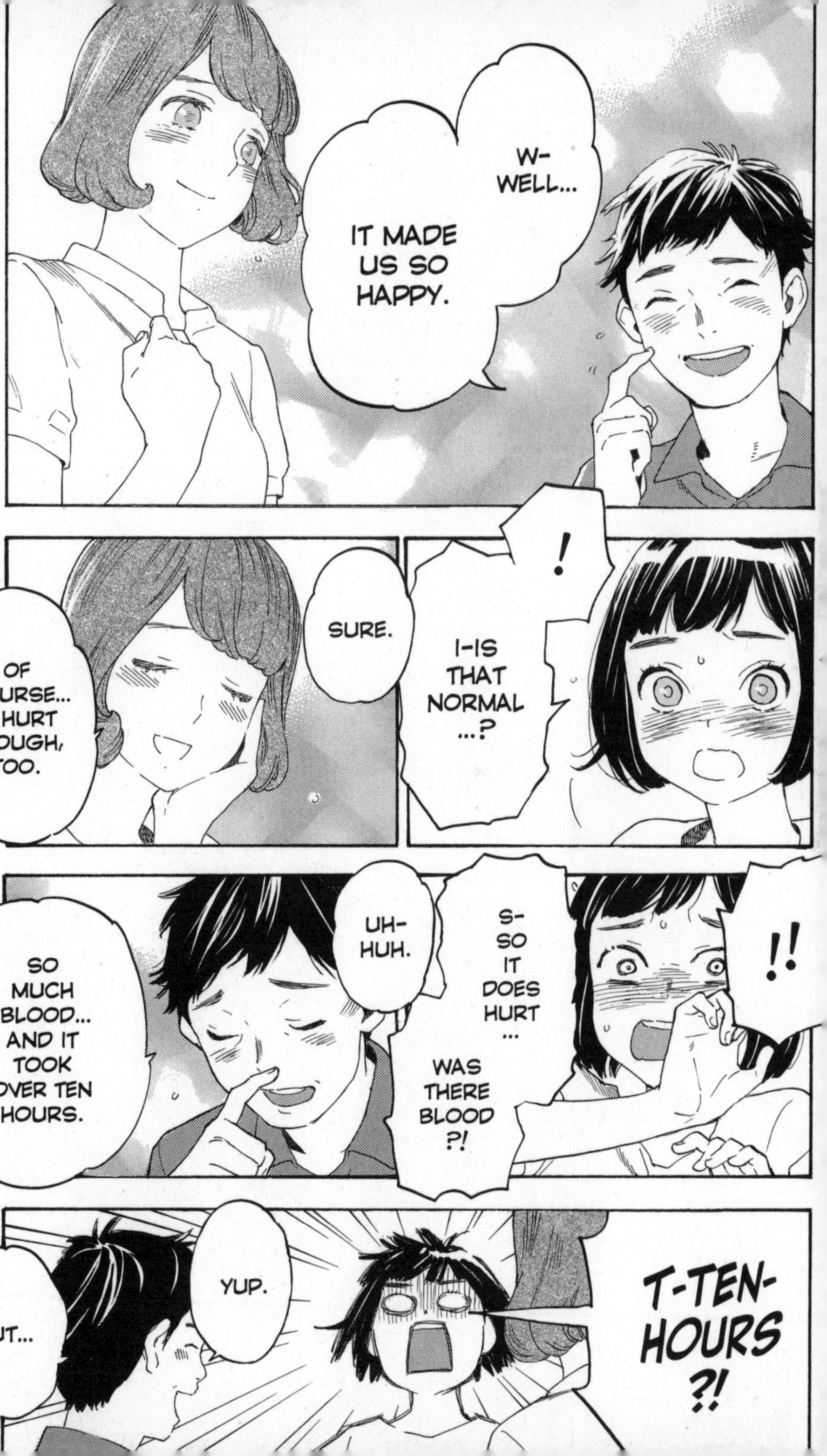
W-WELL... IT MADE US SO HAPPY.
!
I-IS THAT NORMAL...?
SURE.
OF COURSE... IT HURT THOUGH, TOO.
!!
S-SO IT DOES HURT... WAS THERE BLOOD?!
UH-HUH.
SO MUCH BLOOD... AND IT TOOK OVER TEN HOURS.
T-TEN-HOURS?!
YUP.
BUT...

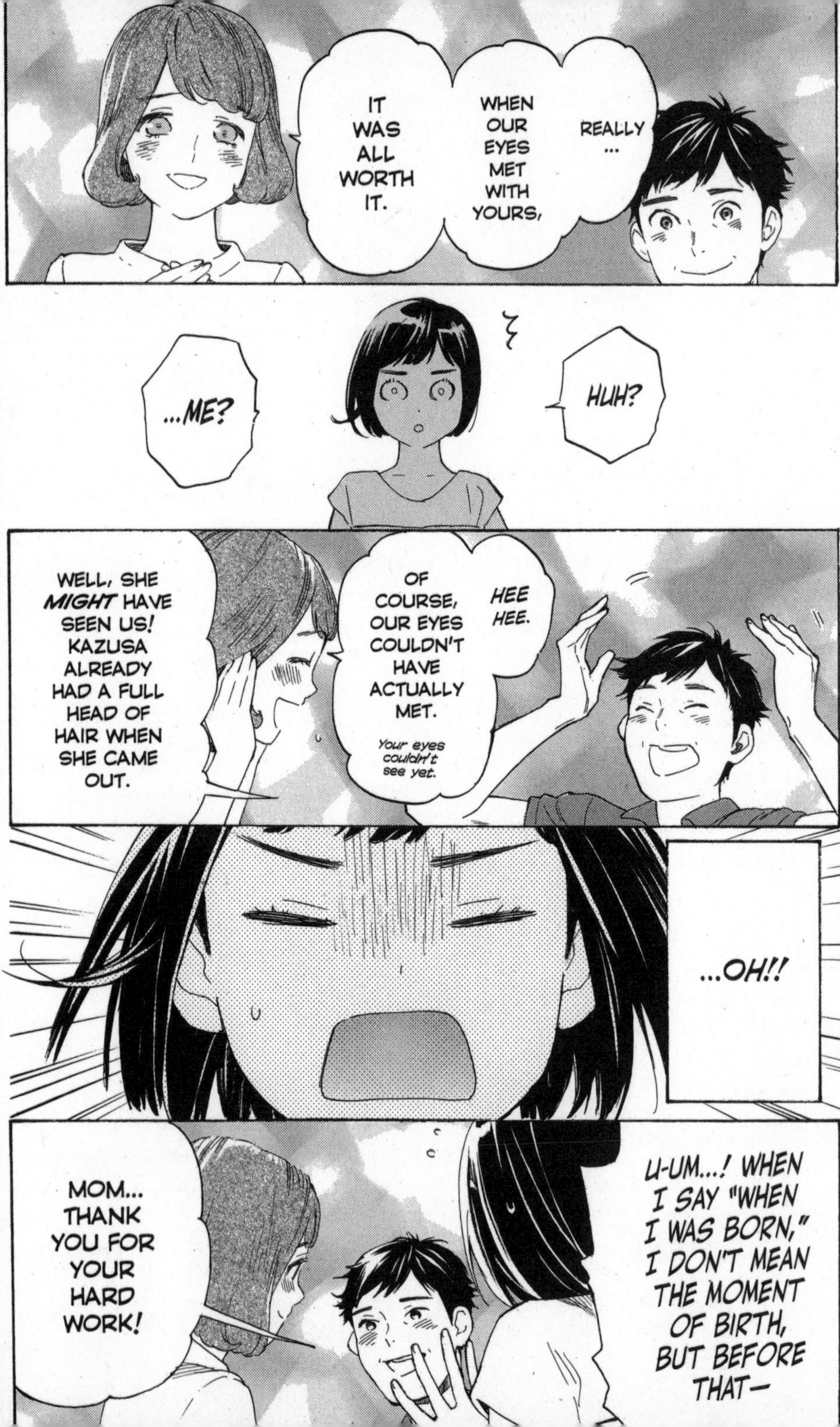
REALLY...
WHEN OUR EYES MET WITH YOURS,
IT WAS ALL WORTH IT.
HUH?
...ME?
HEE HEE.
OF COURSE, OUR EYES COULDN'T HAVE ACTUALLY MET.
Your eyes couldn't see yet.
WELL, SHE MIGHT HAVE SEEN US! KAZUSA ALREADY HAD A FULL HEAD OF HAIR WHEN SHE CAME OUT.
...OH!!
U-UM...! WHEN I SAY "WHEN I WAS BORN," I DON'T MEAN THE MOMENT OF BIRTH, BUT BEFORE THAT—
MOM... THANK YOU FOR YOUR HARD WORK!

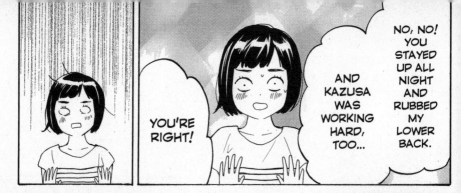

NO, NO! YOU STAYED UP ALL NIGHT AND RUBBED MY LOWER BACK.
AND KAZUSA WAS WORKING HARD, TOO...
YOU'RE RIGHT!
THANK YOU, KAZUSA!!
IT'S BEEN SO LONG SINCE THE THREE OF US HAVE SLEPT LIKE THIS... HOW EXCITING!
SHOULD WE MAKE THIS A MONTHLY THING?

Hitoto> Milo-saaan

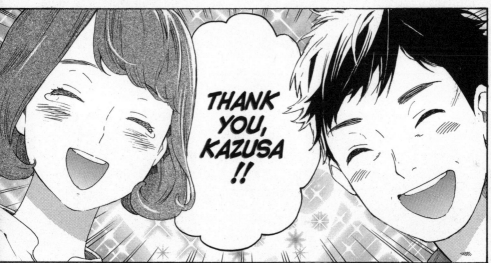

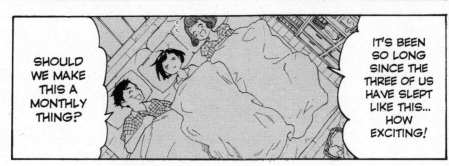

Hitoto> Say something, Milo-san.
You're horrible for ignoring me.
I know you're online.

OH.

Milo> You probably haven't heard of it

Milo> You probably haven't heard of it
but my username isn't from the "Venus de Milo."
It's from "The strong kid's MILO."

Milo> (left the room)

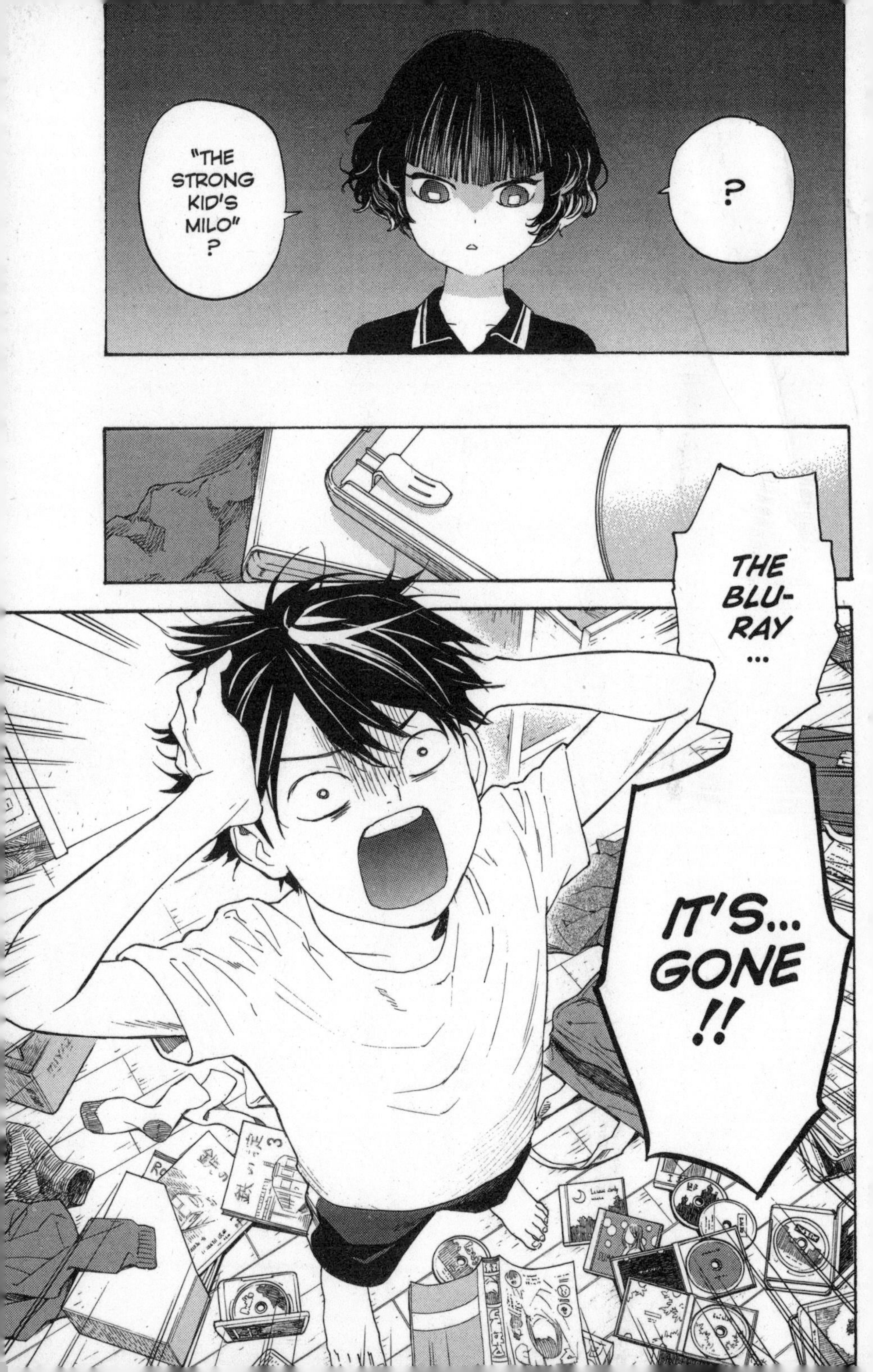
?
"THE STRONG KID'S MILO" ?
THE BLU-RAY ...
IT'S... GONE !!

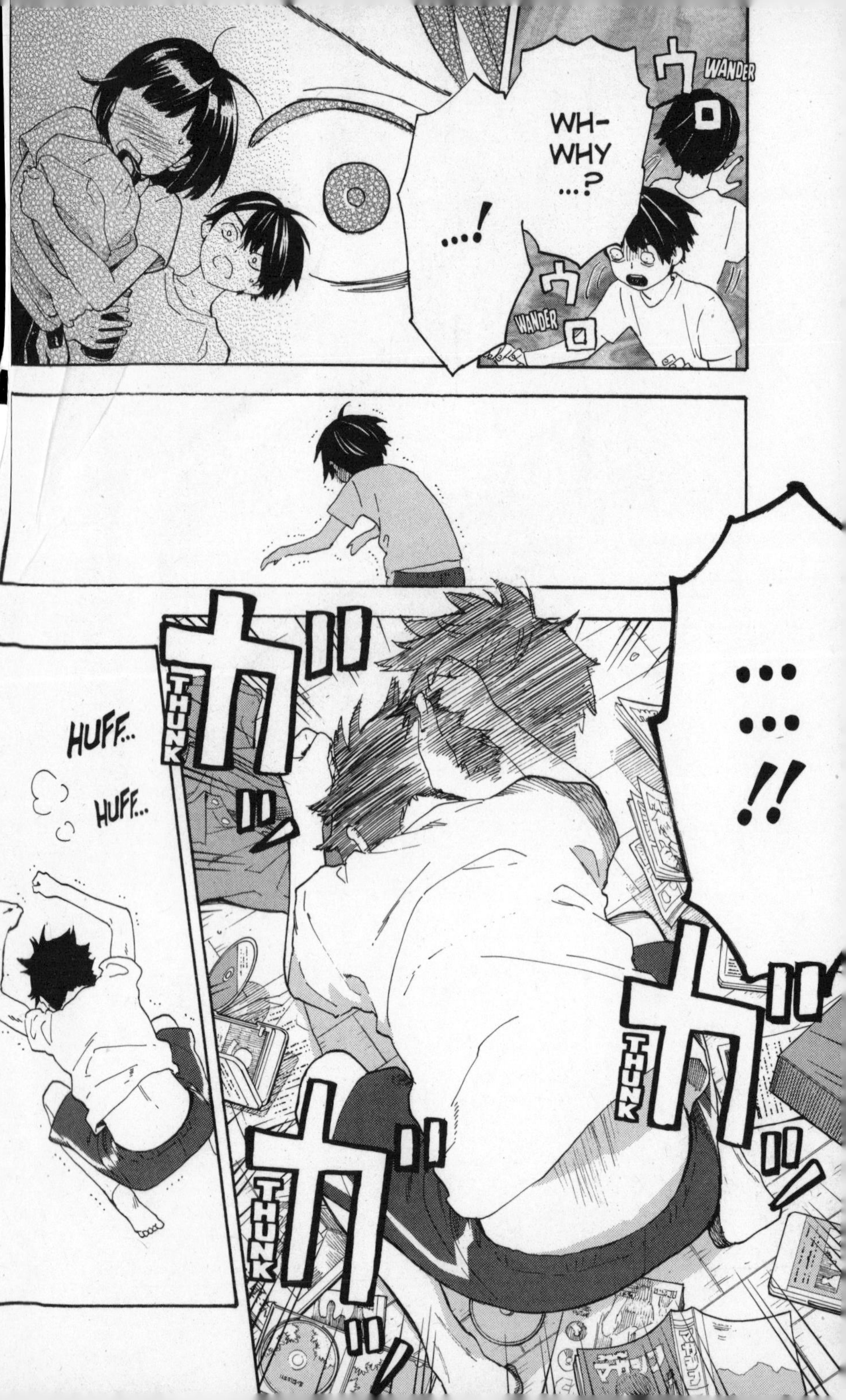
ウロ
WANDER
WH-
WHY
...?
...!
ウロ
WANDER
...
...
!!
ガッ
THUNK
ガッ
THUNK
ガッ
THUNK
HUFF...
HUFF...

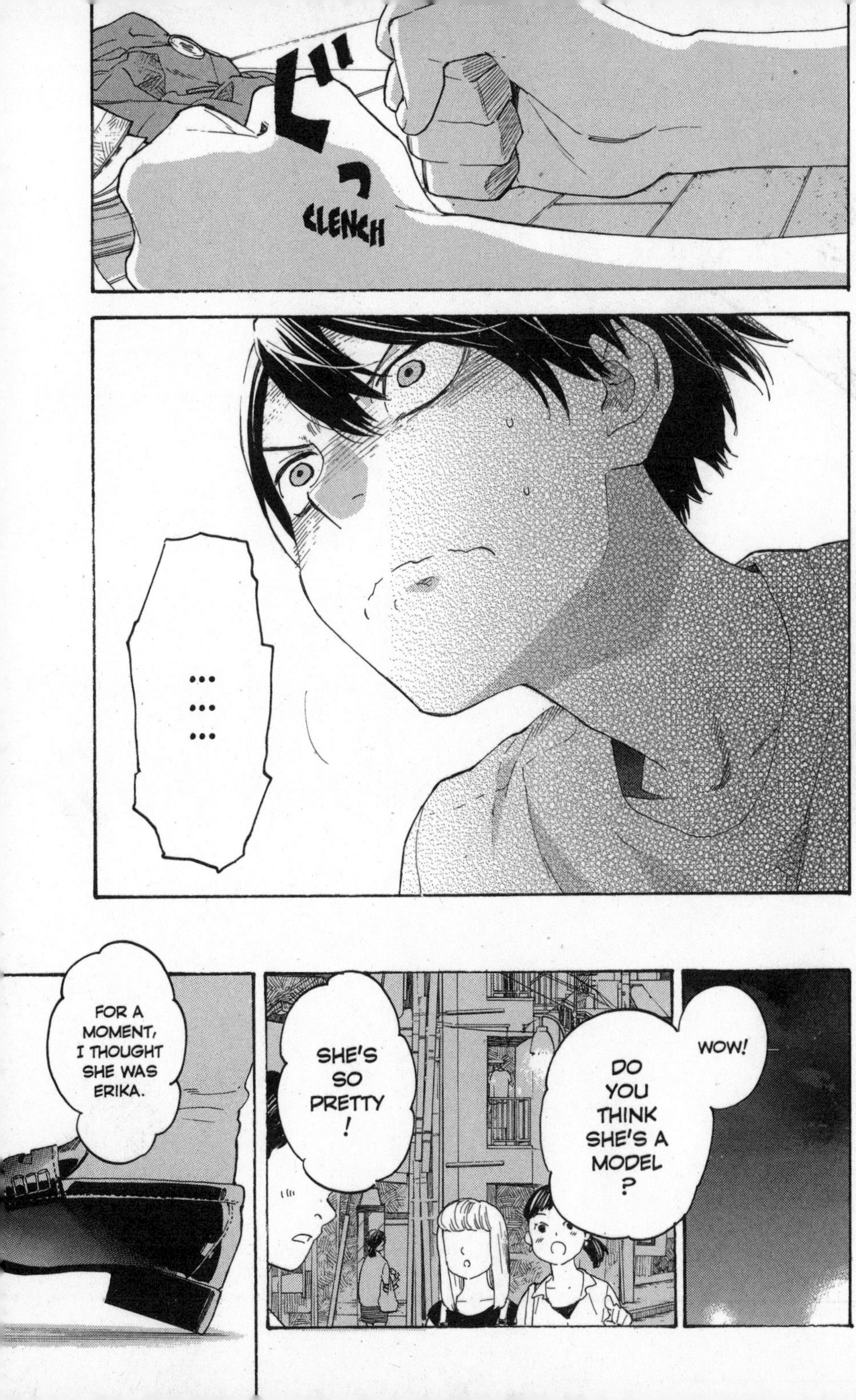
CLENCH
....
WOW!
DO YOU THINK SHE'S A MODEL?
SHE'S SO PRETTY!
FOR A MOMENT, I THOUGHT SHE WAS ERIKA.

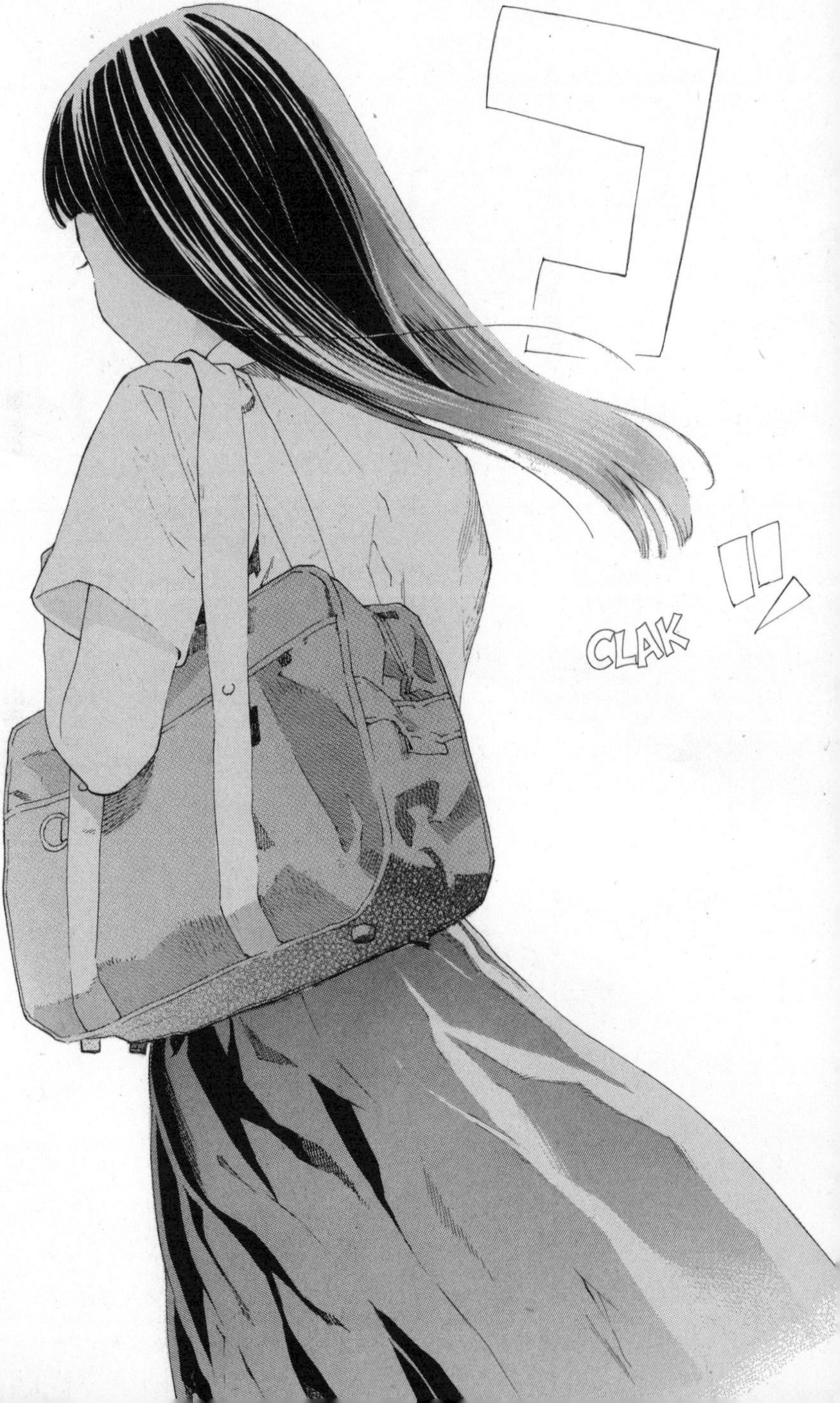
CLAK

Meeting 8

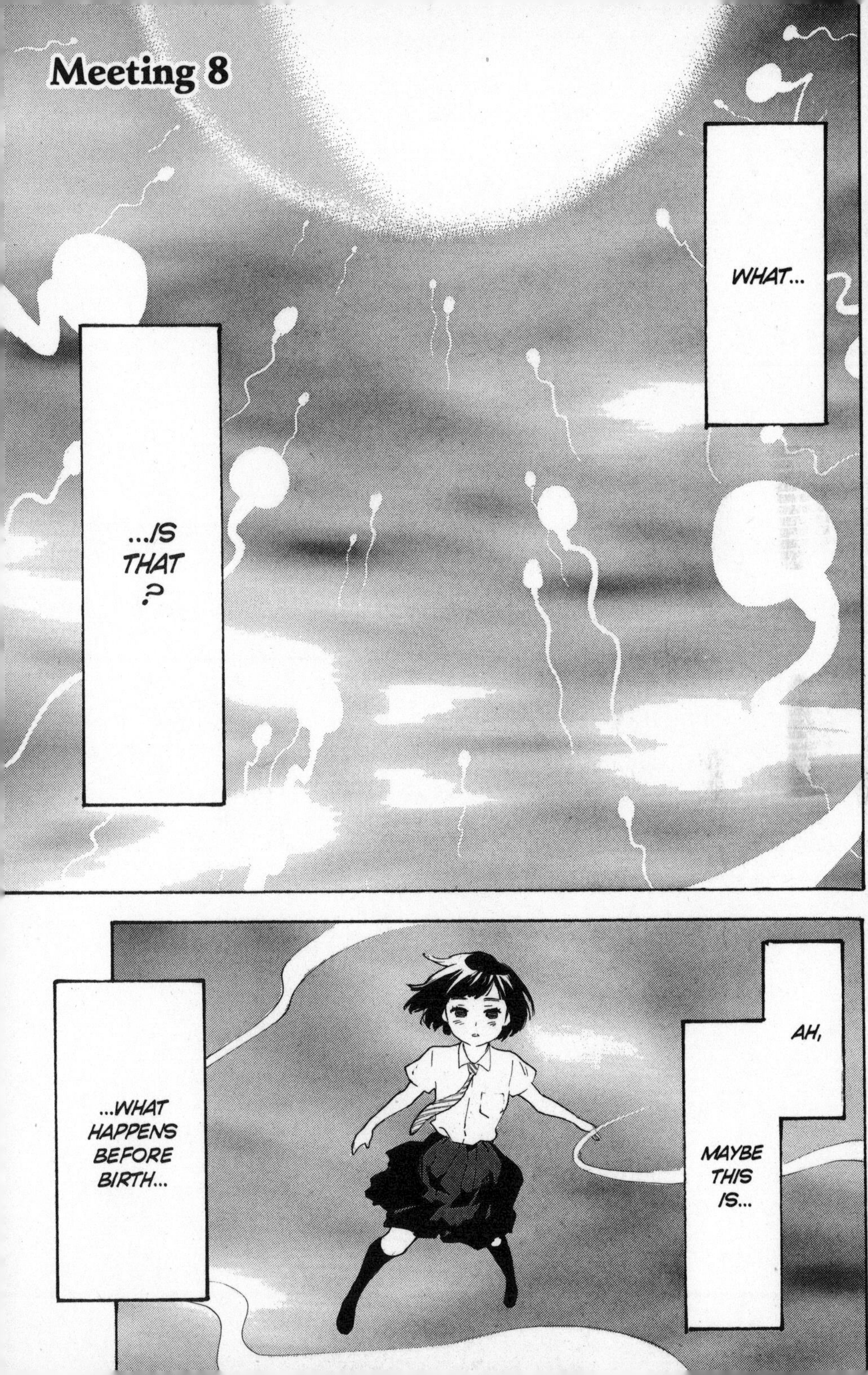
WHAT...
...IS THAT?
AH,
MAYBE THIS IS...
...WHAT HAPPENS BEFORE BIRTH...

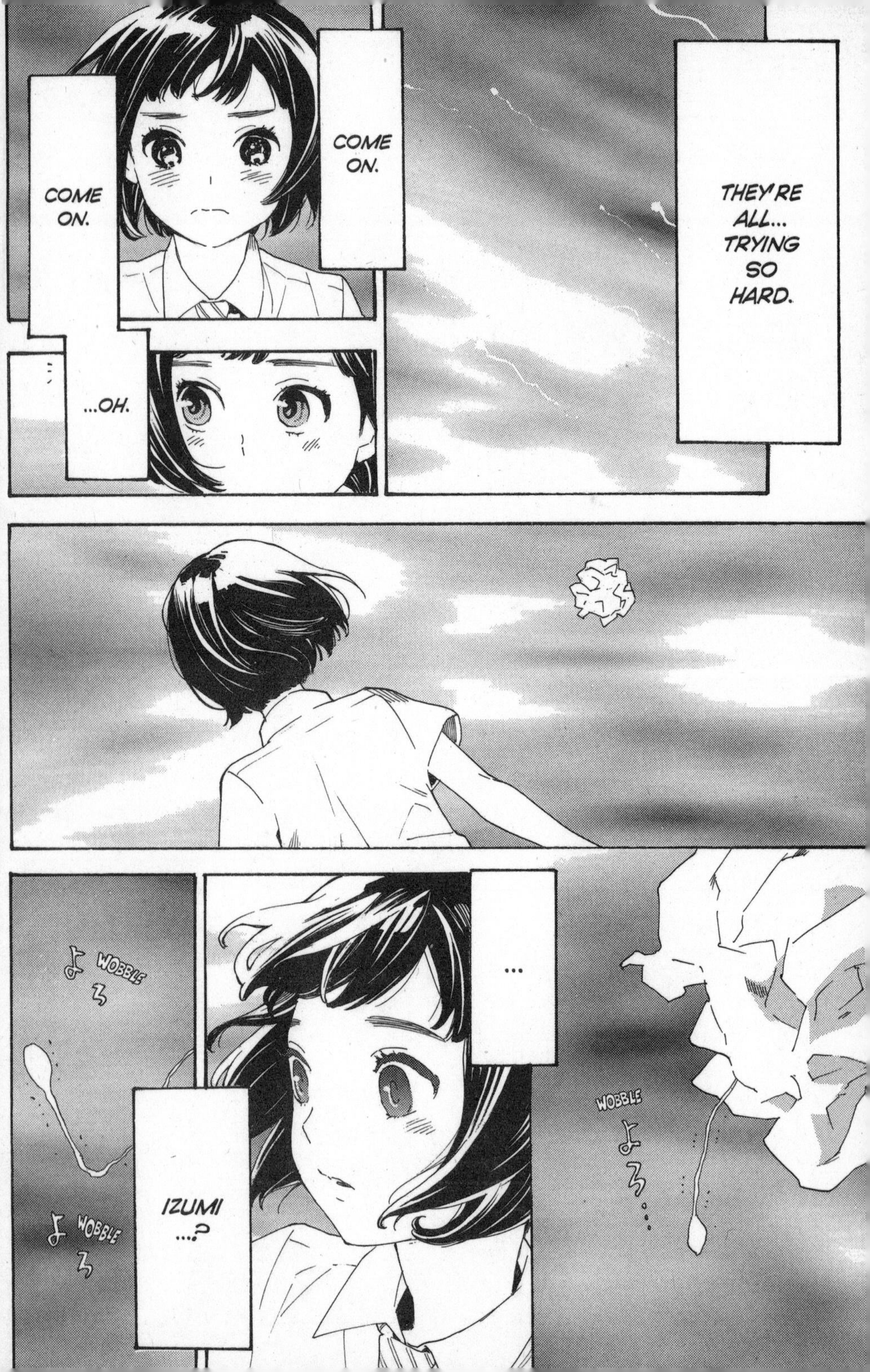
THEY'RE ALL... TRYING SO HARD.
COME ON.
COME ON.
...OH.
WOBBLE
よろ...
...
IZUMI ...?
WOBBLE
よろ
WOBBLE
よろ

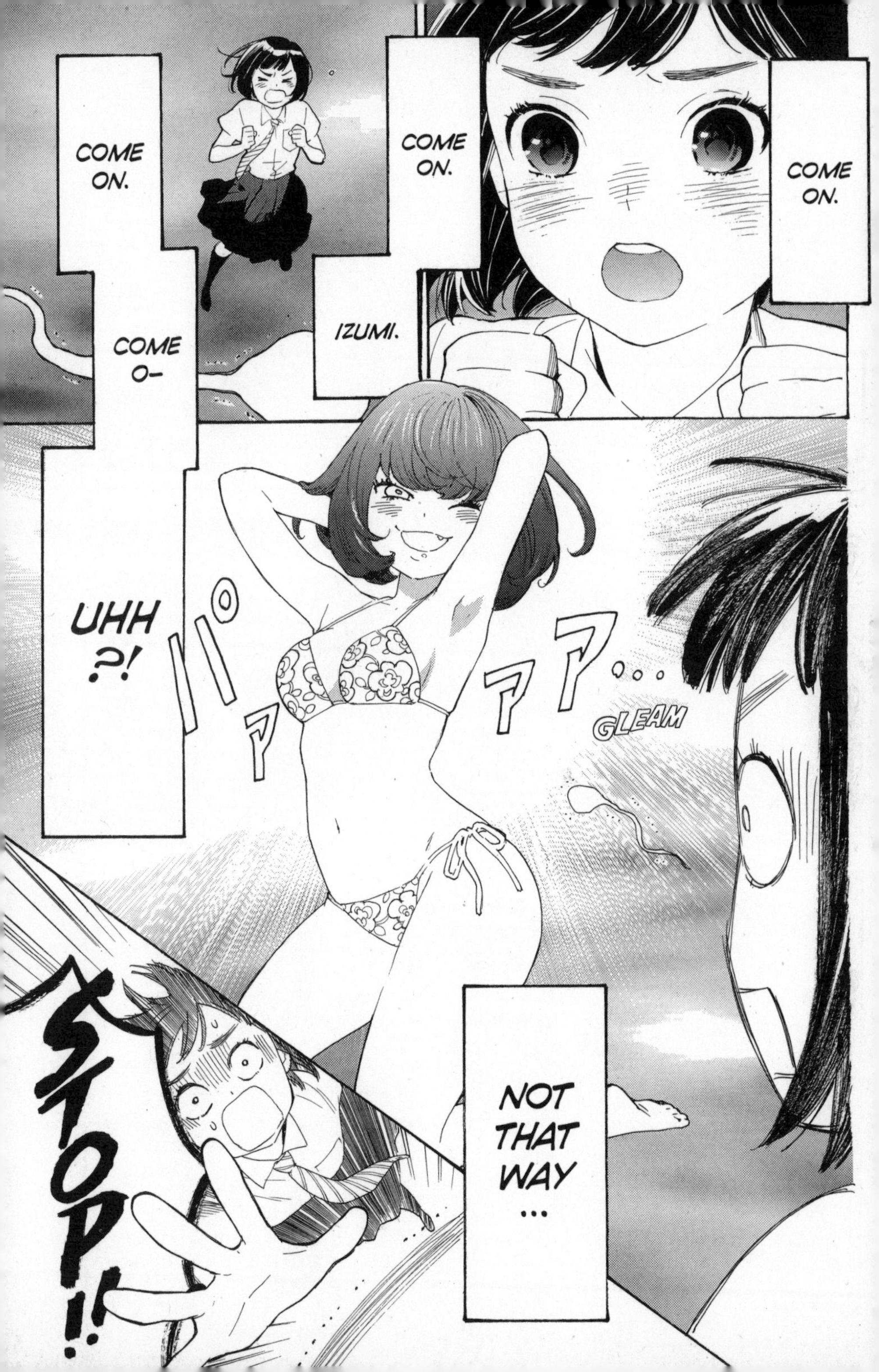
COME ON.
COME ON.
IZUMI.
COME ON.
COME O-
パァァァ...
GLEAM
UHH ?!
NOT THAT WAY ...
STOP!!

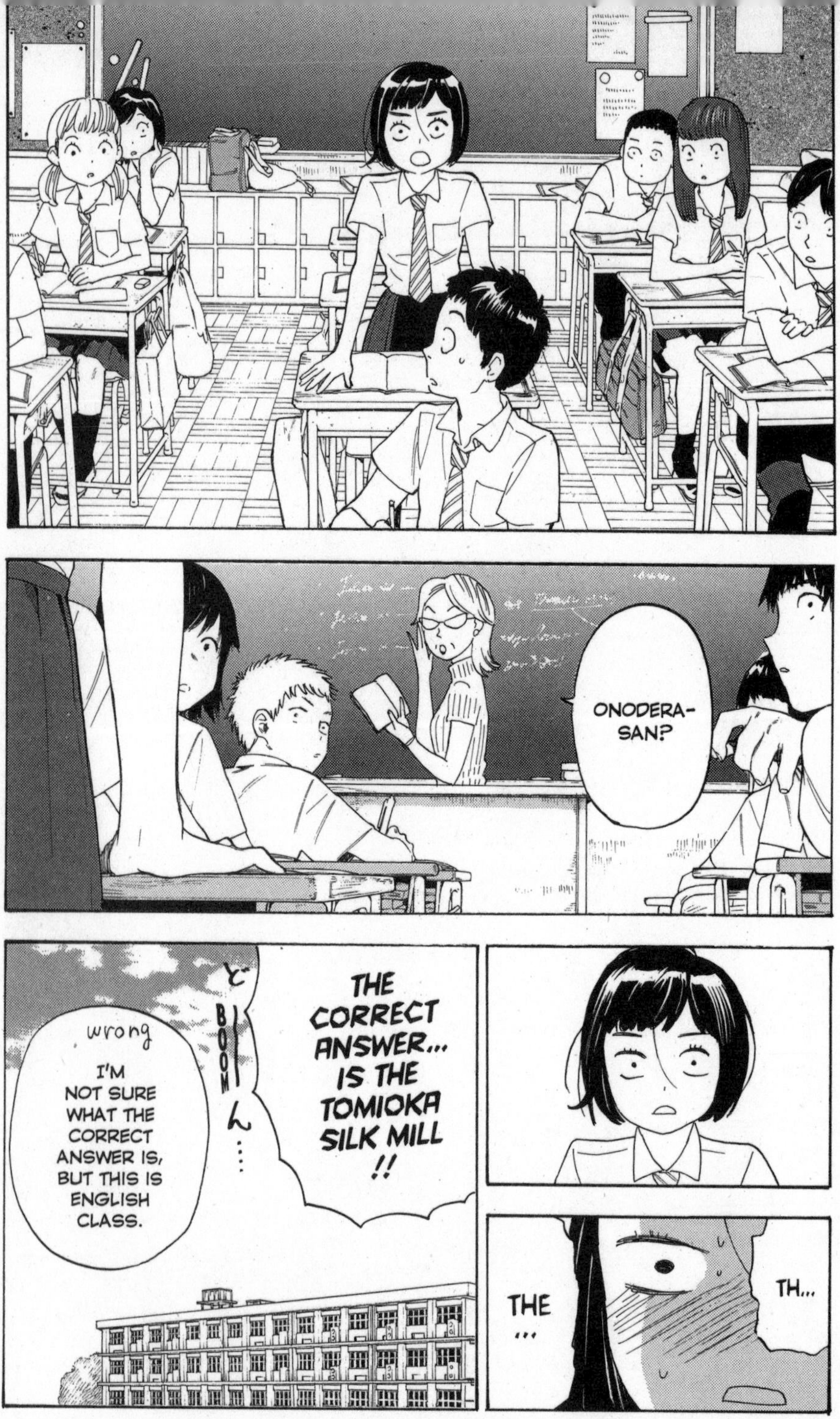
ONODERA-SAN?
TH...
THE ...
THE CORRECT ANSWER... IS THE TOMIOKA SILK MILL !!
どーん.... BOOM
wrong
I'M NOT SURE WHAT THE CORRECT ANSWER IS, BUT THIS IS ENGLISH CLASS.

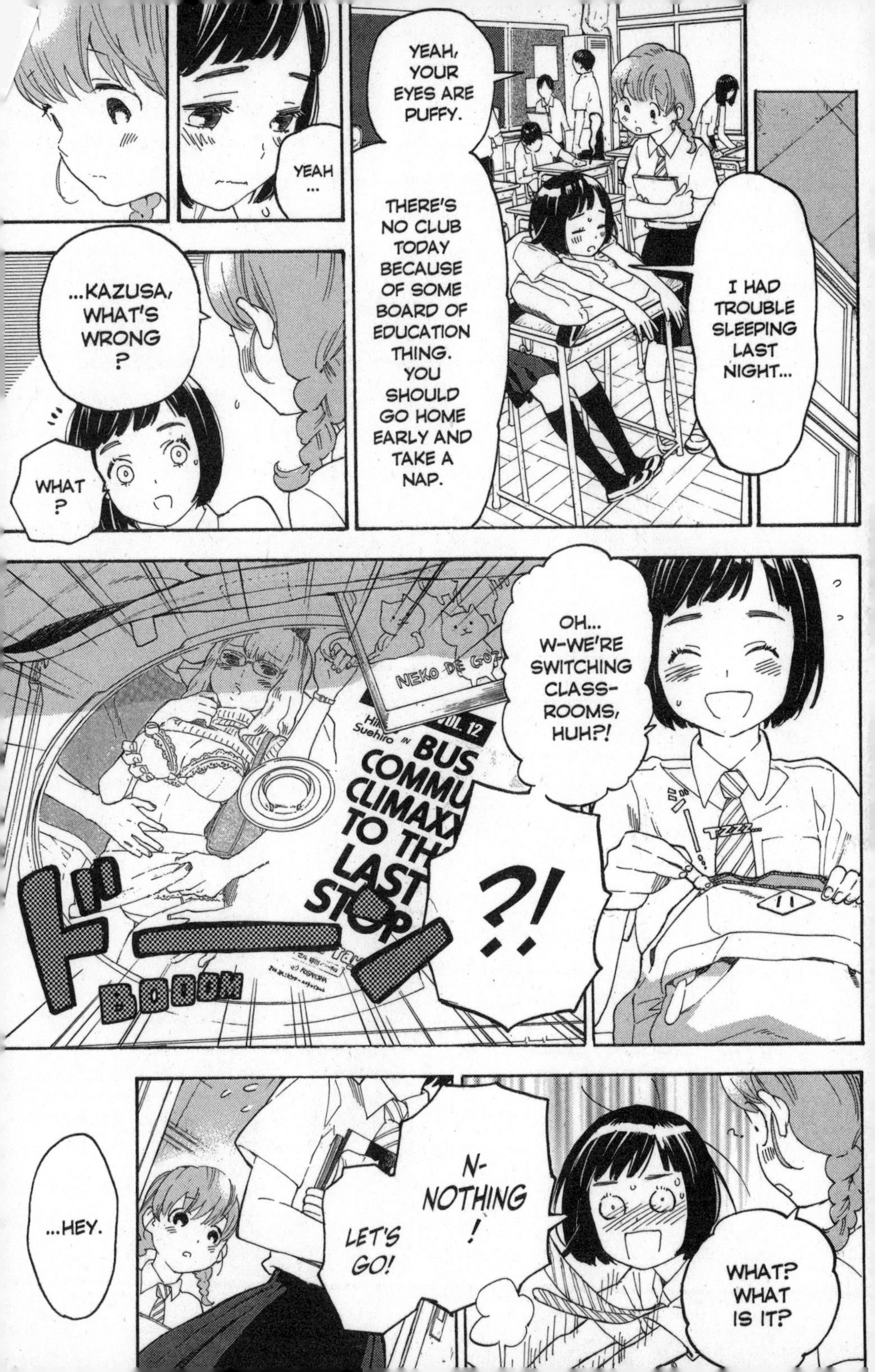
I HAD TROUBLE SLEEPING LAST NIGHT...
YEAH, YOUR EYES ARE PUFFY.
THERE'S NO CLUB TODAY BECAUSE OF SOME BOARD OF EDUCATION THING. YOU SHOULD GO HOME EARLY AND TAKE A NAP.
YEAH ...
...KAZUSA, WHAT'S WRONG ?
WHAT ?
OH... W-WE'RE SWITCHING CLASS-ROOMS, HUH?!
?!
NEKO DE GOZ
VOL. 12
BUS COMMU CLIMAXX TO TH LAST STOP
WHAT? WHAT IS IT?
N-NOTHING !
LET'S GO!
...HEY.

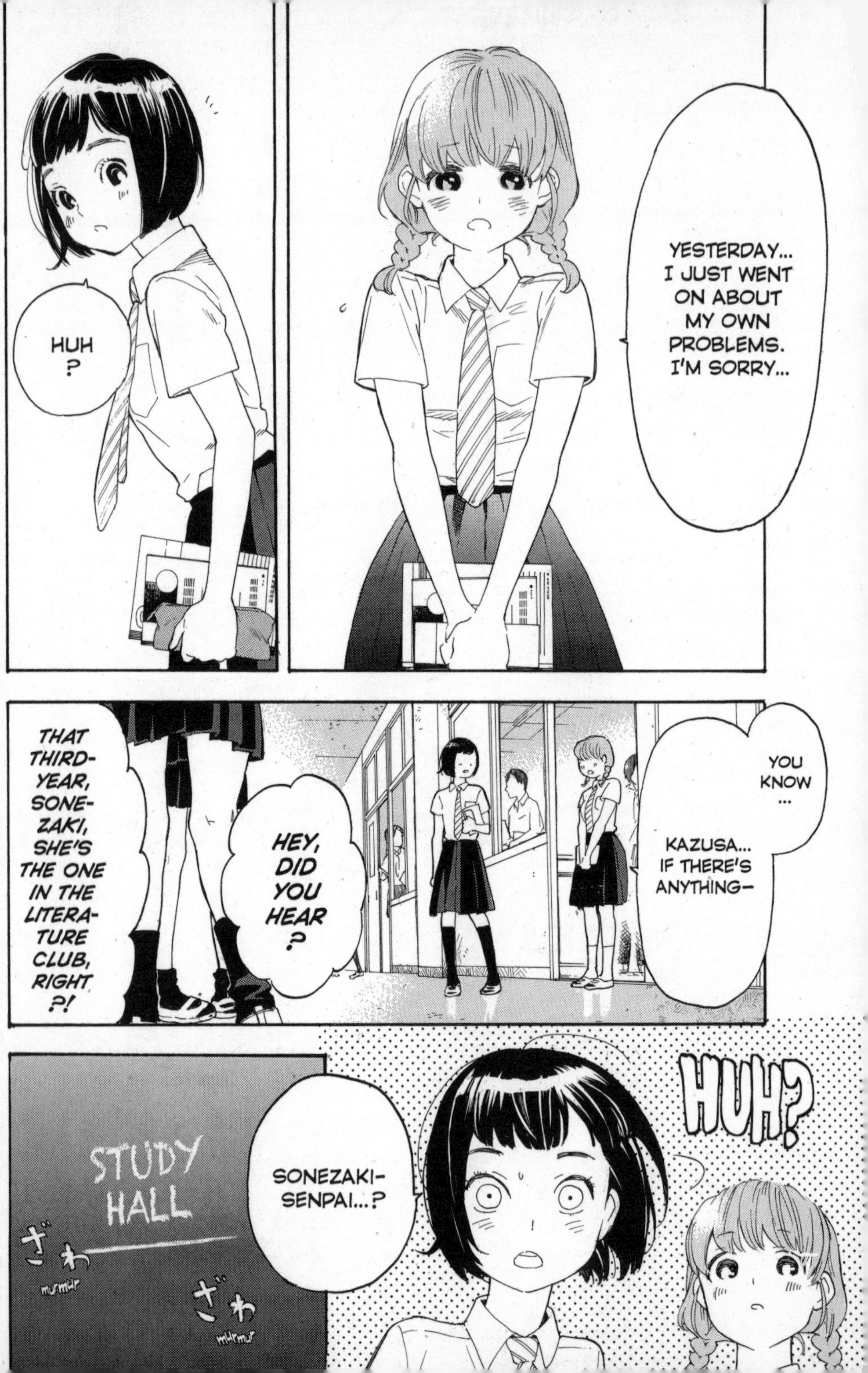
YESTERDAY... I JUST WENT ON ABOUT MY OWN PROBLEMS. I'M SORRY...
HUH ?
YOU KNOW ...
KAZUSA... IF THERE'S ANYTHING—
HEY, DID YOU HEAR ?
THAT THIRD-YEAR, SONEZAKI, SHE'S THE ONE IN THE LITERATURE CLUB, RIGHT ?!
HUH?
SONEZAKI-SENPAI...?
STUDY HALL
ざわ
murmur
ざわ
murmur

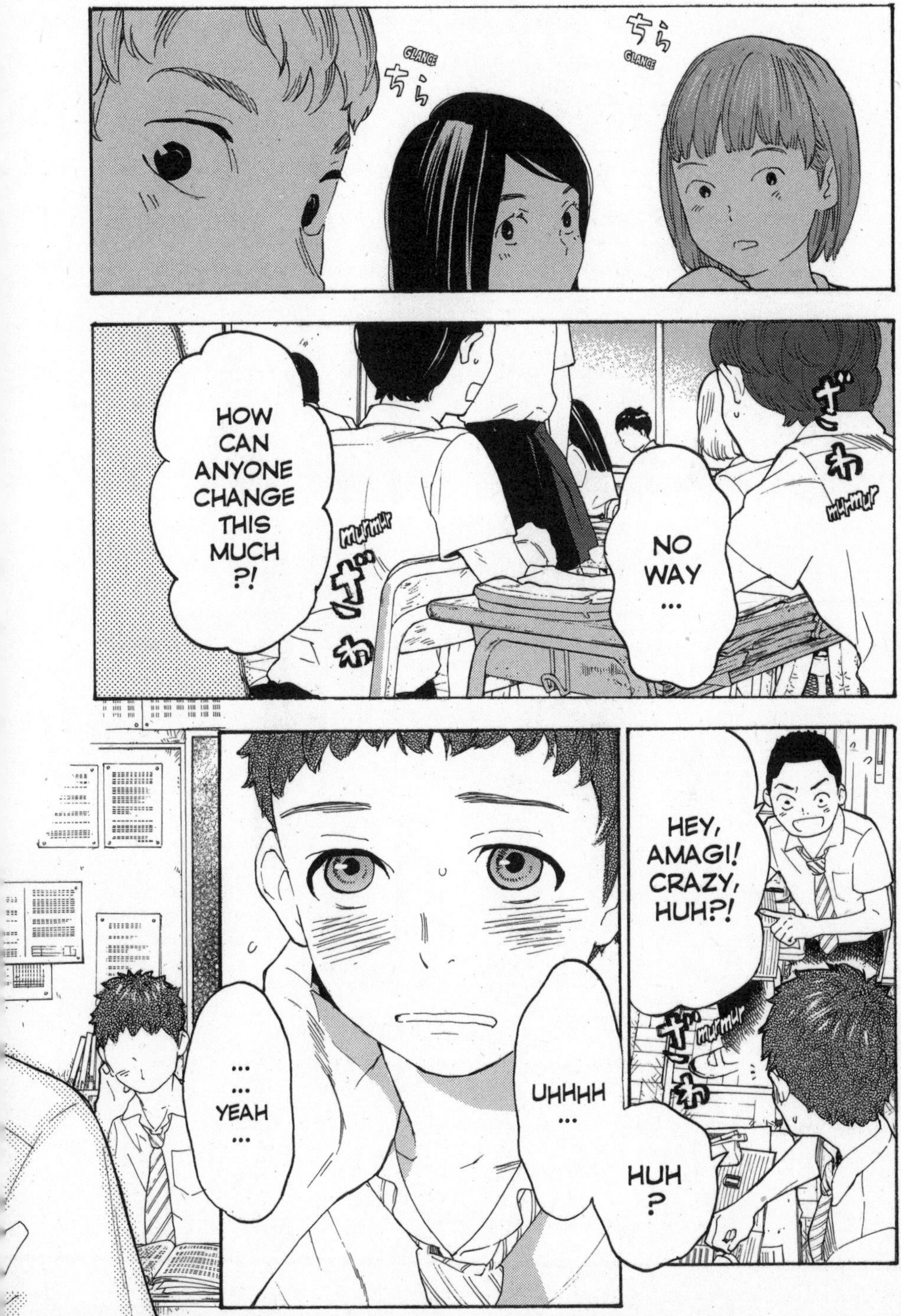
ちら
GLANCE
GLANCE
ちら
ざわ
murmur
NO WAY ...
HOW CAN ANYONE CHANGE THIS MUCH ?!
murmur
ざわ
HEY, AMAGI! CRAZY, HUH?!
ざわ
murmur
UHHHH ... HUH ?
... ... YEAH ...

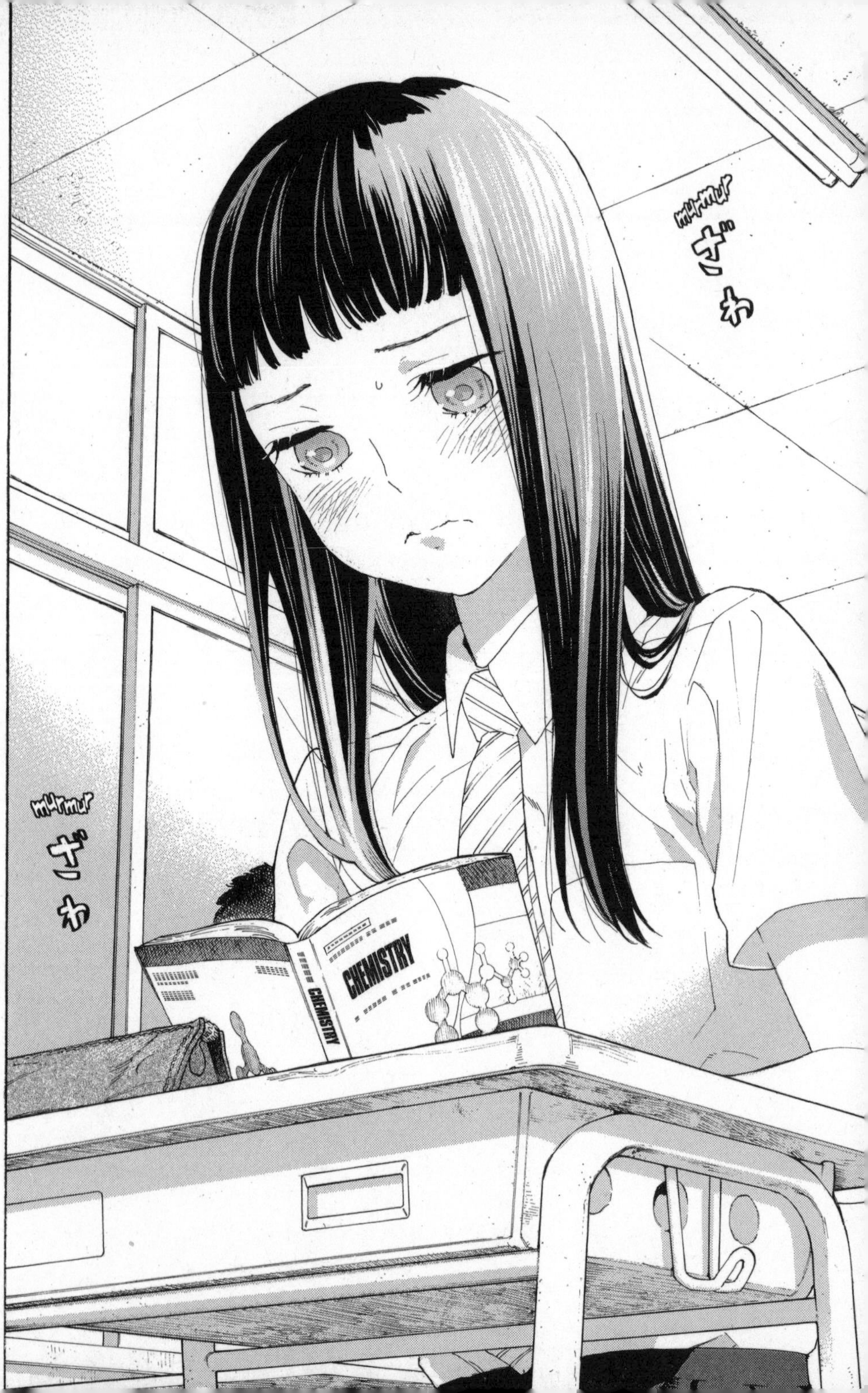
murmur
ざわ
murmur
ざわ
CHEMISTRY
CHEMISTRY

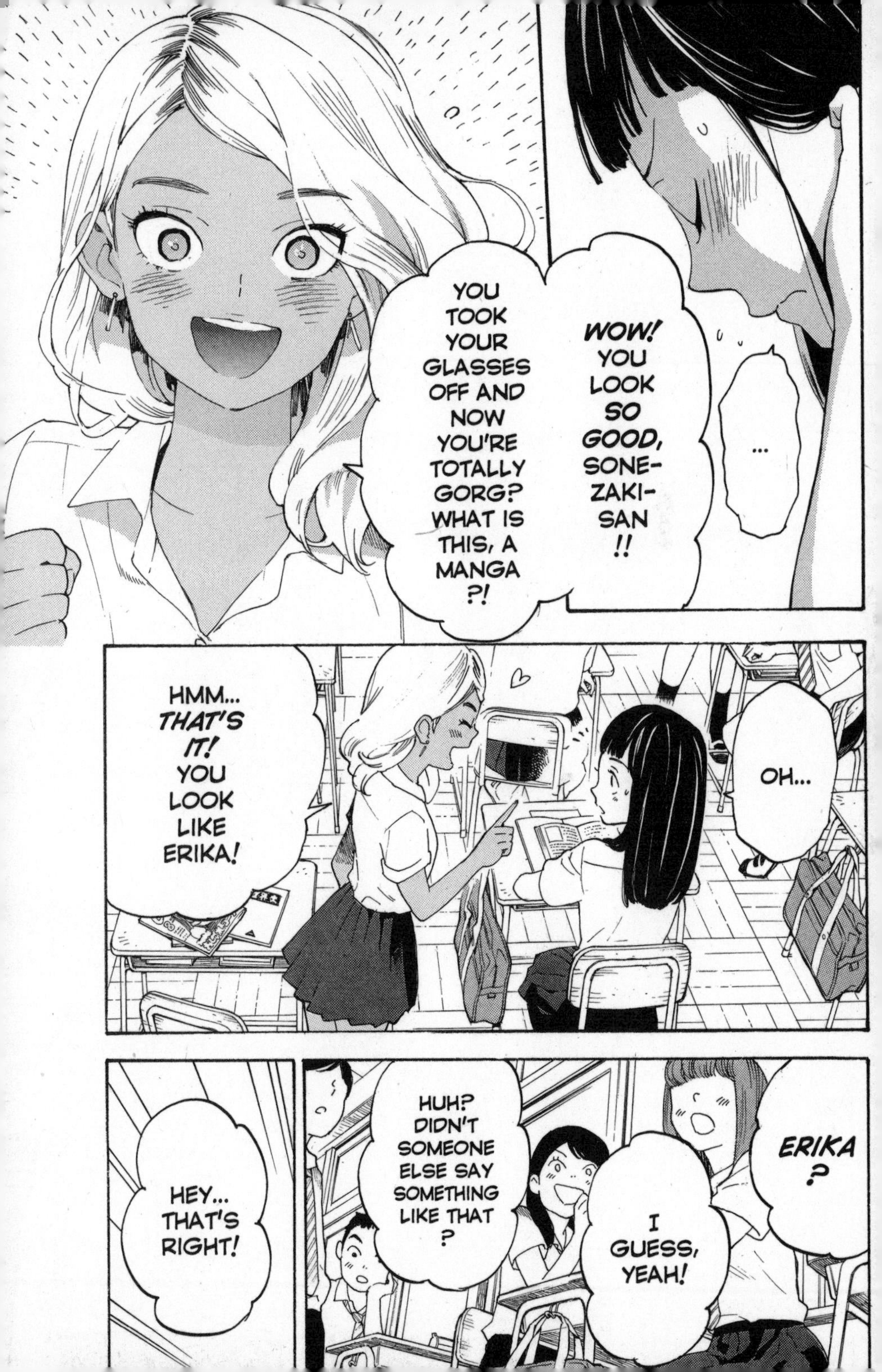
...
WOW! YOU LOOK SO GOOD, SONE-ZAKI-SAN!!
YOU TOOK YOUR GLASSES OFF AND NOW YOU'RE TOTALLY GORG? WHAT IS THIS, A MANGA?!
OH...
HMM... THAT'S IT! YOU LOOK LIKE ERIKA!
ERIKA?
I GUESS, YEAH!
HUH? DIDN'T SOMEONE ELSE SAY SOMETHING LIKE THAT?
HEY... THAT'S RIGHT!

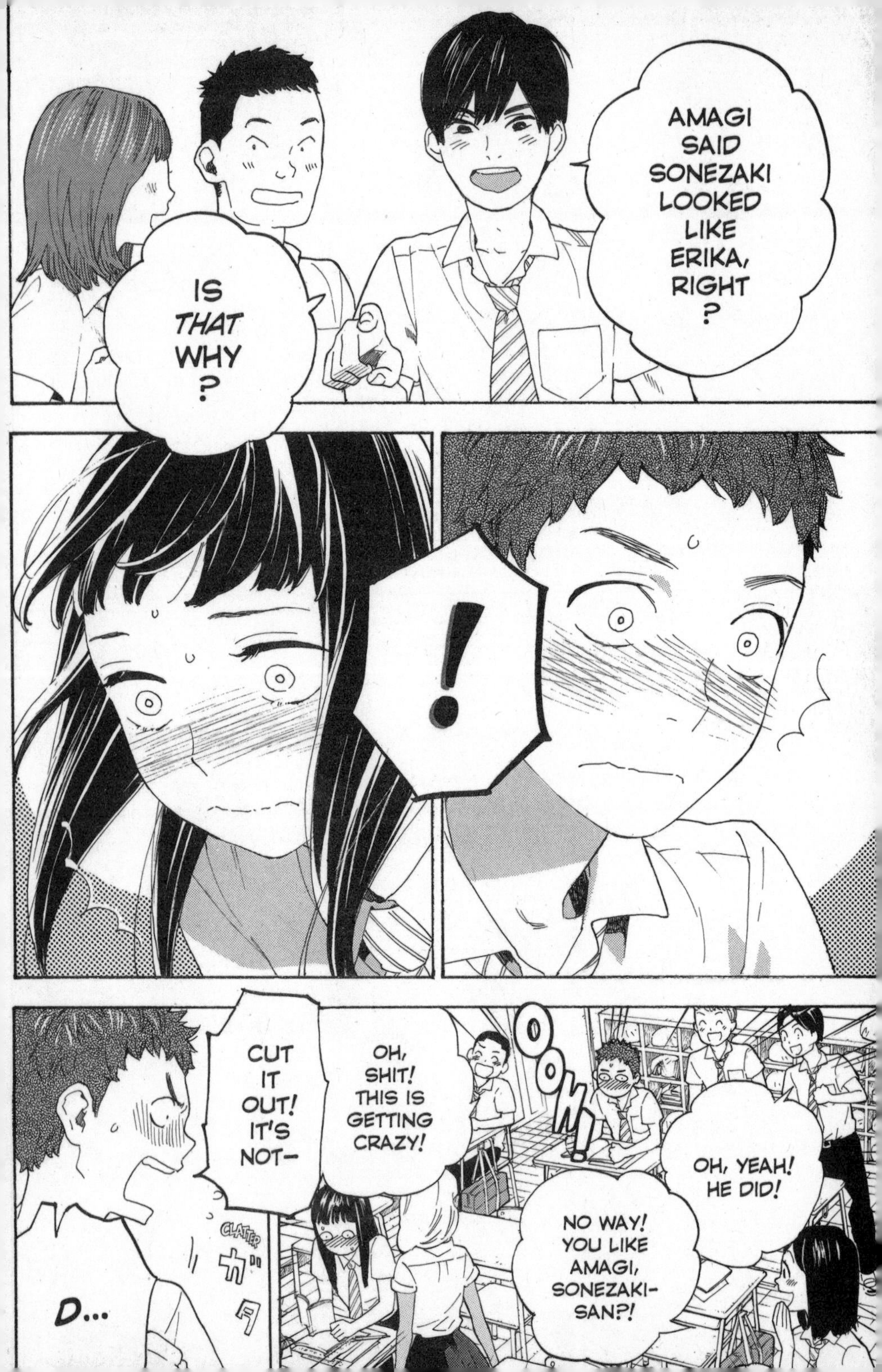
AMAGI SAID SONEZAKI LOOKED LIKE ERIKA, RIGHT?
IS *THAT* WHY?
!
NO WAY! YOU LIKE AMAGI, SONEZAKI-SAN?!
OH, YEAH! HE DID!
OOH!
OH, SHIT! THIS IS GETTING CRAZY!
CUT IT OUT! IT'S NOT—
CLATTER
カタ
D...

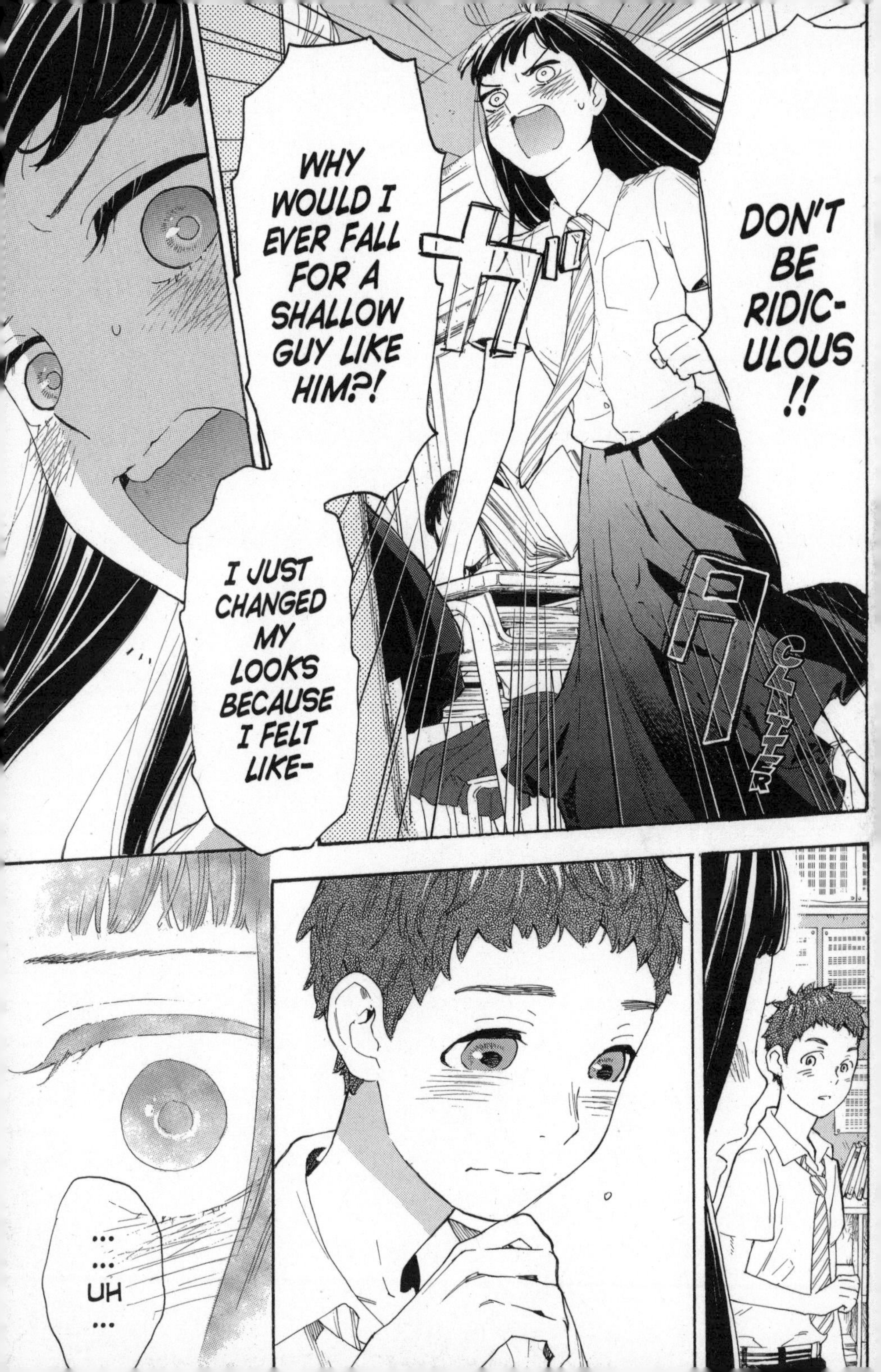
DON'T BE RIDIC-ULOUS!!
WHY WOULD I EVER FALL FOR A SHALLOW GUY LIKE HIM?!
I JUST CHANGED MY LOOKS BECAUSE I FELT LIKE-
CLATTER
... ... UH ...

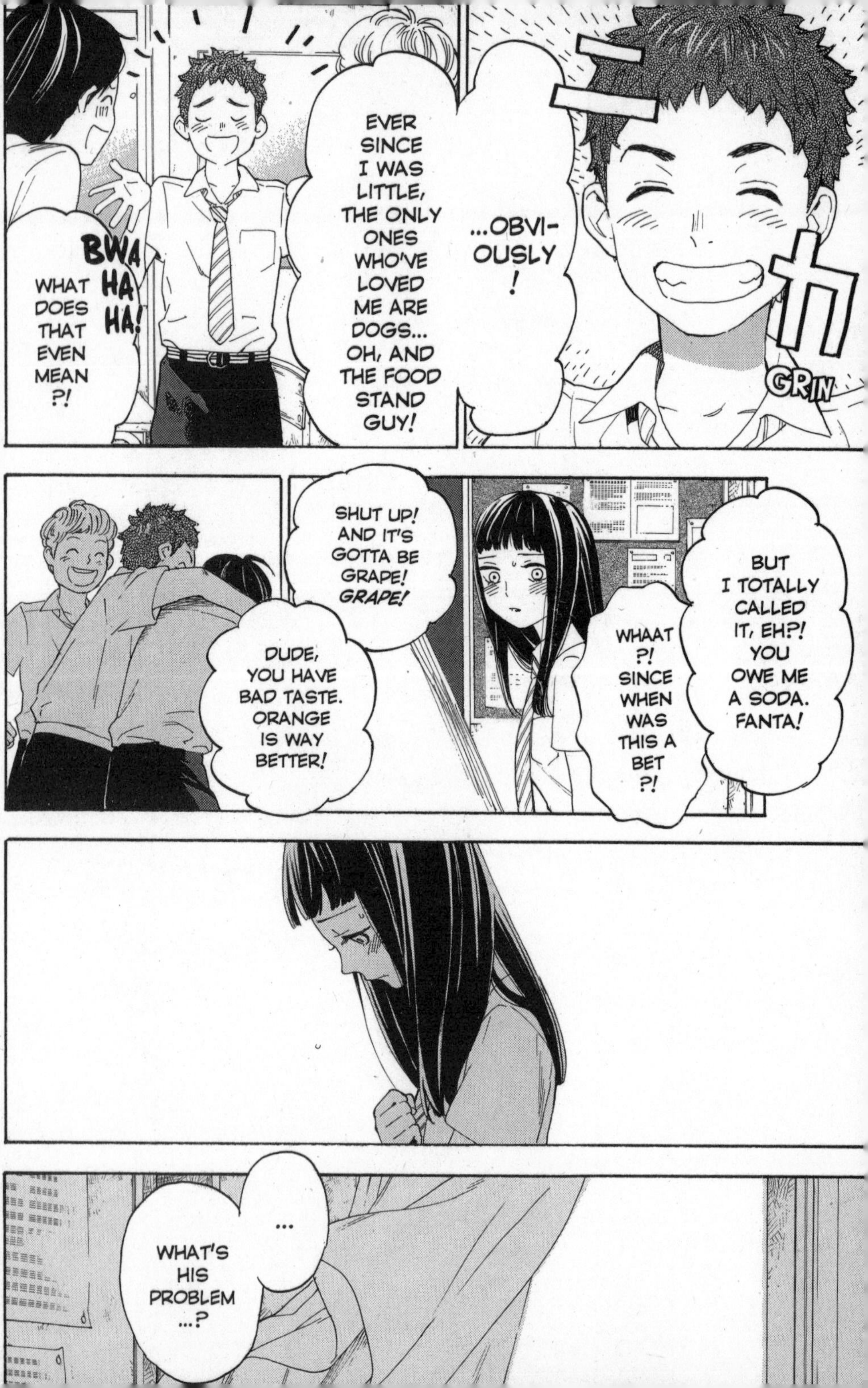
...OBVIOUSLY!
カ
GRIN
EVER SINCE I WAS LITTLE, THE ONLY ONES WHO'VE LOVED ME ARE DOGS... OH, AND THE FOOD STAND GUY!
BWA HA HA!
WHAT DOES THAT EVEN MEAN?!
BUT I TOTALLY CALLED IT, EH?! YOU OWE ME A SODA. FANTA!
WHAAT?! SINCE WHEN WAS THIS A BET?!
SHUT UP! AND IT'S GOTTA BE GRAPE! *GRAPE!*
DUDE, YOU HAVE BAD TASTE. ORANGE IS WAY BETTER!
...
WHAT'S HIS PROBLEM...?

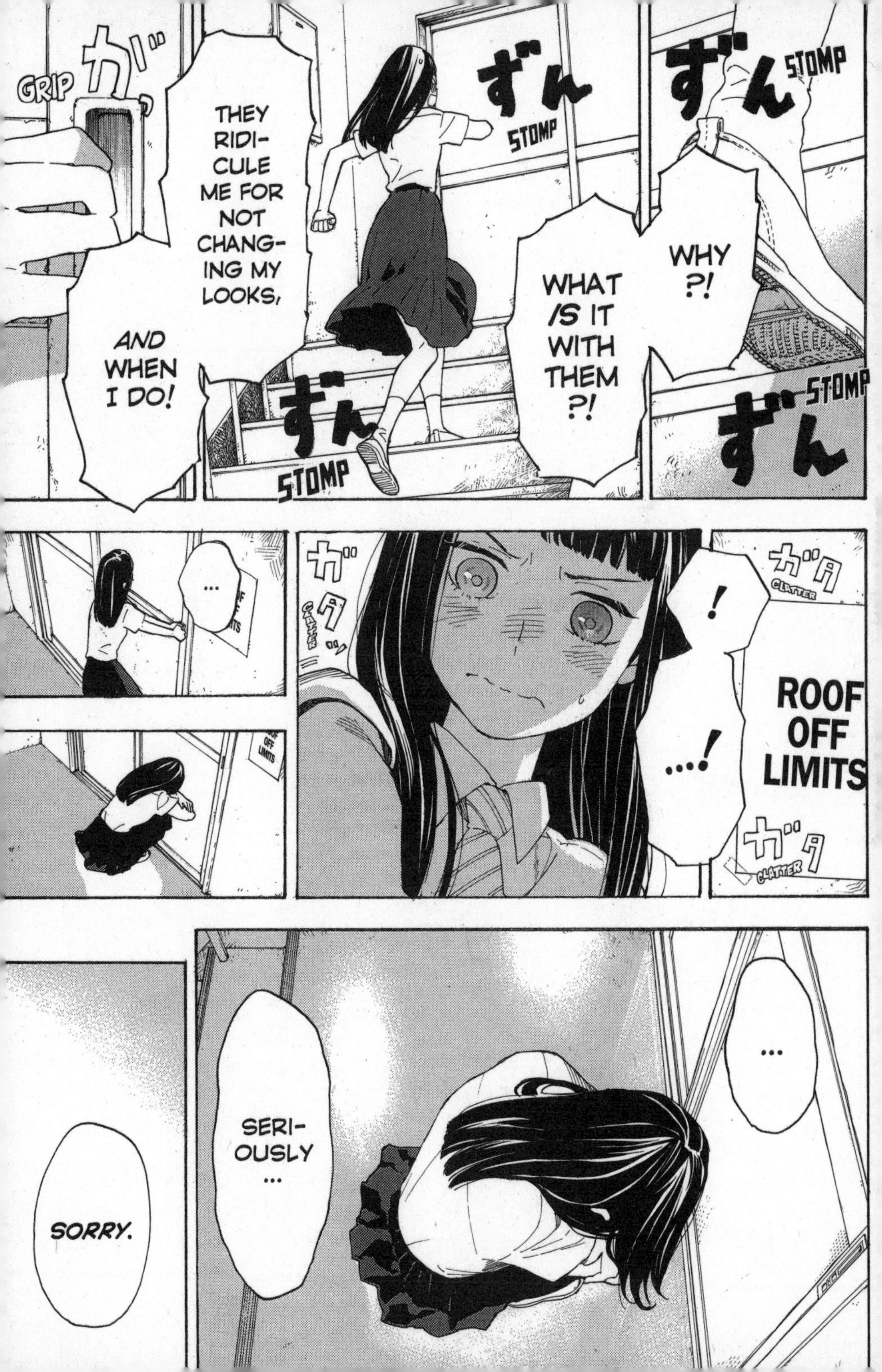
ずん
STOMP
WHY?!
STOMP
ずん
WHAT IS IT WITH THEM?!
ずん
STOMP
ずん
STOMP
THEY RIDICULE ME FOR NOT CHANGING MY LOOKS,
AND WHEN I DO!
GRIP
ガッ
ガタ
CLATTER
!
...!
ROOF OFF LIMITS
ガタ
CLATTER
ガタッ
CLATTER
...
...
SERIOUSLY...
SORRY.

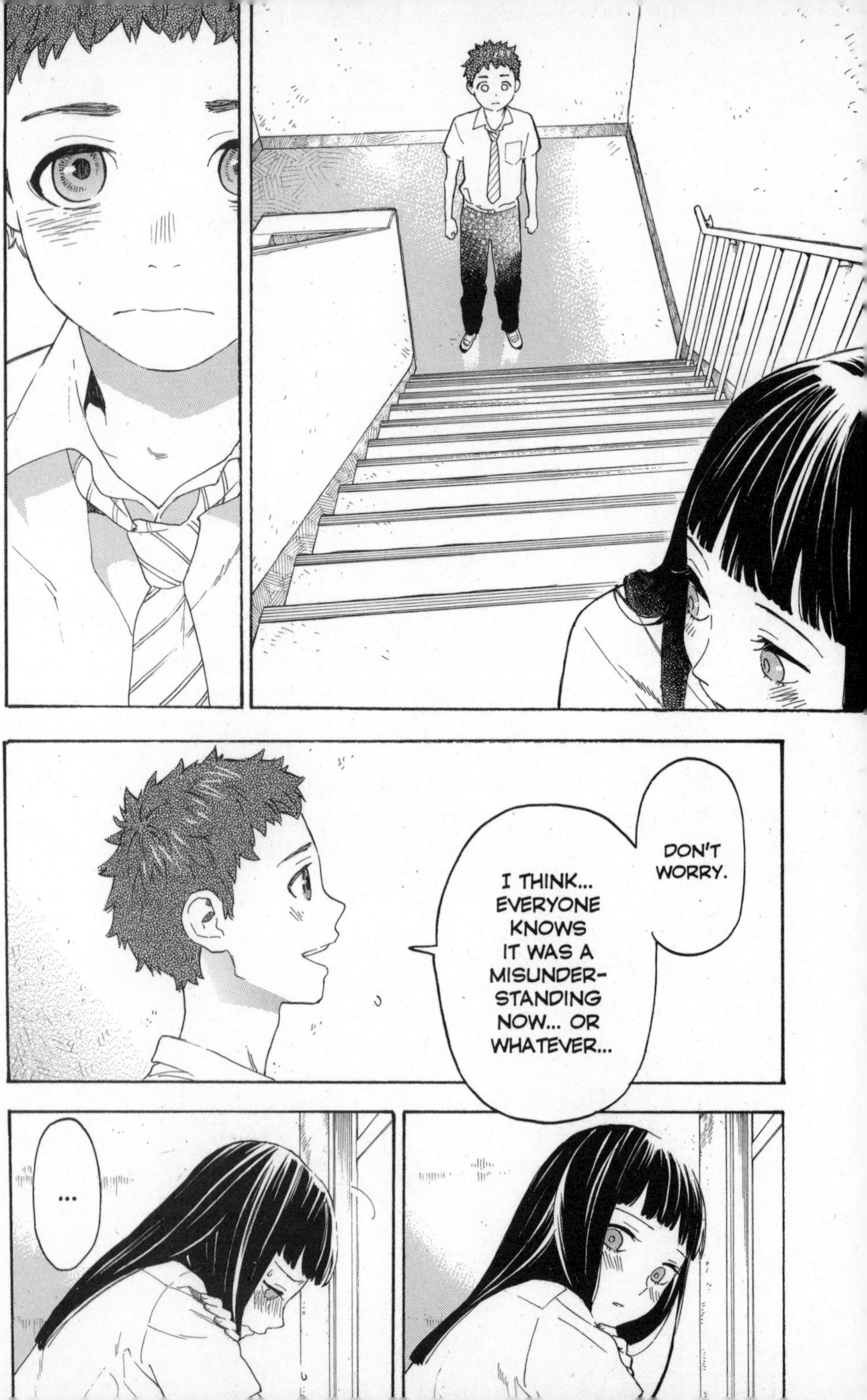
DON'T WORRY.
I THINK... EVERYONE KNOWS IT WAS A MISUNDER-STANDING NOW... OR WHATEVER...
...

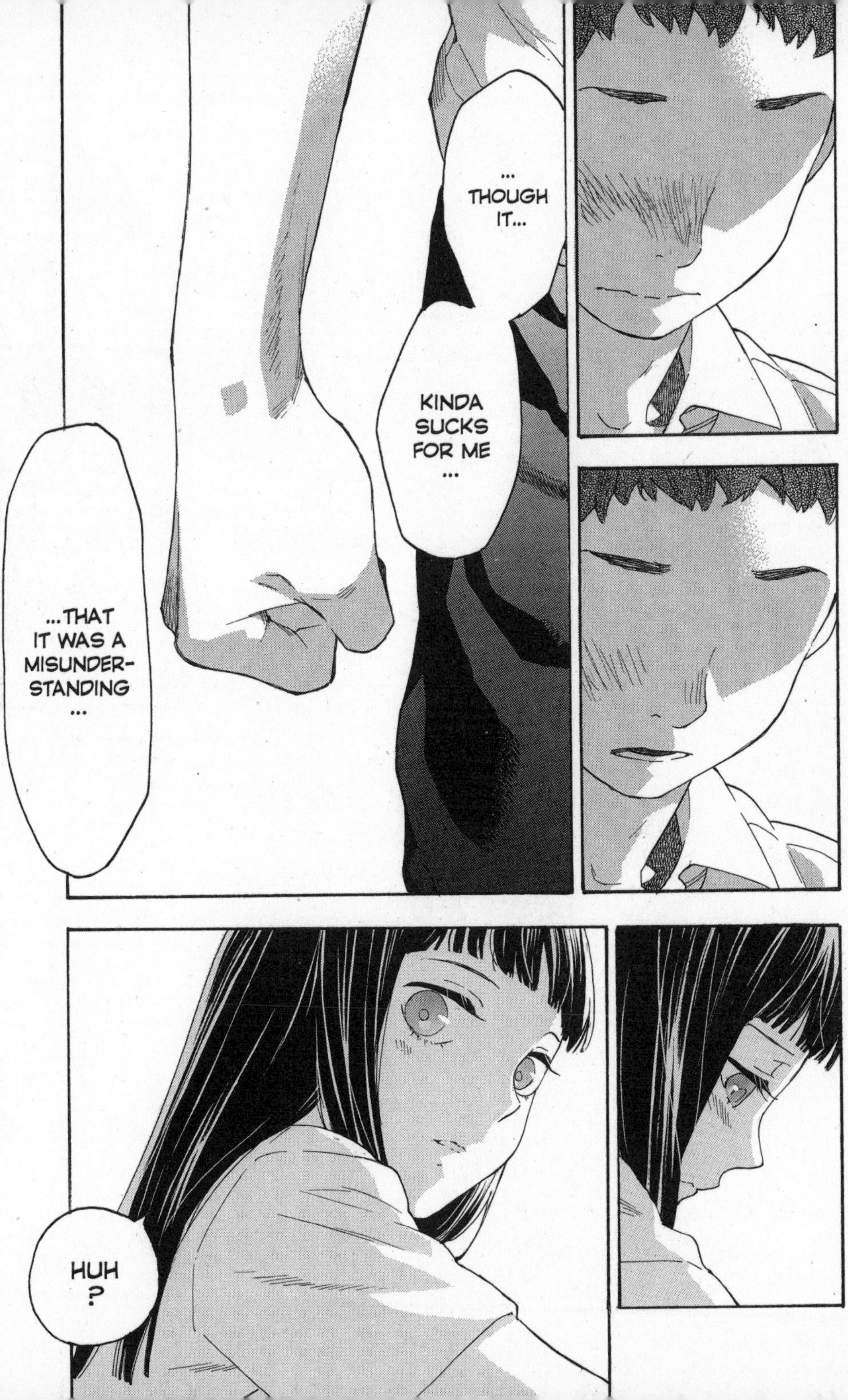
...THOUGH IT...
KINDA SUCKS FOR ME ...
...THAT IT WAS A MISUNDER-STANDING ...
HUH ?

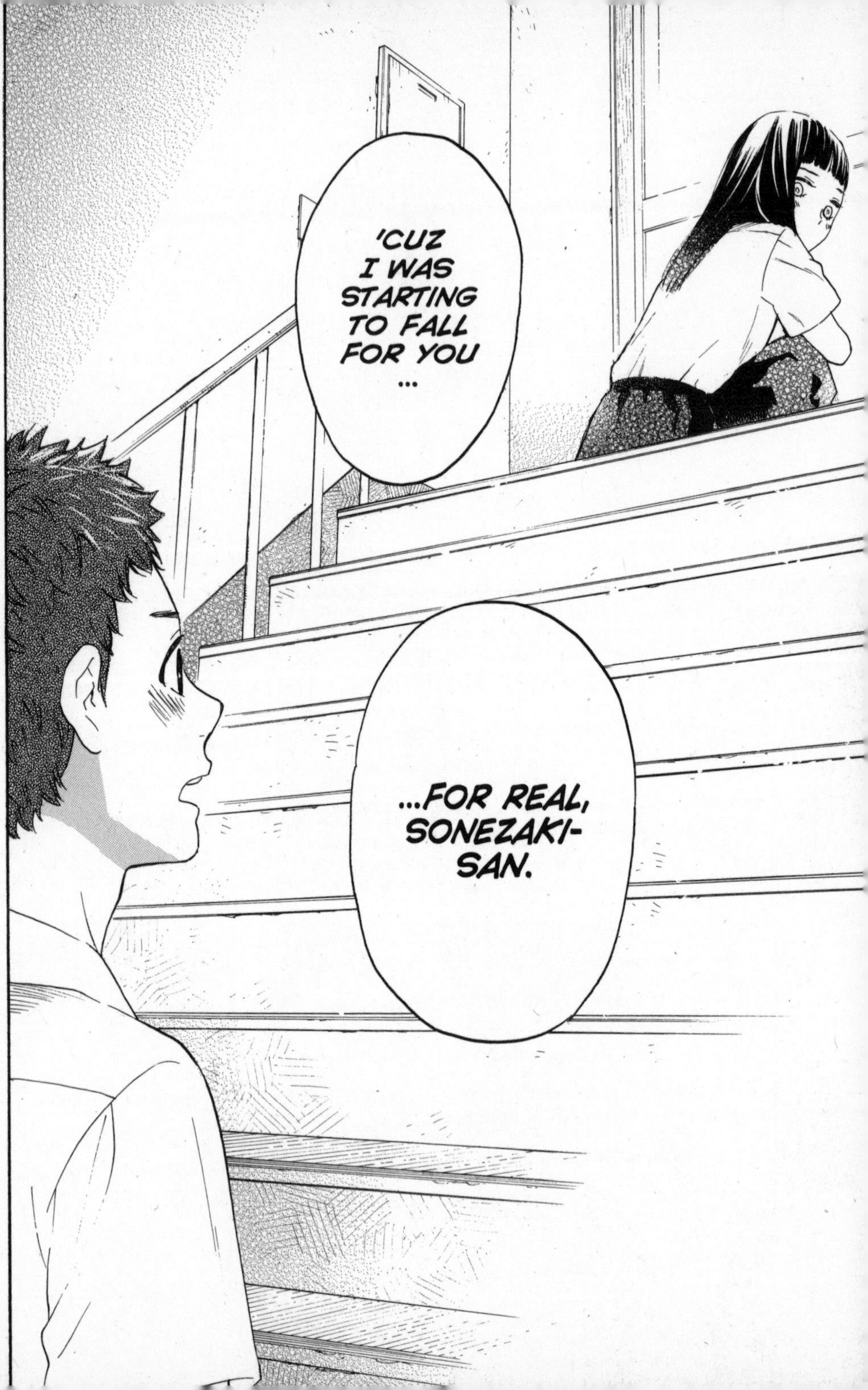
'CUZ I WAS STARTING TO FALL FOR YOU ...
...FOR REAL, SONEZAKI-SAN.

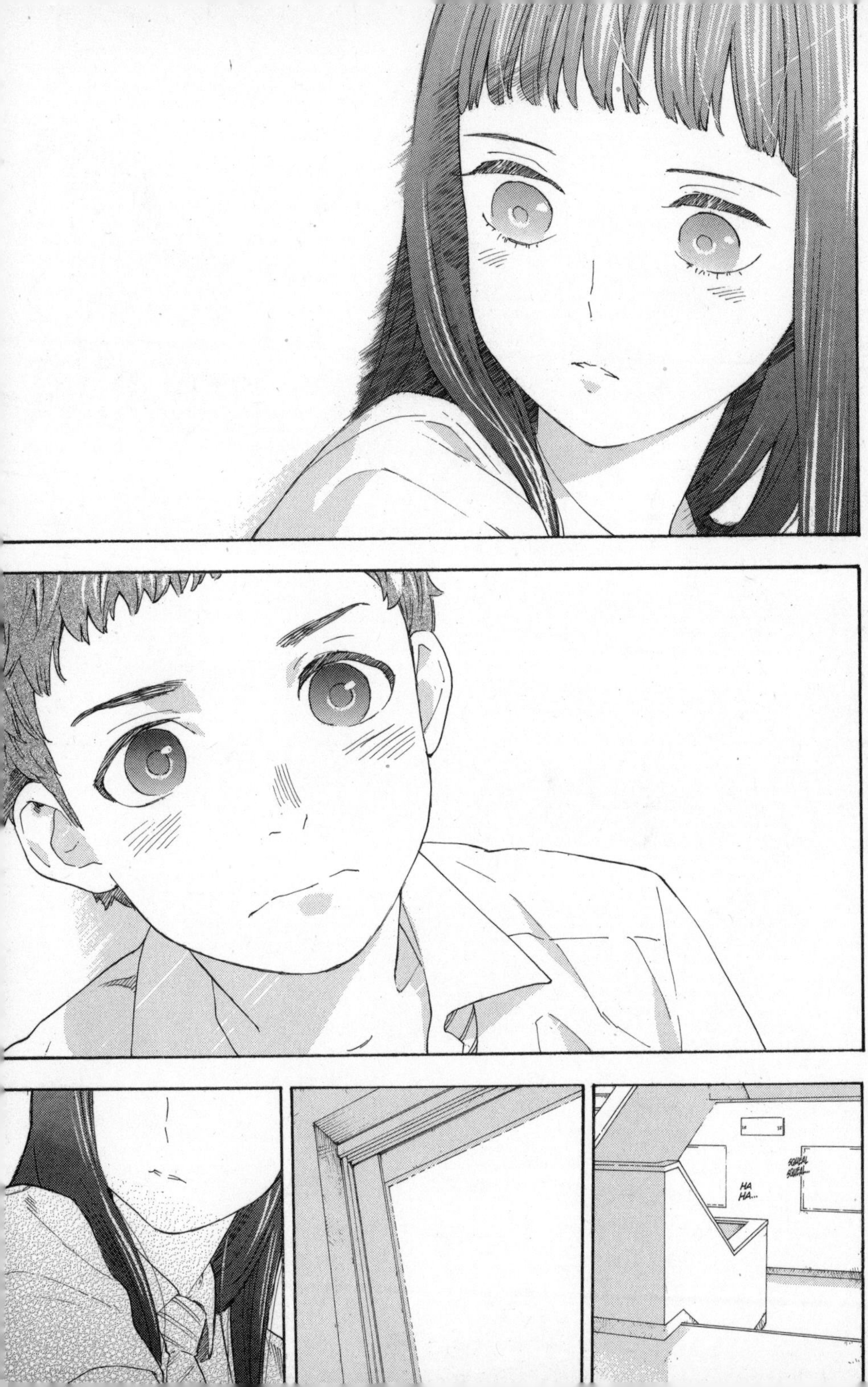
SQUEAL SQUEAL...
HA HA...

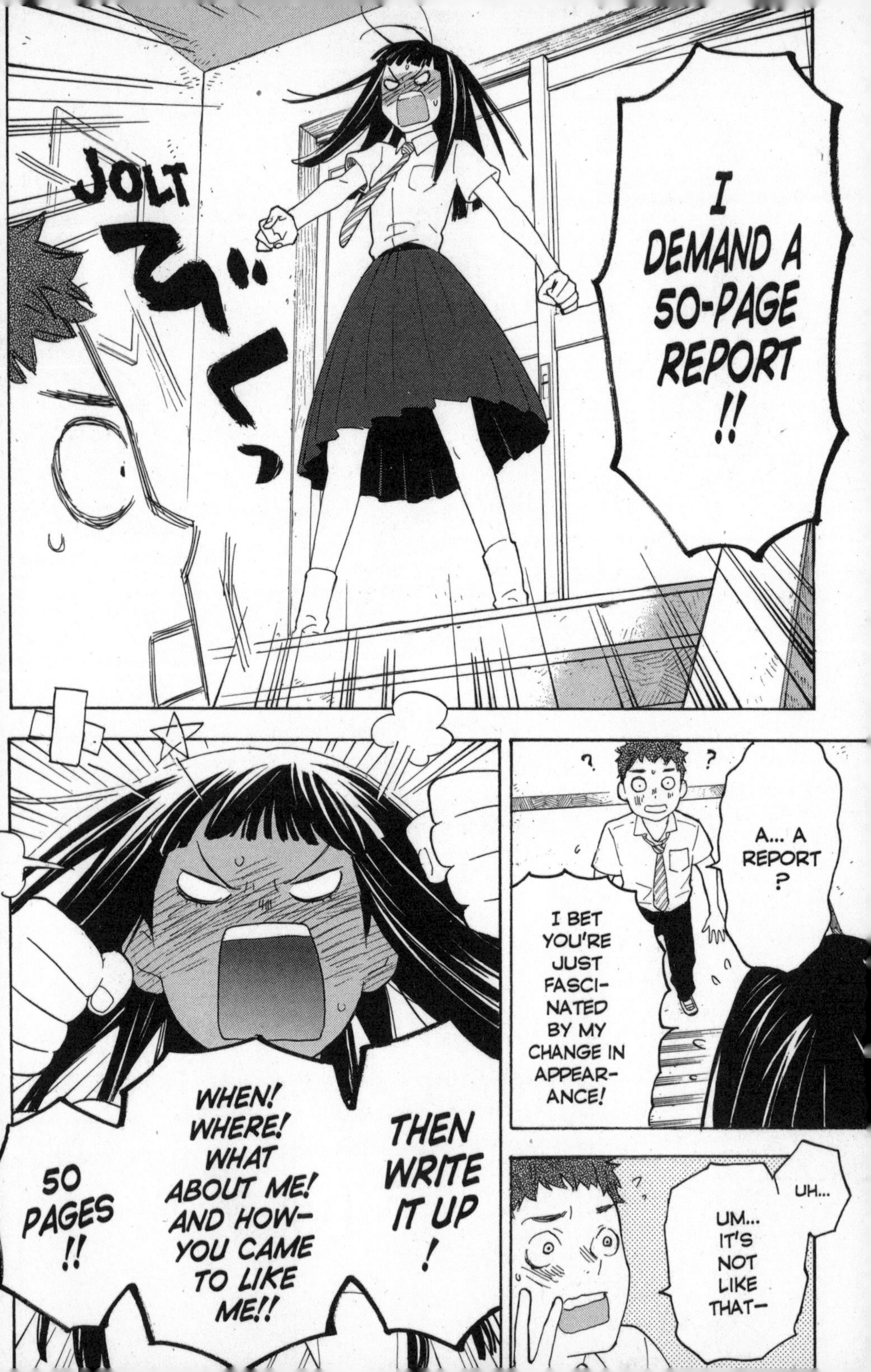
I DEMAND A 50-PAGE REPORT !!
JOLT
A... A REPORT ?
I BET YOU'RE JUST FASCI-NATED BY MY CHANGE IN APPEAR-ANCE!
UH...
UM... IT'S NOT LIKE THAT—
THEN WRITE IT UP !
WHEN! WHERE! WHAT ABOUT ME! AND HOW-YOU CAME TO LIKE ME!!
50 PAGES !!

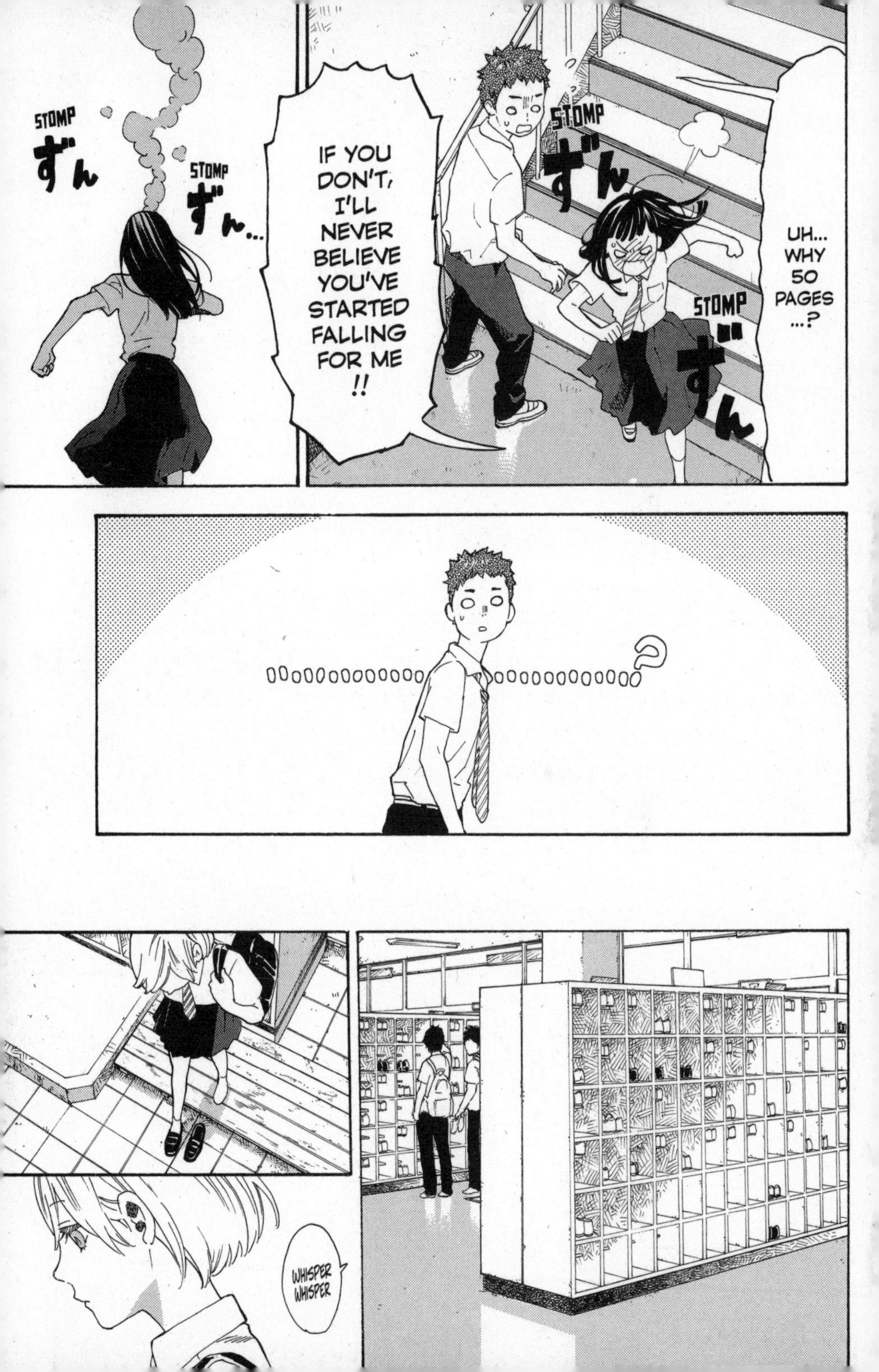
UH... WHY 50 PAGES ...?
STOMP
ずん
IF YOU DON'T, I'LL NEVER BELIEVE YOU'VE STARTED FALLING FOR ME !!
STOMP
ずん
STOMP
ずん
STOMP
ずん...
WHISPER WHISPER

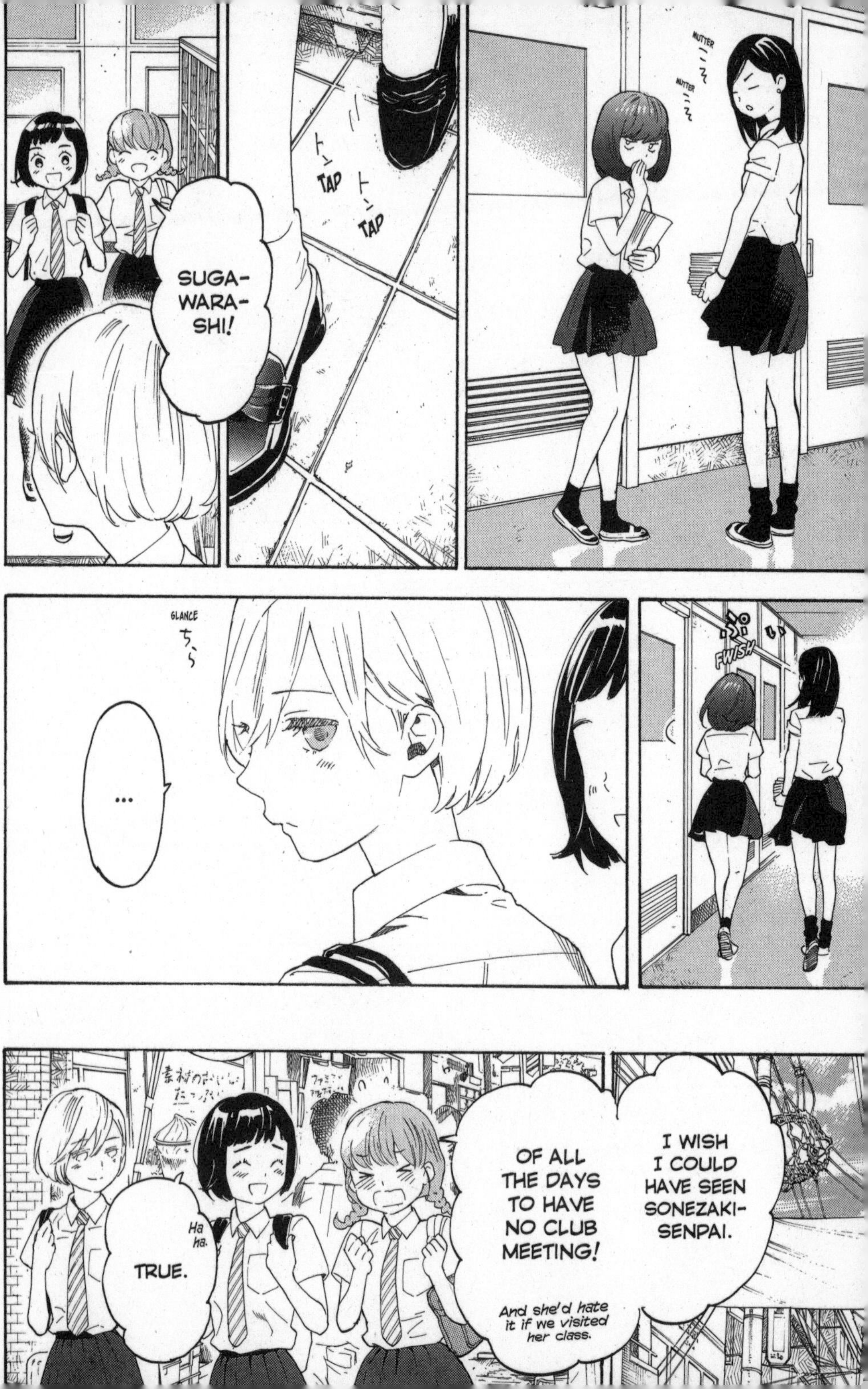
MUTTER
MUTTER
TAP
TAP
SUGA-WARA-SHI!
FWISH
GLANCE
ちら
...
I WISH I COULD HAVE SEEN SONEZAKI-SENPAI.
OF ALL THE DAYS TO HAVE NO CLUB MEETING!
And she'd hate it if we visited her class.
Ha ha.
TRUE.

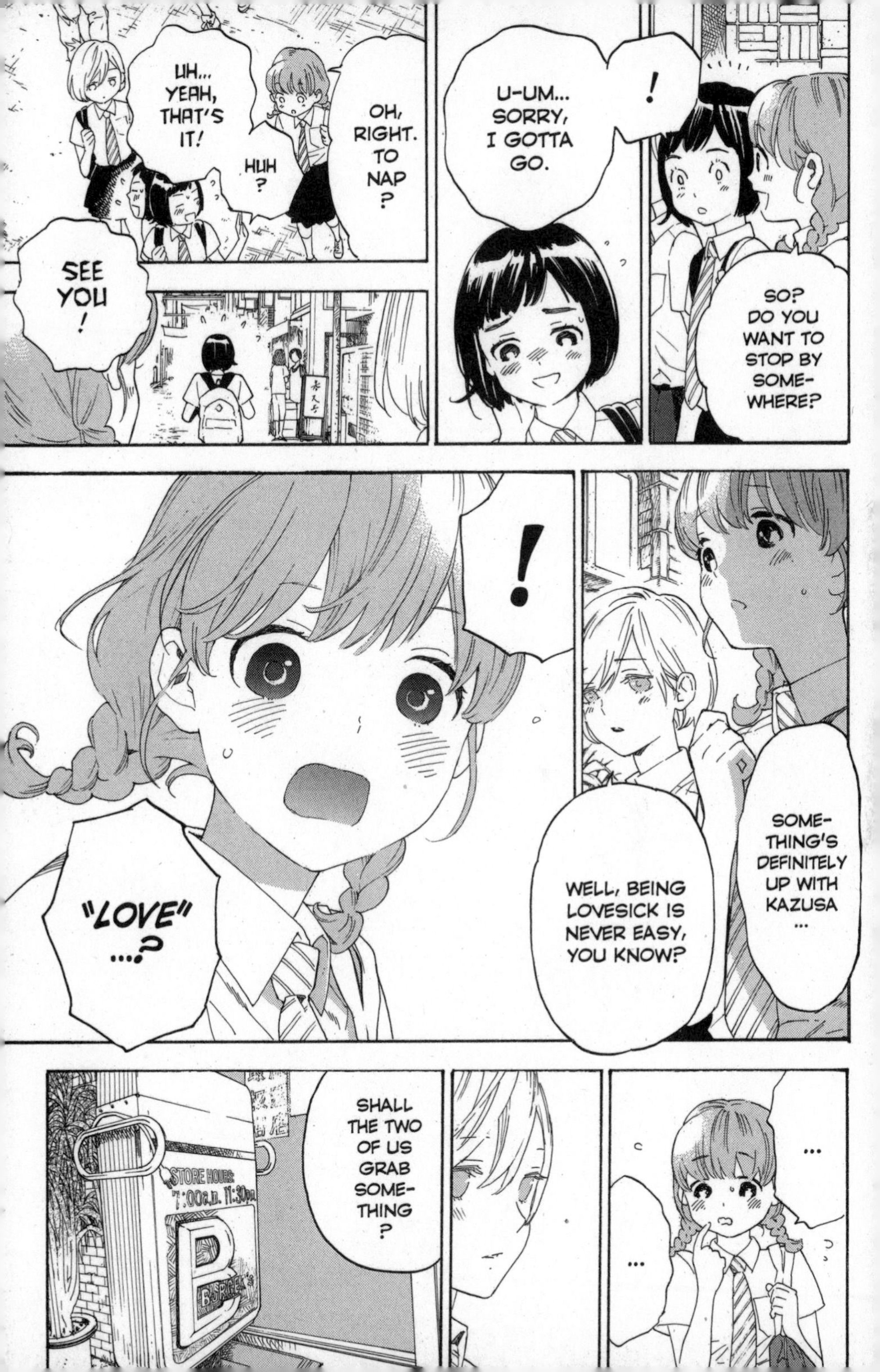
SO? DO YOU WANT TO STOP BY SOME-WHERE?
!
U-UM... SORRY, I GOTTA GO.
OH, RIGHT. TO NAP?
HUH?
UH... YEAH, THAT'S IT!
SEE YOU!
SOME-THING'S DEFINITELY UP WITH KAZUSA...
WELL, BEING LOVESICK IS NEVER EASY, YOU KNOW?
!
"LOVE" ...?
...
...
SHALL THE TWO OF US GRAB SOME-THING?
STORE HOURS:

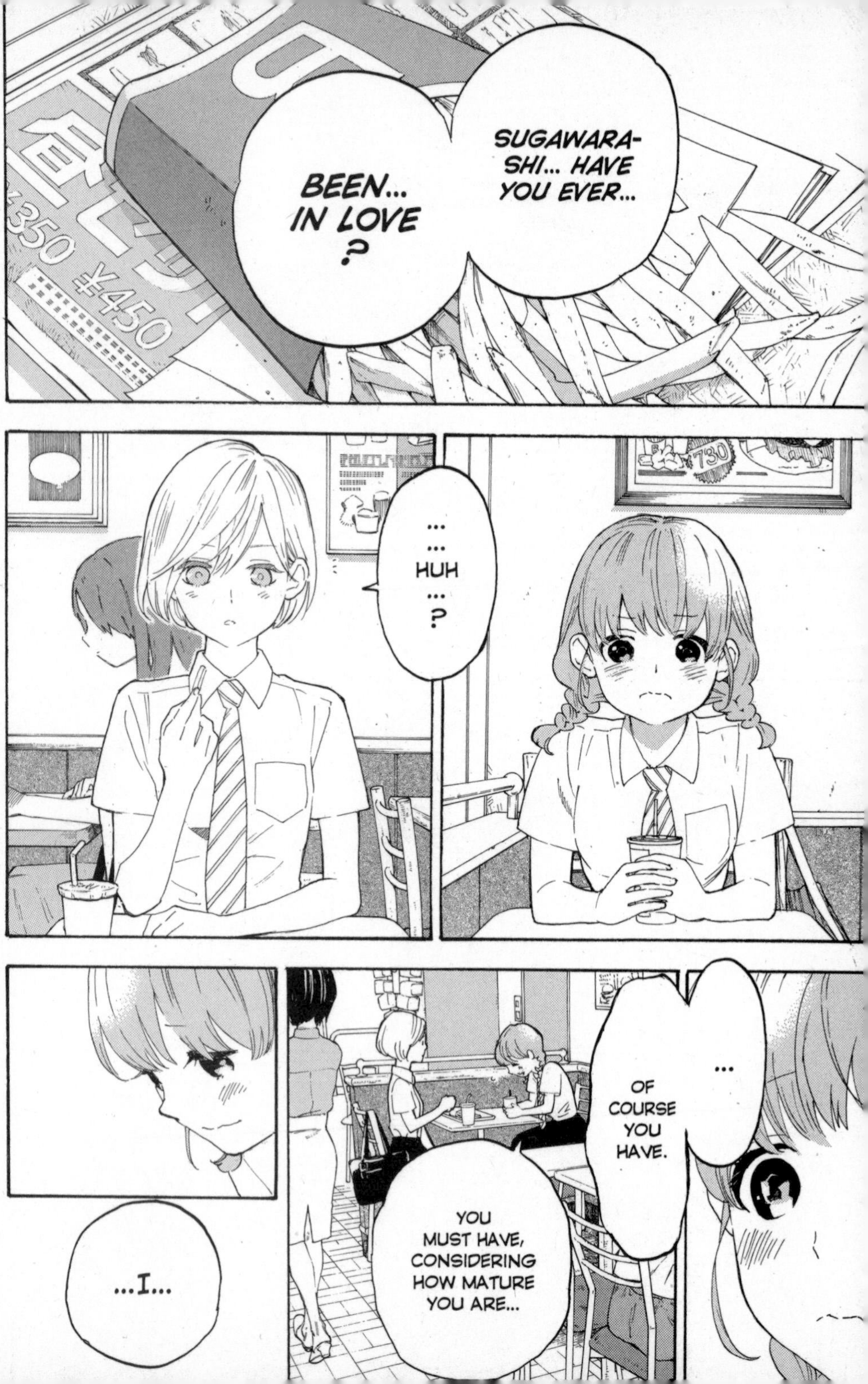
SUGAWARA-SHI... HAVE YOU EVER...
BEEN... IN LOVE ?
... ... HUH ... ?
... OF COURSE YOU HAVE.
YOU MUST HAVE, CONSIDERING HOW MATURE YOU ARE...
...I...

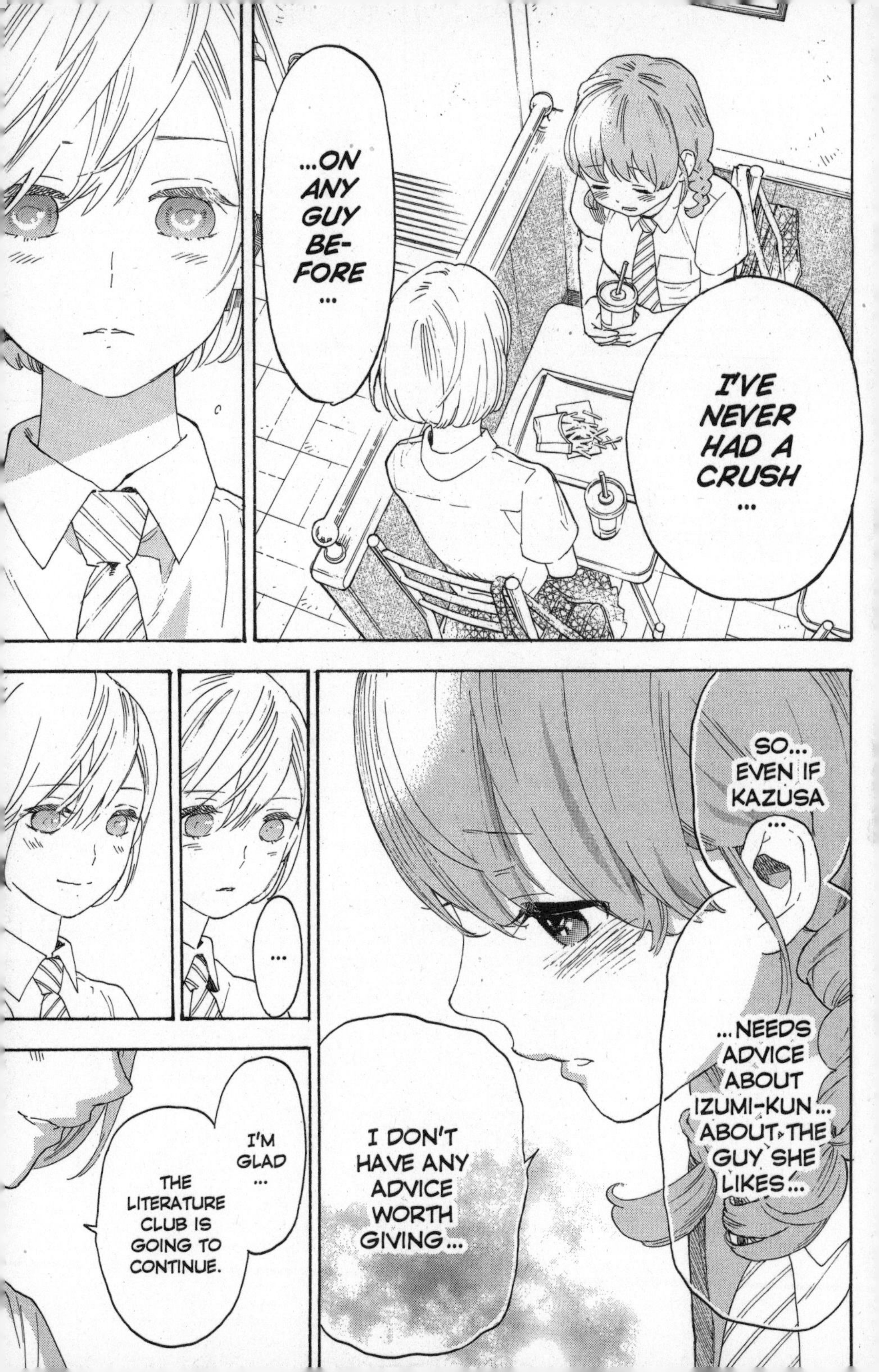
I'VE NEVER HAD A CRUSH...
...ON ANY GUY BE-FORE...
SO... EVEN IF KAZUSA...
...NEEDS ADVICE ABOUT IZUMI-KUN... ABOUT THE GUY SHE LIKES...
I DON'T HAVE ANY ADVICE WORTH GIVING...
...
I'M GLAD...
THE LITERATURE CLUB IS GOING TO CONTINUE.

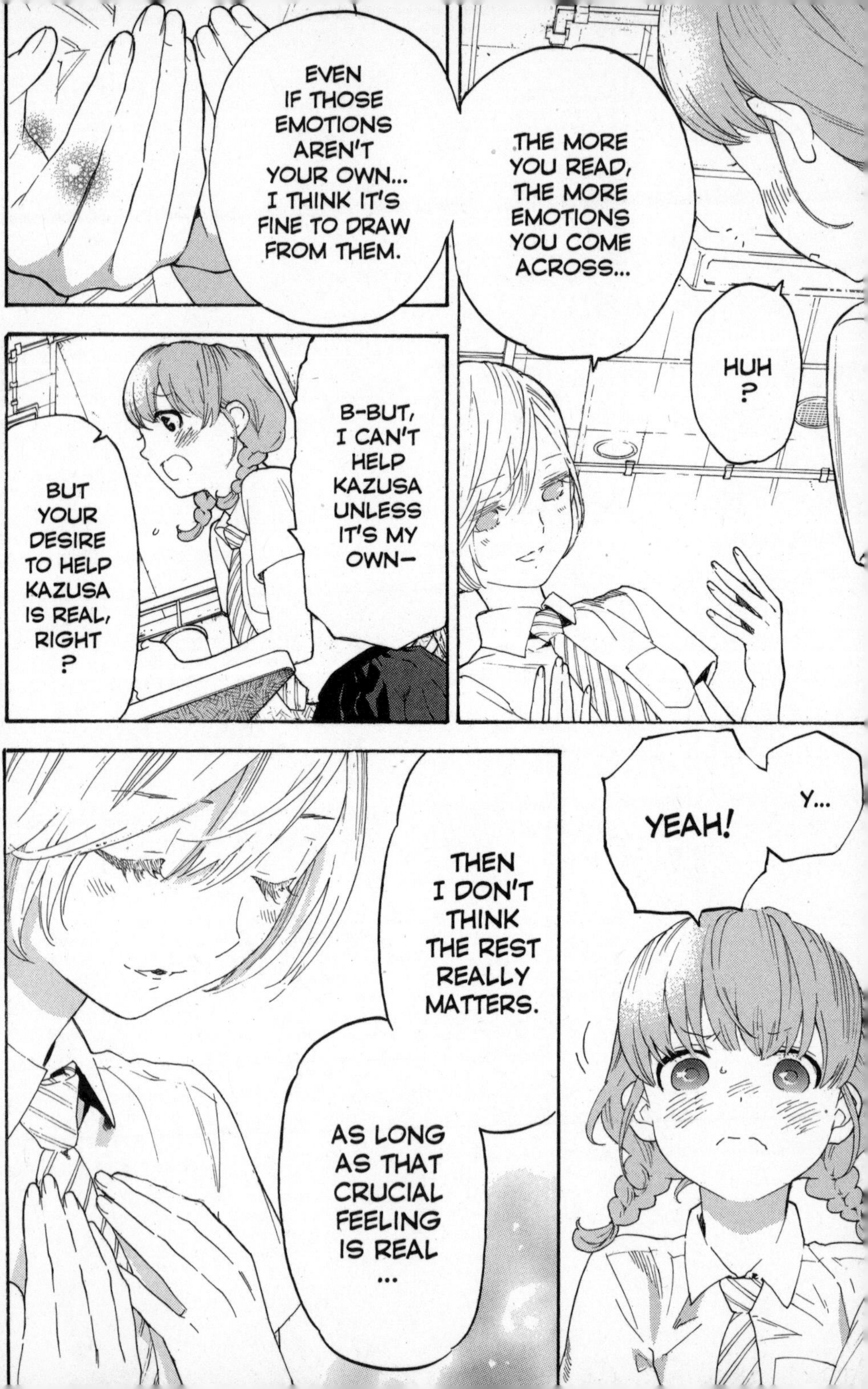
THE MORE YOU READ, THE MORE EMOTIONS YOU COME ACROSS...
EVEN IF THOSE EMOTIONS AREN'T YOUR OWN... I THINK IT'S FINE TO DRAW FROM THEM.
HUH?
B-BUT, I CAN'T HELP KAZUSA UNLESS IT'S MY OWN—
BUT YOUR DESIRE TO HELP KAZUSA IS REAL, RIGHT?
Y... YEAH!
THEN I DON'T THINK THE REST REALLY MATTERS.
AS LONG AS THAT CRUCIAL FEELING IS REAL...

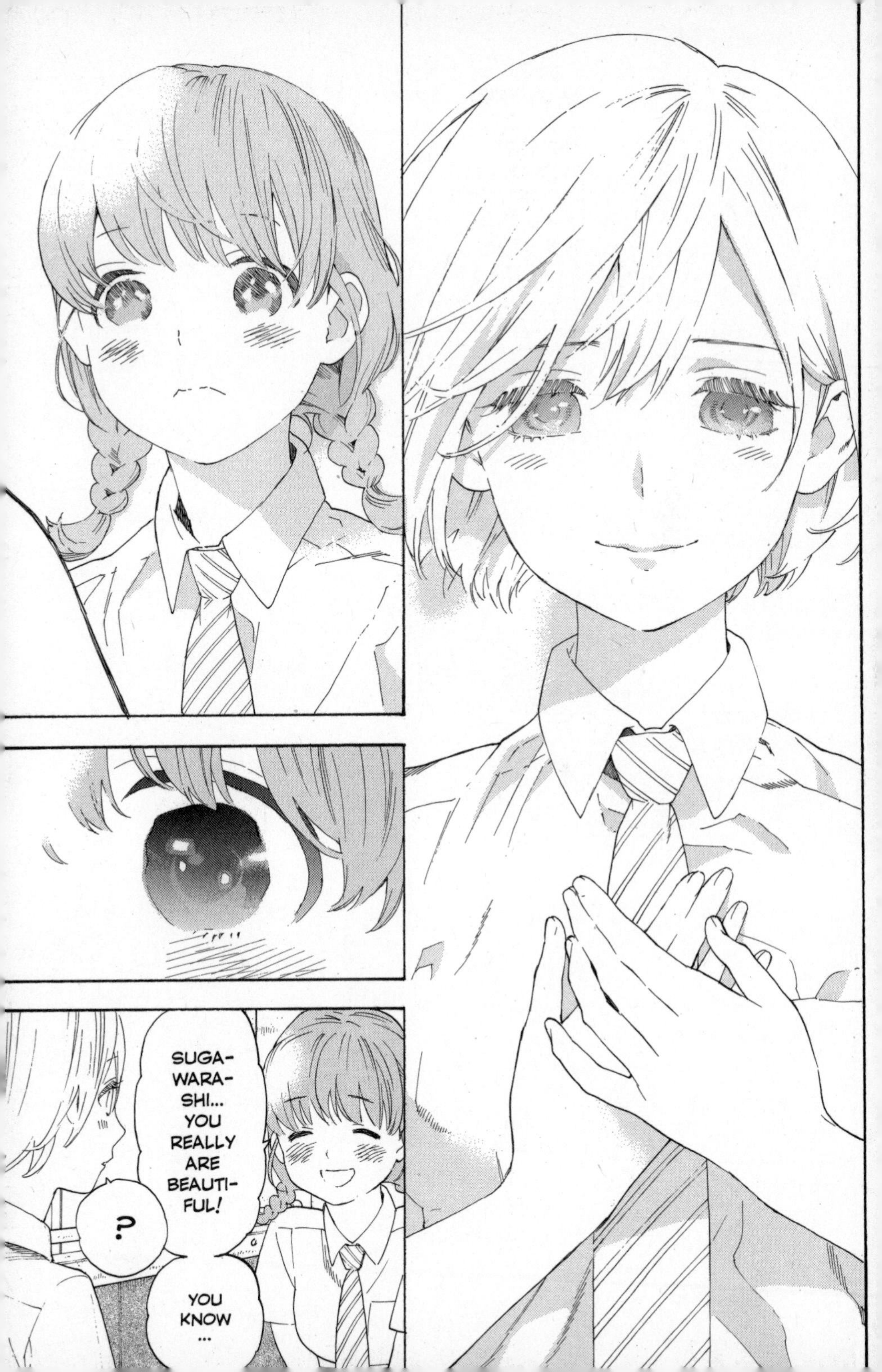
SUGA-WARA-SHI... YOU REALLY ARE BEAUTI-FUL!
?
YOU KNOW ...

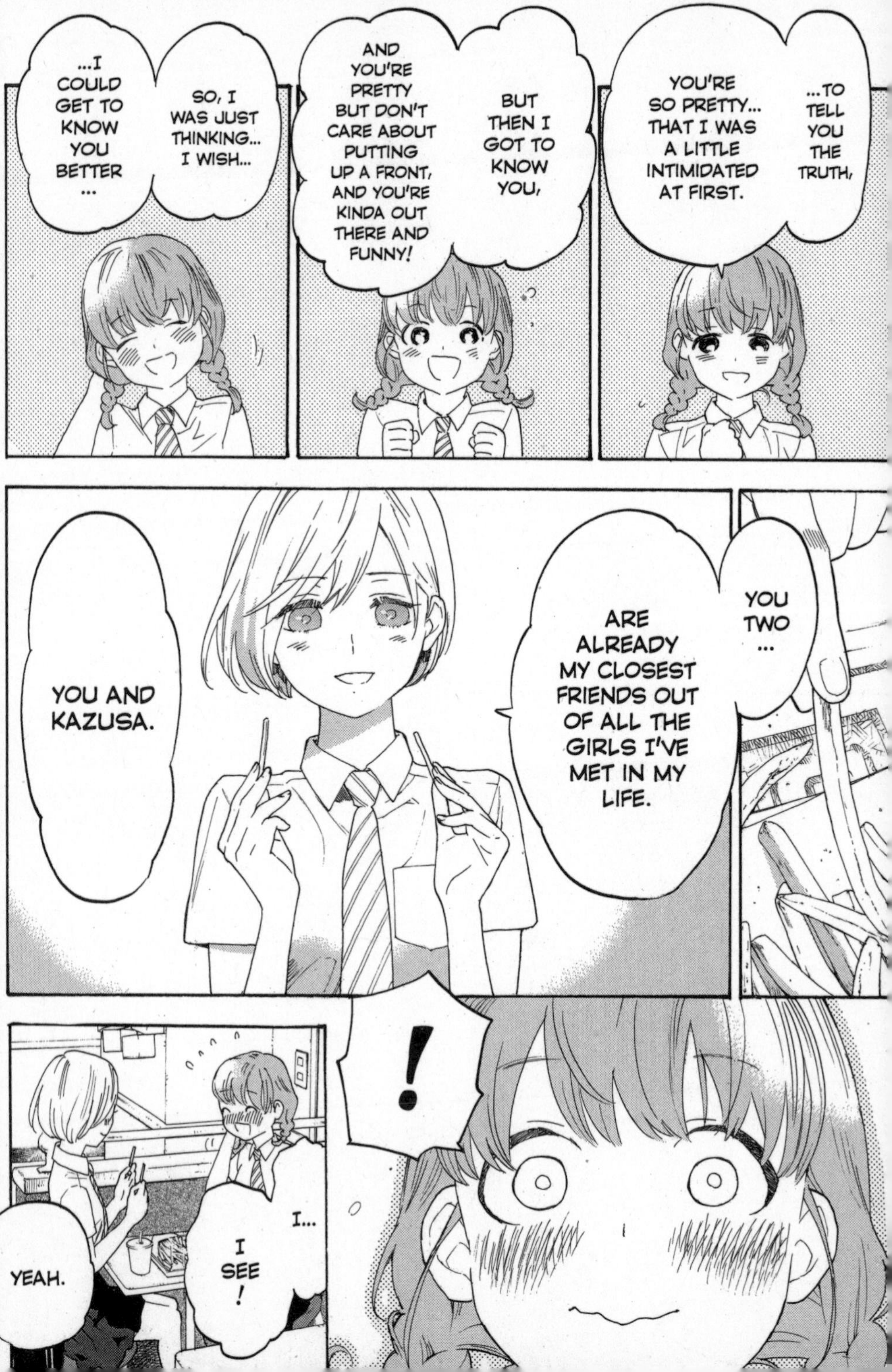
...TO TELL YOU THE TRUTH,
YOU'RE SO PRETTY... THAT I WAS A LITTLE INTIMIDATED AT FIRST.
BUT THEN I GOT TO KNOW YOU,
AND YOU'RE PRETTY BUT DON'T CARE ABOUT PUTTING UP A FRONT, AND YOU'RE KINDA OUT THERE AND FUNNY!
SO, I WAS JUST THINKING... I WISH...
...I COULD GET TO KNOW YOU BETTER...
YOU TWO...
ARE ALREADY MY CLOSEST FRIENDS OUT OF ALL THE GIRLS I'VE MET IN MY LIFE.
YOU AND KAZUSA.
!
I...
I SEE!
YEAH.

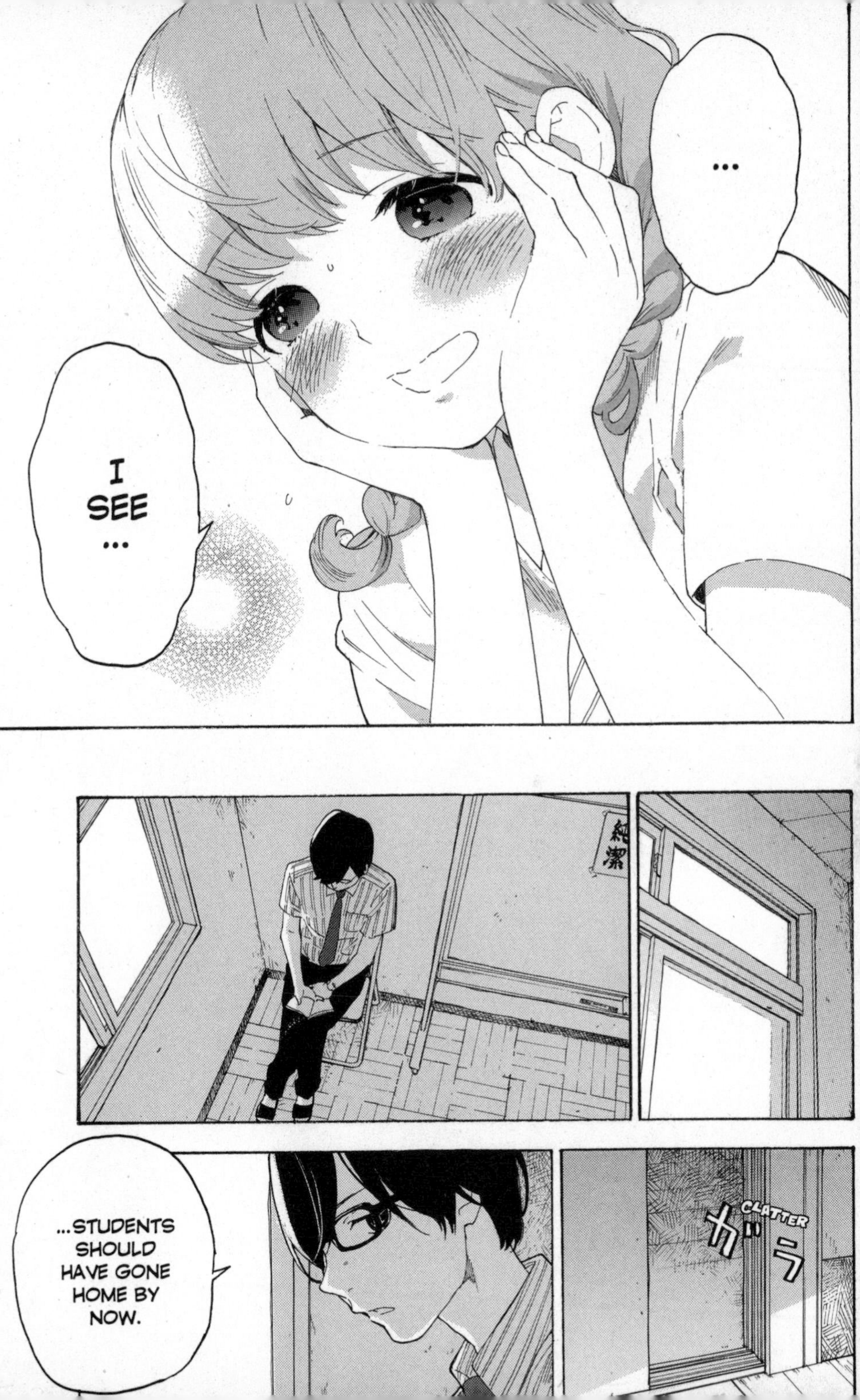
...
I SEE ...
CLATTER
...STUDENTS SHOULD HAVE GONE HOME BY NOW.

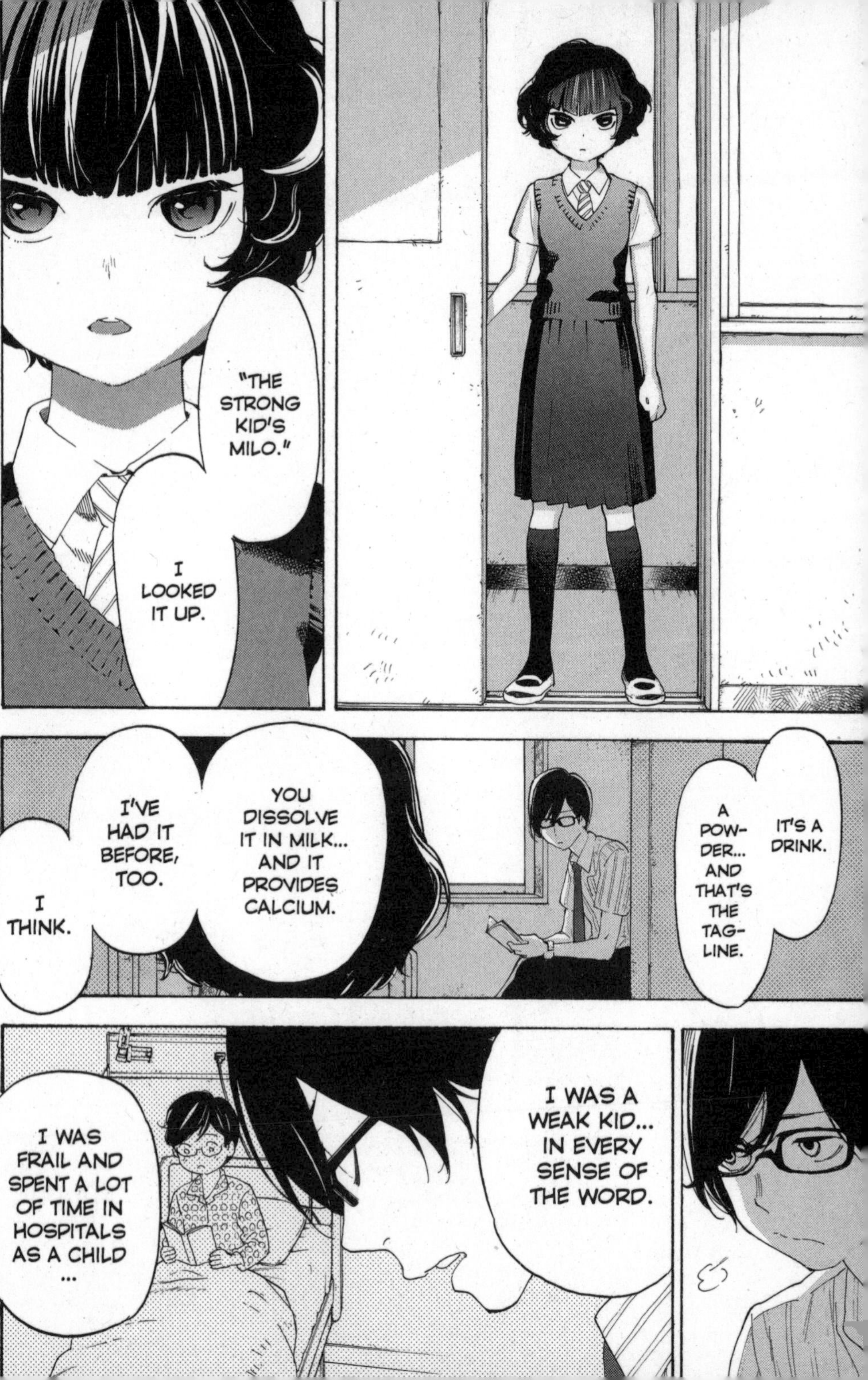
"THE STRONG KID'S MILO."
I LOOKED IT UP.
IT'S A DRINK.
A POWDER... AND THAT'S THE TAGLINE.
YOU DISSOLVE IT IN MILK... AND IT PROVIDES CALCIUM.
I'VE HAD IT BEFORE, TOO.
I THINK.
I WAS A WEAK KID... IN EVERY SENSE OF THE WORD.
I WAS FRAIL AND SPENT A LOT OF TIME IN HOSPITALS AS A CHILD ...

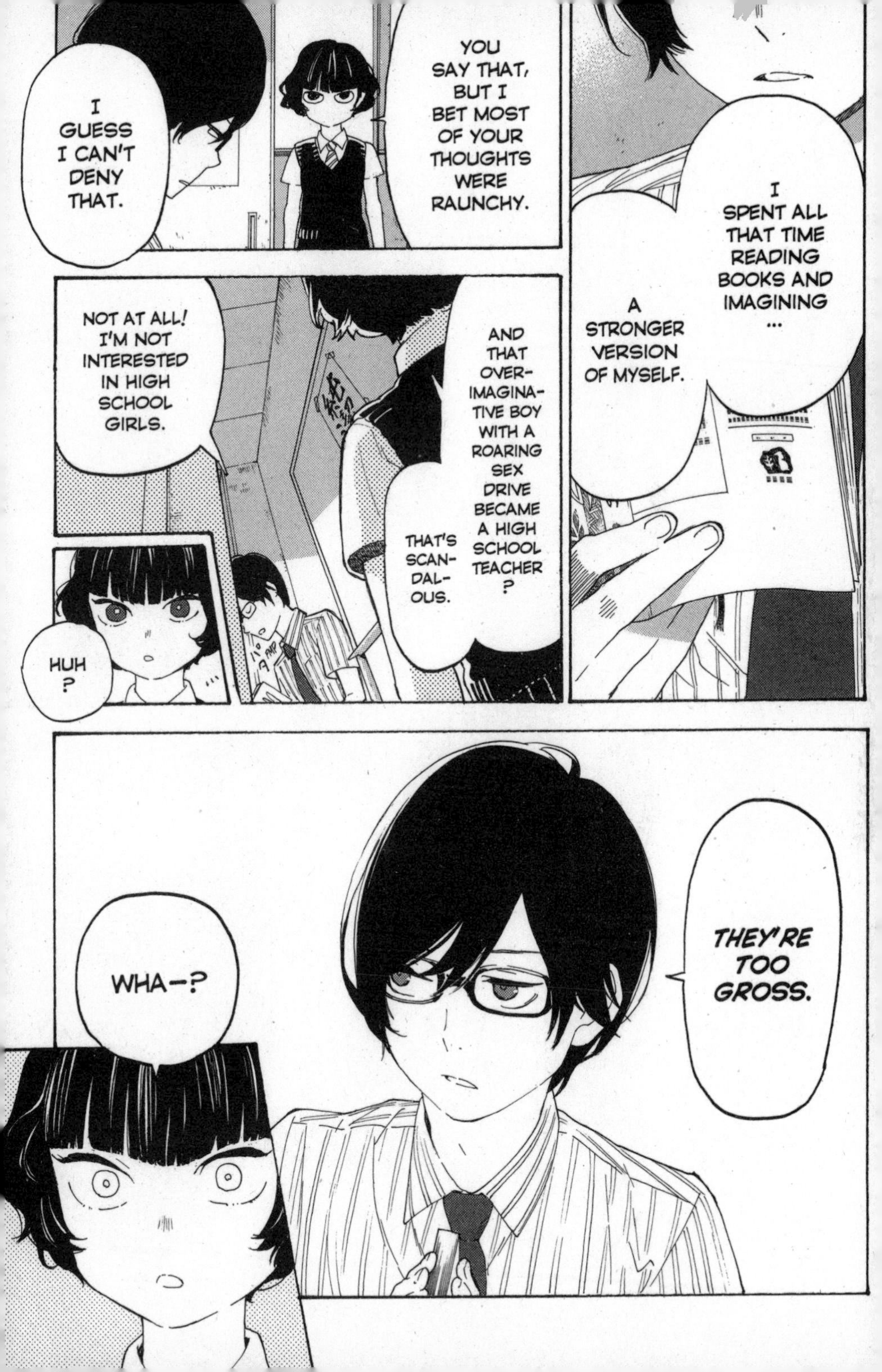
I SPENT ALL THAT TIME READING BOOKS AND IMAGINING ...
A STRONGER VERSION OF MYSELF.
YOU SAY THAT, BUT I BET MOST OF YOUR THOUGHTS WERE RAUNCHY.
I GUESS I CAN'T DENY THAT.
AND THAT OVER-IMAGINA-TIVE BOY WITH A ROARING SEX DRIVE BECAME A HIGH SCHOOL TEACHER?
THAT'S SCAN-DAL-OUS.
NOT AT ALL! I'M NOT INTERESTED IN HIGH SCHOOL GIRLS.
HUH?
THEY'RE TOO GROSS.
WHA-?

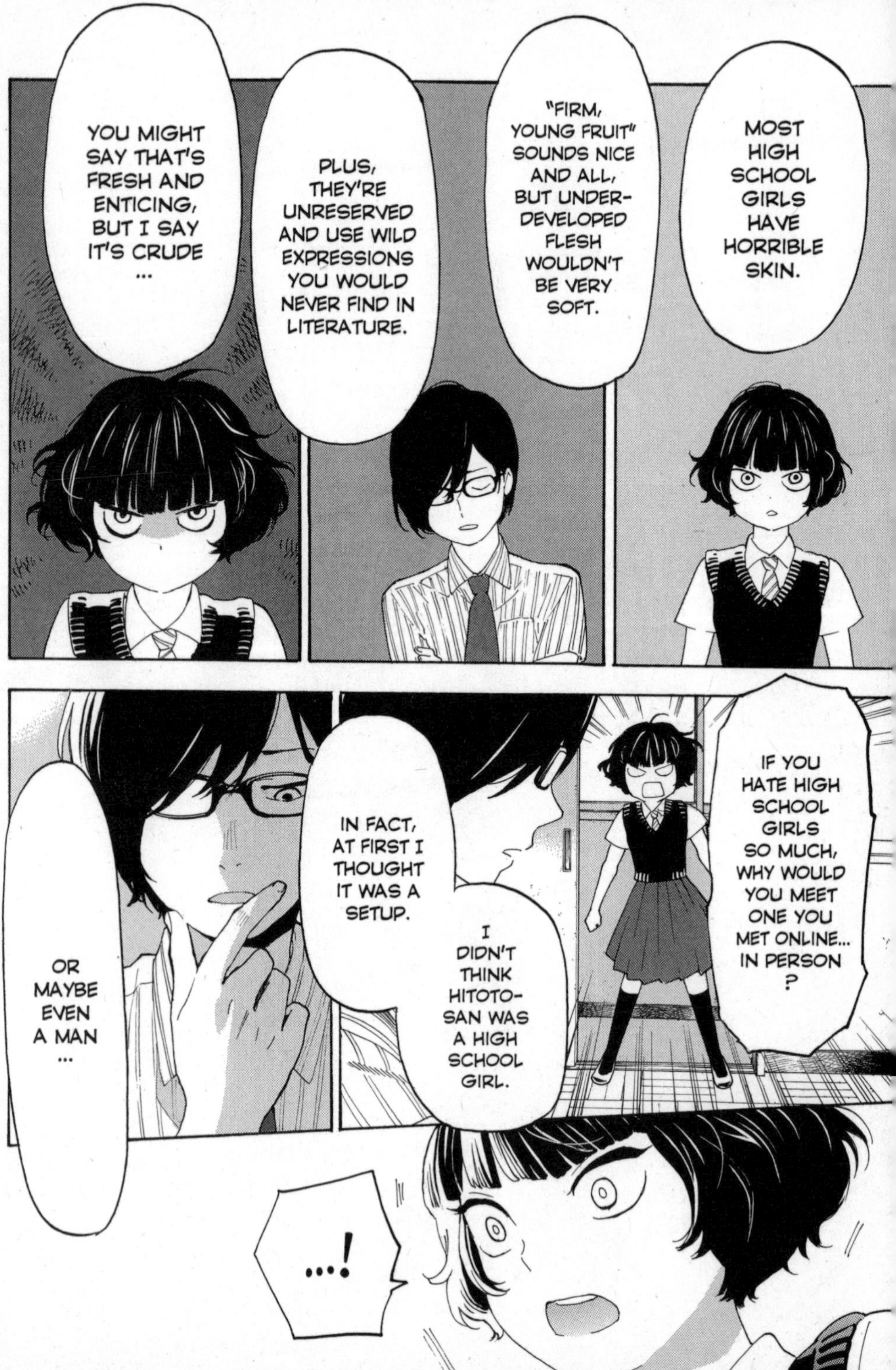
MOST HIGH SCHOOL GIRLS HAVE HORRIBLE SKIN.
"FIRM, YOUNG FRUIT" SOUNDS NICE AND ALL, BUT UNDER-DEVELOPED FLESH WOULDN'T BE VERY SOFT.
PLUS, THEY'RE UNRESERVED AND USE WILD EXPRESSIONS YOU WOULD NEVER FIND IN LITERATURE.
YOU MIGHT SAY THAT'S FRESH AND ENTICING, BUT I SAY IT'S CRUDE ...
IF YOU HATE HIGH SCHOOL GIRLS SO MUCH, WHY WOULD YOU MEET ONE YOU MET ONLINE... IN PERSON ?
I DIDN'T THINK HITOTO-SAN WAS A HIGH SCHOOL GIRL.
IN FACT, AT FIRST I THOUGHT IT WAS A SETUP.
OR MAYBE EVEN A MAN ...
...!

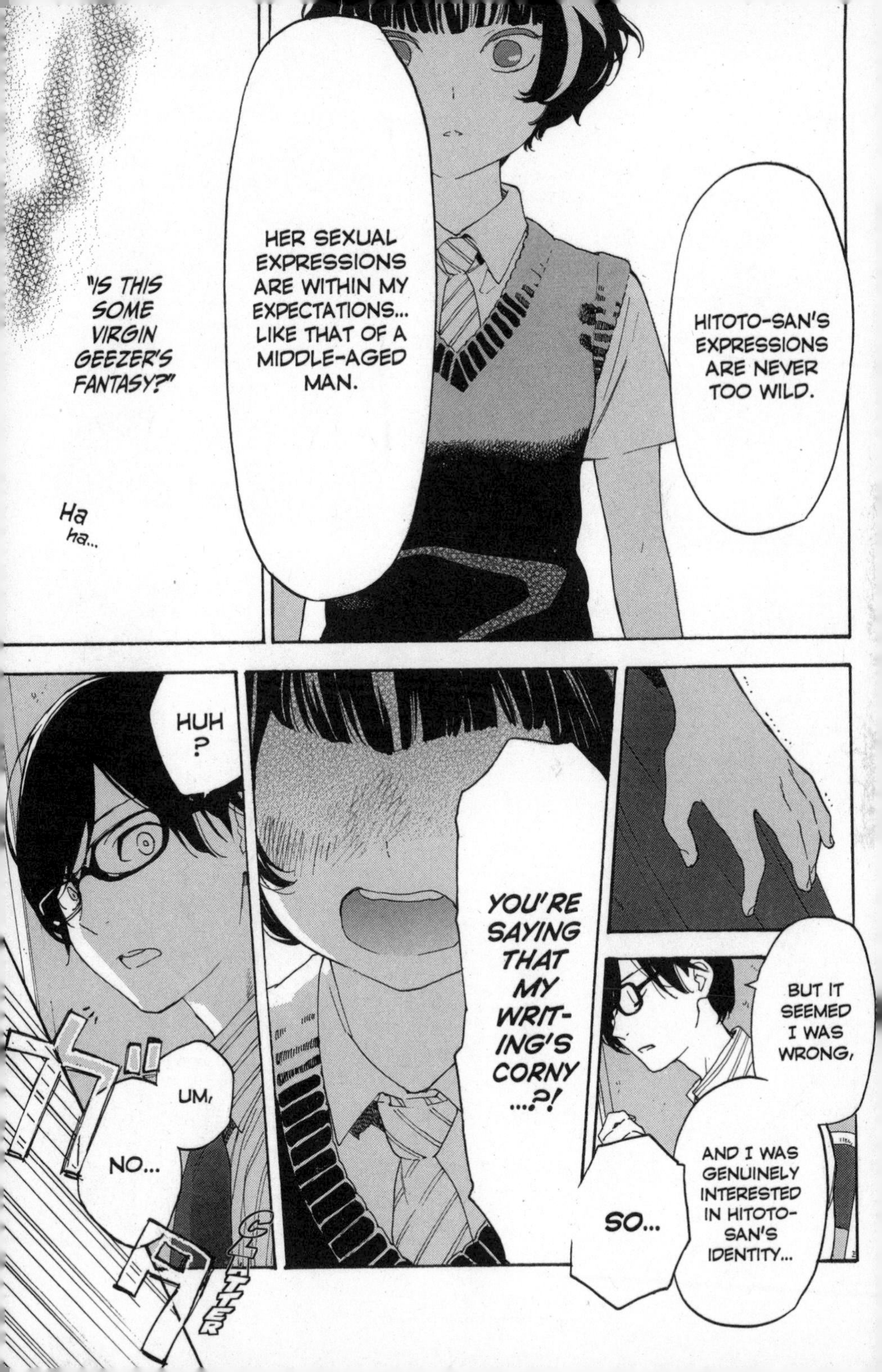
HITOTO-SAN'S EXPRESSIONS ARE NEVER TOO WILD.
HER SEXUAL EXPRESSIONS ARE WITHIN MY EXPECTATIONS... LIKE THAT OF A MIDDLE-AGED MAN.
"IS THIS SOME VIRGIN GEEZER'S FANTASY?"
Ha ha...
BUT IT SEEMED I WAS WRONG,
AND I WAS GENUINELY INTERESTED IN HITOTO-SAN'S IDENTITY...
SO...
YOU'RE SAYING THAT MY WRIT-ING'S CORNY ...?!
HUH ?
UM,
NO...
CLATTER

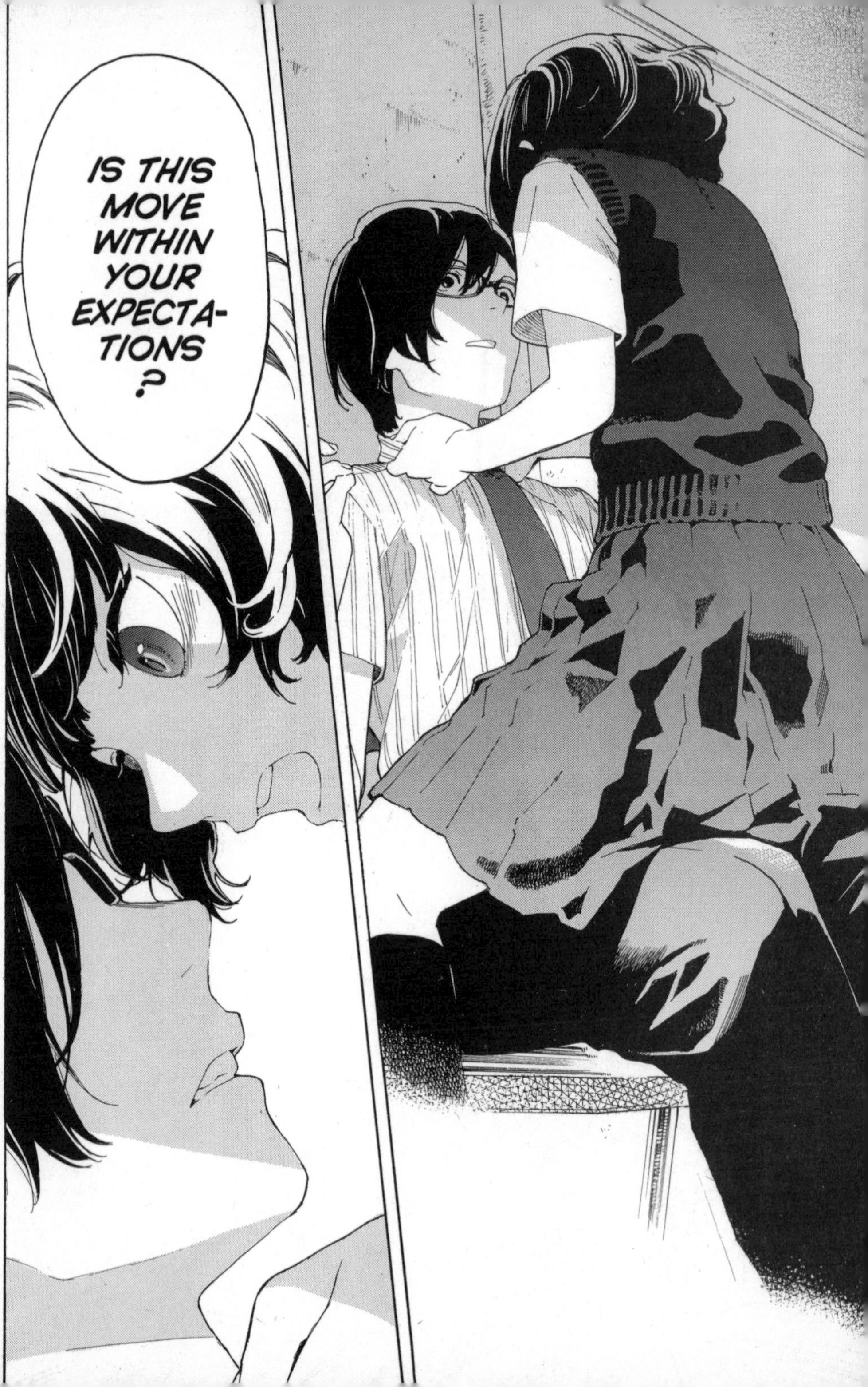
IS THIS MOVE WITHIN YOUR EXPECTA-TIONS?

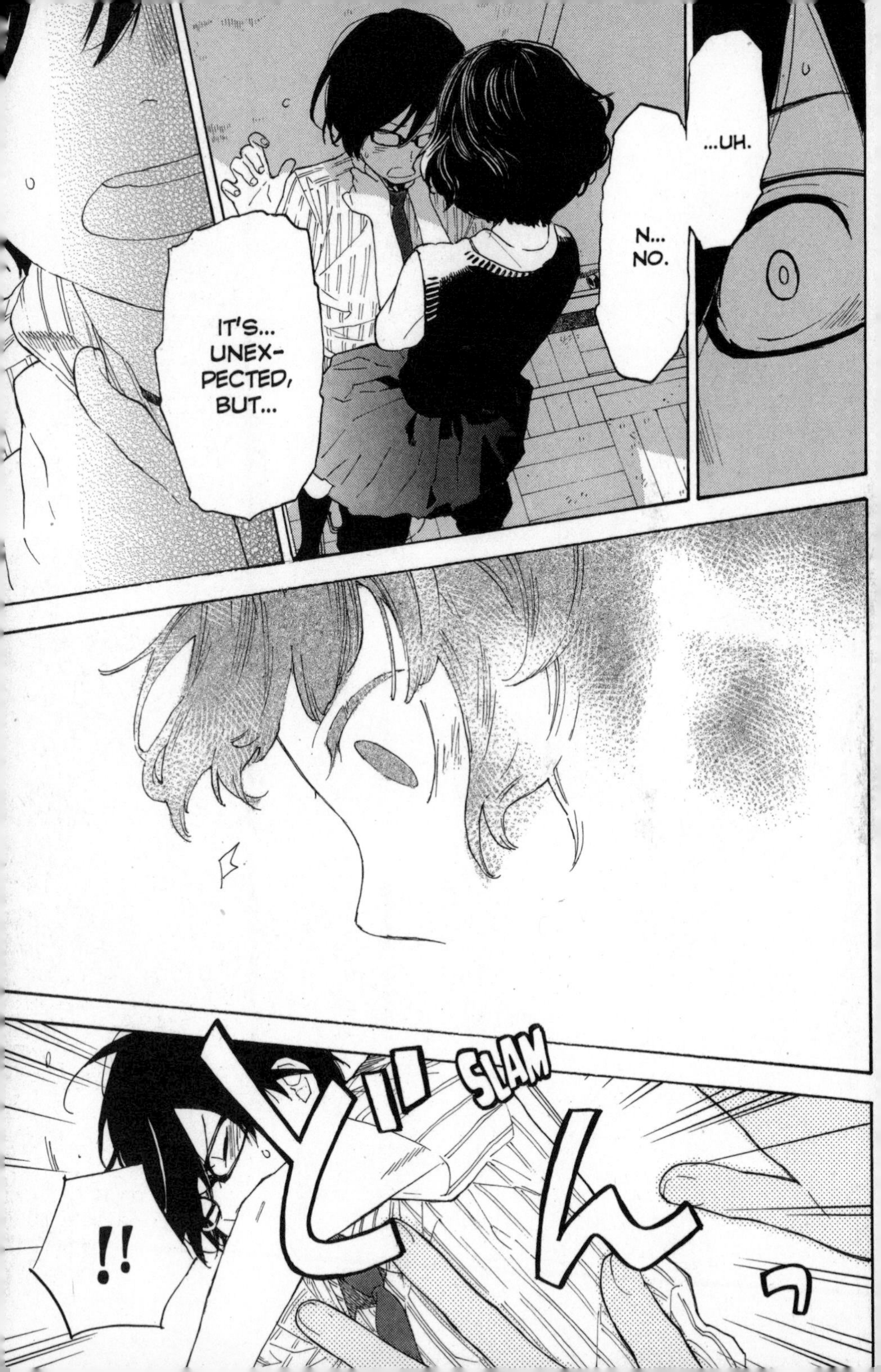
...UH.
N... NO.
IT'S... UNEX-PECTED, BUT...
どんっ
SLAM
!!

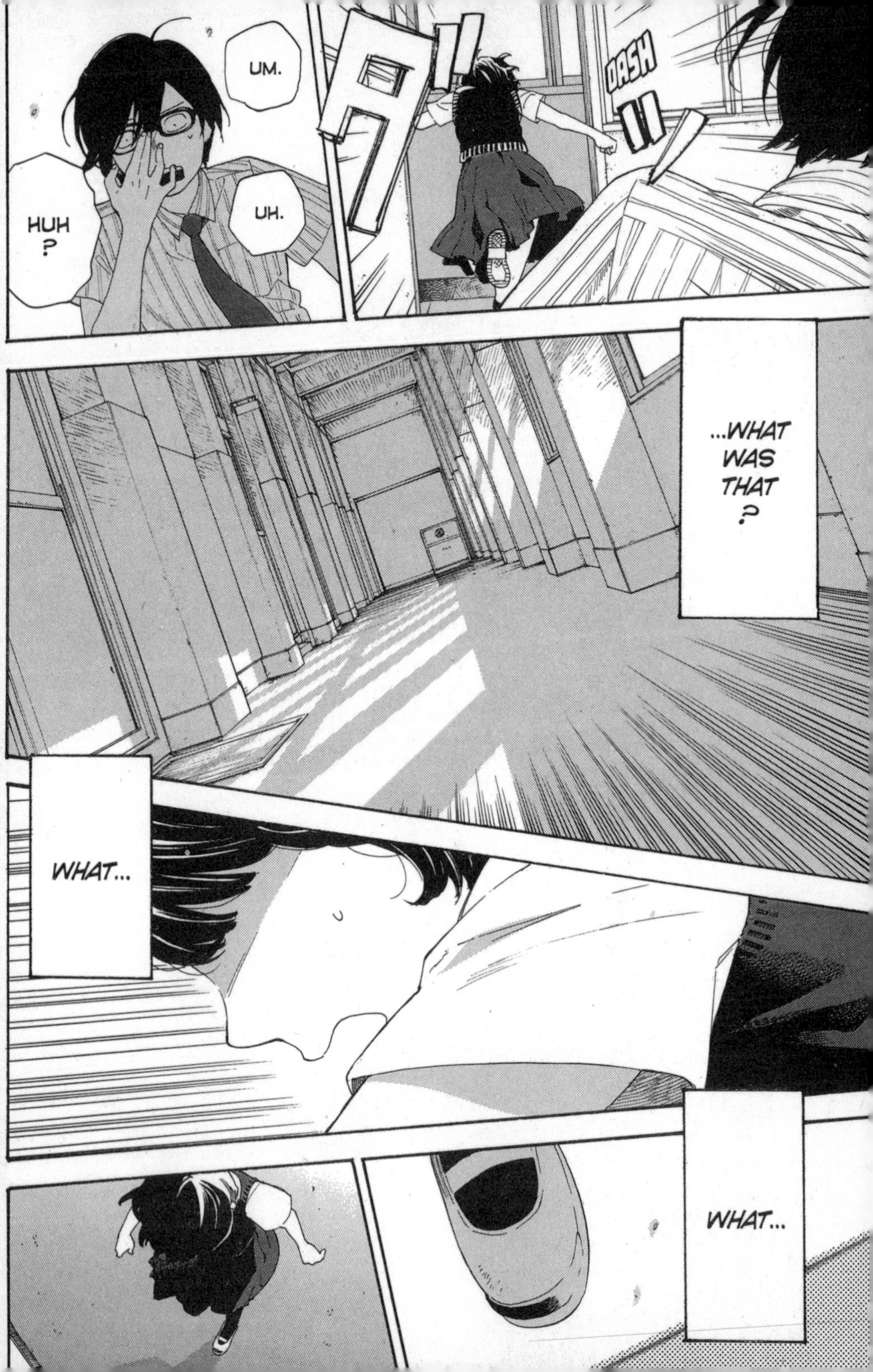
DASH
UM.
UH.
HUH ?
...WHAT WAS THAT ?
WHAT...
WHAT...

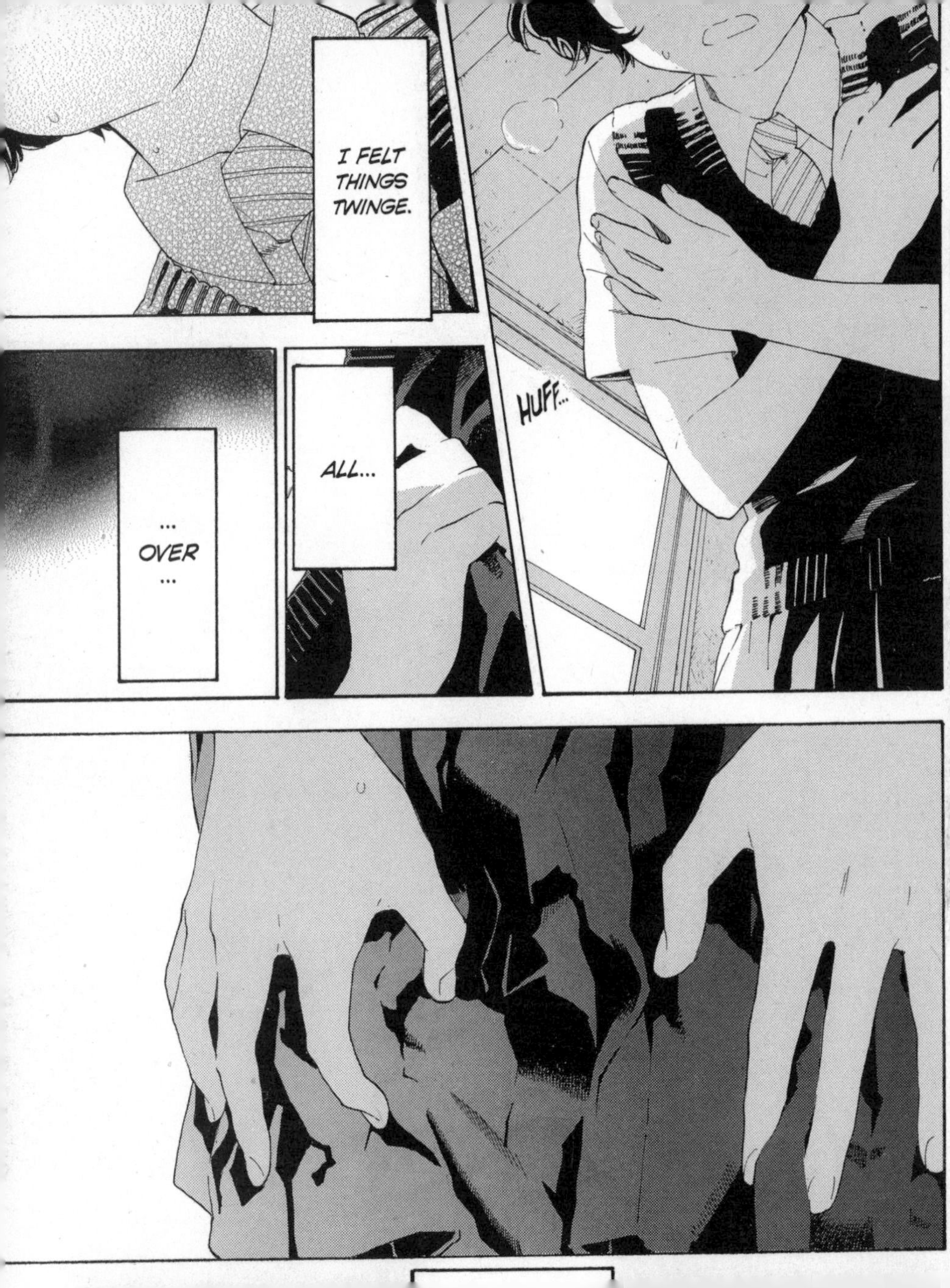
HUFF...
I FELT THINGS TWINGE.
ALL...
... OVER ...

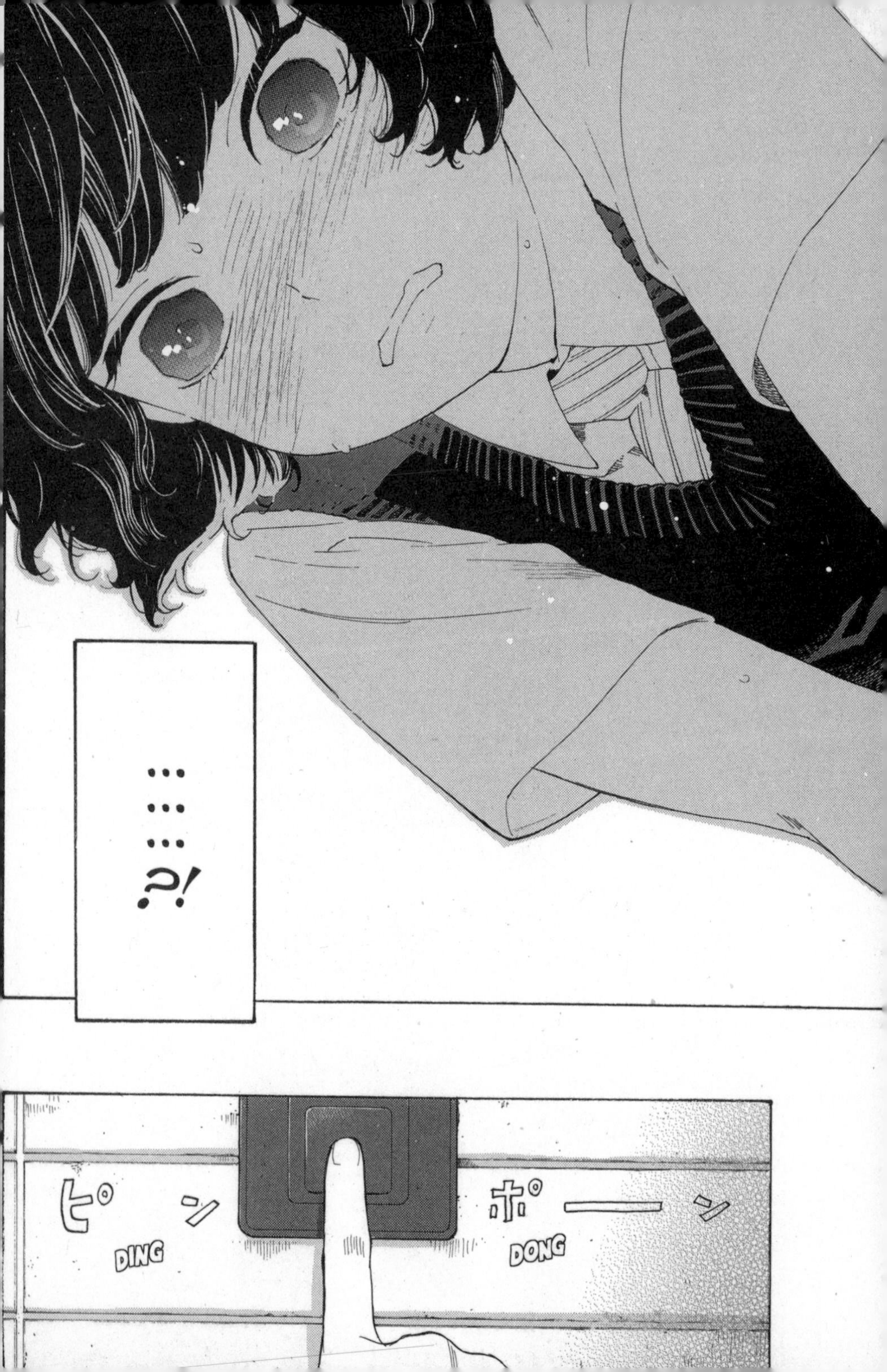
……?!
ピン
DING
ポーーン
DONG

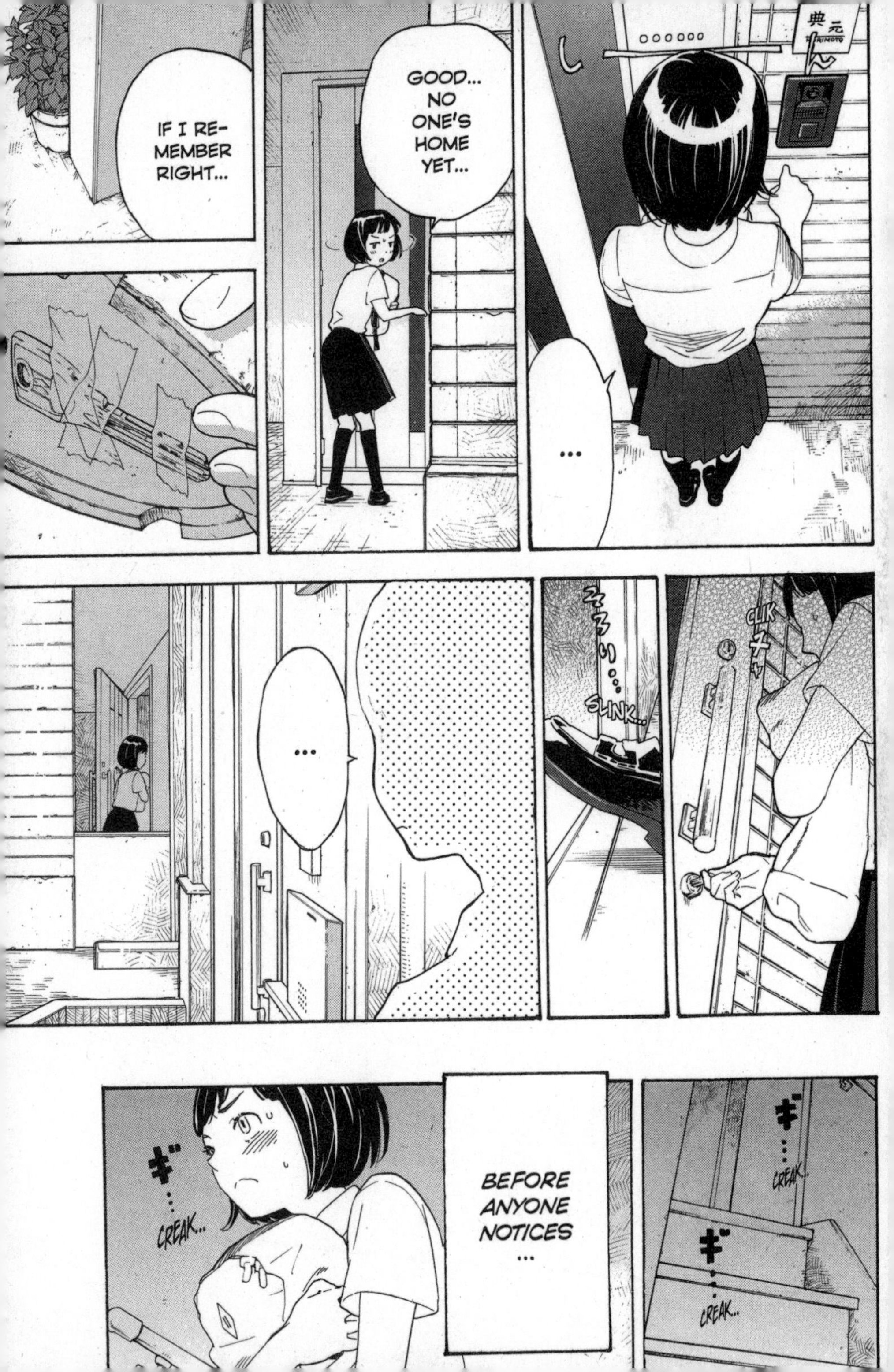
...
GOOD... NO ONE'S HOME YET...
IF I RE-MEMBER RIGHT...
CLIK
SLINK...
...
CREAK...
CREAK...
BEFORE ANYONE NOTICES ...
CREAK...

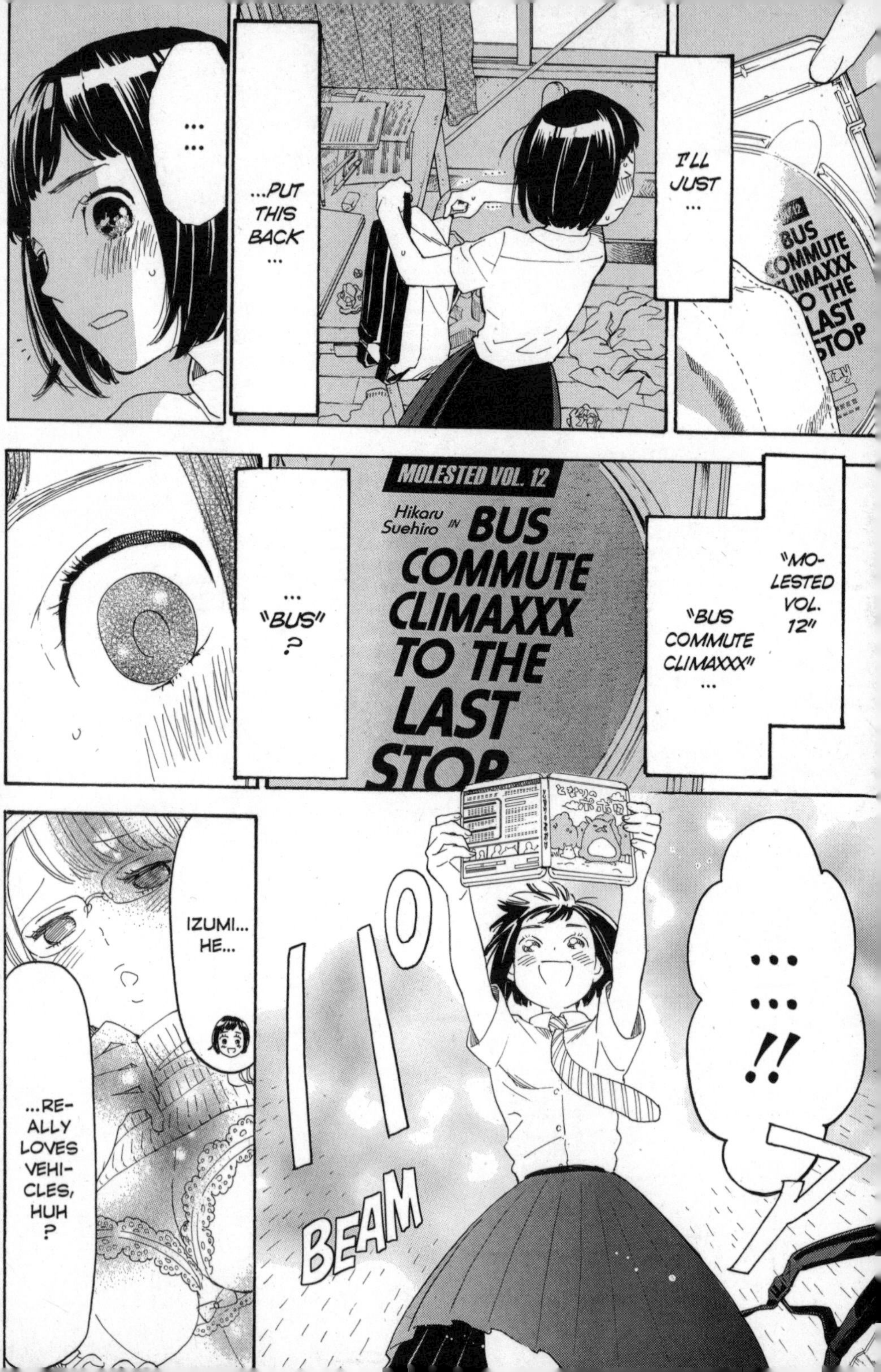

I'LL JUST ...
BUS COMMUTE CLIMAXXX TO THE LAST STOP
...PUT THIS BACK ...
... ...
"MO-LESTED VOL. 12"
"BUS COMMUTE CLIMAXXX" ...
MOLESTED VOL. 12
Hikaru Suehiro IN BUS COMMUTE CLIMAXXX TO THE LAST STOP
... "BUS" ?
... ... !!
BEAM
IZUMI... HE...
...RE-ALLY LOVES VEHI-CLES, HUH ?

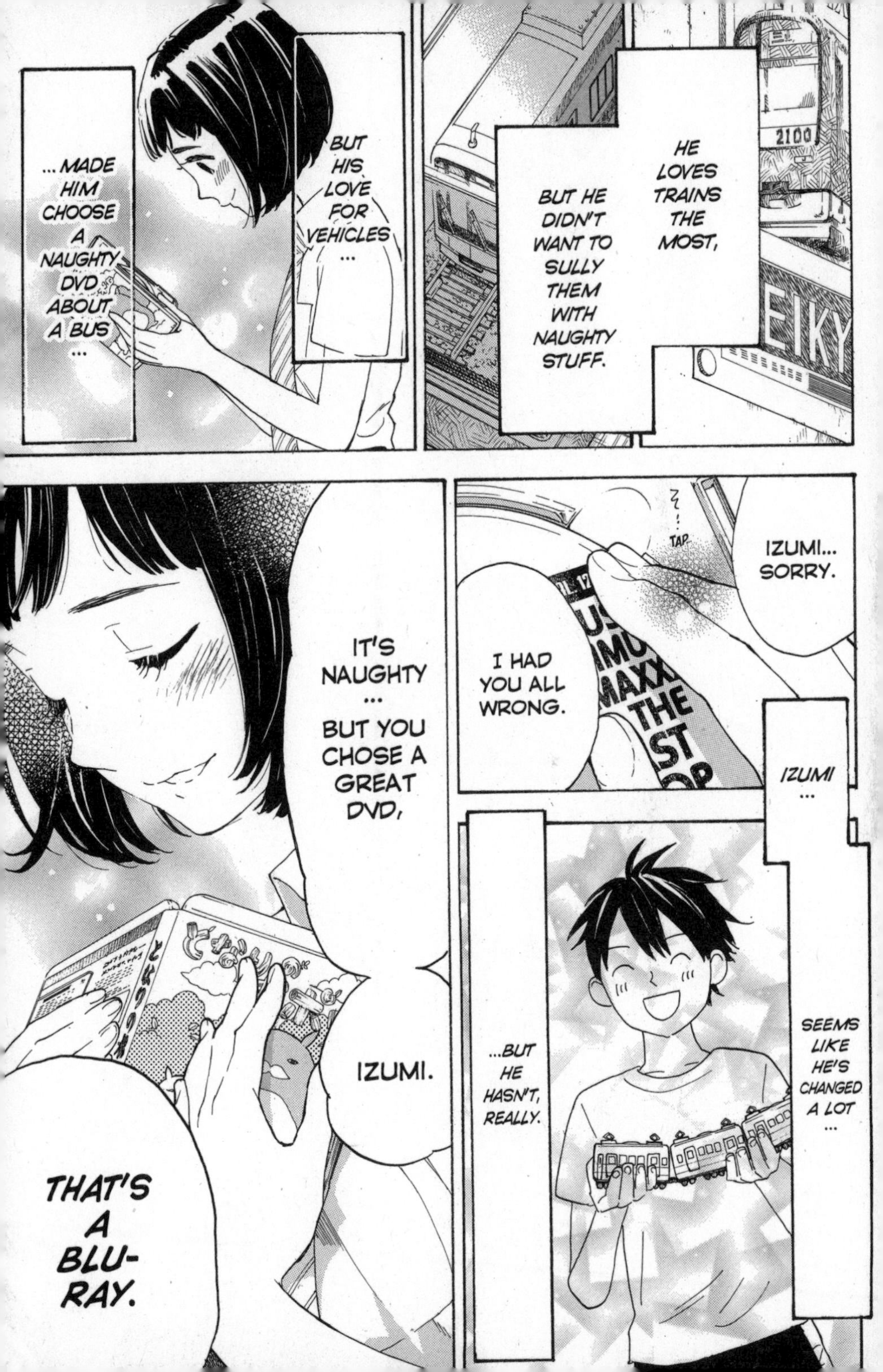
HE LOVES TRAINS THE MOST,
BUT HE DIDN'T WANT TO SULLY THEM WITH NAUGHTY STUFF.
BUT HIS LOVE FOR VEHICLES...
...MADE HIM CHOOSE A NAUGHTY DVD ABOUT A BUS...
TAP
IZUMI... SORRY.
I HAD YOU ALL WRONG.
IZUMI...
SEEMS LIKE HE'S CHANGED A LOT...
...BUT HE HASN'T, REALLY.
IT'S NAUGHTY... BUT YOU CHOSE A GREAT DVD,
IZUMI.
THAT'S A BLU-RAY.

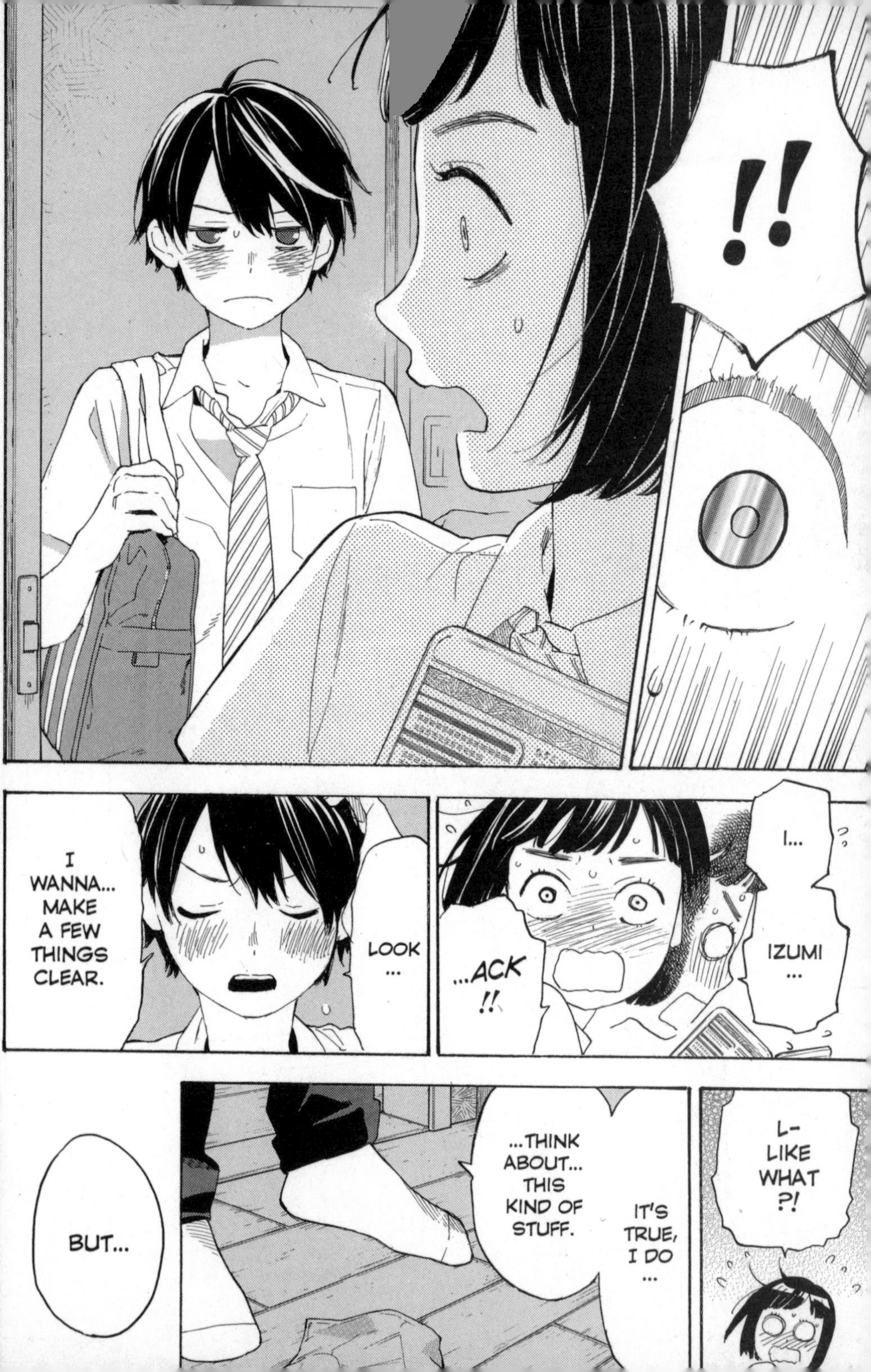
!!
I...
IZUMI ...
...ACK !!
LOOK ...
I WANNA... MAKE A FEW THINGS CLEAR.
L-LIKE WHAT ?!
IT'S TRUE, I DO ...
...THINK ABOUT... THIS KIND OF STUFF.
BUT...

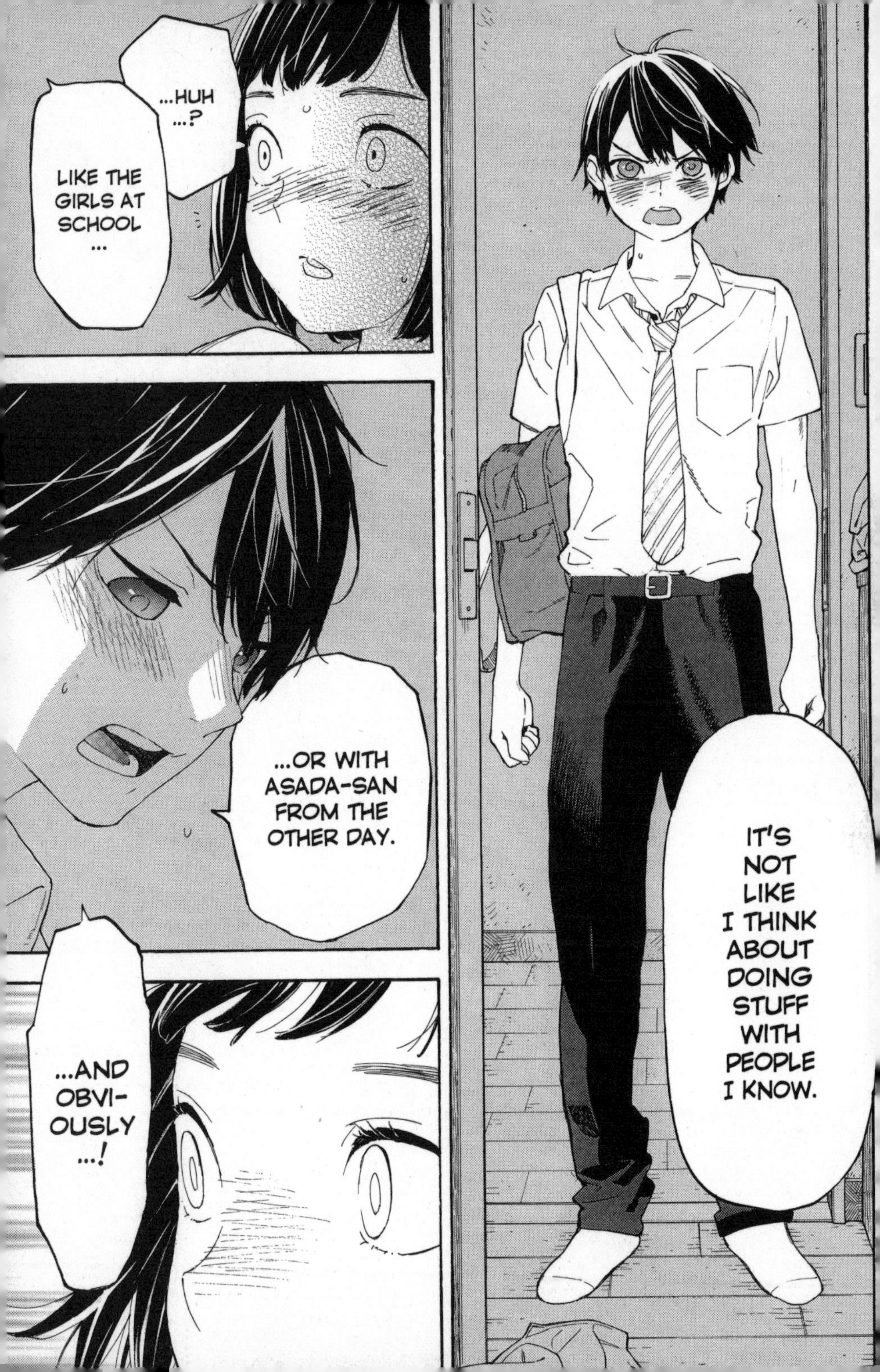
IT'S NOT LIKE I THINK ABOUT DOING STUFF WITH PEOPLE I KNOW.
...HUH ...?
LIKE THE GIRLS AT SCHOOL ...
...OR WITH ASADA-SAN FROM THE OTHER DAY.
...AND OBVI-OUSLY ...!

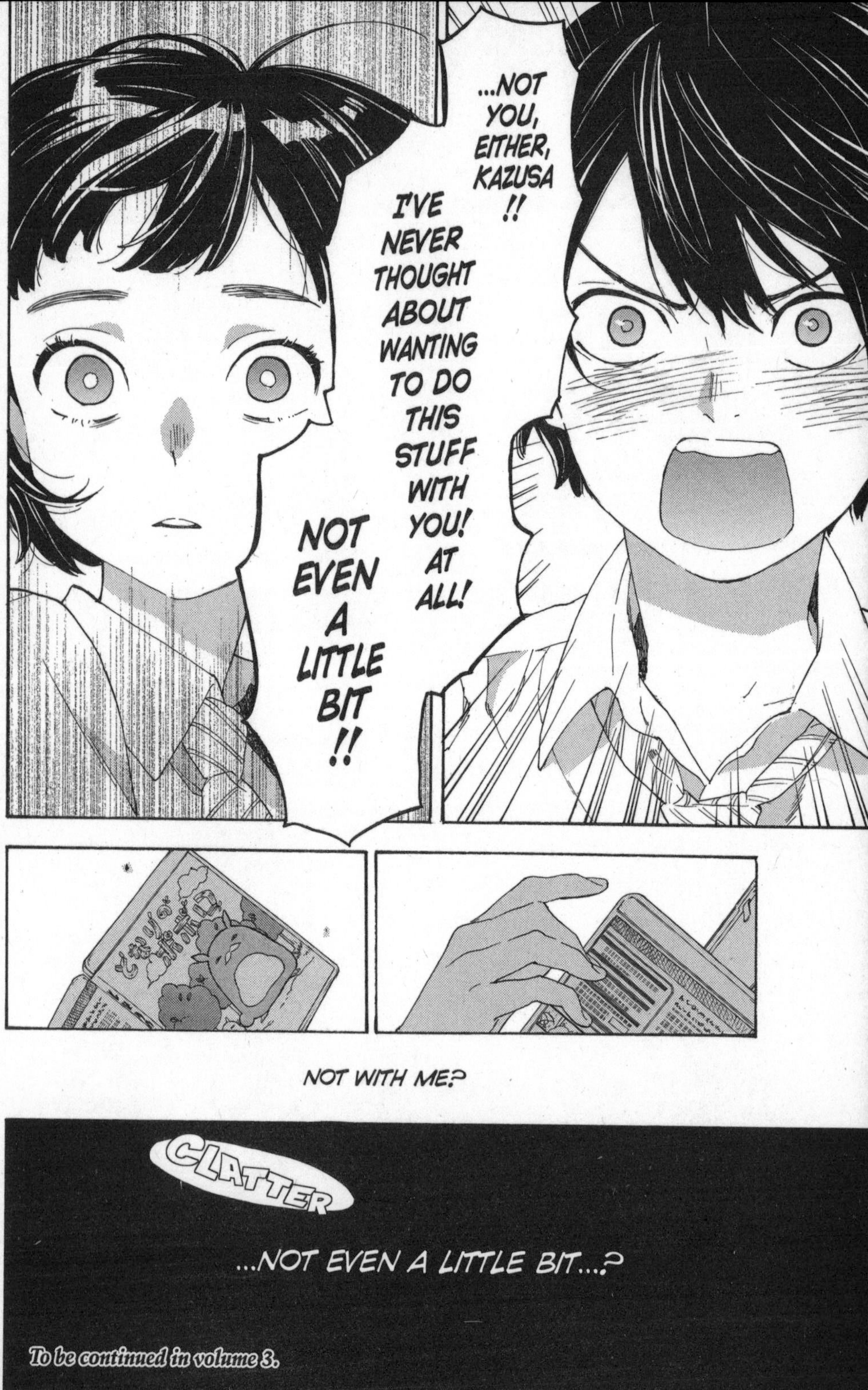
...NOT YOU, EITHER, KAZUSA!!
I'VE NEVER THOUGHT ABOUT WANTING TO DO THIS STUFF WITH YOU! AT ALL!
NOT EVEN A LITTLE BIT!!
NOT WITH ME?
CLATTER
...NOT EVEN A LITTLE BIT...?
To be continued in volume 3.

Next volume preview

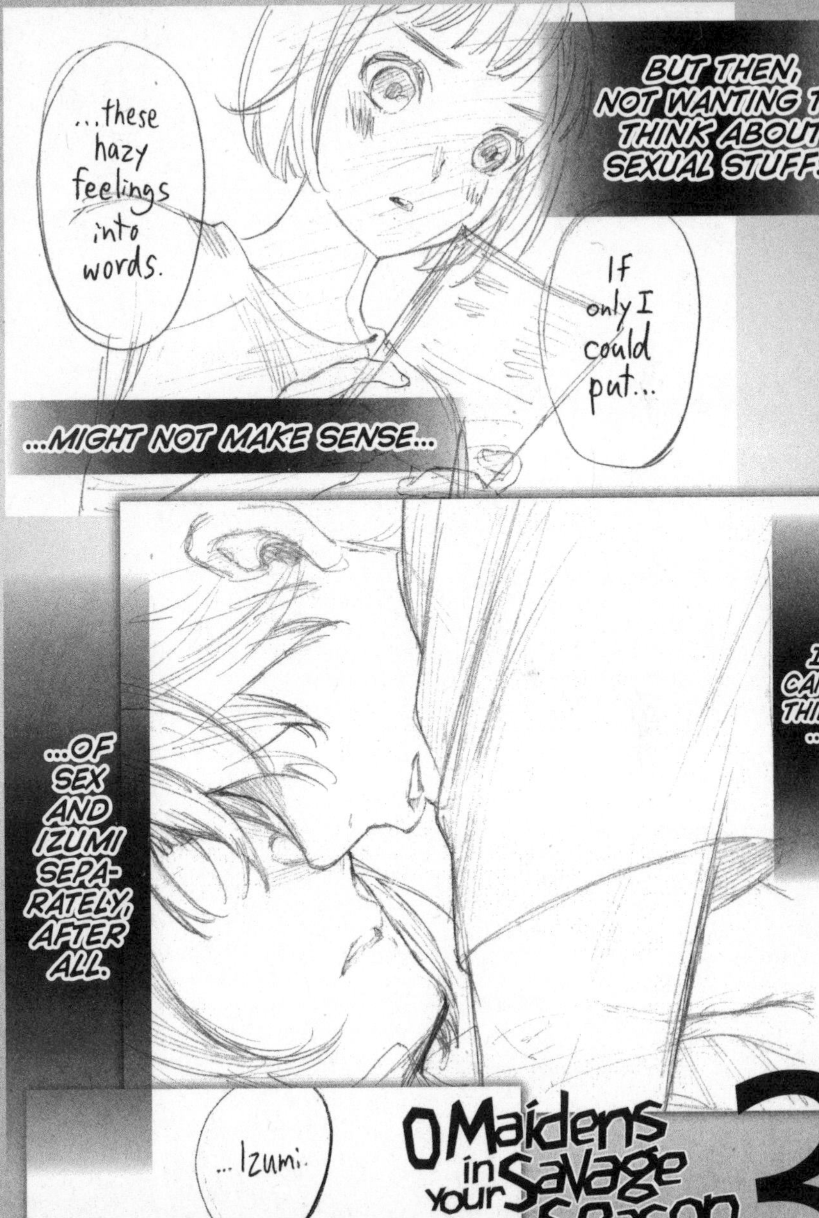
THAT'S BECAUSE... I LIKE IZUMI, AND I'VE GOT "SEX" AND "LOVE" ALL JUMBLED UP...
BUT THEN, NOT WANTING TO THINK ABOUT SEXUAL STUFF...
If only I could put...
...these hazy feelings into words.
...MIGHT NOT MAKE SENSE...
I CAN'T THINK...
...OF SEX AND IZUMI SEPARATELY, AFTER ALL.
...Izumi.

O Maidens in your Savage Season 3

Coming Soon

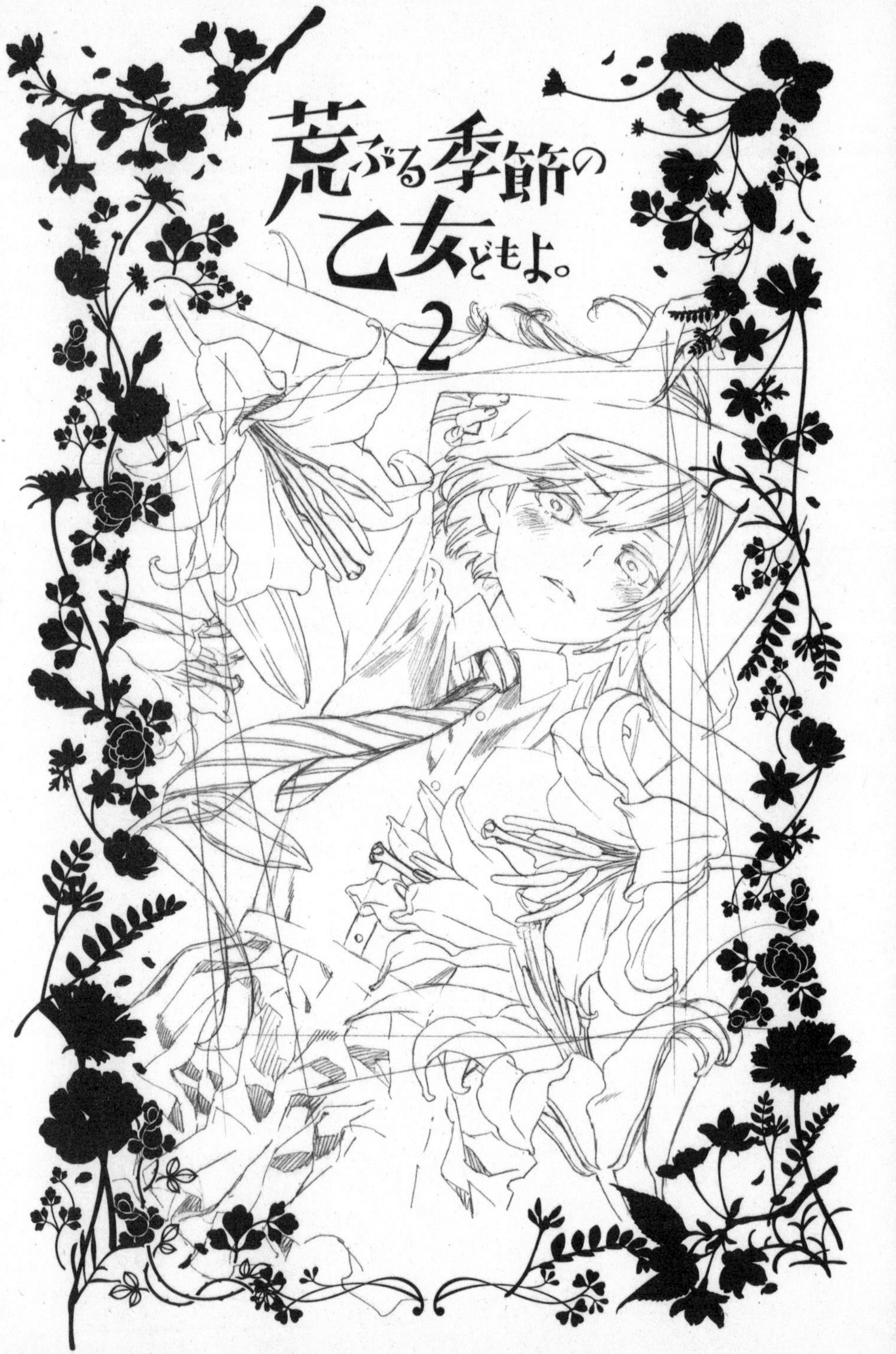
荒ぶる季節の
乙女どもよ。
2

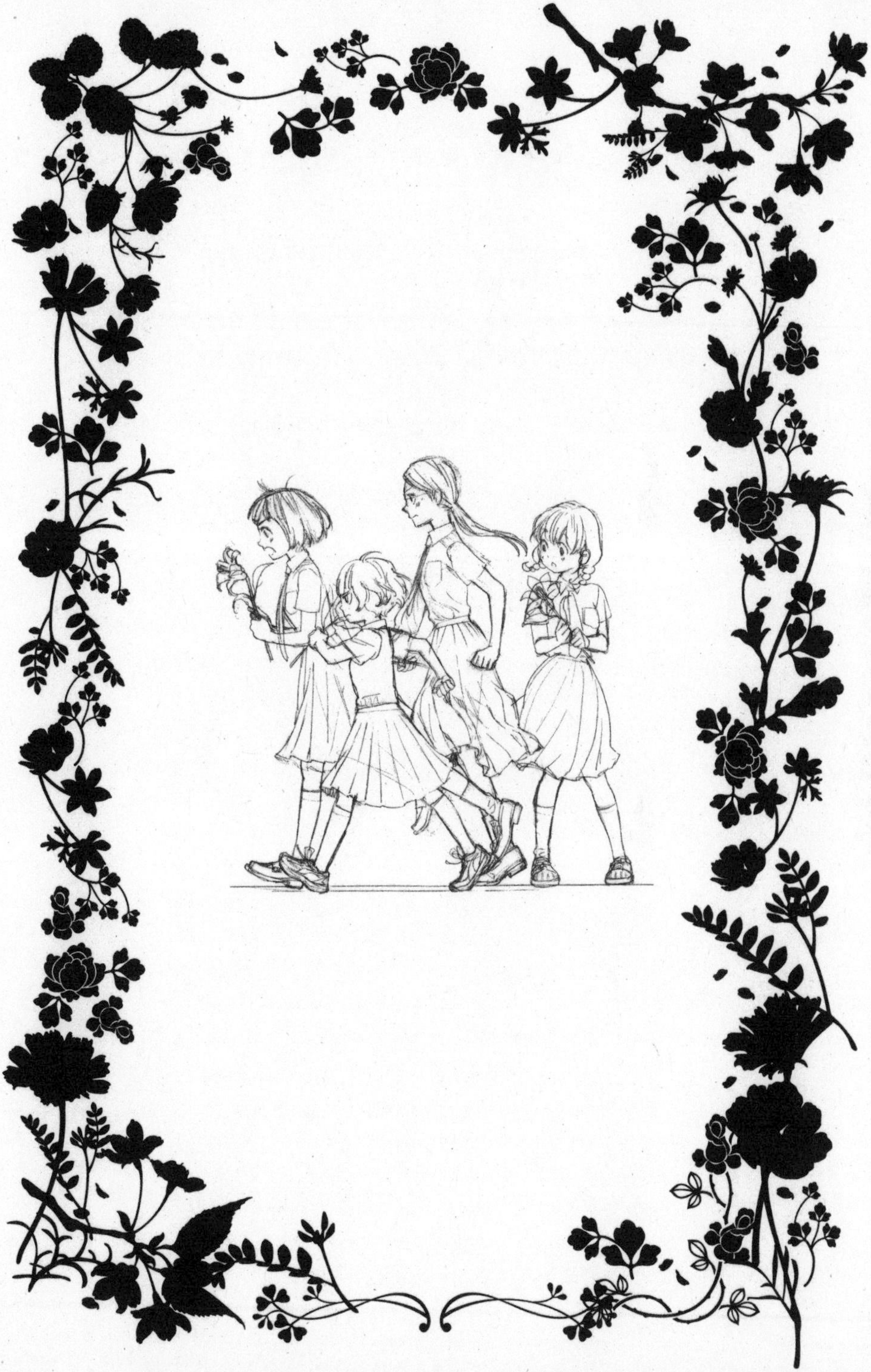

To like someone is a beautiful thing.

The heart palpitates. The feeling of love is pure and
exhilarating. Your heart gets all warm inside…

And yet, my mind can't handle it.

That thing keeps going around in circles inside my head.

Oh, if only I could go off on a three-day trip
in search of love that's free of *that*…

O Maidens
in your Savage
your Season

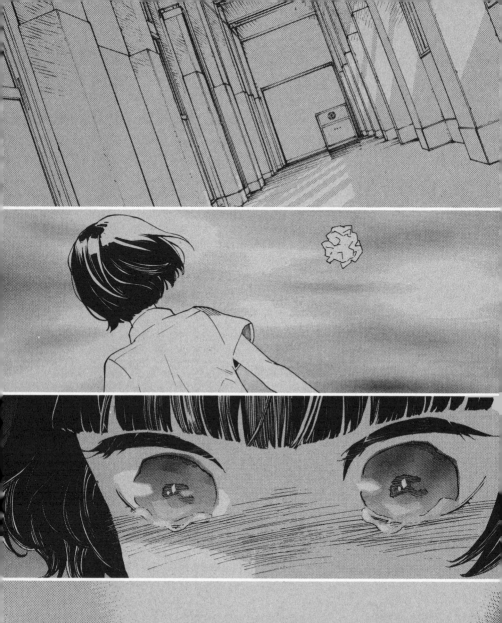

O Maidens in Your Savage Season, volume 2

Translation Notes

page 2

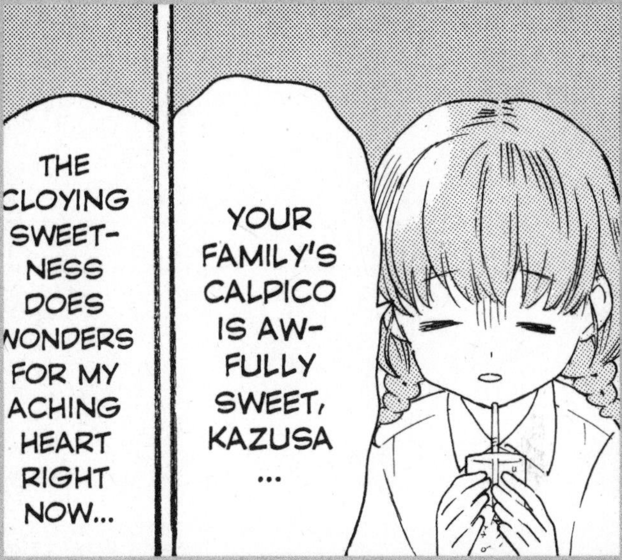
YOUR FAMILY'S CALPICO IS AW-FULLY SWEET, KAZUSA ...
THE CLOYING SWEET-NESS DOES WONDERS FOR MY ACHING HEART RIGHT NOW...

Calpico

Calpico is a popular milk-based concentrate that makes a sweet-and-tangy beverage when mixed with water. Each house dilutes the drink to their liking, so every person grows up with their family's own Calpico taste.

page 8

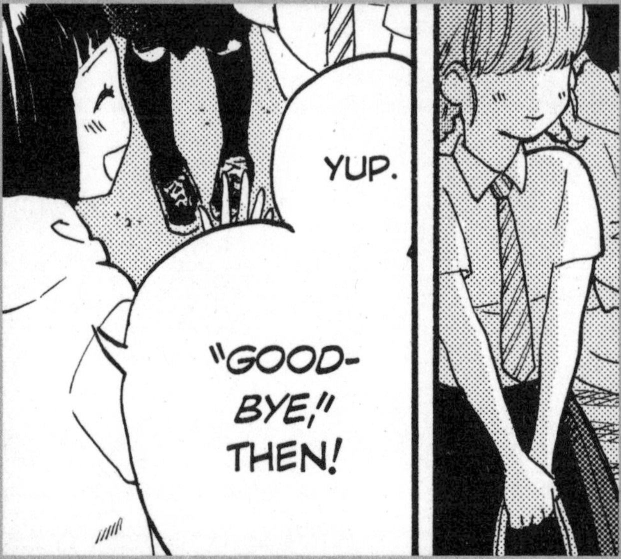
YUP.
"GOOD-BYE," THEN!

Good-bye

The last unfinished work by celebrated 20th- century author Osamu Dazai. The Literature Club members sometimes make a reference to it when bidding each other farewell.

DO YOU MEAN A MIDSUMMER NIGHT'S DREAM OR THE HUNTER'S MOON?! EXPLAIN YOURSELF!!

A *Midsummer Night's Dream* and *The Hunter's Moon*

Both works involve fairy kingdoms. *A Midsummer Night's Dream* is a play by Shakespeare, and *The Hunter's Moon* is a fantasy novel by O.R. Melling.

page 48

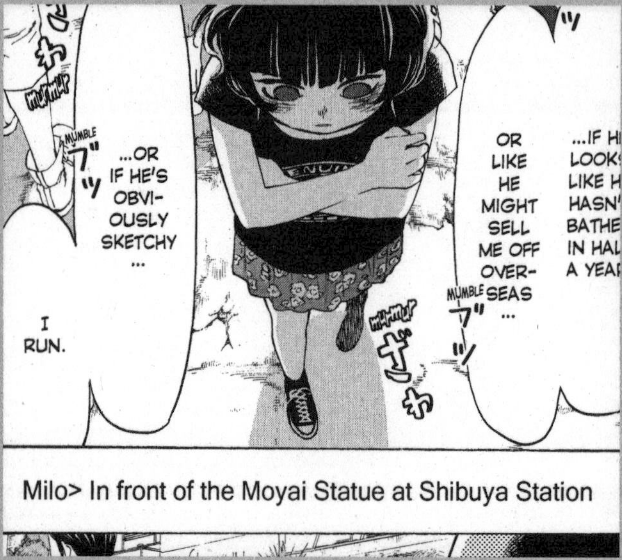
...IF H LOOK LIKE H HASN' BATHE IN HAL A YEA
OR LIKE HE MIGHT SELL ME OFF OVER-SEAS ...
MUMBLE
...OR IF HE'S OBVI-OUSLY SKETCHY ...
MUMBLE
I RUN.
Milo> In front of the Moyai Statue at Shibuya Station

Moyai Statue at Shibuya Station

Moyai Statue is the second most popular meeting spot at Shibuya Station after the famous Hachiko Statue. It looks similar to the Moai Statues from Easter Island, but was actually a donation from the volcanic island of Niijima, where the old Japanese meaning of *moyai*, "to cooperate," is still used, hence the homage.

"MY TEARS WERE BITTER, LIKE TEARS OF SHAME OVER A HUMILATION."

"THE KI REEKED DESIR I WEPT I ACCEF THEM

The Setting Sun

The book they are reading is *The Setting Sun* by Osamu Dazai, a novel about the decline of a small aristocratic family in the transitional period of postwar Japan. Kazuko, the daughter of the family, has a complicated relationship with a married novelist.

(English translation excerpt by Donald Keene, from the 1968 New Directions edition.)

pages 84 & 93

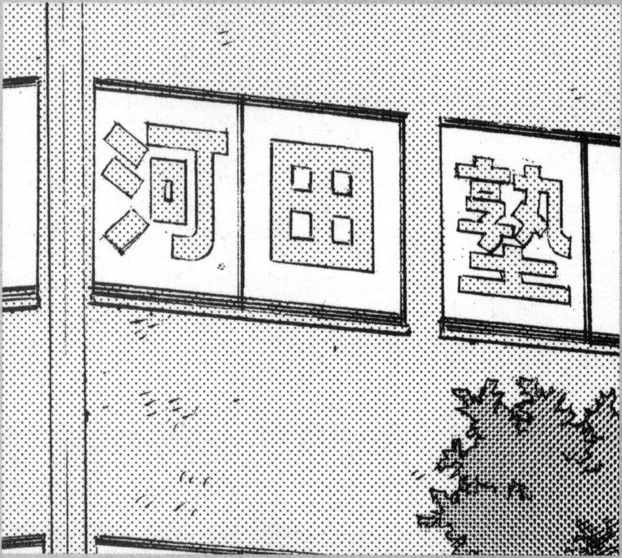
河田塾

Cram school

Many Japanese students attend special programs, or *juku*, outside of normal school hours to study for college or high school entrance exams. The exams are often the sole determining factor in admissions.

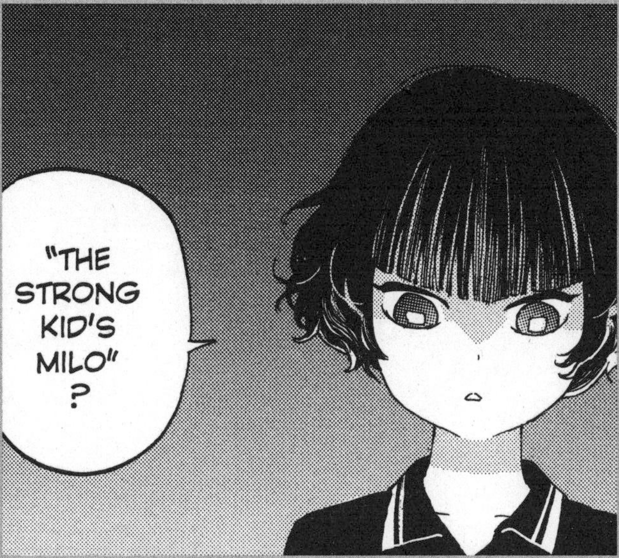
"THE STRONG KID'S MILO" ?

The strong kid's MILO

MILO is a chocolate and malt powder produced by Nestlé that is most often enjoyed mixed with milk. In Japan, the product was originally sold with the slogan "The strong kid's MILO" for its nutritional value.

page 122

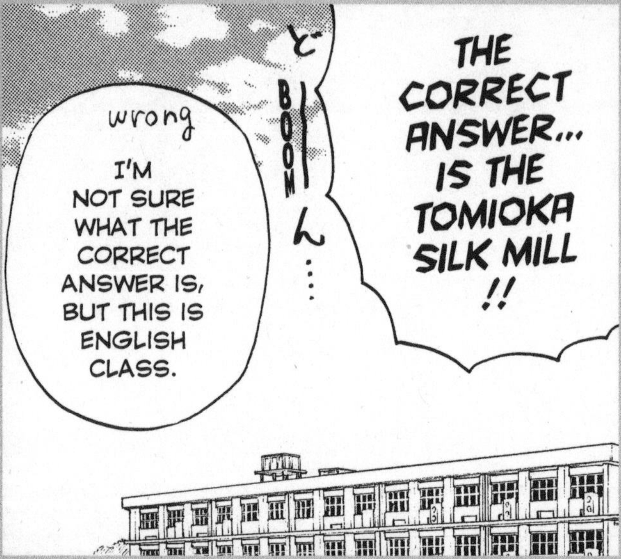
THE CORRECT ANSWER... IS THE TOMIOKA SILK MILL !!
ど BOOM ん......
wrong
I'M NOT SURE WHAT THE CORRECT ANSWER IS, BUT THIS IS ENGLISH CLASS.

Tomioka Silk Mill

This was Japan's first modern factory for processing raw silk, established in 1872, and is now on the UNESCO World Heritage List. All Japanese students learn about this at some point in history class.

O Maidens in your Savage Season

Yuri Is My Job!

miman

Hime is a picture-perfect high school princess, so when she accidentally injures a café manager named Mai, she's willing to cover some shifts to keep her façade intact. To Hime's surprise, the café is themed after a private school where the all-female staff always puts on their best act for their loyal customers. However, under the guidance of the most graceful girl there, Hime can't help but blush and blunder! Beneath all the frills and laughter, Hime feels tension brewing as she finds out more about her new job and her budding feelings...

KC KODANSHA COMICS

"A quirky, fun comedy series... If you're a yuri fan, or perhaps interested in getting into it but not sure where to start, this book is worth picking up."
— Anime UK News

ANIME OUT NOW FROM SENTAI FILMWORKS!

A BL romance between a good boy who didn't know he was waiting for a hero, and a bad boy who comes to his rescue!

Masahiro Setagawa doesn't believe in heroes but wishes he could: He's found himself in a gang of small-time street bullies, and with no prospects for a real future. But when high school teacher (and scourge of the streets) Kousuke Ohshiba comes to his rescue, he finds he may need to start believing after all... in heroes, and in his budding feelings, too.

Hitorijime My Hero

Memeco Arii

KC KODANSHA COMICS

O Maidens in Your Savage Season volume 2 is a work of fiction.
Names, characters, places, and incidents are the products of
the author's imagination or are used fictitiously.
Any resemblance to actual events, locales, or
persons, living or dead, is entirely coincidental.

A Kodansha Comics Trade Paperback Original

Published in the United States by Kodansha Comics, an imprint of
Kodansha USA Publishing, LLC, New York.

Publication rights for this English edition arranged through
Kodansha Ltd, Tokyo.

First published in Japan in 2017 by Kodansha Ltd, Tokyo,
as *Araburu Kisetsu no Otomedomoyo* volume 2.

ISBN 978-1-63236-819-5

Printed in the United States of America.

www.kodanshacomics.com

9 8 7 6 5 4 3 2 1
Translation: Sawa Matsueda Savage
Lettering: Evan Hayden
Editing: Haruko Hashimoto
Kodansha Comics edition cover design by Phil Balsman